Accessible XHTML™ and CSS Web Sites
Problem - Design - Solution

Jon Duckett

WILEY

Wiley Publishing, Inc.

Accessible XHTML™ and CSS Web Sites Problem - Design - Solution

Published by
Wiley Publishing, Inc.
10475 Crosspoint Boulevard
Indianapolis, IN 46256
www.wiley.com

ISBN: 0-7645-8306-9

ISBN-13: 978-0-7645-8306-3

Manufactured in the United States of America

10 9 8 7 6 5 4 3 2 1

1MA/TQ/QT/QV/IN

For general information on our other products and services or to obtain technical support, please contact our Customer Care Department within the U.S. at (800) 762-2974, outside the U.S. at (317) 572-3993 or fax (317) 572-4002.

Wiley also publishes its books in a variety of electronic formats. Some content that appears in print may not be available in electronic books.

Library of Congress CataloginginPublication Data

Duckett, Jon.
 Accessible XHTML and CSS Web sites problem design solution / Jon Duckett.
    p. cm.
 Includes index.
 ISBN 0-7645-8306-9 (paper/Web site)
 1. XHTML (Document markup language) 2. Cascading style sheets. 3. Web sitesDesign. I. Title.
 QA76.76.H94D836 2005
 006.7'4dc22

                            2005000593

About the Author

Jon Duckett published his first Web site in 1996 while studying for a BSc (Hons) in psychology at Brunel University, London. Since then he has helped create a wide variety of Web sites and has coauthored more than ten programmingrelated books on topics from ASP to XML (via many other letters of the alphabet) that have covered diverse aspects of Web programming, including design, architecture, and coding.

After graduating, Jon worked for Wrox Press, first in their Birmingham (U.K.) offices for three years and then in Sydney (Australia) for another year. He is now a freelance developer and consultant based in a leafy suburb of London, working for a range of clients spread across three continents.

When not stuck in front of a computer screen, Jon enjoys writing and listening to music.

Credits

Acquisitions Editor
Jim Minatel

Senior Development Editor
Kevin Kent

Production Editor
William A. Barton

Technical Editor
WileyDreamtech India Pvt Ltd

Copy Editor
Luann Rouff

Editorial Manager
Mary Beth Wakefield

Vice President & Executive Group Publisher
Richard Swadley

Vice President and Publisher
Joseph B. Wikert

Project Coordinator
Erin Smith

Graphics and Production Specialists
April Farling
Lauren Goddard
Denny Hager
Lynsey Osborn
Julie Trippetti

Quality Control Technician
John Greenough
Joe Niesen
Carl William Pierce

Media Development Specialist
Kit Malone

Proofreading and Indexing
TECHBOOKS Production Services

Preface

This book is designed to help existing Web page authors update their skills. We all know that technology can move at a blistering pace, and sometimes it can seem very hard to keep up with the changes. This book will help keep you up to speed by teaching you about three of the hottest issues for Web page authors to learn about: XHTML, CSS, and accessibility.

You'll be glad to know that, because this book is for those of you who already know how to write Web pages in HTML, I won't be boring you with the basics of how to write a Web page from scratch. Rather, it will enable you to extend the knowledge you already have by presenting examples and information that reflect the way the Web has changed in the past decade.

Since the birth of the Web, many new technologies have been released, and almost as many have vanished without a trace. XHTML and CSS, however, have emerged as mature technologies that are likely to be around for many years to come. They were specifically designed to replace HTML, and as you would expect, you will find many advantages in writing Web pages using XHTML and CSS as opposed to writing them in HTML, although they share a lot of similarities, as you will see.

You should also be aware that companies increasingly face legal obligations to ensure that their Web sites meet accessibility standards. These standards are intended to ensure that as many people as possible are able to access the content of a site, without discriminating against any groups of users. Therefore, it is important to learn how to build pages that meet these accessibility requirements.

Contents

Contents

Contents

Contents

Contents

Contents

Introduction

In this book, I will show you how XHTML and CSS actually make it easier and quicker to write and maintain pages. I will also show you how the correct use of XHTML and CSS enable you to create Web pages that work in many different types of browsers (not only in different versions of Netscape and Internet Explorer, but also on the various devices that can access the Web these days, such as mobile phones and TV set top boxes).

While XHTML *is* the successor to HTML, it is not a completely new language. In fact, much of the markup you already know remains exactly the same, so you should be creating XHTML pages in no time at all. However, some new rules control the way you write your elements (or tags) and attributes, and where they can appear in the document. In addition, you are encouraged not to use any of the elements or attributes that controlled the appearance or presentation of pages, such as the `<font>` element and attributes such as `bgcolor`, `color`, and `face`. While you may think that this would result in some very boring pages, this is the point when CSS steps in.

CSS, or Cascading Style Sheets, is the new way to control the presentation (and sometimes even the layout) of your pages. CSS uses rules, which are applied to certain elements, to indicate how the content of that element should appear. An example of a CSS rule might be one that says the content of all `<h1>` elements should be displayed in an Arial typeface.

Although CSS is a new language for you to learn, having already learned HTML, you have a big advantage because many of the socalled *properties* in CSS are very similar to attributes, such as the `face` attribute on a `<font>` element or the `bgcolor` and `color` attributes.

The third topic covered in this book is accessibility, and you may already be well aware of how very important it is to ensure that your pages are accessible to everyone (especially if you don't want a court order to rebuild your site). Accessibility focuses on making Web sites site accessible to as many people as possible, and this particularly affects those with disabilities, such as those who might not be able to read small fonts or who might have motor control difficulties. In the same way that architects have had to design public buildings so that they are accessible by a wheelchair, Web designers must learn to create pages that are accessible to those who may not be able to read as easily as you or I, or who might not have such good control over a mouse.

In the last section of this book, you will learn about guidelines developed by both the U.S. government and the W3C (the World Wide Web Consortium, an organization dedicated to creating specifications for the Web) to help ensure that Web sites are accessible to as many people as possible. Adhering to these guidelines not only ensures that you will stay on the right side of the law, it also ensures a larger potential audience for your sites.

Although you can find books dedicated to each of these topics, if you have already been creating Web sites with HTML, there really is no need to wade through several thick books; rather, you just need to bring your existing skills up to date. That's where this book comes in. Using this one volume, you can update your existing skills, and by doing so you should find that your skills remain marketable for a good time to come.

This book introduces each of these new technologies by taking a Web site written in HTML 3.2 (a fictional site that was built in the late 1990s) and updating it to use XHTML and CSS and to ensure that it meets the accessibility guidelines. You will meet this fictional site in Chapter 1, and each subsequent chapter addresses the different skills you need to learn to update the site. At the end of each chapter, you will see how the site has been adapted following the principles you learned in that chapter.

Who This Book Is For

This book is written for anyone who has learned to use HTML to create Web pages and wants to remain current with changes that have occurred over the past few years regarding how to write them, but who does not want to read a separate book on each of the key topics.

It is possible to cover XHTML, CSS, and accessibility in this one book because it is assumed that the reader has already written Web pages in HTML, and therefore knows what elements and attributes HTML contains and how a Web page is constructed. By not repeating these basics, it is possible to get on with the topic in hand: learning how these technologies have evolved.

The book has been designed so that you can dip into each topic separately, without having to read the rest of the book, so if you want to learn about accessibility right now, you can go straight to Chapter 7. Similarly, if you only want to learn the differences between HTML and XHTML at the moment, you need only read Chapter 2 for now.

The book is also ideal for Web developers who use serverside languages such as ASP/ASP.NET, PHP, JSP, or ColdFusion, because developing in these languages usually requires that you write code that creates HTML to send to the browser. Therefore, if you use one of these languages, you can benefit from this book by learning how to send accessible XHTML and CSS to the browser instead of plain old HTML.

Indeed, the example site that runs throughout this book has been designed with serverside developers in mind. While the original site is written in plain HTML, it could easily have been HTML that is generated from database content; for example, the product list pages demonstrate how any tabular data could be represented, and the individual product pages could easily have been generated by any kind of content management system.

In other words, whatever level you are at, if your job involves creating Web pages to send to a browser, this book will help you keep your skills up to date.

What This Book Covers

By the end of this book, you will have evolved from being an HTML author to being an author able to write Web pages that are attractive, accessible, and that conform to the new Web standards of XHTML and CSS.

To begin, you will learn the differences between HTML and XHTML. You will learn to write both *Strict* and *Transitional* XHTML 1.0. You will also be introduced to the way in which XHTML is likely to develop in the future, with XHTML 1.1 (also known as modularized XHTML).

You will then be shown how to use CSS1 and CSS2 to control the presentation of your documents—for example, how to control typefaces and fonts used in your documents, colors of backgrounds, text, and lines, and so on. You will also learn how CSS2 positioning can be used to control the layout of Web pages and the positioning of items upon them (rather than rely on tables).

Finally, you will learn how to ensure that the pages you write meet the accessibility guidelines set forth by the U.S. government in Section 508 of the Rehabilitation act (generally shortened to just Section 508 in the Web design community) and by the W3C in the Web Accessibility Initiative (WAI) guidelines.

What You Need to Use This Book

All you need to work through this book is a PC with a Web browser such as Netscape 6 or later and Internet Explorer 6, and a simple text editor such as Notepad (Windows) or SimpleText (Mac). Ideally, you should try to download more than one Web browser because, as you will see in this book, different browsers have differing levels of support for some of the latest technologies.

If you have a Web page editor program, such as Macromedia Dreamweaver or Microsoft FrontPage, you are welcome to use it, but this book does not cover how to use those programs. Rather, it focuses on the code that they would generate.

The sample code for this book is available on the Web (www.wrox.com), so you need an Internet connection if you wish to download that code. Once you have downloaded it, however, you will be able to run and test it on any PC with a recent Web browser.

How This Book Is Organized

This book is part of the *Problem Design Solution* series. As such, it teaches the subjects it addresses in three steps: looking at specific problems, looking at possible ways these problems could be solved, and finally showing the solution to the problem that was posed in the beginning.

Throughout the book, your challenge is to update a fictional Web site that was supposedly created in the late 1990s using HTML 3.2. Now, in 2005, you need to be able to update the site to take advantage of XHTML and CSS and to ensure that it adheres to accessibility requirements. Each chapter addresses separate problems, such as converting the site from HTML to XHTML, and ensuring that the site meets the Section 508 guidelines for accessibility.

❑ The first chapter of the book introduces the First Promotions Web site. It will show you how the site was originally written, which will probably look very familiar to you. You will then learn why we are going to update the site. The question answered here is, Why is it important to learn these new skills?

❑ Chapter 2 deals with converting the site from HTML to XHTML. It begins by looking at the differences between HTML and XHTML—in particular, some new rules that govern how you write your elements and attributes and where they may appear. The chapter then proceeds to describe how you remove all of the elements and attributes that controlled the presentation of the page— elements such as the `<font>` element, and attributes such as the `bgcolor` and `face` attributes. By the end of the chapter, you will have a rather plainlooking site that is written in Strict XHTML 1.0.

❑ The next three chapters are devoted to making the site look more attractive again using CSS. Along the way, you will learn how CSS makes it a lot easier to control the presentation of the pages you design; and how it makes your XHTML pages more useful and gives them a longer life span. Chapter 3 introduces how CSS works and starts to control the presentation of pages. Chapter 4 looks at many more of the CSS properties that control how your pages appear. Chapter 5 then describes how you can use CSS to control layout and to position elements on the page, rather than rely on tables.

❑ Chapters 6 and 7 focus on accessibility and ensure that you are writing pages that adhere to the guidelines created by the U.S. government in Section 508 and by the W3C's Web Accessibility Initiative.

❑ Chapter 8 reviews what you have learned throughout the book, and describes how you can apply your new skills with XHTML and CSS to develop for many different types of devices, from mobile phones to TV set top boxes. It also addresses the directions the Web is likely to take in the future and how these technologies are likely to continue to develop. After all, if you keep one eye on the future, it will be easier to write code that will last longer.

Finally, at the end of the book are some very helpful appendixes: The first covers the new finished version of the site, the second covers all of the elements in XHTML and the attributes they can carry, while the third covers the properties of CSS and their possible values. These are followed by appendixes on escape characters and MIME types. The appendixes should act as a helpful reference as you continue to practice writing accessible pages in XHTML and CSS.

Conventions

To help you get the most from the text and keep track of what's happening, I've used a number of conventions throughout the book:

> **Boxes like this one hold important, nottobe forgotten information that is directly relevant to the surrounding text.**

Tips, hints, tricks, and asides to the current discussion are offset and placed in italics like this.

As for styles in the text:

❑ I *italicize* important words when they are first introduced.

❑ I show keyboard strokes like this: Ctrl+A.

❑ I show filenames, URLs, and code within the text like so: `version="10"`.

❑ I present code in two different ways:

```
In code examples, I highlight new and important code with a gray background.
```

```
The gray highlighting is not used for code that's less important in the present
context or has been shown before.
```

Source Code

As you work through the examples in this book, you may choose either to type in all the code manually or to use the source code files that accompany the book. All of the source code used in this book is available for download at www.wrox.com. Once at the site, simply locate the book's title (either by using the Search box or by using one of the title lists) and click the Download Code link on the book's details page to obtain all the source code for the book.

Because many books have similar titles, you may find it easiest to search by ISBN: 0-7645-8306-9.

Once you download the code, just decompress it with your favorite compression tool. Alternatively, you can go to the main Wrox code download page at www.wrox.com/dynamic/books/download.aspx to see the code available for this book and all other Wrox books.

Errata

I've made every effort to ensure that there are no errors in the text or in the code. However, no one is perfect, and mistakes do occur. If you find an error in this book, such as a spelling mistake or a faulty piece of code, I would be very grateful for your feedback. By sending in errata, you may save another reader hours of frustration; and at the same time, you will be helping to provide even higher quality information.

To find the errata page for this book, go to www.wrox.com and locate the title using the Search box or one of the title lists. Then, on the book's details page, click the Book Errata link. On this page, you can view all errata that have been submitted for this book and posted by Wrox editors. A complete book list, including links to each book's errata, is also available at www.wrox.com/miscpages/booklist.shtml.

If you don't spot "your" error on the Book Errata page, go to www.wrox.com/contact/techsupport.shtml and complete the form there to send us the error you have found. We'll check the information and, if appropriate, post a message to the book's errata page and fix the problem in subsequent editions of the book.

p2p.wrox.com

For author and peer discussion, join the P2P forums at http://p2p.wrox.com. The forums are a Webbased system for you to post messages relating to Wrox books and related technologies and interact with other readers and technology users. The forums offer a subscription feature to e-mail you topics of interest of your choosing when new posts are made to the forums. Wrox authors, editors, other industry experts, and your fellow readers are present on these forums.

At http://p2p.wrox.com, you will find several different forums that will help you not only as you read this book, but also as you develop your own applications. To join the forums, just follow these steps:

1. Go to http://p2p.wrox.com and click the Register link.
2. Read the terms of use and click Agree.

3. Complete the required information to join as well as any optional information you wish to provide and click Submit.

4. You will receive an e-mail with information describing how to verify your account and complete the joining process.

You can read messages in the forums without joining P2P, but in order to post your own messages, you must join.

Once you join, you can post new messages and respond to messages other users post. You can read messages at any time on the Web. If you would like to have new messages from a particular forum e-mailed to you, click the Subscribe to this Forum icon by the forum name in the forum listing.

For more information about how to use the Wrox P2P, be sure to read the P2P FAQs for answers to questions about how the forum software works as well as many common questions specific to P2P and Wrox books. To read the FAQs, click the FAQ link on any P2P page.

1

Introducing the Site

In what has been a relatively short life to date, the Web has grown at a tremendous pace. When I first started learning HTML, I would not have imagined that so many people would be using the Web today. Nor, while sitting at my desktop PC, would I have imagined that by now I would need to write pages that could be accessed through such a variety of devices — such as mobile phones and TV set top boxes. These new devices are quite different from the desktop PC — they have differently sized screens and different amounts of power and memory available to them, and they enable users to access information in very different ways. Given the growth of the Web and the way in which it has changed, it is hardly surprising that those of us who build Web sites might need to update our skills, and that the tools we use to get the job done also need modernizing.

This chapter describes why it is important to learn to write sites using XHTML and CSS, and why it is so important to make your sites accessible. You will also be introduced to the example site that you will be working on throughout this book.

In this chapter, you will:

❑   Examine some of the problems caused by traditional HTML

❑   Find out why it is important to separate styling from content

❑   Meet the example First Promotions site. This is the site that you will be updating throughout the book.

❑   Learn about the aims of redesigning the site

❑   Find out more about the benefits that you will accrue by creating accessible sites in XHTML and CSS.

By the end of the chapter, you will understand the reasons why you need to update your skills and sites, and what you will be doing to the example site in this book.

Problems with HTML

As the Web evolved, so did HTML. Several versions of HTML have been released by the W3C (the World Wide Web Consortium — the body responsible for maintaining many Web standards). The first versions of HTML enabled you to use markup to describe the structure of a document, but did not offer much control over how that document looked. By the time HTML 4 was released, it had become a much more complex language than its original version. The features that were first added to HTML over the years afforded Web designers a lot of control over the appearance of a page. For example, they enabled Web page authors to control the exact width of tables (to the pixel); the size and weight of fonts; the colors and images used as backgrounds; and so on.

The addition of these new rules that offered designers control over the appearance of pages meant that it was possible to create attractive pages that worked great on your average desktop computer. However, problems soon started to manifest:

❑ Various browsers developed different ways of doing the same thing, which meant sites would not look or work the same in all browsers.

❑ Different users had different sized screens and different screen resolutions, so pages would not look the same on all computers.

❑ New devices started to access the Web; it was no longer just desktop PCs, but also TV set top boxes, mobile phones, and so on, and each new device had different capabilities. For example, a page containing a table that was 700 pixels wide would not fit on a phone that had a display only 128 pixels wide.

❑ If you (or your boss) wanted to change some aspect of the site design, such as the colors or fonts used, every page had to be changed because this information was in the HTML for every page.

❑ As designers used more HTML code to control the layout of a page, the source code of the page became longer and more complicated to write. This in turn introduced greater scope for errors when authoring or editing a site.

❑ If you did not have 20/20 vision, it could be hard to read some of the text on the sites, and if you had severe vision impairments, you would not be able to navigate some sites at all.

As a result, some companies started to create several versions of their Web sites, with versions for different browsers and devices; they even created text-only versions of sites intended to meet disability requirements. Obviously, this means a lot of extra work, and often results in versions of the site that are not as up-to-date as others. Clearly, this solution is far from ideal.

To summarize, traditional HTML posed the following problems:

❑ As HTML developed, a lot of stylistic rules were introduced to the language that enabled Web page authors to control the appearance of their pages; however, these same enhancements to the language meant that the rules governing how the page should appear were mixed in with the actual content of the page, and that many pages would work as intended only on desktop PCs.

❑ Because the Web is such a powerful medium, it needs to be made accessible to the widest range of users as possible. That includes those with disabilities who might not be able to read, hear, or move a mouse as well as others can.

Therefore, you can see that the changes you have to make to the way you build sites merely reflect changes in the Web's popularity and how people use it. In this chapter, you will see how and why the languages for writing Web pages have changed.

Design

After HTML 4.0, the W3C (which is responsible for developing the HTML specification) decided that it was time for a large-scale overhaul in the way people write Web sites. The problems described in the preceding section indicated to the W3C that these changes needed to reflect the following simple fact:

> **Different users require different presentations of the same information.**

Three common reasons why you would need to present the information on your Web site in different ways are as follows:

❑   Different pieces of technology used to view the Web have different capabilities, and they are not all capable of displaying a single design adequately for all users.

❑   The information made available online can often be very useful in other formats, such as in print or on a projector as part of a conference.

❑   Some people have difficulty accessing information in a way that others might find easy; for example, those with visual impairments might not be able to read text on a computer screen.

This last point is especially important because the Web is fundamentally changing the way in which people go about their everyday lives — from being able to shop, bank, and pay bills online to the introduction of electronic voting — so you cannot exclude sections of the community who have disabilities.

Indeed, the Web can have a more profound effect upon the lives of people with disabilities, some of whom may find leaving their home harder than those without any disabilities. Therefore, it is essential that advances in technology include everyone.

The W3C's solution to this problem was to strip out all the *presentational* markup that had been added to HTML over the years to control how pages looked; this is the markup such as the <font> and <center> elements, and the bgcolor and color attributes. The HTML markup that was left described the structure and semantics of a document, such as the title of a document, where paragraphs start and end, what text represents a heading, and so on. This did not mean that Web designers would lose control over how their documents appeared; rather, they would use something called a *style sheet*, which is a separate document, to indicate how the page should be displayed. Indeed, style sheets have several other advantages described throughout the chapter.

The result of this separation of style and content led to the W3C's development of two standards, which the browser manufacturers are expected to support and the Web page authors are expected to learn: *XHTML* and *CSS*. Don't let this put you off, however. In reality, both languages are very similar to the HTML you already know, which makes learning these technologies rather quick and simple.

Before looking at how the languages of the Web have changed, the following section clarifies a few key terms to ensure that your understanding of them matches mine. I then want to elaborate a little on how and why we ended up where we are today, learning these new languages, and the differences between presentational and structural markup.

Clarifying terminology

The following terms might seem obvious to you, but people often refer to the same things by slightly different names. A quick review of these definitions will ensure that you understand any concepts presented in the following discussion before you start updating your skills:

A *tag* is a set of characters surrounded by angled brackets; for example, here is a familiar *opening tag*:

```
<td>
```

Meanwhile, here is its corresponding closing tag. Anything in between these tags is used as a table cell (or *table data* — hence, the letters td):

```
</td>
```

An *element* refers to both an opening tag and a closing tag, plus anything between them. For example, here is a table cell element:

```
<td>234.5</td>
```

The bit between the opening tag and the closing tag is referred to as *element content*.

Elements can "carry" *attributes*, which provide further information about the element that carries them. Attributes always sit inside the opening tag of an element. For example, here is the align attribute:

```
<td align="right">
```

This attribute indicates that the content of this table cell should be aligned to the right.

Some elements do not have a closing tag; for example, the <img> element can carry several attributes, but does not have any element content — there is nothing between an opening and closing tag:

```
<img src="/images/120x80_logo.gif" alt="Acme Logo" width="120" height='80'>
```

Elements that have no content are called *empty elements*. You will see in Chapter 2 that empty elements are written differently in XHTML, so you will have to start writing all of your <img>, <br>, and <hr> tags in a new way.

Figure 1-1 illustrates all of these concepts.

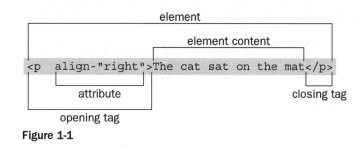

Figure 1-1

A Little Background to HTML

Removing all of the styling rules from HTML might seem like a backward step, rather than an exciting new progression of the language — you may well be wondering why we didn't have separate style sheets from the start if they are such a great idea. To understand why HTML evolved the way it did — that is, why HTML introduced all this stylistic markup such as the <font> elements and bgcolor attributes if they were only going to be removed, you need to look at how HTML developed into the language you know and use today. As is often the case, the answer appears obvious with hindsight — if only we could have foreseen that the problem would occur in the first place.

HTML was originally designed as a markup language to describe the *structure* and *semantics* of a document. The elements and attributes of HTML were supposed to indicate things such as the title of a document, what part of the text was a heading, what of the text was a paragraph, what data belonged in a table, and so on. In its earliest form, the Web was intended to transmit scientific documents so that the research community had quick and easy access to published work. Here is an example of a document that might have been generated for the scientific community (see the file ch01_eg01.html for the download):

```html
<html>
  <head>
    <title>The Effect of the Internet on Psychological Theories of Self</title>
  </head>
  <body>
    <h1>The Effect of the Internet on Psychological Theories of Self</h1>
    <h2>Abstract</h2>
      <p>This paper looks that the role in which Internet users can adopt different
      online personae, and the effects this has on psychoanalytic theories of
      self and personal identity.</p>
      <p>While psychologists have long suggested that our concept of self should
      reflect a single, unitary, rational self, many people will adopt online
      personae that are very different than that which they display in person.</p>
      ...
  </body>
</html>
```

While this kind of document was highly practical, and enabled academics to share information with far greater ease than relying on printed journals, the presentation of these documents was rather gray and uninteresting, as you can see in Figure 1-2, which shows you what this document would look like in a browser.

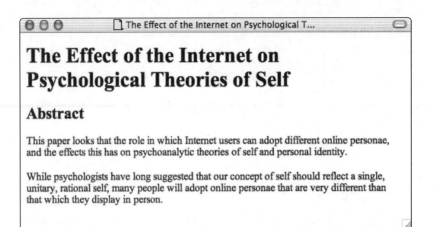

The Effect of the Internet on Psychological T...

The Effect of the Internet on Psychological Theories of Self

Abstract

This paper looks that the role in which Internet users can adopt different online personae, and the effects this has on psychoanalytic theories of self and personal identity.

While psychologists have long suggested that our concept of self should reflect a single, unitary, rational self, many people will adopt online personae that are very different than that which they display in person.

Figure 1-2

At the time, many people were quick to see the potential of the Web. These users started creating Web pages for all different kinds of purposes, from personal home pages to huge corporate sites advertising a company's products and services. It wasn't long before Web page authors wanted to control how their sites looked, and they expected the same level of control over their pages' appearance as print designers had over their creations. For example, Web designers wanted to be able to control the fonts and colors used in documents, and where their text would appear on a page. As a result, the major browser manufacturers started adding new elements and attributes to control the appearance of Web pages; both Netscape and Microsoft were desperately trying to win a greater share of the browser market by giving Web designers more control over pages shown in their browsers. The W3C also introduced many of these elements and attributes into successive versions of HTML.

This new markup is known as *presentational* or *stylistic* markup, because it affects the way that pages look. (It does not describe the structure and semantics of the document, which was the initial intention of HTML.) Prime examples of this new type of markup are the `<center>` and `<font>` elements and the `bgcolor` and `color` attributes.

Designers were quick to learn tricks that enabled them to control the layout of pages (the positioning of content on the screen) in a similar way to print designers. Two common techniques included the use of tables as layout grids for pages and the use of transparent single-pixel GIF images (commonly known as the single pixel or transparent GIF trick) to position elements.

The following example shows the same page you just met in `ch01_eg01.html`, but this time it has had stylistic markup added to control its presentation. The new file, called `ch01_eg02.html`, is much longer with the stylistic markup added to the page:

```html
<html>
  <head>
    <title>The Effect of the Internet on Psychological Theories of Self</title>
  </head>
  <body bgcolor="#000000">
    <center>
    <table width="650" border="1" bordercolor="#666666" cellpadding="10"
           cellspacing="0">
```

```
      <tr>
        <td bgcolor="#999999">
          <font face="Arial, Helvetica, sans-serif" size="5" color="#FFFFFF">
            <h1>The Effect of the Internet on Psychological Theories of Self</h1>
          </font>
        </td>
      </tr>
      <tr>
        <td bgcolor="#EFEFEF">
          <font face="Arial, Helvetica, sans-serif" size="4" color="#000066">
            <h2>Abstract</h2>
          </font>
          <font face="Arial, Helvetica, sans-serif" size="2" color="#333333">
            <p>This paper looks that the role in which Internet users can adopt
            different online personae, and the effects this has on psychoanalytic
            theories of self and personal identity.</p>
            <p>While psychologists have long suggested that our concept of self
            should reflect a single, unitary, rational self, many people will adopt
            online personae that are very different than that which they display in
            person.</p>
            ...
          </font>
        </td>
      </tr>
    </table>
  </center>
  </body>
</html>
```

Even though the layout of the document is still quite basic, the size of the page has ballooned; the number of characters (not including spaces) has almost doubled, with ch01_eg01.html containing 529 characters and ch01_eg02.html containing 928 characters. This extra complexity increases the chances of making an error, both when authoring the page in the first place and when making any alterations to the pages. Figure 1-3 shows you what ch01_eg02.html looks like in the browser.

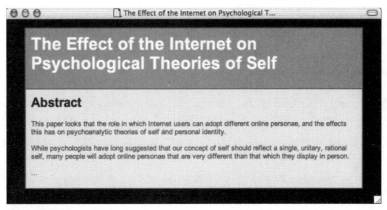

Figure 1-3

When the rules that govern the presentation of the Web page are intermingled with the actual content of the pages, changing any aspect of the presentation of your site (such as the typeface used for headings or the background color of the page) means changing *every* page of the site. When you consider that many pages are littered with `<font>` tags and a whole host of presentational attributes, it becomes even harder to find the markup you want to change. Therefore, you can see why the stylistic markup introduces more scope for error.

At the same time that the browser manufacturers were writing their browsers to understand new markup, they were also trying to make it easy for authors to write pages, so they would incorporate code that helped users display pages even if the HTML contained errors. This meant that a lot of HTML authors got into bad habits; even some of the leading authoring tools generated sloppy code. Furthermore, because the browser manufacturers were making the browsers capable of rendering pages even if they contained errors, the amount of disk space and memory required to run a browser had to increase.

None of these developments were inherently bad. Indeed, if it had not been possible to create attractive pages, and if it had not been as easy as to write Web pages as it is today, then it is unlikely that the Web would have ever become as popular as it is now. As you have already seen, however, with all of the extra stylistic markup and the tricks that designers were employing to control the layout of their sites, Web pages were becoming much larger. The markup no longer just described the structure of the page or provided information about its content; it also contained a lot of markup that was there only to control the presentation of the page for one kind of device: the desktop PC.

Browser issues

The problems associated with writing pages that contain rules governing how a page should look were exacerbated by the fact that the way in which people viewed Web sites was changing just as rapidly as the audiences were growing. As I have already hinted, advances in technologies meant the following:

- ❑ Computer processors and graphics cards improved.
- ❑ Higher-resolution screens became available.
- ❑ Larger screens fell in price and became more widespread.
- ❑ Devices other than desktop computers were accessing the Web, such as mobile phones and TV set top boxes; even refrigerators were being developed with built-in browsers.

Each of these advancements brought a new set of challenges:

- ❑ As processors and graphics cards improved, more users were encouraged to use higher screen resolutions.
- ❑ Because larger screens were becoming more widespread, more people were using these higher resolutions.
- ❑ Sites that were designed to fit on a screen at 640 × 480 resolution look smaller on a 1024 ×768 resolution screen and can therefore be harder to read at high resolutions.
- ❑ New devices often had smaller screens, lower resolution, less power available, and less memory available.

Most challenging were the new types of devices that were now accessing the Web, such as mobile phones, PDAs (personal digital assistants, such as the Blackberry and Palm Pilot), and set top boxes, because the screens could be very different from desktop PCs (not just slightly larger or with a bit better resolution). You certainly don't want to have to consider rewriting a Web site for each new kind of device that can access the Web.

The problems highlighted here are, once again, tied into the way HTML developed. If the content of the page were separated from the rules that govern how the page appears on a desktop PC, you could make the same content available to numerous devices by creating only one new set of presentational rules for each device that each page of the Web site could use (rather than rewriting every page again to be styled for a particular kind of device).

Of course, creating a new version of a site from scratch for each type of device that can access the Web is not a practical solution, and as you are about to see, you can learn a number of lessons by looking at how early mobile devices accessed the Web. It is fair to say that these events spurred the W3C's efforts to push forward the development of new versions of XHTML.

Lessons from the mobile world

When mobile phone manufacturers wanted to create Internet-enabled handsets, they knew that the HTML pages commonly available on the Web were not suitable for their devices. Not only were Web pages designed for screens much larger and more complex than theirs, but these phones had far less memory and power available to run them.

Memory was a key point because, as mentioned earlier, browsers designed to run on desktop computers had become bloated with code that enabled them to display pages even if they were not written correctly. When you consider that Netscape 7.2's system requirements are 26MB of hard disk space and 64MB of RAM, it is not hard to imagine that this is too much for your average mobile phone.

Because mobile phones presented such a different way of accessing the Web, the mobile phone manufacturers developed their own languages designed to make Web content available to their phones. This resulted in several competing languages that were designed to offer Web content on different mobile devices — examples include Wireless Markup Language (WML), which was part of the Wireless Application Protocol (WAP) group of specifications, Compact HTML, and Handheld Device Markup Language (HDML). When you look closely at all of these languages, however, you can see that they have something in common — they all act like a subset of HTML, and enable users to do the following:

❑   Create titles, headings, and text

❑   Link between pages

❑   Embed simple images

❑   Create basic tables

❑   Collect information from users via simple forms

What these languages lacked were the more advanced features of Web browsers, such as the capability to display complex layouts using tables and collect information using complex form controls, or the capability to display Flash movies and run powerful scripting languages.

These languages also require that the author write the page using a strict syntax — the browsers on these mobile devices were not as forgiving of sloppy coding as the major browsers on desktop computers.

By creating their own smaller languages, the mobile phone companies were able to create smaller browsers that would require less memory, eat up less power, and would therefore be able to run on their phones. With hindsight, you can see that they were all reinventing the wheel, when they could have just used a select few of the HTML elements and attributes, but this is not what happened.

At various points in the history of the Web, you might well have thought that each new device to access the Web was going to require its own new language that reflected the capabilities of that device. This would have meant creating several different versions of each and every page for each device. If you have ever struggled to get a site to work in both Internet Explorer *and* Netscape, then this idea would proba-bly have filled you with dread. Furthermore, if each new device required its own language, then it would have been harder for these devices to gain acceptance, because content would have to be devel-oped especially for them if they were going to be a success.

As you will see in the last chapter of this book, the W3C's solution has made it possible for all devices, both today and in the future, to use languages based upon XHTML; but you have a way to go before you can look at working with multiple devices.

> *In reality, when it comes to developing sites for different platforms, rather than creating static sites for each device, the pages are more likely to be dynamically generated from content in a database. Therefore, as you will see in this book, it is very important to ensure that the database holds XHTML, which can be repurposed for different devices.*

Accessibility

Many Web designers got into the habit of designing sites with pixel-precision accuracy. They used tables for layout whose width was measured in pixels; they used fixed-sized fonts; they commonly relied on a lot of images to make attractive layouts. This helped to ensure that the site looked the same on different computers (or at least on different browsers on desktop computers). However, it introduced a lot of problems for anyone who had less than 20/20 vision or perfect control over their mouse.

Many computer users with visual impairments use devices known as *screen readers* to read the content of the screen to them. These devices have complicated sets of keyboard shortcuts that enable the user to operate the software without necessarily seeing what is on the screen. Screen readers are just one of the many types of devices available to users with disabilities, and in many countries it is now a legal requirement that all Web pages are accessible to those with disabilities.

Some of the problems facing users with visual impairments when visiting Web sites include the following:

❑ Tables are used for layout, and often screen readers process tables in a way that makes pages hard to understand, reading things to users in the wrong order.

❑ Poor choices of color combinations can make it very hard to read text.

❑ Text can be specified in fixed-size fonts, making it impossible for users to increase the size when needed.

These problems, yet again, could be solved if the rules that indicate how a document should be presented were separated from the actual content of the document (and followed accessibility guidelines). For example, users with screen readers might want to remove all visual formatting (after all, they will not *see* the page) and let their software concentrate on the actual content of the page.

When it comes to accessibility, a number of other issues affect the way you go about designing and building Web pages, and these go beyond the issue of separating style from content. That is why two chapters are dedicated to the topic after you have learned all about XHTML and CSS. Here are some of the problems that users face, which are dealt with in those chapters:

❑ When dealing with forms, it is not always clear what information should be entered into a form control such as a text box, or which radio button should be selected. It is therefore important to label all form controls.

❑ If a page contains a large header (possibly with a lot of navigation items), a user with a screen reader will have to listen to all of this information before getting to the content of a page, which could be very tedious if the information is repeated on each page. It would be better if this information could be skipped.

❑ If images are used to represent text that is necessary for understanding the site and these images do not make use of the `alt` attribute (to provide a text alternative for those who cannot read what the image says), then users with screen readers will not know what the text on the image said.

Learning how to build sites in XHTML and CSS is the first step in creating accessible Web sites, so you should understand these basics before you continue on and learn about the range of other design considerations specifically related to accessibility issues, which are addressed in Chapters 6 and 7.

If you create an accessible site, you also reap other benefits (beyond those of meeting accessibility laws and helping those with disabilities):

❑ Increase the number of potential visitors to your site (and therefore potentially increase income), because the site is accessible to people it might not have been before.

❑ Make the content of your site accessible to those using your site in different situations. For example, if your site can be accessed by a screen reader, it is likely that it could also be used by an emerging market of voice browsers that can be used in different situations, such as while driving or jogging, when hands cannot be used to navigate using a mouse.

❑ Create code that will be available to a whole host of devices other than desktop PCs.

Separating style from content

At the very core of the problems you have been introduced to up to now is that most traditional HTML pages contained rules that controlled how they were presented. There was, therefore, a simple solution: Stop authors from mixing presentational (or stylistic) markup in with the markup that dictated the structure of the document.

The idea of *separating style from content* meant taking HTML back to its roots, when markup only described the structure and semantics of a document, not how it appeared. At first, these simple HTML documents might seem like a step backward to the days when the Web was a rather gray and drab place; but in reality, the documents can be just as visually attractive.

Rather than put the rules that govern how a document should appear in the same document that holds the real content that people read, you put those rules in a separate document known as a *style sheet*. For example, a rule in the style sheet might indicate that all level 1 headings should be written in a dark blue, size 5, Arial font.

This approach has many other advantages. For example, several documents can share the same style sheet, making it possible to create a single set of rules to be used to style every page of a site. Conversely, each document could be attached to different style sheets to make the same content appear in a different manner.

If you still need convincing, here is a summary of the key advantages of separating style rules from content:

❑   The content has been freed up. It can be presented in a lot of different ways for different users.

❑   You have simpler source documents, which will be easier to write.

❑   When you have simpler source documents, you are less likely to create errors when editing the documents.

❑   You can create the style rules once and use them for each page of your site, rather than repeat them in each page.

❑   It becomes much easier to maintain the style of a site, not only because it acts as a template for all pages, but because it also enables you to change a font or color across the whole site by just altering the one style sheet.

❑   If you want your content to be made available on different devices, you only need to write a new style sheet for each different device, rather than rewrite the whole site for each device.

❑   Once the browser has automatically downloaded the style sheet when it accesses the first page that uses it, it will be quicker to download subsequent pages that use the same style sheet because the browser stores a copy of the style sheet, and subsequent pages will be smaller because they do not contain style rules.

As you can see, in addition to solving the problems discussed so far, the separation of style from content brings a lot of other advantages, too.

Putting the "X" in XHTML

At the same time that the W3C decided to remove stylistic markup from HTML, they also decided that they would go one step further and rewrite HTML in a language you may well have heard of: *XML*. XML is a language that is used to write markup languages (and is therefore sometimes referred to as a *meta-markup language*). When the W3C was making these changes, XML was gaining wide acceptance in all areas of programming; it can be used on any platform because (like HTML) it uses plain text to hold the data, and it has been one of the most widely used new technologies in the past decade.

Reformulating HTML in XML would prepare the language for the next decade and beyond. Therefore, to reflect the change, rather than release HTML 5.0, the W3C decided to highlight the new family of documents by calling it XHTML (rather like Microsoft released Windows XP instead of Windows 2003, or Macromedia released Dreamweaver MX instead of Dreamweaver 6).

Several languages that you may have heard of are written in XML, including Scalable Vector Graphics (SVG), MathML (a language dedicated to writing mathematical equations), Extensible Stylesheet Language Transformations (XSLT), and XML Schemas. You can also find hundreds of business-orientated markup languages written in XML.

Making HTML compliant with the rules of XML has many advantages. You will learn more about these advantages in Chapters 2 and 8, but they include the following:

❑ XML requires a stricter syntax than HTML did — as you will see in Chapter 2. This in turn has other advantages:

  ❑ Browser manufacturers can write smaller browsers that can handle the XHTML pages. These smaller browsers are ideal for small devices that do not have as much memory or power available to them as desktop computers.

  ❑ You can perform complex operations, processing, and transformation upon the data held within the XHTML page. This means that the data is no longer solely used for visual presentation.

❑ Many tools and languages have been written to work with XML, all of which are then available to XHTML documents, including tools such as XSLT and Simple API for XML (SAX) processors.

In October 1999, the W3C released XHTML 1.0 — this was the reformulation of HTML in XML syntax. As you will see in Chapter 2, there are actually three versions of XHTML 1.0:

❑ **Strict XHTML 1.0** — which also removed all the old stylistic markup

❑ **Transitional XHTML 1.0** — which enabled Web page authors to continue to use the stylistic markup of HTML 4.1 while adopting XML syntax. This was largely designed to support older browsers known as *legacy* browsers.

❑ **Frameset XHTML 1.0** — which is used to create frameset documents.

Don't worry if this sounds complicated; it will all become clear in Chapter 2. Strict XHTML 1.0 is just a subset of Transitional XHTML 1.0, while Frameset XHTML 1.0 introduces only a handful of different markup to create frames. Best of all, each of the elements and attributes should be familiar to you already from HTML — after all, XHTML is just the latest incarnation of HTML.

The Story Behind CSS

Because Strict XHTML 1.0 documents contain no presentational markup, if you want them to look visually attractive, you have to link them to a style sheet that controls how the document is to be presented.

The W3C had already created a style sheet language that would be ideal for use with Web pages long before they came up with XHTML. *CSS* or *Cascading Style Sheets* were already being used by many HTML authors to control basic aspects of the style of documents, such as fonts and background colors.

CSS1 was actually released in December 1996, while CSS2, which expanded upon CSS1, was released in May 1998. Because Web designers were already using CSS to control the appearance of Web pages, and because of its benefits, it was the obvious choice for use with XHTML.

One thing that makes CSS relatively easy to learn is that its so-called *properties,* which control how the content of an element is displayed, are very similar to the attribute names you have used in HTML. However, CSS is also a very powerful language that enables you to do much more than is possible with the basic stylistic markup of HTML. For example, CSS offers the following:

- ❑ Very fine-grained control over the presentation of a page
- ❑ Control over the layout of a document without relying on tables (as you will see in Chapter 5)
- ❑ Properties for presenting a document in paged media (what most people would call print)
- ❑ Properties for aural versions of documents — which may be used by users with visual impairments or anyone on the move who cannot look at a screen

Chapters 3, 4, and 5 ensure that you can create attractive layouts using CSS.

Using Style Sheets

To solve the problems associated with viewing a Web site in different browsers and on different devices and to make sites more accessible, you have seen that the best approach is to separate the markup that describes the structure of a document's content from the rules that indicate how it should be displayed.

Separating design from content suggests the following:

- ❑ You are going to have to take your HTML skills back to basics and forget about the stylistic markup that was added to later versions of HTML. The main content of a page can now be written in Strict XHTML, which contains only markup to describe the structure and semantics of a document.
- ❑ The rules governing how a page should be displayed are written in a separate document to which the XHTML page links. This document is a style sheet written in CSS.

It is hard to look at examples in depth without learning more about each of the relevant languages. However, the following example is a version of the document you met in ch01_eg01.html written in XHTML. It is followed by a CSS style sheet used to control presentation of the page.

As you can see in this example, even the table (which was used for layout purposes) has been removed and replaced with <div> elements, which act as grouping elements to which styles can be attached (ch01_eg03.html):

```
<?xml version="1.0" encoding="iso-8859-1"?>
<!DOCTYPE html PUBLIC "-//W3C//DTD XHTML 1.0 Strict//EN"
        "http://www.w3.org/TR/xhtml1/DTD/xhtml1-strict.dtd">
<html xmlns="http://www.w3.org/1999/xhtml">
  <head>
    <title>The Effect of the Internet on Psychological Theories of Self</title>
```

```
    <link rel="stylesheet" type="text/css" href="ch01_eg03.css" />
    <meta http-equiv="Content-Type" content="text/html; charset=iso-8859-1" />
  </head>
  <body>
    <div class="page">
      <div class="heading">
            <h1>The Effect of the Internet on Psychological Theories of Self</h1>
      </div>
      <div class="body">
            <h2>Abstract</h2>
            <p>This paper looks that the role in which Internet users can adopt
            different online personae, and the effects this has on psychoanalytic
            theories of self and personal identity.</p>
            <p>While psychologists have long suggested that our concept of self
            should reflect a single, unitary, rational self, many people will adopt
            online personae that are very different than that which they display in
            person.</p>
            ...
      </div>
    </div>
  </body>
</html>
```

The following code represents the accompanying style sheet (ch01_eg03.css). Do not worry if this looks complicated at first; when you start to look at the language in Chapter 3, you will notice that a lot of it reflects features you learned with HTML attributes:

```
body {
  background-color:#000000;
  font-family: arial, verdana, sans-serif;}

div.page {
  width:650px;
  border-style:solid; border-width:1px; border-color:#666666;}

div.heading {
  background-color:#999999;
  padding:10px;}

div.body {
  background-color:#EFEFEF;
  padding:10px;}

h1 {
  font-size:22pt;
  color:#000066;}
h2 {
  font-size:18pt;
  color:#000066;}
p {
  font-size:14pt;
  color:#000000;}
```

While it might seem like a hassle to write a style sheet like this for one document, it can really save time if you are creating numerous pages that use the same styles; after all, you do not have to add the presentation rules to each document that uses them.

As you go through this book, you will see in more detail how the solution of separating style from content has many advantages. Indeed, in the future, as new devices are invented that need new capabilities, this solution can be extended — rather than having to create a new languages for each new device.

Furthermore, if you design your Web pages according to the XHTML and CSS standards, it should come as a relief to you that you will also be able to view them in older browsers that were written before these standards came out.

Introducing the Sample Site

Throughout this book, you are going to be working with one example site. The site is a fictional company that sells items known as "promotional" or "corporate" gifts, such as pens, bags, note pads, and stress reliever toys that have company names or logos on them. This next section introduces you to the site, including how it is organized and coded. You will be updating the site throughout subsequent chapters.

The fictional company whose site you are working on is called First Promotions, and their catalog and price list form the main part of the site. The company does not take orders online because they need to obtain the customer's logo (in addition to the text that should appear on the merchandise) before they start on the order. This often requires working with designers to ensure that the artwork is supplied in the correct formats (it also gives the sales team the benefit of direct contact with the customer). Once the artwork has been received, the design has to be approved before anything is actually produced.

> *If you are familiar with a server-side language, such as ASP/JSP/PHP, this example should be highly relevant to you, even though the site is written in HTML. After all, each of these technologies sends HTML back to the browser, and therefore teaches you how to correctly write the code to send back to the client.*

For the purposes of this book, pretend that First Promotions built a site in the late 1990s. That is the site you are going to meet now; it certainly uses techniques that were commonplace back then, and the style could do with a makeover while you are at work on it.

You can test the site for yourself by going to www.firstPromotions.co.uk and selecting the option to view the original version of the site. The complete code for the original and finished versions of the site is also available for download (along with the rest of the code for this book) from www.wrox.com.

Figure 1-4 shows you the home page of the First Promotions site.

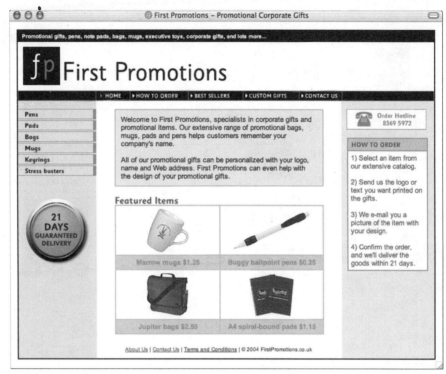

Figure 1-4

You can see from Figure 1-4 that the home page has a header and some navigation items underneath the logo, and then the rest of the page is divided into three columns. This is a very common layout.

As already mentioned, the main purpose of the site is to act as a catalog and price list for the company. You can see the sections of the catalog in the left-hand column—this is referred to as *category navigation*. Each of these links will take you to a product list page, which shows summary information for all of the items in that category. You can see an example of a product list page in Figure 1-5, which shows the product list page for the Bags category.

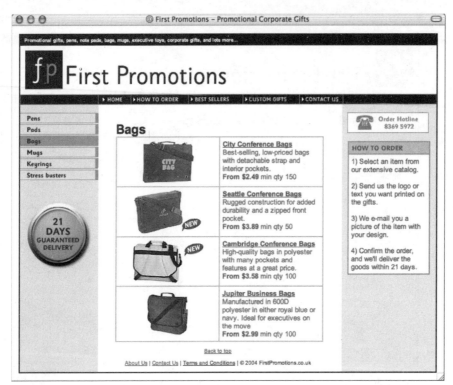

Figure 1-5

This page follows the same three-column layout that the home page does, and the list pages for all categories are identical in all but the products they contain.

When users click on the image or title of an item, they are taken to an individual product page. You can see an example of one of these product pages in Figure 1-6. As you can see from this screenshot, the product pages use a two-column layout. By removing the third column, more space is available to show the product in detail.

Across the top of each page, and at the bottom of the main column, you can see additional navigation links to pages that contain information on topics such as how to contact the company, how to place an order, information about the company, and so on. These pages all follow the same structure as the home page, with a three-column layout. The only exception is the best sellers page, which uses the same structure as the product list pages.

In summary, the site contains three main types of pages:

❑   Home page

❑   Product lists page

❑   Product details page

Figure 1-6

Every page follows one of these three designs. The following sections describe each one of these in a little more detail. You do not need to study every line of code in minute detail, but you should get a good idea of how the site is built because you will be coming back to it throughout the rest of the book. The code for the original version of the site is also reproduced here so that you can refer to it later as you work on the updates.

Home page

As with any site, the home page is the first that most visitors will see when they access the site. It tells users what they can expect to find on the site, and provides a base from which they can navigate the site.

Figure 1-7 shows a line drawing superimposed over the home page, indicating the location of the tables that control the layout of the page.

The whole page is written inside a single-cell table, which fixes the width of the table and draws a border around the page. Inside this table are three other tables.

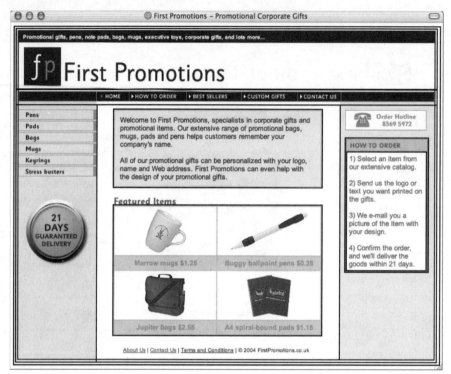

Figure 1-7

At the top you can see the first table containing the heading, with the company logo and aim of the site. Beneath this is a second table containing links to individual pages that feature other information, such as how to order products, contact details, and the best-selling items. The third table contains the main body of the page. This third table has three columns:

❑ Column 1 contains the navigation for different sections (and the guarantee stamp image)

❑ Column 2 contains the main content of the page, which is what the user came to see

❑ Column 3 contains additional information, such as ordering details

Here is the code for the home page (index.html), which starts out as you might expect:

```
<html>
<head>
  <title>First Promotions - Promotional Corporate Gifts</title>
```

The following script is generated by Macromedia Dreamweaver when you add a rollover image:

```javascript
<script language="JavaScript" type="text/JavaScript">
<!--
function MM_swapImgRestore() { //v3.0
  var i,x,a=document.MM_sr; for(i=0;a&&i<a.length&&(x=a[i])&&x.oSrc;i++)
  x.src=x.oSrc;
}

function MM_preloadImages() { //v3.0
  var d=document; if(d.images){ if(!d.MM_p) d.MM_p=new Array();
  var i,j=d.MM_p.length,a=MM_preloadImages.arguments; for(i=0; i<a.length; i++)
  if (a[i].indexOf("#")!=0){ d.MM_p[j]=new Image; d.MM_p[j++].src=a[i];}}
}

function MM_findObj(n, d) { //v4.01
  var p,i,x;  if(!d) d=document; if((p=n.indexOf("?"))>0&&parent.frames.length) {
  d=parent.frames[n.substring(p+1)].document; n=n.substring(0,p);}
  if(!(x=d[n])&&d.all) x=d.all[n];
  for (i=0;!x&&i<d.forms.length;i++) x=d.forms[i][n];
  for(i=0;!x&&d.layers&&i<d.layers.length;i++) x=MM_findObj(n,d.layers[i].document);
  if(!x && d.getElementById) x=d.getElementById(n); return x;
}

function MM_swapImage() { //v3.0
  var i,j=0,x,a=MM_swapImage.arguments; document.MM_sr=new Array;
  for(i=0;i<(a.length-2);i+=3)
   if ((x=MM_findObj(a[i]))!=null){document.MM_sr[j++]=x; if(!x.oSrc) x.oSrc=x.src;
      x.src=a[i+2];}
}
//-->
  </script>
</head>
```

On the `<body>` element, you can see several stylistic attributes such as the `bgcolor` and `link` attributes. The `onLoad` attribute is generated by Dreamweaver (as was the script) to preload rollover images:

```html
<body bgcolor="#FFFFFF" alink="#0000CC" vlink="#003366" link="#0066CC"
  onLoad="MM_preloadImages('images/interface/nav_order_on.gif',
   'images/interface/nav_bestSellers_on.gif','images/interface/nav_custom.gif',
   'images/interface/nav_contactUs_on.gif','images/interface/nav_pens_on.gif',
   'images/nav_nav_pads_on.gif','images/interface/nav_bags.gif',
   'images/interface/nav_mugs_on.gif', 'images/interface/nav_stress_on.gif')">
```

Now you get to the content of the page, which is held within a `<center>` element to make it appear in the middle of the page. The whole page is created inside one `<table>` element that is given a `width` of 800 pixels so that the width of the page is fixed, and it is surrounded by a single-pixel border. This table has just one cell, containing the rest of the page.

Inside the single cell of the table that contains the page are three other tables: one containing the masthead (or header) for the page, the second containing the navigation, and the third containing the main body of the page. First, here is the table containing the masthead for the page:

```
<center>
<table border="1" cellpadding="0" cellspacing="0" width="800"
    bordercolor="#000066"><tr><td>

<!-- masthead -->
<table border="0" cellpadding="5" cellspacing="0" width="800">
  <tr>
    <td bgcolor="#000066">
      <font face="Arial, Helvetica, sans-serif" size="6" color="#FFFFFF">
        <b> Promotional gifts, pens, note pads, bags, mugs, executive toys,
          corporate gifts, and lots more...</b>
      </font>
    </td>
  </tr>
  <tr>
    <td><img src="images/branding/logo_400x80.gif" alt="logo" border="0"></td>
  </tr>
</table>
```

The second table contains the navigation. As you can see, the table for the navigation contains code to create rollover images on each item in the top navigation bar:

```
<!-- navigation -->
<table border="0" cellpadding="0" cellspacing="1" width="800" bgcolor="6699FF">
  <tr>
    <td width="150" bgcolor="#000066"></td>
    <td bgcolor="#000066">
      <img src="images/interface/nav_home_on.gif" width="64" height="17"border="0">
    </td>
    <td bgcolor="#000066">
      <a href="order.html" onMouseOut="MM_swapImgRestore()"
        onMouseOver="MM_swapImage('HowToOrder','',
         'images/interface/nav_order_on.gif',1)">
        <img src="images/interface/nav_order.gif" alt="How to Order"
            name="HowToOrder" width="110" height="17" border="0">
      </a>
    </td>
    <td bgcolor="#000066">
      <a href="bestSellers.html" onMouseOut="MM_swapImgRestore()"
        onMouseOver="MM_swapImage('BestSellers','',
         'images/interface/nav_bestSellers_on.gif',1)">
        <img src="images/interface/nav_bestSellers.gif" alt="Best Sellers"
            name="BestSellers" width="104" height="17" border="0">
      </a>
    </td>
    <td bgcolor="#000066">
      <a href="custom.html" onMouseOut="MM_swapImgRestore()"
        onMouseOver="MM_swapImage('CustomGifts','',
         'images/interface/nav_custom_on.gif',1)">
        <img src="images/interface/nav_custom.gif" alt="Custom Gifts"
          name="CustomGifts" width="107" height="17" border="0">
      </a>
    </td>
```

```
        <td bgcolor="#000066">
            <a href="contact.html" onMouseOut="MM_swapImgRestore()"
              onMouseOver="MM_swapImage('ContactUs','',
                'images/interface/nav_contactUs_on.gif',1)">
                <img src="images/interface/nav_contactUs.gif" alt="Contact Us"
                    name="ContactUs" width="82" height="17" border="0">
            </a>
        </td>
        <td width="180" bgcolor="#000066"></td>
    </tr>
</table>
```

The third and final table contains the main page. This table contains one row with three table cells; there is one cell for each column in the layout.

The first column contains the product navigation, which again contains rollover images just like the top navigation. To make the code readable, I have added white space between each element; however, in the download code, there are no spaces between the navigation links and spacer images (otherwise, you can find gaps between them in Internet Explorer):

```
<!-- main page -->
<table border="0" cellpadding="0" cellspacing="0" width="800">
  <tr>
    <td width="150" bgcolor="#D9ECFF" valign="top">
        <img src="images/interface/1px.gif" height="15" width="150">
        <a href="products/pens/index.html" onMouseOut="MM_swapImgRestore()"
            onMouseOver="MM_swapImage('Pens','',
              'images/interface/nav_pens_on.gif',1)">
            <img src="images/interface/nav_pens.gif" alt="Pens" name="Pens" width="150"
                height="19" border="0">
        </a>
        <img src="images/interface/1px.gif" height="2" width="150">
        <a href="products/pads/index.html" onMouseOut="MM_swapImgRestore()"
            onMouseOver="MM_swapImage('Pads','',
              'images/interface/nav_pads_on.gif',1)">
            <img src="images/interface/nav_pads.gif" alt="Pads" name="Pads" width="150"
                height="19" border="0">
        </a>
        <img src="images/interface/1px.gif" height="2" width="150">
        <a href="products/bags/index.html" onMouseOut="MM_swapImgRestore()"
            onMouseOver="MM_swapImage('Bags','',
              'images/interface/nav_bags_on.gif',1)">
            <img src="images/interface/nav_bags.gif" alt="Bags" name="Bags" width="150"
                height="19" border="0">
        </a>
        <img src="images/interface/1px.gif" height="2" width="150">
        <a href="mugs.html" onMouseOut="MM_swapImgRestore()"
            onMouseOver="MM_swapImage('Mugs','',
              'images/interface/nav_mugs_on.gif',1)">
            <img src="images/interface/nav_mugs.gif" alt="Mugs" name="Mugs" width="150"
                height="19" border="0">
        </a>
```

```
    <img src="images/interface/1px.gif" height="2" width="150">
    <a href="products/keyrings/index.html" onMouseOut="MM_swapImgRestore()"
       onMouseOver="MM_swapImage('Keyrings','',
        'images/interface/nav_keyrings_on.gif',1)">
      <img src="images/interface/nav_keyrings.gif" alt="Key rings"
         name="Key rings" width="150" height="19" border="0">
    </a>
    <img src="images/interface/1px.gif" height="2" width="150">
    <a href="products/stressbusters/index.html" onMouseOut="MM_swapImgRestore()"
       onMouseOver="MM_swapImage('StressBusters','',
        'images/interface/nav_stress_on.gif',1)">
      <img src="images/interface/nav_stress.gif" alt="Stress busters"
         name="StressBusters" width="150" height="19" border="0">
    </a>
    <img src="images/interface/1px.gif" height="40" width="150">
    <center>
     <img src="images/interface/guarantee.jpg" height="126" width="127">
    </center>
  </td>
```

The second column holds the main message of the page. The first thing you see in this column is an introductory paragraph telling users what the company does. This paragraph is held in its own table to make the text look like it is in a box of its own:

```
<td width="470" bgcolor="#FFFFFF" valign="top">
  <center>
  <img src="images/interface/1px.gif" height="15" width="1">
    <table border="1" cellpadding="10" cellspacing="0" bordercolor="#C5C5C5"
         bgcolor="#EFEFEF" width="400">
      <tr>
        <td>
          <font face="Arial, Helvetica, sans-serif" size="2" color="#000066">
            Welcome to First Promotions, specialists in corporate gifts and
            promotional items. Our extensive range of promotional bags,
            mugs, pads and pens helps customers remember your company's
            name.<br><br>

            All of our promotional gifts can be personalized with your logo,
            name and Web address. First Promotions can even help with
            the design of your promotional gifts.</font>
        </td>
      </tr>
    </table>
  </center>
  <br>
```

Beneath the introductory paragraphs on the home page is a simple table containing some featured items. Note how the image that says "featured items" is indented using a single-pixel transparent GIF. These featured items link directly to pages that show the full details of the items in the catalog:

```
<img src="images/interface/1px.gif" width="35" height="1">
<img src="images/interface/featuredItems.gif">
<center>
  <table border="1" cellpadding="5" cellspacing="0" bordercolor="#C5C5C5"
      bgcolor="#D6D6D6" width="400">
    <tr>
      <td width="200" bgcolor="#FFFFFF" align="center">
        <a href="products/mugs/mug2.html">
          <img src="products/mugs/images/mugs2_thumb.gif" border="0">
        </a>
      </td>
      <td width="200" bgcolor="#FFFFFF" align="center">
        <a href="products/pens/pen2.hml">
          <img src="products/pens/images/pens2_thumb.gif" border="0">
        </a>
      </td>
    </tr>
    <tr>
      <td width-"200" align="center">
        <font face="Arial, Helvetica, sans-serif" size="2" color="6699FF">
          <b>Marrow mugs from $1.25</b>
        </font>
      </td>
      <td width="200" align="center">
        <font face="Arial, Helvetica, sans-serif" size="2" color="6699FF">
          <b>Buggy ballpoint pens from $0.25</b>
        </font>
      </td>
    </tr>
    <tr>
      <td width="200" bgcolor="#FFFFFF" align="center">
        <a href="products/bags/bag4.html">
          <img src="products/bags/images/bags4_thumb.gif" border="0">
        </a>
      </td>
      <td width="200" bgcolor="#FFFFFF" align="center">
        <a href="products/pads/pad3.html">
          <img src="products/pads/images/pad3_thumb.gif" border="0">
        </a>
      </td>
    </tr>
    <tr>
      <td width="200" align="center">
        <font face="Arial, Helvetica, sans-serif" size="2" color="6699FF">
          <b>Jupiter bags $2.55</b>
        </font>
      </td>
      <td width="200" align="center">
        <font face="Arial, Helvetica, sans-serif" size="2" color="6699FF">
          <b>A4 spiral-bound pads $1.15</b>
        </font>
      </td>
    </tr>
  </table>
```

At the bottom of the center column, you can see the footer links:

```
    <font face="Arial, Helvetica, sans-serif" size="1" color="#0000CC">
     <br><br>
      <a href="about.html">About Us</a> |
      <a href="contact.html">Contact Us</a> |
      <a href="terms.html">Terms and Conditions</a> |
      &copy; 2004 FirstPromotions.co.uk
      <br><br>
     </font>
    </center>
   </td>
```

The third and final column contains the information about ordering that you can see on the right-hand side of the home page. This part of the page uses nested tables to create boxes around parts of the text:

```
   <td width="180" bgcolor="#EFEFEF" valign="top">
     <img src="images/interface/1px.gif" height="15" width="1">
     <center>
       <img src="images/interface/orderHotline.gif" width="155" height="38"> <br>
       <img src="images/interface/1px.gif" height="15" width="1">
       <table border="1" cellpadding="0" cellspacing="0" bordercolor="#FF9900"
              width="155">
         <tr>
           <td>
             <img src="images/interface/howToOrder.gif" width="153" height="21">
           </td>
         </tr>
         <tr>
           <td bgcolor="#FFFFFF">
             <table border="0" cellpadding="5" cellspacing="0">
               <tr>
                 <td>
                   <font face="Arial, sans-serif" size="2" color="#904C2D">
                   1) Select an item from our extensive catalog.<br><br>
                   2) Send us the logo or text you want printed on the
                      gifts.<br><br>
                   3) We e-mail you a picture of the item with your
                      design.<br><br>
                   4) Confirm the order, and we'll deliver the goods within
                      21 days.<br>
                   </font>
                 </td>
               </tr>
             </table>
           </td>
         </tr>
       </table>
       <br><br>
     </center>
   </td>
  </tr>
</table>
```

```
</td></tr></table>
</center>
</body>
</html>
```

As you can see when you browse through the site, the pages that you get to when using the top and the bottom navigation are of a very similar structure — the main content is the middle of an otherwise identical three-column layout — the only exception being the best sellers page, which follows the structure of the product list pages that you are about to meet.

Product list pages

Each of the six categories has its own folder in the directory structure of the site. Each of these folders has a file called index.html that contains a list of all the products in that category; hence, it is known as a product list page. This page uses a three-column layout, just like the home page, and indeed the only real difference between this page and the home page is the center column of the table that forms the main part of the page.

Let's start looking at this page inside the <body> tags. Because the logo and masthead, the top navigation, and the left navigation are virtually identical to those in the home page, I'll skip over them. There are only two notable differences:

❑   The image indicating that the user is in the Bags section of the site is "on."

❑   All URLs to images and links to other pages are preceded by ../../, indicating that the relative URLs given are from the folder above the parent folder for this file.

```
<center>
<table border="1" cellpadding="0" cellspacing="0" width="800"
        bordercolor="#000066">
  <tr><td>

<table border="0" cellpadding="5" cellspacing="0" width="800">
<!-- LOGO AND MASTHEAD HERE -->
</table>

<table border="0" cellpadding="0" cellspacing="1" width="800" bgcolor="6699FF">
<!-- TOP NAVIGATION GOES HERE -->
</table>

<table border="0" cellpadding="0" cellspacing="0" width="800">
    <tr>
      <td width="150" bgcolor="#D9ECFF" valign="top">
<!-- LEFT NAVIGATION GOES HERE -->
      </td>
```

The real changes are in the middle column in the third table (which is the table that holds the main content of the page that changes). First, there are a couple of transparent single-pixel GIFs that position the heading in the desired place. The heading indicates which category the user is accessing — in this case, Bags:

```
<td width="470" bgcolor="#FFFFFF" valign="top">
  <center>
    <img src="../../images/interface/1px.gif" height="15" width="1">
  </center><br>
  <img src="../../images/interface/1px.gif" height="1" width="35">
  <font face="Arial, Helvetica, sans-serif" size="5" color="#000066">
    <b>Bags</b>
  </font><br>
```

The main part of the product list page is a table that shows the different products available in the category. There is one row for each product, with an image of that product in the left-hand cell and a description of that product in the right-hand cell. Both the image and the title link to the page that contains details about that product:

```
<center>
  <table border="1" cellpadding="5" cellspacing="0" bordercolor="#C5C5C5"
        bgcolor="#D6D6D6" width="400">
    <tr>
      <td width="200" bgcolor="#FFFFFF" align="center">
        <a href="bag1.html">
          <img src="images/bags1_thumb.gif" border="0">
        </a>
      </td>
      <td width="200" bgcolor="#FFFFFF" valign="top">
        <font face="Arial, Helvetica, sans-serif" size="2" color="#666666">
          <b><a href="bag1.html">City Conference Bags</a></b><br>
            Best-selling, low-priced bags with detachable strap and
              interior pockets.<br>
          <b>From $2.49</b> min qty 150
        </font>
      </td>
    </tr>
    <tr>
      <td width="200" bgcolor="#FFFFFF" align="center">
        <a href="bag2.html">
          <img src="images/bags2_thumb.gif" border="0">
        </a>
      </td>
      <td width="200" bgcolor="#FFFFFF" valign="top">
        <font face="Arial, Helvetica, sans-serif" size="2" color="#666666">
        <b><a href="bag2.html">Seattle Conference Bags</a></b><br>
          Rugged construction for added durability and a zipped front
            pocket.<br>
          <b>From $3.89</b> min qty 50
        </font>
      </td>
    </tr>
    <tr>
      <td width="200" bgcolor="#FFFFFF" align="center">
        <a href="bag3.html">
          <img src="images/bags3_thumb.gif" border="0">
        </a>
      </td>
    </tr>
```

```
        <td width="200" bgcolor="#FFFFFF" valign="top">
          <font face="Arial, Helvetica, sans-serif" size="2" color="#666666">
            <b><a href="bag3.html">Cambridge Conference Bags</a></b><br>
              High-quality bags in polyester with many pockets and features
                at a great price.<br>
              <b>From $3.58</b> min qty 100
          </font>
        </td>
      </tr>
      <tr>
        <td width="200" bgcolor="#FFFFFF" align="center">
          <a href="bag4.html">
            <img src="images/bags4_thumb.gif" border="0">
          </a>
        </td>
        <td width="200" bgcolor="#FFFFFF" valign="top">
          <font face="Arial, Helvetica, sans-serif" size="2" color="#666666">
            <b><a href="bag4.html">Jupiter Business Bags</a></b><br>
              Manufactured in 600D polyester in either royal blue or navy.
                Ideal for executives on the move<br>
              <b>From $2.99</b> min qty 100
          </font>
        </td>
      </tr>
    </table>
```

As with all of the pages, this column contains some footer links at the bottom:

```
        <font face="Arial, Helvetica, sans-serif" size="1" color="#0000CC">
        <!-- FOOTER LINKS GO HERE -->
        </font>
        </center>
      </td>
```

The rest of the page, including the right-hand column, has exactly the same content as the home page, so I won't repeat that here:

```
        <td width="180" bgcolor="#EFEFEF" valign="top">
        <!-- RIGHT COLUMN GOES HERE -->
        </td>
      </tr>
    </table>

    </td></tr></table>
    </center>
```

Remember that there are six product categories—pens, bags, mugs, pads, keyrings, and stress busters. Each category has its own folder in the directory structure. In the folder for each category is a file called index.html, which is the product list for that product category.

Product details page

When users click on any of the items on the product list (or the featured items on the home page), they will be taken to an individual product page containing the detailed information for that product, along with prices for the products.

Because more information needs to go on the product details pages than the other pages, you have only two columns in the main part of this page. Figure 1-8 shows the product details page for the Jupiter bag, with lines superimposed over the locations where tables control the layout.

Figure 1-8

As before, the entire page is contained inside a table that controls the width of the page and draws a border around the edge of it. Inside this table are three more tables, the first containing the masthead, the second the navigation, and the third the main body of the page. This third table contains only two cells, one for the left navigation and the one for the product details.

Now have a look at the code behind this page (`bag4.html`). The start of the page is the same as both the home page (except that the URLs start with `../../`) and the product list pages, so I'll start in the body of the page. As with the other pages, a table with a single cell holds the entire content of the page. Inside this cell are tables for the masthead and navigation:

```
<center>

<table border="1" cellpadding="0" cellspacing="0" width="800"
        bordercolor="#000066"><tr><td>

<table border="0" cellpadding="5" cellspacing="0" width="800">
  <!-- MASTHEAD -->
</table>

<table border="0" cellpadding="0" cellspacing="1" width="800" bgcolor="6699FF">
  <!-- TOP NAVIGATION -->
</table>
```

Next is the third table, which is the one that creates the columns in the main part of the page. As with the other pages, the first column (which is held in the first cell of this table) contains the navigation — you don't need to look at this again.

The second column is a lot wider at 650 pixels and provides a lot more room to display the details of the selected product:

```
<!-- main page -->
<table border="0" cellpadding="0" cellspacing="0" width="800">
  <tr>
    <td width="150" bgcolor="#D9ECFF" valign="top">
      <!-- LEFT NAVIGATION -->
    </td>
    <td width="650" bgcolor="#FFFFFF" valign="top">
```

Now you are in the cell that represents the main product information part of the page. This cell contains two tables — the first holds the title of the product and the link to all of the bags:

```
    <br>
    <center>
    <table border="0" cellpadding="0" cellspacing="0" width="550">
      <tr>
       <td>
         <font face="Arial, Helvetica, sans-serif" size="5" color="#000066">
           <b>Jupiter Business Bags</b>
         </font>
       </td>
       <td align="right" valign="top">
         <a href="/products/bags/index.html">
           <font face="Arial, Helvetica, sans-serif" size="1" color="#000066">
             <b>View All Bags</b>
           </font>
         </a>
       </td>
      </tr>
    </table><br>
```

Although it may not look like it, the second table contains just one cell. That is because it is a wrapper table, and it in turn contains another table. This single-celled table is used to create a line around the information it contains and is made up of two rows and two columns:

- ❏ Row 1, column 1 contains the image of the bag.

- ❏ Row 1, column 2 contains the description of the bag.

- ❏ Row 2, column 1 contains the prices.

- ❏ Row 2, column 2 contains printing information.

Let's start with the first row, which contains the image and description and is fairly straightforward:

```
<table border="1" bordercolor="#666666" cellpadding="0"
    cellspacing="0" width="550"><tr><td>

  <table border="0" cellpadding="10" cellspacing="0" bgcolor="#FFFFFF"
      width="550">
    <tr>
    <td width="350" bgcolor="#FFFFFF" align="center" valign="top">
      <img src="images/bags4.jpg" border="0">
    </td>
    <td width="200" bgcolor="#EFEFEF" valign="top">
      <font face="Arial, Helvetica, sans-serif" size="2" color="#666666">
        <b>Manufactured in high-quality 600D polyester in either black or
           navy and featuring two plastic turn locks and additional pen
           holders underneath the flap.</b>
        <br><br><br>
        <b>PRODUCT SPECIFICATIONS</b><br>
        <b>Product size:</b> 32 x 9 x 36 cm<br>
        <b>Print area:</b> 200 x 120 mm<br>
        <b>Product colors:</b> black, navy<br>
        <b>Lead time:</b> 3-4 weeks <br><br>
      </font>
    </td>
  </tr>
```

The following code shows the second row. The first column of row two contains more nested tables that control the layout of the prices for the products. The second column of row two just contains the printing information:

```
<tr>
  <td bgcolor="#EFEFEF" align="center" valign="top">
    <table border="0" cellpadding="2" cellspacing="2">
      <tr>
        <td bgcolor="#D6D6D6">
          <font face="Arial, sans-serif" size="2"><b>Quantity</b></font>
        </td>
        <td bgcolor="#D6D6D6">
          <font face="Arial, sans-serif" size="2"><b>100</b></font>
        </td>
```

```
                    <td bgcolor="#D6D6D6">
                       <font face="Arial, sans-serif" size="2"><b>250</b></font>
                    </td>
                    <td bgcolor="#D6D6D6">
                       <font face="Arial, sans-serif" size="2"><b>500</b></font>
                    </td>
                    <td bgcolor="#D6D6D6">
                       <font face="Arial, sans-serif" size="2"><b>1000</b></font>
                    </td>
                 </tr>
                 <tr>
                    <td bgcolor="#D6D6D6">
                       <font face="Arial, sans-serif" size="2"><b>Unit price</b></font>
                    </td>
                    <td><font face="Arial, sans-serif" size="2">$4.25</font></td>
                    <td><font face="Arial, sans-serif" size="2">$3.66</font></td>
                    <td><font face="Arial, sans-serif" size="2">$3.44</font></td>
                    <td>
                       <font face="Arial, Helvetica, sans-serif" size="2">$3.22</font>
                    </td>
                 </tr>
                 <tr>
                    <td bgcolor="#D6D6D6">
                       <font face="Arial, sans-serif" size="2">
                         <b>Additional colors (each)</b>
                         </font>
                    </td>
                    <td><font face="Arial, sans-serif" size="2">$0.50</font></td>
                    <td><font face="Arial, sans-serif" size="2">$0.45</font></td>
                    <td><font face="Arial, sans-serif" size="2">$0.45</font></td>
                    <td><font face="Arial, sans-serif" size="2">$0.45</font></td>
                 </tr>
              </table>
           </td>
           <td width="200" bgcolor="#FFFFFF" valign="top">
             <font face="Arial, Helvetica, sans-serif" size="2" color="#666666">
               <b>Price includes a single-color print in one position.<br><br>
               Screens cost £35 per color, per position.</b>
             </font>
           </td>
        </tr>
     </table>
  </td>
</td></tr></table>
```

Remember that this page has only two columns, so the bottom of the page finishes at the end of this cell, which still contains the footer links:

```
<font face="Arial, Helvetica, sans-serif" size="1" color="#0000CC">
<!-- FOOTER LINKS -->
</font>
</center>
</td>
```

```
            </tr>
          </table>
      </td>
    </tr>
  </table>

  </td></tr></table>
  </center>
```

At this point you have seen the structure of every page on this site. Only the content of the pages differs, but it would probably help if you also took a look at the directory structure.

Site structure

Having looked at how all of the pages are written for the First Promotions site, it is helpful to see how the directory structure is set up. Figure 1-9 shows the corresponding folder structure for the site.

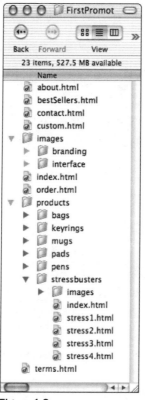

Figure 1-9

The main home page is called `index.html`, and it sits in the root directory, along with an `images` folder, a `products` folder, and the following pages:

Filename	Purpose
`aboutUs.html`	Introduces information about the company
`bestSellers.html`	Contains details about the best-selling items
`contact.html`	Contact information to get in touch with the company
`custom.html`	How to place orders for custom items that are not in the catalog
`order.html`	How to order items from the catalog
`terms.html`	Terms and conditions of using the site

Inside the `images` folder are two more folders. The first one is called `branding` and contains images such as the logo; the second folder is called `interface` and contains images used to create the user interface, such as the navigation buttons.

Inside the `products` folder are six subfolders — one for each of the six different product categories that First Promotions offers: pens, bags, mugs, pads, keyrings, and stress busters. Each of these folders contains the following:

❑   An `index.html` page that provides an overview of all the products in that category

❑   A folder called `images` that contains the photographs of the products in that category (there is a thumbnail and full-size copy of each image)

❑   A page for each product that provides more details about the product and pricing information

Before you continue with subsequent chapters, it would be helpful to either try the site out at `www.FirstPromotions.co.uk` or to download a copy from `www.wrox.com` along with the rest of the source code for this book and get it running on your own computer. This will help you in the coming pages as you look at the site in more detail.

Updating the site

Throughout the book, you will be making changes to the site as you learn each topic. By the end of the book, you will have a new site that is XHTML compliant, whose style and layout is controlled by CSS, and which meets the W3C and Section 508 accessibility guidelines. The design will also be more modern. Figure 1-10 shows a screenshot of the home page that you will end up with after all your efforts.

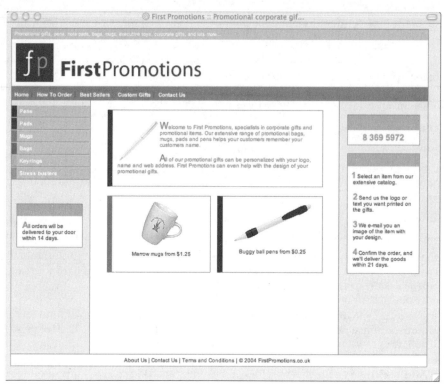

Figure 1-10

Your updating of the site will take the following course throughout the book:

1. While you look at XHTML (and the differences between HTML and XHTML), you will take the HTML structure that you have just been introduced to and change it to make the site XHTML-compliant. By the end of Chapter 2, all of the code will use XHTML syntax, and the presentational markup in the site will have been removed. As a result, the site will look a lot less styled, but that is okay because you will make it more attractive again in the chapters on CSS. The XHTML pages should also be easier to maintain because they will not be cluttered with presentational markup.

Having learned how to write XHTML pages, you will be able to write content that can be served to devices that use XHTML browsers and don't necessarily support all of the features of HTML. In addition, because XHTML is written in XML, all of your pages could be used in conjunction with any of the existing XML tools, such as XSLT, DOM, and SAX-aware processors.

2. Chapters 3 and 4 will show you how to use CSS to control the presentation of the site, and by the end of Chapter 4, the site will look much as it does now, but it will use a CSS style sheet, rather than presentational markup, to control its appearance. This achieves a separation of style from content, and makes the updating and maintenance of styles much easier. Then, should you want to change a color or font across the whole site, you can do so by making an alteration to the one style sheet. Because the presentational rules are contained in the one style sheet, rather than being repeated in every page (and because browsers keep a copy of this style sheet locally once it has been downloaded), it should make the size of the files in your site smaller, which will enable the site to download faster. The use of style sheets to control presentation also means that you can attach different style sheets to the same XHTML documents to present them in different ways for different purposes and devices.

3. In Chapter 5, you will see how the layout of the pages can be controlled by CSS. Rather than relying on tables to create the masthead and navigation at the top of the page, and using cells to create columns in the main body of the page, these sections of the site will be rebuilt contained within <div> elements, which are then positioned using CSS. Using CSS to control page layout means that tables are used only for tabular data, which is what they were originally intended to contain, and that you can change the layout of your entire site simply by altering the one style sheet. It should make your XHTML pages simpler and help make your site more accessible.

4. Chapters 6 and 7 look at the topic of accessibility in greater detail, and throughout these chapters you will learn techniques to ensure that your site meets the requirements of the W3C and Section 508 guidelines. Once you have created an XHTML version of the site that uses CSS to control presentation and layout, you are already a long way towards creating an accessible site; however, you need to be aware of many more issues, which are covered in these chapters. You will be looking at different aspects of a site and the guidelines that cover each aspect; for example, providing text alternatives to nontext content (such as images, video, and audio) so that visually impaired users can still use the site to creating accessible forms and tables. You will also be introduced to some tools that you can use to help ensure that your site meets accessibility requirements.

5. Finally, in Chapter 8 you will see how XHTML is looking toward the future and evolving to cope with the plethora of new devices that can access the Internet. In this chapter, you will learn that the move to XHTML will provide you with a solid foundation for devising pages for all kinds of new devices. You will even see a sample of what a site can look like on a mobile phone.

The code for the final version of the site is available in the code download along with the rest of the code samples for the book. You can also see it online by visiting www.FirstPromotions.co.uk and selecting the option to view the final site.

Summary

In this chapter, you have learned both how the Web has changed over time and how Web page authors must adapt skills to reflect those changes. You have seen how, as technology advanced, the size and resolutions of the monitors used when accessing the Web improved, and how the variety of devices capable of viewing Web pages ballooned. This means that you can no longer create one design for a Web page and expect it to work on all devices that access the Internet.

Although the successive versions of HTML introduced all sorts of elements and attributes that helped Web page authors control the appearance of their pages, it is now necessary to stop using that stylistic or presentational markup in the same document as the content you expect people to read. Instead, you should be separating the markup that describes the structure of a document from the stylistic rules that indicate how a Web page should be displayed. The presentation rules should be placed in a separate style sheet written using a language called Cascading Style Sheets, or CSS for short.

HTML has therefore been replaced with a new language that has removed the stylistic markup. It also has a slightly refined syntax because the successor to HTML has been written in a language called XML; hence the name has changed to XHTML. The reformulation of HTML in XML helps ensure that the most widely used language on the Web today will remain just as popular for many years to come, even if new devices with different capabilities start to emerge. This topic is discussed in more detail in Chapter 8.

Finally, you have seen that you have to make numerous changes to the way you design your Web pages if you are going to meet legal requirements that expect all Web pages to be accessible to those with disabilities. Learning to write sites in XHTML and CSS is the first step along the road to building accessible Web sites, although you will find a lot more tips and techniques you need to learn from Chapters 6 and 7 to create truly accessible sites.

Moving from HTML to XHTML

In this chapter, you will learn everything you need to know to progress from writing HTML documents to writing fully XHTML-compliant documents. XHTML is the future of HTML; it is HTML 4 rewritten using the syntax of a language called XML. If you have not heard of XHTML, the good news is that most of the elements and attributes in the XHTML recommendation are the same as those you are familiar with from HTML 4; however, the bad news is that the rules for XHTML are quite a lot stricter than HTML, so you have to be more careful about how you write pages in XHTML, and for a lot of people this means breaking a few habits that they have acquired over the years.

Apart from the rules being stricter, and the necessity of learning a few new rules, the other major difference with XHTML is that it aims to separate style from content. This means that all of the elements and attributes that were there just to control the presentation of documents are on their way out, as styling a document now becomes the responsibility of CSS style sheets. It also means that frames are dealt with in a different way.

In this chapter, you will:

- ❑ Learn the differences between HTML and XHTML

- ❑ Look at the three different types of XHTML documents you can write — strict, transitional, and frameset — and learn the differences between each document type

- ❑ Learn why you have to be stricter about how you write XHTML documents

- ❑ Find out how to remove all of the styling elements and attributes from your HTML documents

- ❑ Discover how frames are dealt with in XHTML

- ❑ Learn about more of the benefits that you will accrue by creating accessible sites in XHTML and CSS

By the end of the chapter, not only will you know how to create XHTML documents, but you will also have converted the sample site to be XHTML-compliant.

Problem

To bring the sample site up to date using established Web standards to build the site, you must remove all of the styling from the HTML pages and convert the markup from HTML to XHTML 1.0.

Rather than create HTML 5, the W3C introduced XHTML. While previous updates to HTML simply consisted of new elements and attributes being added (and a few old ones either removed or marked for future removal from the language), this update is quite different. In fact, XHTML is different enough from HTML 4 that we are left with a new *family* of documents — XHTML documents.

Although XHTML documents are backwardly compatible with HTML documents and can be viewed just like normal HTML documents in older browsers, there are many new restrictions governing how you author XHTML documents that did not apply when writing HTML. You need to learn all of these new rules in order to create what are known as *valid* XHTML documents.

As mentioned in Chapter 1, there are three versions of XHTML 1.0, and you will need to learn the differences between each of these versions. In particular, you need to learn which elements and attributes have been removed from the version called Strict XHTML 1.0, which is the version that does not contain any stylistic elements and attributes, and no longer permits the use of frames. After all, in this new way of creating Web sites, we have to separate the content from the markup that controls the way that content is presented.

Because XHTML is a lot less forgiving than HTML, you also need to learn how to ensure that your site is XHTML-compliant using a tool called a *validator*. If you do not use a validation tool and your page contains errors, some browsers might not be able to display it at all.

Design

The purpose of any type of markup is to add meaning to a document; you can even think of going through a book with a highlighter pen as adding markup to a document. As you saw in Chapter 1, when HTML first appeared, the purpose of the markup was to explain the structure of a document — what text represents a heading, what is a paragraph, what is a bulleted point, and so on. As it grew in popularity, however, HTML started to include markup that controlled the appearance of documents. For example, the `<font>` element was introduced to control the font that a section of text appeared in, the `bgcolor` attribute was introduced to control background colors, and so on. XHTML aims to return the markup function to solely describing the structure and semantics of the document.

Almost all of the HTML and XHTML elements are interpreted by Web browsers and presented in a different manner from each other. For example, the `<h1>` to `<h6>` elements are all presented differently than the content of a `<p>` element; list items in an `<ol>` element are presented differently than those in a `<ul>` element. However, all of these elements describe the structure of the document, what is a heading, what is an item in a numbered list, and so on. The way the content of these elements is presented reflects the structure that the markup imposes — which is why the heading elements get smaller from `<h1>` through to `<h6>`, and why the `<li>` elements create separate numbered items or bulleted points depending on whether they are contained inside an `<ol>` or `<ul>` element.

Elements that describe the structure of a document are very different from those that just affect the presentation of the document without adding any meaning. Therefore, it is these purely presentational elements and attributes that are going to be cut from XHTML — not the ones you are used to that describe the structure of documents, even though browsers display the content of structural markup in different ways.

This means that you will already be familiar with the elements and attributes used in XHTML 1.0. However, you do need to learn four things:

❑ What the three versions of XHTML are

❑ How to change the way you write your HTML markup so that it obeys the rules (or syntax) of XML

❑ Which elements are allowed to appear in each of the three versions of XHTML 1.0

❑ Where each element is allowed to appear in a document

You would be forgiven for thinking that it would be easier if there were just one version of XHTML 1.0 — not three. However, the W3C introduced these three variations to make the adoption of XHTML easier. To understand why there are three versions, and to learn XHTML, you first need to understand the differences between the three versions. You will often hear these three versions of XHTML 1.0 referred to as three different *document types*:

❑ **Strict XHTML 1.0** uses XHTML syntax, so you need to obey the rules of XML documents. It also removes markup that controls only the presentation of documents. Finally, it no longer allows the use of elements used to create frames.

❑ **Transitional XHTML 1.0** still allows you to use all the markup that was in HTML 4. However, it does use XML syntax, so you need to make sure that you obey the rules of a language written in XML.

❑ **Frameset XHTML 1.0** is just there to enable you to continue to create documents that use frames, but to do so using XML syntax.

The following sections take a closer look at each of these different versions of XHTML. Which version you choose to use will depend on the project you are working on at the time, although when you are comfortable using CSS to style your documents you will probably aim to use Strict XHTML 1.0 where possible.

Strict XHTML

Strict XHTML 1.0 shows you how the W3C *want* people to write their Web pages. There are two key differences between Strict XHTML 1.0 and HTML 4 — namely, Strict XHTML:

❑ Uses XML syntax, so your documents must follow the rules of any language written in XML

❑ Does not contain any of the stylistic markup, such as the `<center>` and `<font>` elements and attributes such as the `bgcolor` and `color` attributes, and does not support frames

This means that you get not only the benefits of a language that is XML-compliant but also one that separates style from content. You will see exactly which elements and attributes have been removed later in this chapter in the section "The Differences Between Transitional and Strict XHTML 1.0."

Note that not only have several elements and attributes been removed from the Strict XHTML 1.0 specification, but Strict XHTML 1.0 is more restrictive over which elements are allowed to appear within other elements. You will learn more about this shortly in the section "Greater Structure in Strict XHTML." Before looking at Strict XHTML in depth, it helps to learn how to create documents using Transitional XHTML.

Each version of HTML and XHTML has its own *Document Type Definition (DTD)*. This is a document that contains the rules specifying what elements are allowed in a document, what attributes those elements can carry, and where the elements are allowed to appear within a document. You might have seen a DTD referenced at the beginning of some HTML documents in what is known as a *Document Type Declaration* (or `!DOCTYPE` declaration). The `!DOCTYPE` declaration is used to indicate what version of a language the document is written according to. In the following example, the `!DOCTYPE` declaration indicates that a document has been written according to the rules of the Strict XHTML 1.0 DTD that are written in the `xhtml1-strict.dtd` document:

```
<!DOCTYPE html PUBLIC "-//W3C//DTD XHTML 1.0 Strict//EN"
    "http://www.w3.org/TR/xhtml1/DTD/xhtml1-strict.dtd">
```

The names Document Type Definition and Document Type Declaration are very similar and can be somewhat confusing. The Document Type Definition indicates the rules of a markup language, whereas the Document Type Declaration indicates which rules a particular document is following.

Transitional XHTML

The W3C was aware that not everyone would be able to remove all stylistic markup from their documents immediately; after all, many people would still be expected to build sites that looked fantastic in browsers that did not support the styling of documents with CSS. However, the W3C still wanted these people to be able to benefit from a language that used XML syntax; therefore, to help the authors' transition from HTML to XHTML, they created the Transitional XHTML 1.0 document type.

Transitional XHTML does use the new XML syntax; however, it also lets you continue to use all of the elements and attributes you have had at your disposal in HTML 4. In some ways, therefore, Transitional XHTML is the easiest form of XHTML 1.0 that you can start to learn.

The `!DOCTPYE` declaration for Transitional XHTML 1.0 documents references the `xhtml1-transitional.dtd` document that contains the rules for Transitional XHTML 1.0:

```
<!DOCTYPE html PUBLIC "-//W3C//DTD XHTML 1.0 Transitional//EN"
    "http://www.w3.org/TR/xhtml1/DTD/xhtml1-transitional.dtd">
```

Frameset XHTML

Although browsers have been supporting frames for a long time, they made it into the official W3C recommendation only in HTML 4.0. They have also been removed from the Strict XHTML recommendation.

Again, the W3C realized that some people would continue to want to use frames (just like some people would need to continue to use presentational markup) and recognized that these people should be able to benefit from making their markup compliant with XML syntax. Therefore, they created Frameset XHTML 1.0, which allows users to continue using frames but requires that authors follow the rules of XML syntax.

The !DOCTPYE declaration for Frameset XHTML 1.0 documents references the xhtml1-frameset.dtd document that contains the rules for Frameset XHTML 1.0:

```
<!DOCTYPE html PUBLIC "-//W3C//DTD XHTML 1.0 Frameset//EN"
   "http://www.w3.org/TR/xhtml1/DTD/xhtml1-frameset.dtd">
```

An example XHTML document

To see just how similar HTML is to XHTML, take a look at the following example of an XHTML page — it should look very familiar to you, and the biggest difference is reflected in the first few lines. Note how even the file extension remains .html. Here is ch02_eg01.html:

```
<?xml version="1.0" encoding="iso-8859-1"?>
<!DOCTYPE html PUBLIC "-//W3C//DTD XHTML 1.0 Transitional//EN"
        "http://www.w3.org/TR/xhtml1/DTD/xhtml1-transitional.dtd">
<html xmlns="http://www.w3.org/1999/xhtml">

<head>
  <title>Sample XHTML Document</title>
  <meta http-equiv="Content-Type" content="text/html; charset=iso-8859-1" />
</head>

<body>

  <img src="images/wrox_logo.gif" alt="Wrox Logo" width="50" height="50" />
  <h1>A Simple Login Form</h1>

  <form action="login.php" method="post" name="frmLogin">

    <table>
      <tr>
        <td>Username</td>
        <td><input type="text" name="txtUserName" size="20" /></td>
      </tr>
      <tr>
        <td>Password</td>
        <td><input type="password" name="txtPassword" size="20" /></td>
      </tr>
      <tr>
        <td></td>
        <td>
         <input type="submit" value="Log in" />
        </td>
      </tr>
    </table>

  </form>

</body>
</html>
```

As shown in Figure 2-1, when you look at this page in a Web browser, the XHTML page also looks identical to what you would expect of an HTML page.

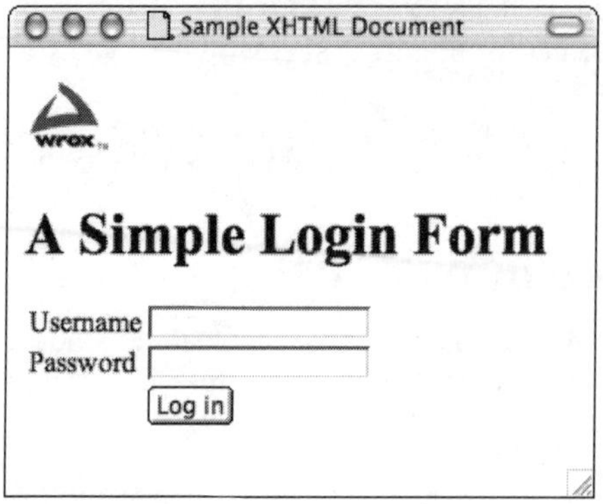

Figure 2-1

To start learning how to write the three different types of XHTML document, you need to learn the following, which is covered in this order in the chapter:

❑ First, you need to learn how to write HTML using the stricter syntax of XML because all versions of XHTML require you to modify the way you write your documents. Having learned this stricter syntax, you will be able to write Transitional XHTML documents.

❑ It would then be beneficial to look at why the W3C chose to rewrite HTML using XML syntax; it might help you ensure that you obey the stricter syntax you learned.

❑ Finally, you need to learn which of the elements that you were allowed to use in HTML 4.0 and Transitional XHTML are no longer allowed when you write Strict XHTML. At the same time, it helps to look at the tightening of structure in Strict XHTML and how some elements are no longer allowed to contain other elements. By the end of this section, you will be able to write Strict XHTML documents, too.

You will start off, therefore, by learning to write your documents using the syntax of XML.

Writing documents using XML syntax

While HTML and XHTML are very similar, you need to learn a few rules in order to write Web pages using any version of XHTML. In this section, you will take a closer look at XHTML and discover the core differences in writing XHTML markup so that it meets the strict requirements of XML syntax. In particular, you will learn the following:

❑ XHTML documents can start with the optional XML declaration.

❑ XHTML documents should contain a Document Type Declaration (before the opening HTML tag).

❑ All element and attribute names must be written in lowercase.

❑ You must close all tags correctly.

❑ The <html> element must be the root element.

❑ All markup must nest correctly.

❑ All attributes must have a value.

- ❑ All attribute values must be written in quotes.

- ❑ All documents should be given a title.

- ❑ Comments may be stripped out by the Web server or processing application.

- ❑ You need to escape the < and & characters.

- ❑ Scripts and style rules should be placed within CDATA sections or in external files.

Once you have learned about these differences, you will be able to write Transitional XHTML — after all, the elements and attributes at your disposal are the same as the ones in HTML 4.

Including the optional XML declaration

Any XML document can start with what is known as an *XML declaration*. As you already know, XHTML uses XML syntax, so any XHTML document is also considered to be an XML document. This means that any XHTML document can start with the following optional declaration:

```
<?xml version="1.0" ?>
```

Whether you use the XML declaration or not is up to you, but the purpose of the XML declaration is to tell processing applications that the document is written in XML (and which version it is written in), so it may help some applications determine the language in which your document was written.

Currently (early 2005), there are two versions of XML — XML 1.0 and XML 1.1. Either of these values could be used in the version attribute. (If you subscribe to any kind of programming newsletter or news-group, or read any IT magazines, you are likely to hear if a new version of XML comes out because it is so widely used in programming.)

If you do include the XML declaration, be aware of a very important rule:

> **When including an XML declaration, nothing — not even a single space — can appear before the opening angled bracket.**

The XML declaration can also carry an optional encoding attribute, which is used to indicate the character encoding in which the document was written. For example, if your document were written in Windows Notepad or Macromedia Dreamweaver, you are likely to be using a text encoding known as iso-8859-1:

```
<?xml version="1.0" encoding="iso-8859-1"?>
```

It becomes important to use the encoding attribute when you are dealing with anything other than the most common characters — for example, if you are using characters that do not belong to the ASCII character set shown as follows:

	!	"	#	$	%	&	'	(	)	*	+	,	-	.	/
0	1	2	3	4	5	6	7	8	9	:	;	<	=	>	?
@	A	B	C	D	E	F	G	H	I	J	K	L	M	N	O
P	Q	R	S	T	U	V	W	X	Y	Z	[	\	]	^	_
`	a	b	c	d	e	f	g	h	i	j	k	l	m	n	o
p	q	r	s	t	u	v	w	x	y	z	{	|	}	~	DEL

Full coverage of character encodings is beyond the scope of this book; however, you can find out more information at www.w3.org/International/O-charset.

Another way to indicate the encoding used in a document is to add the following <meta> tag inside the <head> element of an XHTML document, as follows:

```
<meta http-equiv="Content-Type" content="text/html;charset=iso-8859-1" />
```

To be extra vigilant, when using characters other than those in the ASCII character set, you should use a combination of both of these techniques.

Starting XHTML documents with a Document Type Declaration

As you have already seen, a Document Type Declaration (also known as a !DOCTYPE declaration) is a statement indicating the document type — for example, whether it is written according to the rules of Transitional XHTML 1.0, Strict XHTML 1.0, Frameset XHTML, or any other document type.

Each of the three variations of XHTML 1.0 (Strict, Transitional, and Frameset) uses a slightly different Document Type Declaration.

If you are writing Strict XHTML 1.0, you must include a !DOCTYPE declaration, which looks like the following:

```
<!DOCTYPE html PUBLIC "-//W3C//DTD XHTML 1.0 Strict//EN"
    "http://www.w3.org/TR/xhtml1/DTD/xhtml1-strict.dtd">
```

The only thing allowed to appear before a Document Type Declaration in an XHTML document is the XML declaration. The !DOCTYPE declaration should then be immediately followed by the opening <html> tag.

When writing Transitional XHTML documents, you do not need to include a !DOCTYPE declaration, although it is good practice to include one. Here you can see the !DOCTYPE declaration for Transitional XHTML:

```
<!DOCTYPE html PUBLIC "-//W3C//DTD XHTML 1.0 Transitional//EN"
    "http://www.w3.org/TR/xhtml1/DTD/xhtml1-transitional.dtd">
```

Again, the only thing that should be allowed to appear before a Document Type Declaration in an XHTML document is the XML declaration. The !DOCTYPE declaration should then be followed by the opening <html> tag.

An XHTML 1.0 Frameset document should use the following !DOCTYPE declaration:

```
<!DOCTYPE html PUBLIC "-//W3C//DTD XHTML 1.0 Frameset//EN"
    "http://www.w3.org/TR/xhtml1/DTD/xhtml1-frameset.dtd">
```

These !DOCTYPE declarations may look familiar to you because HTML documents were allowed (and indeed were intended) to have Document Type Declarations like these.

Making the <html> element the root element

The *root element* of any document is the element that contains the entire document; it is the first and last tag in the document. Despite being called XHTML, XHTML documents still use the <html> element as the root element of the document. (There is no new <xhtml> element.) Whereas some browsers allowed you to skip the <html> tags and just use the <body> tags to contain the document, this would not be correct XHTML, and it might cause some processors to generate an error, so you should always use the <html> element.

The <html> element is kept as the root element of XHTML documents because it allows older browsers—written before XHTML was released—to process XHTML documents as if they were HTML documents. Because there are few differences between early versions of HTML and Strict XHTML 1.0, and because browsers are programmed to ignore any elements and attributes they do not understand, older browsers can usually deal with Strict XHTML quite well.

The only things that can appear before the opening tag of the <html> root element are the XML declaration and the Document Type Declaration, no other markup. Therefore, the opening <html> tag directly follows the Document Type Declaration, and the closing </html> tag must be the last tag in the document.

The <html> element can also carry an attribute called xmlns. This is a very special attribute in XML and indicates something known as the *namespace* for the markup used in the document. You do not need to understand all about XML namespaces for the moment, although you will read about them in Chapter 8. For now, you just need to know that if you are writing any type of XHTML 1.0 documents, then the xmlns attribute and namespace is as follows:

```
<html xmlns="http://www.w3.org/1999/xhtml">
```

The final point to note about this root element is that the <html> tags must be written in lowercase characters to meet the criteria of the next requirement.

Writing all element and attribute names in lowercase letters

In HTML, you could write element and attribute names in uppercase or lowercase characters, or indeed in a mix of the two. Therefore, HTML browsers would treat all three of the following tags as if they were from the same element:

```
<html> <HTML> <HtMl>
```

XML, however, is case-sensitive, and therefore so is XHTML. This means that the three preceding tags would be treated as if they belonged to different elements.

In XHTML, all element and attribute names should be written in lowercase letters. Of course, the content between the opening and closing tags of an element, and attribute values, may contain a mix of uppercase and lowercase characters; this rule affects only the characters between the angled brackets and the attribute values.

For example, the following would *not* be correct XHTML:

```
<HTML XMLNS="http://www.w3.org/1999/xhtml">
<body>
Some text goes here.
</BODY>
</HTML>
```

47

Conversely, the code that follows would be valid XHTML:

```
<html xmlns="http://www.w3.org/1999/xhtml">
<body>
Some text goes here.
</body>
</html>
```

This is one of the habits that many experienced HTML developers find hard to break, especially if they have been using uppercase characters for several years, but it can be achieved with practice.

Closing all tags correctly

For every element that has content, there must be an opening tag and a corresponding closing tag. This might sound obvious, but many HTML browsers allowed you to omit some closing tags, even if the element had content. For example, HTML browsers would allow you to write bulleted lists like the following, missing the closing </li> tags:

```
<ul>
  <li>Point one
  <li>Point two
  <li>Point three
</ul>
```

The preceding code would not be valid XHTML because there are no closing tags on the <li> elements. To create valid XHTML, you would have to write the list as follows, with the closing </li> tags:

```
<ul>
  <li>Point one</li>
  <li>Point two</li>
  <li>Point three</li>
</ul>
```

Similarly, many browsers would display HTML tables correctly even if table cells did not have correct closing </td> tags for each cell; each time these browsers came across a new opening <td> tag, they would assume that the previous cell had been finished.

For example, the following code is *not* a correct example of how to write an HTML table, although it would be displayed correctly in most HTML browsers:

```
<table>
  <tr>
    <td>Row one Cell one
    <td>Row one Cell two
  </tr>
  <tr>
    <td>Row two Cell one
    <td>Row two Cell two
  </tr>
</table>
```

Here is how this table should be written in XHTML, with each opening `<td>` tag having a corresponding closing `</td>` tag:

```
<table>
  <tr>
    <td>Row one Cell one</td>
    <td>Row one Cell two</td>
  </tr>
  <tr>
    <td>Row two Cell one</td>
    <td>Row two Cell two</td>
  </tr>
</table>
```

Almost every element should have both an opening and closing tag, with one exception that you will meet in the next section.

Using closing slashes for empty elements

The only time when an element does not need a closing tag is when no content appears between the opening and closing tags. For example, the `<br>` and `<hr>` elements in HTML did not have any element content. These are known as *empty elements*.

In XHTML, empty elements must explicitly state that they have no content between an opening and closing tag. They therefore have a forward slash character before the right-angled bracket in the opening tag, so you would write these tags like so:

```
<br /> <hr />
```

Note that there is a space between the characters that make up the element name and the forward slash. If this space were not present, some older browsers might ignore the element.

Another common example of an empty element is the `<img>` element, used to include images in a document, which should now be written like this:

```
<img src="/images/logo.gif" width="150" height="25" alt="Wrox Press Logo" />
```

Nesting all markup correctly

This next point goes hand in hand with the fact that all elements must be closed correctly. With XHTML, not only do you have to provide a closing tag for every element that is not empty; you also need to ensure that any element that starts inside another element closes within that same element. This is probably best described through the use of an example.

In the following line, the opening `<u>` tag starts before the opening `<b>` tag, but the closing `</u>` tag comes before the closing `</b>` tag:

```
A is for <u><b>a</u>pple</b>
```

For the elements to nest correctly, the `<u>` element should sit completely within the `<b>` element:

```
A is for <b><u>a</u>pple</b>
```

In the preceding example, you can see that the entire <u> element lives, or *nests*, inside the <b> element.

One area in which it is common to encounter problems with getting elements to nest correctly is in complex tables. Take a look at the following, slightly more complex example and see if you can spot the errors:

```
<table>
  <tr>
    <td><a href="index.html"><img src="index.html" /></td></a>
    <td><b><h1>Wrox Press</b></h1></td>
  </tr>
  <tr>
    <td colspan="2">
      <table>
        <tr>
          <td><a href=index.html">Home</a></td>
          <td><a href=services.html">Our Services</a>
          <td><a href=contact.html">Contact Us</a></td>
        </td>
      </tr>
    </table>
  </tr>
</table>
```

The preceding example contains quite a few problems, and the lines with corrections are highlighted in the next snippet of code.

❑ The first line that is highlighted had the closing </a> tag outside the closing </td> tag.

❑ The second error was the incorrect nesting of the <b> element. Both <b> tags should have been either inside the <h1> element or outside the <h1> element, rather than one inside and one outside.

❑ The third highlighted line missed a closing </td> tag.

❑ The final error was that the closing </td> tag for the cell in the second row of the table was in completely the wrong place.

You can nest tags correctly by trying to create them symmetrically. You cannot close an element until any child elements that have been opened within that element have been closed:

```
<table>
  <tr>
    <td><a href="index.html"><img src="index.html" /></a></td>
    <td><b><h1>Wrox Press</h1></b></td>
  </tr>
  <tr>
    <td colspan="2">
      <table>
        <tr>
          <td><a href=index.html">Home</a></td>
          <td><a href=services.html">Our Services</a></td>
          <td><a href=contact.html">Contact Us</a></td>
        </tr>
```

```
      </table>
    </td>
  </tr>
</table>
```

If you use a tool such as Macromedia Dreamweaver to write your XHTML pages, you can set it to high-light any errors that occur if your elements do not nest correctly.

Giving all attributes a value

HTML allowed something called *attribute minimization*. This meant that you did not necessarily need to provide a value for every attribute. For example, when creating a checkbox in an HTML form, you could use the checked attribute (without a value) to indicate that the item should be checked by default when the form loads:

```
<input type="checkbox" name="chkInsurance" checked /> I would like insurance.
```

In XHTML, all attributes must have a value, and any attributes that previously could be minimized in HTML should be given a value that is the same as the attribute name. For example, the preceding check-box would look like this in XHTML:

```
<input type="text" name="chkInsurance" checked="checked" />I would like insurance.
```

In this case, you can see how the checked attribute has been given a value of checked.

Here is a list of all the attributes that could be minimized in HTML:

```
compact, nowrap, ismap, declare, noshade, checked, disabled, readonly, multiple,
selected, noresize, defer
```

Writing all attribute values in quotes

In HTML, although many authors did provide attribute values in quotation marks, it was not strictly required in all versions. Indeed, some popular authoring tools did not write attribute values using quotes at all until more recent editions. Whenever you write a value for an attribute in XHTML, you must provide the value in double quotation marks, as shown in the following example:

```
<form action="login.php" method="post" name="frmLogin">
```

The following code would *not* be correct:

```
<form action=login.php method=post name=frmLogin>
```

Giving all documents a title

All XHTML documents should contain a <title> element inside the <head> element of the document. This title should be as descriptive as possible, explaining what the user might find in that page. You should avoid using only the site or company name as the content of the <title> element on every page.

For example, here is a descriptive title for a page:

```
<title>Reef Imaging Catalogue of Real Estate Signboards for Sydney and NSW</title>
```

The `<title>` element is also one of the key pieces of information that search engines use to determine whether your pages match keyword criteria entered by users during searches, so creating good, accurate titles such as the following is very important:

```
<title>The Film Channel's Reviews of the Top 10 Films of 1975</title>
```

Using the id attribute over the name attribute

HTML makes use of the `name` attribute on several elements in order to allow that element to be identified. For example, it is used on the rollover images so that the scripts can identify which image should be changed. Similarly, the `name` attribute is often used on forms to allow access to individual form controls via script.

HTML 4.0 introduced the capability to use the `id` attribute instead of the `name` attribute — after all, the `name` attribute is used as an ID or identifier for that element. In XHTML, you should always use this new `id` attribute, rather than the `name` attribute. Furthermore, the value of this attribute has to be unique within the document. For example, you are not allowed to have two images carry an `id` attribute whose value is `home`, even if they are the same image.

The value of an `id` attribute must be a letter or an underscore, followed by letters, digits, hyphens, underscores, colons, or full stops. You may not start the value of an `id` attribute with a number or the letters *xml* (in any combination of uppercase or lowercase).

Unfortunately, not all browsers respond to the `id` attribute in the same way that they do to the `name` attribute (including Netscape 4 and the Mac version of IE 5). For example, if you are creating links within a document, some browsers will not respond to elements that use the `id` attribute. As a result, you might like to consider using both attributes, although (as you will see) this means you are able to write only Transitional XHTML, not Strict XHTML.

Realizing comments may be stripped out

While XHTML comments are written in exactly the same way as HTML comments, there is no requirement for the Web server to send comments to the browser (it may strip them out), so you should not rely on them to convey any information to the user. Why might the Web server strip them out? The stripping out of comments might help reduce bandwidth, especially when serving Web pages to devices that access the Web with a very low bandwidth or slow connection.

In addition, because XHTML comments are the same as HTML comments, you cannot use the characters `<!--` between the opening and closing tags of an element, or in an attribute value.

Specifying the language of an element

When specifying the language of an element, you should not only use the `lang` attribute, but also the `xml:lang` attribute. The `xml:lang` attribute is the native XML equivalent, and it takes precedence over the `lang` attribute, which is included for backward compatibility. For example:

```
<p lang="en-GB" xml:lang="en-GB">My favourite colour is yellow.</p>
<p lang="en-GB" xml:lang="en-US">My favorite color is yellow.</p>
```

Escaping characters

The ampersand and left angle bracket characters must not be used in text and should be escaped using numeric character references or the strings & and <, respectively. The right angle bracket may also be represented with the string >.

To allow attribute values to contain both single and double quote characters, the apostrophe or single quote character (') may be represented as ' and the double-quote character as &quote;.

Escape characters are covered in greater detail in Appendix D.

Using external scripts and style sheets or CDATA sections

In the <script> and <style> elements of XHTML, the < and & characters are treated as the start of markup, and entities such as < and & are recognized as entity references for < and &, respectively. This can cause problems for the processing of some scripts and style sheets; therefore, you can wrap your script and styles in a CDATA section to fix this:

```
<script>
<![CDATA[
  function()
]]>
</script>
```

However, some older browsers (IE 5 and Netscape 4 and earlier) will not necessarily recognize CDATA sections, so you are better off (where possible) using external JavaScript documents referenced via the <script> element with a src attribute, and use external style sheets referenced using the <link> element.

That completes the coverage of the differences between the syntax of HTML and all of the versions of XHTML. With a grasp of these differences, you should be able to write Transitional XHTML. You will be looking at plenty of examples of XHTML documents later in the chapter when you look at the sample application again. For the moment, however, I want to turn to why the W3C chose to recreate HTML in this language of XML.

Why XML?

I have not yet explained fully why the W3C chose to make the next version of XHTML in this language called XML. HTML was originally written in a language called Standard Generalized Markup Language (SGML), which, like XML, is a language for creating markup languages. SGML is a very powerful language, far more powerful than HTML. However, with its power comes complexity, and its complexity meant that the major companies creating tools for the Web (such as browsers) had no intention of supporting it. It would have made their programs too complex and therefore too large.

As a result, the W3C created Extensible Markup Language (XML) as simpler alternative to SGML that could be used on the Web. XML was also designed with the idea that it would be used not only to deal with traditional documents, such as those that would be printed, but also to cope with marking up many other kinds of data (particularly data you might find in a relational database or an electronic message between computers).

You have probably heard of XML, even if you do not know what it does and why it does it. To offer a very basic explanation of XML — it enables you to define the names of the tags and attributes that can appear in a markup language and specifies where each of these elements and attributes may appear within a document written in this language (for example, in XHTML a `<title>` element may appear within a `<head>` element). The fact that XML could be used to create a wide variety of markup languages—each specific to the type of data being marked up—really took off as an increasing number of users and companies started to share more and more data between different computers.

All kinds of markup languages have been created in XML, from languages that enable you to mark up data for presentation on the Web to languages that enable manufacturers to order parts from suppliers and to languages that configure software. One of its great strengths is that it is written in plain text and will therefore work on all kinds of computer platforms and operating systems—it is therefore ideal for the Internet.

In addition to being a very popular technology on the Web, there are some other strong advantages to HTML being rewritten in XML, as described in the following sections.

It requires a stricter syntax

By making XHTML follow rules of XML syntax, it forces Web page authors to adhere to a stricter set of rules, which include the following requirements:

- ❏ Use only lowercase characters for all element and attribute names.
- ❏ Close elements correctly (except empty elements, which must have a forward slash at the end of the tag).
- ❏ Nest elements correctly.
- ❏ Place all attribute values in double quotes.
- ❏ Provide values for all attributes.

Alone, these syntax requirements (which were discussed earlier in the chapter) are not really benefits in themselves. However, when you require a stricter syntax, other benefits follow.

Because the syntax is stricter, you can create smaller programs to work with the documents—such as browsers. With a stricter syntax, these programs, for example, do not need to be written to understand what an attribute value is or whether it has quotes around it because all attribute values will appear in quotes. Programs do not need to assume that if a new line item element is opened the previous one had finished and should be treated as if a closing element had already appeared. If all elements are nested correctly, it is easier to process the documents and understand their structure. And so on. Because this stricter syntax allows for smaller browsers, you can therefore make XHTML available to devices that did not have the capacity to work with the full HTML recommendation.

It enables easier programmatic access

Not only is the syntax of XHTML stricter than HTML; so is its structure. The requirements for XHTML documents to nest all elements correctly; close elements; place attribute values in double quotes; and provide values for all attributes result in a stricter document structure, and therefore make it easier to gain programmatic access to Web documents. If there is only one route from point A to point B on a map, you are less likely to get lost; similarly, if all elements have closing tags, and all attributes are in quotes, it is easier to find the information you are looking for.

There are many reasons why you might want to programmatically work with your Web documents, rather than just look at them in a Web browser. For example, you might want to do the following:

❑ Generate XHTML invoices automatically for your customers when they place an order, and store the records in the same format you presented them to the customer

❑ Perform calculations upon the electronic documents you have stored, such as totaling the amount of sales tax paid by a particular customer in March 2004

❑ Create an automated indexing, searching, and retrieval tool that can collect information from reports generated by employees around the world

It is the fixed structure that makes it easier for those writing programs to find what they are looking for in the documents.

It enables the use of XML tools and technology

Because XHTML documents are themselves instances of XML documents, any tool designed to work with XML and XML documents can also be used with XHTML and XHTML documents. If you bear in mind the widespread adoption of XML into all areas of programming, this means that a huge variety of technologies and programs can be used with your XHTML documents.

You have access to technologies such as the following:

❑ **Extensible Stylesheet Language Transformation (XSLT)**, which enables you to take one XML syntax and convert it into another document type. For example, it would be possible to take an XML file that was generated by a database and convert that into an XHTML table.

❑ The W3C **Document Object Model (DOM)**, which is used for XML documents that are held in the memory of an application

❑ The **Simple API for XML (SAX)**, which is used for XML documents that can be read as a stream (this means the entire document is not loaded into memory; rather, it can be read as it goes along — which is very handy if you are working with a lot of large documents).

❑ **Validation tools** that can be used to confirm that your syntax meets the rules of XHTML

The idea behind the Document Object Model and the Simple API (application program interface) for XML is that each indicates a set of functionality that XML processors (programs that work with XML documents) support. For example, any program working with XML will probably need to be able to perform an action such as opening or saving a document, and these actions are known as *methods*. Similarly, all programs might be able to determine similar things about a document, such as the length (number of characters) of an element's content, or the value of an attribute, and these are known as *properties*. The DOM and SAX both provide a list of methods and properties that should be made available by any XML processor that supports them.

Therefore, if an XML processor indicates that it is a DOM processor, it will support all of the methods and properties specified in the DOM recommendation, while a processor that indicates it is a SAX processor will support all of the methods and properties of SAX. This makes it much easier for programmers to use these processors because they all share standard methods and properties and don't require the programmer to learn new ones for each different processor. This quality also increases the adoption of the processor.

55

It provides extensibility

The X in XML stands for *extensible,* so called because it is easy to extend upon a language written in XML. This helps increase the lifetime of a language written in XML, enabling new features to be added later.

It also makes it possible to mix different languages written in XML in the same document. For example, you can use Scalable Vector Graphics (SVG), Mathematical Markup Language (MathML), and XHTML in the same document, because each language is written in XML.

You will learn more about both of these points in Chapter 8 when you look at the future of XHTML.

Now that you know why the W3C chose to write XHTML in XML, it is time to look at the differences between Transitional XHTML (which uses the same elements and attributes as HTML 4, but following XML syntax) and Strict XHTML.

Differences between Transitional and Strict XHTML 1.0

You have already learned how to write Transitional XHTML — you take exactly the same elements and attributes you had available to you in HTML 4 and follow the rules introduced in the section "Writing Using XML Syntax" (which included points such as using all lowercase characters for element and attribute names, making sure you have a closing tag for every element except empty elements, and making sure your elements nest properly). In this section, you will learn about the differences between writing Transitional XHTML 1.0 and Strict XHTML 1.0.

Writing Strict XHTML 1.0 involves the following:

❑   Using XML syntax (which you have already met)

❑   Remembering which elements and attributes you are no longer allowed to use

❑   Working with a stricter structure in which elements are allowed to appear inside other elements

To observe the last two points, you will first look at which elements have been removed from the Strict XHTML 1.0 specification. Then you will look at the relationships between elements in a document. Finally, you will look at which elements have changed. The second of these sections looks at which attributes are no longer allowed and where an element cannot contain an element it could previously contain.

By the end of this section, you should be able to write Strict XHTML as well as Transitional XHTML.

Redundant elements

The following 12 elements have been removed from the HTML 4 and Transitional XHTML recommendations to create Strict XHTML 1.0:

❑   `<applet>` — Instead, you should now use the `<object>` element.

❑   `<basefont>` — Replaced by the CSS `font-family` property, used with the `<body>` element

❑   `<center>` — Replaced by the CSS `text-align` property or CSS positioning techniques

❑   `<dir>` — Use only the `<ul>` and `<li>` elements to create unordered lists.

❑   `<font>` — Replaced by the CSS `font-family` property

- ❑   `<iframe>` — Frames are not part of the Strict XHTML 1.0 document type (you should use the Frameset document type if you must use frames).

- ❑   `<isindex>` — Removed in favor of forms

- ❑   `<menu>` — Use only the `<ul>` and `<li>` elements to create unordered lists.

- ❑   `<noframes>` — Frames are not part of the Strict XHTML 1.0 document type (you should use the Frameset document type if you must use frames).

- ❑   `<s>` — Replaced by the CSS `text-decoration` property

- ❑   `<strike>` — Replaced by the CSS `text-decoration` property

- ❑   `<u>` — Replaced by the CSS `text-decoration` property

None of the preceding elements should appear anywhere in a Strict XHTML document.

Greater structure in Strict XHTML

As I have already hinted, some elements are no longer allowed to contain other elements; for example, there is a long list of elements that cannot be used as *child elements* of the `<body>` element. It is important to understand what this means before you look at which elements can or cannot contain other elements.

In this section, think about the relationship between elements as being similar to family trees, where the relationships between elements are referred to using terms such as parents and children, or grandchildren and ancestors. Understanding the relationship between elements is vital to understanding where elements can be placed.

Take a look at the following simple example, and then you will look at the relationship between the elements in the document:

```
<?xml version="1.0" encoding="iso-8859-1"?>
<!DOCTYPE html PUBLIC "-//W3C//DTD XHTML 1.0 Strict//EN"
    "http://www.w3.org/TR/xhtml1/DTD/xhtml1-strict.dtd">
<html xmlns="http://www.w3.org/1999/xhtml">

<head>
  <title>Sample XHTML Document</title>
  <meta http-equiv="Content-Type" content="text/html; charset=iso-8859-1" />
</head>
<body>
  <h1>About This Book</h1>

  <p>This book from <a href="http://www.wrox.com/">Wrox Press</a>helps you update
  your skills from writing web pages in HTML to creating pages in <em>XHTML and
  CSS</em>, and ensures that your pages meet accessibility requirements.</p>

</body>
</html>
```

To understand the relationships in the preceding code, note the following points:

- ❑   The `<head>` and `<body>` elements are children of the `<html>` element.

- ❑   The `<html>` element is the parent of the `<head>` and `<body>` elements.

❑ The <p> element is a child of the <body> element.

❑ The <a> element (inside the <p> element) is a grandchild of the <body> element.

You are probably used to writing HTML pages without thinking too much about which elements are allowed to appear where — most browsers are very forgiving on this point. However, the rules regarding which elements can contain other elements in Strict XHTML 1.0 are inflexible. Take a look at the following example (based on ch02_eg01.html, which you met earlier in the chapter); I have introduced two errors:

```
<?xml version="1.0" encoding="iso-8859-1"?>
<!DOCTYPE html PUBLIC "-//W3C//DTD XHTML 1.0 Strict//EN"
     "http://www.w3.org/TR/xhtml1/DTD/xhtml1-strict.dtd">
<html xmlns="http://www.w3.org/1999/xhtml">

<head>
  <title>Sample XHTML Document</title>
  <meta http-equiv="Content-Type" content="text/html; charset=iso-8859-1" />
</head>
<body>
  <img src="images/wrox_logo.gif" alt="Wrox Logo" width="50" height="50" />
  <h1>About This Book</h1>

  This book from <a href="http://www.wrox.com/">Wrox Press</a>helps you update
  your skills from writing web pages in HTML to creating pages in <em>XHTML and
  CSS</em>, and ensures that your pages meet accessibility requirements.

</body>
</html>
```

The first error is adding an <img /> element as a child of the <body> element. This would not be allowed, because the <img> element is allowed to be a child of the following elements only:

```
<a>, <abbr>, <acronym>, <address>, <b>, <bdo>, <big>, <button>, <caption>, <cite>,
<code>, <dd>, <del>, <dfn>, <div>, <dt>, <em>, <fieldset>, <h1>, <h2>, <h3>, <h4>,
<h5>, <h6>, <i>, <ins>, <kbd>, <label>, <legend>, <li>, <object>, <p>, <q>, <samp>,
<small>, <span>, <strong>, <sub>, <sup>, <td>, <th>, <tt>, <var>
```

This might seem like quite a long list of possible elements, and a complete discussion of which elements are allowed to be a parent or child of another element is beyond the scope of this book. You can, however, find a helpful reference to the relationships allowed between elements at www.dulug.duke.edu/~mark/docs/dtds/xhtml/xhtml10-strict/index.html.

The second error in this document was the removal of the opening <p> tag and the closing </p> tag from around the description of the book. This introduces an error because you are not allowed to place text inside the <body> element unless it is contained within another element — specifically, it has to be contained within a block-level element.

In Strict XHTML, the text is not allowed to appear as a direct child of the <blockquote>, <body>, <form>, and <noscript> elements, nor are the following elements:

```
<a>, <abbr>, <acronym>, <b>, <bdo>, <big>, <br>, <button>, <cite>, <code>, <dfn>,
<em>, <i>, <img>, <input>, <kbd>, <label>, <map>, <object>, <q>, <samp>, <select>,
<small>, <span>, <strong>, <sub>, <sup>, <textarea>, <tt>, <var>
```

Rather, they must be contained within another element.

While the idea of determining which element may appear as a child of another element might seem quite daunting and complicated, a validation tool will let you know if you have any elements where they are not allowed to be, and a simple distinction between two types of elements will help you learn where elements can appear most of the time: the difference between *block-level* and *inline* elements.

Block-level and inline elements

All elements can be thought of as either block-level or inline elements. The way to distinguish the two is simple:

❑ **Block-level elements** are treated by default in browsers as if they have a line before and after them, such as the `<h1>`, `<p>`, `<ol>`, and `<li>` elements.

❑ **Inline elements** appear within block-level elements, do not necessarily start a new line, and require anything following them to appear on a new line, such as the `<b>`, `<img />`, or `<em>` elements. Whatever follows an inline element does not necessarily start on a new line.

The key differences between these two types of elements in terms of the structure of documents are as follows:

❑ A block-level element cannot appear within an inline element.

❑ An inline element can appear as a child of a block-level element or another inline element. However, an inline element cannot be a direct child of the `<body>` element.

For example, an `<em>` element can appear inside any of the following elements:

```
<a>, <abbr>, <acronym>, <address>, <b>, <bdo>, <big>, <button>, <caption>, <cite>,
<code>, <dd>, <del>, <dfn>, <div>, <dt>, <em>, <fieldset>, <h1>, <h2>, <h3>, <h4>,
<h5>, <h6>, <i>, <ins>, <kbd>, <label>, <legend>, <li>, <object>, <p>, <pre>, <q>,
<samp>, <small>, <span>, <strong>, <sub>, <sup>, <td>, <th>, <tt>, <var>
```

Meanwhile, a `<p>` element can appear only as a child of the following elements:

```
<blockquote>, <body>, <button>, <dd>, <del>, <div>, <fieldset>, <form>, <ins>,
<li>, <map>, <noscript>, <object>, <td>, <th>
```

Therefore, when you see that a `<form>` element can no longer contain an `<img />` element, it just means that a `<form>` element cannot contain the `<img />` element as its own child — although an `<img />` element could appear as a grandchild within a permitted block-level element.

Now that you have learned about these new structural limitations, it is now time to look at the changes to the elements that have remained in Strict XHTML, but whose attributes and permitted child elements have changed.

Changes to elements

The next few subsections look at each of the elements whose attributes and permitted children have changed, and while you do not need to memorize them, they should provide a handy reference. As you will see, many of the attributes that have been removed were there just to control the visual presentation of HTML documents.

<body>

The following attributes have been removed: bgcolor, text, link, vlink, and alink.

In addition to the elements that have been removed from the Strict XHTML recommendation, the following elements are no longer allowed to appear as direct children of the <body> element:

```
<a>, <br />, <span>, <bdo>, <object>, <img>, <map>, <sub>, <sup>, <em>, <strong>,
<dfn>, <code>, <q>, <samp>, <kbd>, <var>, <cite>, <abbr>, <acronym>, <big>,
<small>, <font>, <basefont>, <tt>, <i>, <b>, <u>, <input>, <select>, <textarea>,
<label>, <button>
```

Rather, they should appear within other elements that are allowed to be children of the <body> element.

<script>

The language attribute has been removed. You should use the type attribute instead, whose value is a MIME type (for example, text/javascript).

<noscript>

In addition to the elements that have been removed from Strict XHTML, the <noscript> element is no longer allowed to contain the following elements:

```
<a>, <br />, <span>, <bdo>, <object>, <img />, <map>, <sub>, <sup>, <em>, <strong>,
<dfn>, <code>, <q>, <samp>, <kbd>, <var>, <cite>, <abbr>, <acronym>, <big>,
<small>, <tt>, <i>, <b>, <u>, <input>, <select>, <textarea>, <label>, <button>
```

<a>, <base>, and <link>

The <a>, <base>, and <link> elements no longer require the target attribute because the Strict XHTML 1.0 recommendation does not support frames.

<div>, <hn>, <p>

The <div>, <hn>, and <p> elements no longer carry an align attribute.

<ul>, <ol>, and <dl>

The <ul>, <ol>, and <dl> elements can no longer carry the following attributes: compact, type, and start.

<li>

The <li> element can no longer carry the type or value attributes.

<address>

The <address> element should no longer contain a <p> element.

<blockquote>

The <blockquote> element can no longer have the following elements as children:

```
<a>, <br />, <span>, <bdo>, <object>, <img />, <map>, <sub>, <sup>, <em>, <strong>,
<dfn>, <code>, <q>, <samp>, <kbd>, <var>, <cite>, <abbr>, <acronym>, <big>,
<small>, <tt>, <i>, <b>, <u>, <input>, <select>, <textarea>, <label>, <button>
```

<pre>

The `<pre>` element can no longer carry the `width` attribute. However, it is allowed to contain the `<sup>` and `<sub>` elements.

The `<br />` element can no longer carry the `clear` attribute.

<hr />

The `<hr />` element can no longer carry the following attributes: `align`, `noshade`, `size`, and `width`.

<img />

The `<img />` element can no longer carry the following attributes: `name`, `align`, `border`, `hspace`, and `vspace`.

Each `<img />` element *must* carry the `alt` attribute.

<form>

The `<form>` element can no longer contain either the `name` or `target` attributes.

The `<form>` element can no longer have the following elements as children:

```
<a>, <br />, <span>, <bdo>, <object>, <img />, <map>, <sub>, <sup>, <em>, <strong>,
<dfn>, <code>, <q>, <samp>, <kbd>, <var>, <cite>, <abbr>, <acronym>, <big>,
<small>, <tt>, <i>, <b>, <u>, <input>, <select>, <textarea>, <label>, <button>
```

<caption>, <input>

The `align` attribute is no longer allowed on either the `<caption>` or `<input>` elements.

*The **name** attribute is also required for all **<input>** elements except those whose **type** attribute has a value of **submit** or **reset**.*

<table>

The `<table>` element has removed the following attributes: `bgcolor` and `align`.

<tr>

The `bgcolor` attribute is no longer allowed on the `<tr>` element.

<th> and <td>

The `<th>` and `<td>` elements are no longer allowed to carry the `nowrap`, `bgcolor`, `width`, and `height` attributes.

Having surveyed the differences between Transitional XHTML 1.0 and Strict XHTML 1.0, you are almost ready to start converting the site from HTML to XHTML. Before you do, however, the following sections look at how some authoring tools deal with XHTML and how you can validate your XHTML documents.

XHTML compliance in authoring tools

If you rely on an authoring tool when creating Web pages, you need to make sure that it is generating XHTML-compliant code. The latest versions of the leading authoring tools enable you to both write and validate XHTML (validation is covered in the next section). However, you often have to specify that you are creating pages in XHTML. Moreover, if you are not aware of the rules that were discussed earlier in the chapter, you could easily move an element so that it no longer nests correctly, change the case of characters, or make any number of other errors that would prevent the page from being valid XHTML.

Macromedia Dreamweaver is probably the most widely used professional Web authoring tool, so this section covers how you can ensure that your documents are XHTML-compliant in it. When creating a new document in Dreamweaver, you should see the dialog box shown in Figure 2-2. As you can see, when selecting HTML as the document type, an option in the bottom right-hand corner enables you to make it XHTML-compliant.

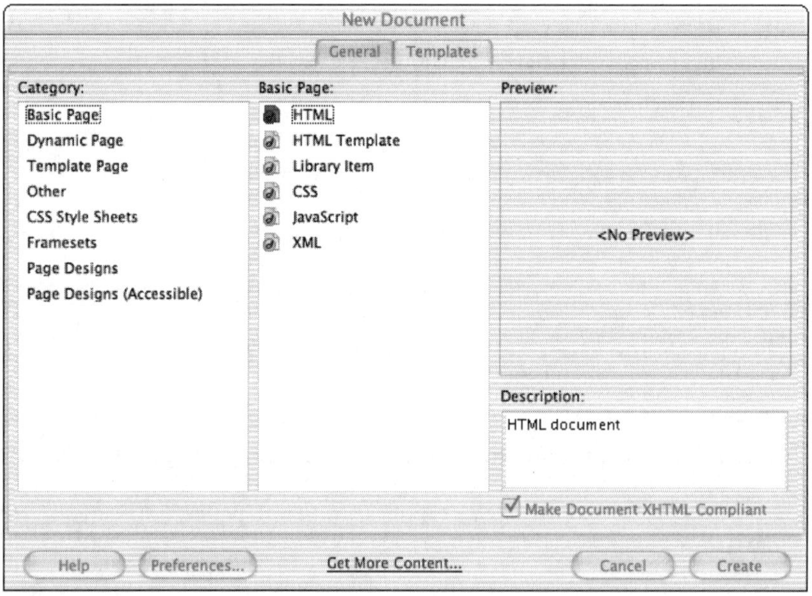

Figure 2-2

By default, this generally creates a document in Transitional XHTML 1.0 (you can check this by looking at the Document Type Declaration) because it uses XML syntax yet still allows your document to contain the same elements and attributes as the much better known earlier versions of HTML. If you want to create a document in Strict XHTML, just change the Document Type Declaration at the top of the page.

You should also select the Preferences button and choose the category Code Format to bring up the details for those settings. In this window, you will see the option for uppercase or lowercase names and attributes. Beneath this is another option for specifying how to deal with items that you want to be centered—you want to choose the `<div>` option, not the `<center>` element, as shown in Figure 2-3.

You can now create your document. After you have created your page (or along the way if you want), you should validate the page to make sure it meets the rules of the XHTML version you have chosen.

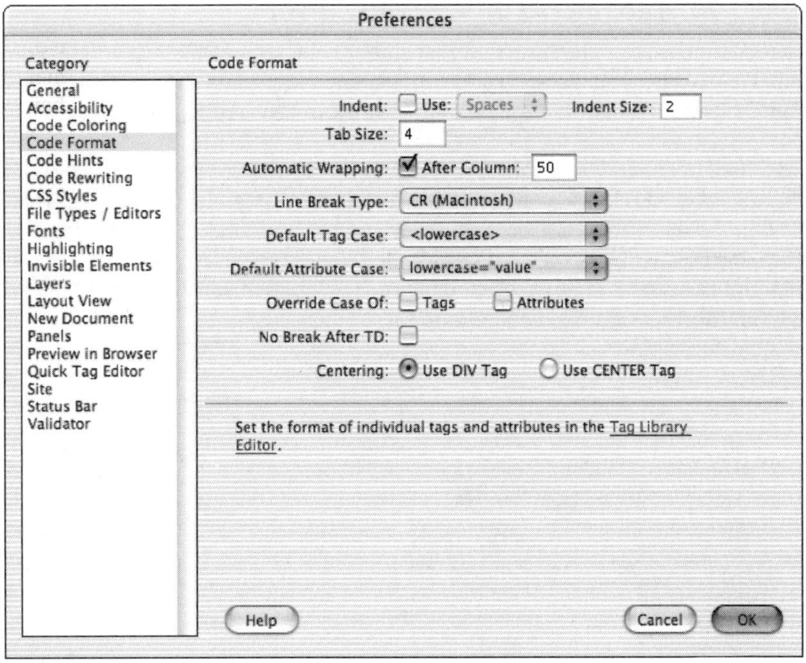

Figure 2-3

Validation

Validation is the process of ensuring that a document you have written meets the rules and requirements of the language. Any XML language can be validated against its Document Type Definition (or another form of schema such as an XML Schema or RelaxNG schema), and XHTML is no exception.

You may remember that the Document Type Declaration (which comes after the optional XML declaration) indicates which Document Type Definition you use—although it does not necessarily indicate where the Document Type Definition can be found.

Many tools enable you to validate your XHTML pages. Most authoring tools can validate your code for you, or you can use an online validation tool such as the one provided by the W3C at `http://validator.w3.org/` to ensure that your pages follow the rules of XHTML.

If you are going to create an entire site based upon a set of template documents, it is always good practice to validate your template documents, rather than wait until you have built your whole site. You can then correct any errors in your first template document, rather than correct every page of your site.

If you create an application that allows users to enter their own markup, it is a good idea to validate the markup the user has entered. You should be able to do this using one of the many validating XML parsers available.

Validating XHTML documents in Dreamweaver

Dreamweaver has a built-in validating tool that enables you to confirm that your markup meets a number of specifications—not just the Strict XHTML recommendation. With the Dreamweaver validation tool, you can validate not only the page you are writing, but the entire site on which you are working.

The validation tool in Dreamweaver does not look at the Document Type Declaration in order to determine which version of XHTML you are writing your document according to. Rather, you need to select it. Go to the Edit menu on Windows or the Dreamweaver menu on a Mac and select Preferences. In the Preferences dialog box, you will see a category called Validator, which will bring up the options shown in Figure 2-4. You can see that I have selected Strict XHTML in this instance, although you could pick Transitional XHTML 1.0 or even older standards.

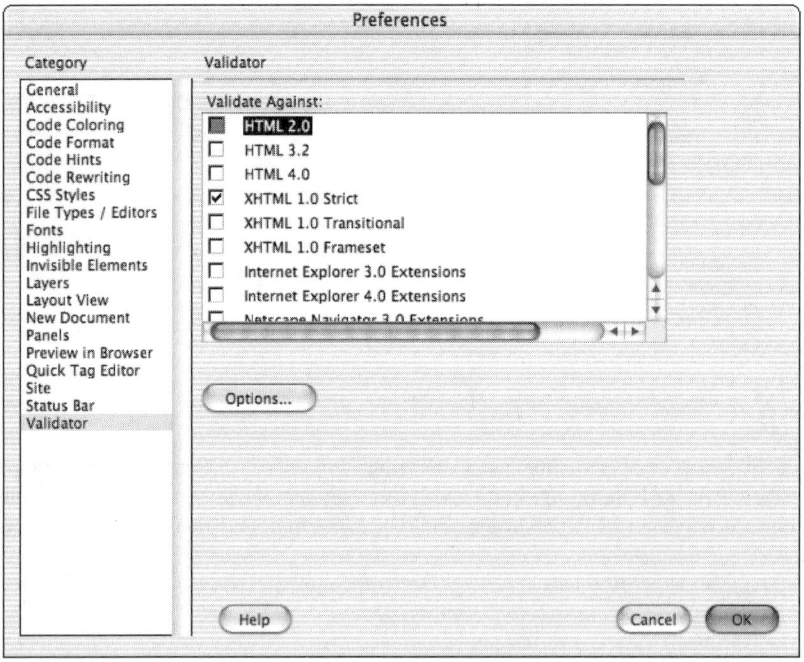

Figure 2-4

Once you have specified which rules you want to validate against, and you are ready to validate your page, go to the Window menu, navigate to the Results option, and select Validation. This will bring up the screen shown in Figure 2-5. Clicking on the arrow just under the word Validation will enable you to validate the document. Figure 2-5 shows you an example of a page that has two errors. You can see the errors just underneath the validation window — the `<img>` tag is an empty element, but it does not have a closing slash before the right-angled bracket and does not have an `alt` attribute.

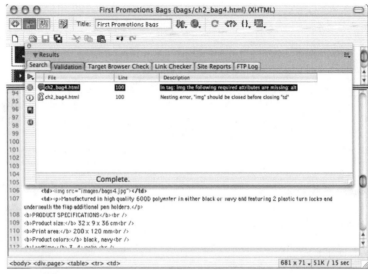

Figure 2-5

As soon as you have fixed these errors (or whatever errors you have encountered) and revalidated the document, you should get a message indicating that "no errors were found" in the location that previously contained the list of errors.

Validating XHTML documents using the W3C validator

It is very easy to confirm online that your XHTML documents meet the Strict XHTML 1.0 guidelines. Check the W3C Web site at `http://validator.w3.org/`. Figure 2-6 shows you the page for the W3C validator.

As you can see, you can either browse to a local file on your hard drive or you can enter the URL of a page that you want to validate. Once you have selected the page you want to check and pressed the Check button, you should see a report showing that either you have errors on your page or your page meets the requirements. Figure 2-7 shows you a report with one error for a missing `alt` attribute on an `<img />` element. As you can see, the report offers quite a lot of information to help you find your errors.

Figure 2-8 shows you a page without any errors that meets the Strict XHTML 1.0 recommendation.

You can see in Figure 2-8 that you are shown a little icon you can use on your page to indicate that it is valid Strict XHTML 1.0. This icon acts as a link to the W3C validator, which you can use to check your page again every time you make changes to it.

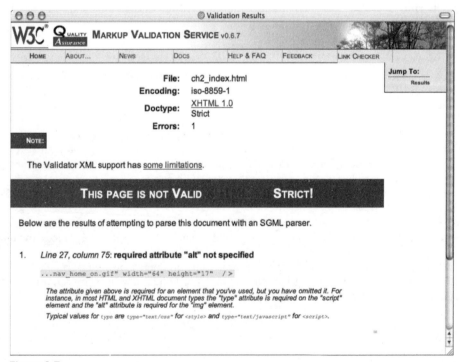

Figure 2-6

Figure 2-7

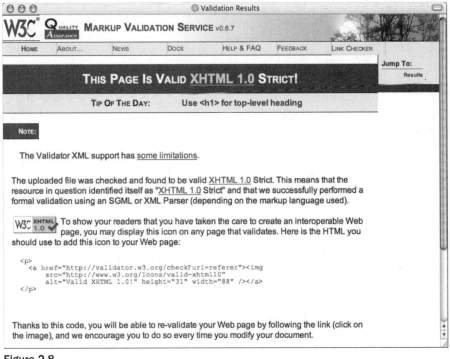

Figure 2-8

Solution

Now it is time to return to the First Promotions site and take one of each of the three types of pages (home page, product list page, and product detail page) and make sure that each is fully XHTML-compliant. This means that you have to do the following:

❑   Add the correct code to the start of pages (adding the optional XML declaration and the !DOCTYPE declaration before the opening <html> element, and the XHTML namespace to the XHTML element).

❑   Strip stylistic markup from the documents.

❑   Ensure that all elements have opening and closing tags and nest correctly and that their names are in lowercase.

❑   Ensure that all attributes are written in lowercase, that they have values, and that these values are in quotes.

❑   Validate each of the pages to ensure that you have obeyed the rules of XHTML.

Before you start, note that most of the element and attribute names were already written in lowercase characters, so there are few alterations in that respect.

You will start by looking at the home page. Remember that all pages have the same header and left navigation, so you need to look at this section of the code only once for the home page.

For the examples in this and the next two chapters, you will still be using tables to control the layout of the document. This means that to a certain extent, the markup is being used to control the presentation of the pages. However, when you reach Chapter 5, you will see how CSS can be used to control the positioning of items on the page, and all of the layout tables can be removed.

Home page

The first page you will be working with to ensure that it is XHTML-compliant is the home page. You can see the how the original home page looked before you start to convert it into XHTML in Chapter 1.

Because it will take a few pages to cover this one Web page, I have split the page into sections under different headings. You will examine this page in the greatest detail because the other pages use exactly the same code for whole sections of the page.

Root element and head

The first task is to ensure that the page starts correctly. In the old site, the page starts with the root `<html>` element, so you should add the optional XML declaration and the Document Type Declaration to indicate that you are going to be writing Strict XHTML. Both of these are placed before the opening `<html>` tag:

```
<?xml version="1.0" encoding="iso-8859-1"?>
<!DOCTYPE html PUBLIC "-//W3C//DTD XHTML 1.0 Strict//EN"
          "http://www.w3.org/TR/xhtml1/DTD/xhtml1-strict.dtd">
<html>
```

Now add the namespace onto the root element of the XHTML document to indicate that all of the markup in this document belongs to the XHTML namespace (you will return to the topic of namespaces in Chapter 8):

```
<?xml version="1.0" encoding="iso-8859-1"?>
<!DOCTYPE html PUBLIC "-//W3C//DTD XHTML 1.0 Strict//EN"
          "http://www.w3.org/TR/xhtml1/DTD/xhtml1-strict.dtd">
<html xmlns="http://www.w3.org/1999/xhtml">
```

Looking at the next line, you can already see the title for the page, which is required in any Strict XHTML document. Because this is the home page, the title explains what the company does, which is an adequate description, although you can add the words `Home Page` at the end of the title if you like.

After the `<title>` element, you can add the `<meta>` tag to specify the encoding of the document; this is in addition to adding it in the XML declaration, although this is not required.

In the original file, the `<title>` element is followed by a `<script>` element that contained a script generated by Macromedia Dreamweaver to handle rollover images. You are going to remove all of this script code and place it in a separate JavaScript file (which is just a text file with a `.js` file extension). This helps keep the document with the content as simple and focused on the content itself as possible, and saves you having to worry about processors that might have trouble with the < and & characters that would otherwise require you to use a CDATA section (you might remember that older browsers do not always understand CDATA sections).

When dealing with scripts in XHTML, use scripts only to *enhance* a page; you should never write a page that can be viewed only if the user's browser supports JavaScript, because users might have JavaScript turned off, or their browser might not support JavaScript at all.

When you place your scripts in an external file, the <script> element only needs to indicate where the JavaScript file is; it does not contain any code itself. The <script> element carries a type attribute to indicate the type of file to which it is pointing (a text file that contains JavaScript), and an src attribute to indicate the source of the file. Note that the <script> element should not be turned into an empty element; you should always use an opening and closing tag for it.

> The **type** attribute should have what is known as a MIME type as its value. You can find a list of common MIME types in Appendix E.

You can see the entire <head> element of the document here, with the <title>, <meta>, and <script> elements as they will appear in the home page:

```
<head>
  <title>First Promotions - Promotional Corporate Gifts  - Home Page</title>
  <meta http-equiv="content-type" content="text/html;charset=iso-8859-1" />
  <script type="text/javascript" src="scripts/rollover.js"></script>
</head>
```

The rollover.js file, which resides in the scripts folder, simply contains the code that would have been in between the opening <script> tag and the closing </script> tag:

```
function MM_swapImgRestore() { //v3.0
 var i,x,a=document.MM_sr;
 for(i=0;a&&i<a.length&&(x=a[i])&&x.oSrc;i++) x.src=x.oSrc;
}

function MM_preloadImages() { //v3.0
  var d=document; if(d.images){ if(!d.MM_p) d.MM_p=new Array();
    var i,j=d.MM_p.length,a=MM_preloadImages.arguments; for(i=0; i<a.length; i++)
    if (a[i].indexOf("#")!=0){ d.MM_p[j]=new Image; d.MM_p[j++].src=a[i];}}
}

function MM_findObj(n, d) { //v4.01
  var p,i,x;  if(!d) d=document; if((p=n.indexOf("?"))>0&&parent.frames.length) {
    d=parent.frames[n.substring(p+1)].document; n=n.substring(0,p);}
  if(!(x=d[n])&&d.all) x=d.all[n]; for (i=0;!x&&i<d.forms.length;i++)
      x=d.forms[i][n];
  for(i=0;!x&&d.layers&&i<d.layers.length;i++)
  x=MM_findObj(n,d.layers[i].document);
  if(!x && d.getElementById) x=d.getElementById(n); return x;
}

function MM_swapImage() { //v3.0
  var i,j=0,x,a=MM_swapImage.arguments; document.MM_sr=new Array;
  for(i=0;i<(a.length-2);i+=3)
  if ((x=MM_findObj(a[i]))!=null){document.MM_sr[j++]=x; if(!x.oSrc) x.oSrc=x.src;
      x.src=a[i+2];}
}
```

Going back to the index.html file, you next change the opening <body> tag. You have to remove the stylistic attributes from this element, which means the bgcolor, alink, vlink, and link attributes are gone. You can see what this element looks like in the original home page here:

```
<body bgcolor="#FFFFFF" alink="#0000CC" vlink="#003366" link="#0066CC"
  onLoad="MM_preloadImages('/images/interface/nav_order_on.gif',
 '/images/interface/nav_bestSellers_on.gif','/images/interface/nav_custom.gif',
 '/images/interface/nav_contactUs_on.gif','/images/interface/nav_pens_on.gif',
 '/images/nav_nav_pads_on.gif','/images/interface/nav_bags.gif',
 '/images/interface/nav_mugs_on.gif','/images/nac/nav_stickers_on.gif',
 '/images/interface/nav_stress_on.gif')">
```

Without the stylistic attributes, it should look like the following (note that the onLoad attribute was one of the few attribute names to contain an uppercase character, so this has been altered to be all lowercase):

```
<body
  onload="MM_preloadImages('/images/interface/nav_order_on.gif',
 '/images/interface/nav_bestSellers_on.gif','/images/interface/nav_custom.gif',
 '/images/interface/nav_contactUs_on.gif','/images/interface/nav_pens_on.gif',
 '/images/nav_nav_pads_on.gif','/images/interface/nav_bags.gif',
 '/images/interface/nav_mugs_on.gif','/images/nac/nav_stickers_on.gif',
 '/images/interface/nav_stress_on.gif')">
```

You should also remove the <center> element, which had been the first element inside the <body> of the page. When removing this element, do not forget to remove the matching closing tag that is near the end of the document. In my experience, it is far more practical to remove the opening and closing tags at the same time; otherwise, you might end up either forgetting to delete a closing tag or accidentally deleting the wrong tags when you get further down the page.

Masthead and top navigation

Inside the <body> element, following the <center> element, was a single-celled table, which was used to hold all of the content and draw a line around the edge of it. This table has been removed and replaced with a <div> element. The <div> element—which you may have come across before (especially if you have worked with layers)—is designed to group together a related set of elements. In this case, the <div> element is grouping together all of the elements that make up the page and is therefore given a class attribute whose value is page, to indicate that this <div> holds and represents the entire page:

```
<div class="page">
```

You will learn more about using the class attribute when you learn about CSS; suffice it to say that it is a very helpful way of applying the same style to a group of elements.

Next up in the original document is the table that held the masthead. Quite a few changes need to be made here, so here is the original table to look at, followed by the new version:

```
<table border="0" cellpadding="5" cellspacing="0" width="800">
  <tr>
    <td bgcolor="#000066">
      <font face="Arial, Helvetica, sans-serif" size="-6"   color="#FFFFFF">
        <b> Promotional gifts, pens, note pads, bags, mugs, executive toys,
          corporate gifts, and lots more...</b>
```

```
          </font>
        </td>
      </tr>
      <tr>
        <td>
          <img src="/images/branding/logo_400x80.gif" alt="logo" border="0">
        </td>
      </tr>
    </table>
```

The changes to be made are as follows:

❑　The opening `<table>` tag loses all of its attributes.

❑　The first `<td>` element loses its `bgcolor` attribute.

❑　The `<font>` and `<b>` elements are removed from inside the first table cell.

❑　The `<img />` element is an empty element and therefore needs a forward slash character added before the right angled-bracket in the tag.

❑　The `border` attribute is removed from the `<img />` element.

The resulting table should look like this (which you can see is a lot simpler and a lot clearer):

```
  <table>
    <tr>
      <td> Promotional gifts, pens, note pads, bags, mugs,
          executive toys, corporate gifts, and lots more...</td>
    </tr>
    <tr>
      <td><img src="/images/branding/logo_400x80.gif" alt="logo" /></td>
    </tr>
  </table>
```

Next up is the table that contains the navigation. With this table, you should make the following changes:

❑　All attributes are removed from the opening `<table>` tag.

❑　The `bgcolor` and `width` attributes are removed from each `<td>` tag.

❑　The `onmouseover` and `onmouseout` attributes are made all lowercase.

❑　The `<img />` tags are given a forward slash character before the closing angled bracket.

❑　All the `name` attributes on the `<img />` elements are replaced with `id` attributes.

```
  <table>
    <tr>
      <td></td>
      <td>
        <img src="images/interface/nav_home_on.gif" width="64" height="17"
            alt="home" />
      </td>
      <td>
```

```
    <a href="order.html" onmouseover="MM_swapImage('HowToOrder','',
      'images/interface/nav_order_on.gif',1)" onmouseout="MM_swapImgRestore()">
      <img src="images/interface/nav_order.gif" alt="How to Order"
          id="HowToOrder" width="110" height="17" />
    </a>
  </td>
  <td>
    <a href="bestSellers.html" onmouseover="MM_swapImage('BestSellers','',
      'images/interface/nav_bestSellers_on.gif',1)"
      onmouseout="MM_swapImgRestore()" >
      <img src="images/interface/nav_bestSellers.gif" alt="Best Sellers"
          id="BestSellers" width="104" height="17" />
    </a>
  </td>
  <td>
    <a href="custom.html" onMouseOver="MM_swapImage('CustomGifts','',
      'images/interface/nav_custom_on.gif',1)" onMouseOut="MM_swapImgRestore()" >
      <img src="images/interface/nav_custom.gif" alt="Custom Gifts"
          id="CustomGifts" width="107" height="17" />
    </a>
  </td>
  <td>
    <a href="contact.html" onMouseOver="MM_swapImage('ContactUs','',
      'images/interface/nav_contactUs_on.gif',1)"
      onMouseOut="MM_swapImgRestore()" >
      <img src="images/interface/nav_contactUs.gif" alt="Contact Us"
          id="ContactUs" width="82" height="17" />
    </a>
  </td>
  <td></td>
</tr>
</table>
```

You might think it a little odd that the `<img />` element can retain its `width` and `height` attributes if you are removing presentational markup, but these attributes are permitted to stay because the size of the image is a property of the image itself. (Even though it is possible to make an image appear smaller or larger than it really is in a browser by setting the width and the height to be the size you want the image to appear, using these attributes does not affect the image file itself.) Specifying the size of an image can also help a page load quicker because the browser does not have to wait for the image to load before knowing how much space to allocate for it.

Left navigation — column one

The main part of the `index.html` page is in one table divided into three columns — left navigation, the main part of the page with the actual content of the site, and the right column that contains information about ordering. Each column lives in its own table cell.

To begin, the `<table>` element, which holds the main part of the page, should have all attributes removed from it:

```
<table>
  <tr>
```

The first column lives in the first cell of the table; it has had the following changes made:

- ❏ All of the attributes on the `<td>` element have been removed.

- ❏ The `onmouseover` and `onmouseout` attributes have been converted to all lowercase characters.

- ❏ All images have to be written using the correct XML syntax for empty elements.

- ❏ All images need their `border` attributes removed.

- ❏ All single-pixel transparent images need an `alt` attribute with empty quotes.

- ❏ All images need their `name` attributes removed and replaced with `id` attributes.

```
<td>
    <img src="images/interface/1px.gif" height="15" width="150" />
    <a href="products/pens/index.html" onmouseout="MM_swapImgRestore()"
      onmouseover="MM_swapImage('Pens','','images/interface/nav_pens_on.gif',1)">
        <img src="images/interface/nav_pens.gif" alt="Pens" id="Pens" width="150"
            height="19" />
    </a>
    <img src="images/interface/1px.gif" height="2" width="150" alt="" />
    <a href="products/pads/index.html" onmouseout="MM_swapImgRestore()"
      onmouseover="MM_swapImage('Pads','','images/interface/nav_pads_on.gif',1)">
        <img src="images/interface/nav_pads.gif" alt="Pads" id="Pads" width="150"
            height="19" />
    </a>
    <img src="images/interface/1px.gif" height="2" width="150" alt="" />
    <a href="products/bags/index.html" onmouseout="MM_swapImgRestore()"
       onmouseover="MM_swapImage('Bags','',
        'images/interface/nav_bags_on.gif',1)">
        <img src="images/interface/nav_bags.gif" alt="Bags" id="Bags" width="150"
            height="19" />
    </a>
    <img src="images/interface/1px.gif" height="2" width="150" alt="" />
    <a href="mugs.html" onmouseout="MM_swapImgRestore()"
       onmouseover="MM_swapImage('Mugs','',
        'images/interface/nav_mugs_on.gif',1)">
        <img src="images/interface/nav_mugs.gif" alt="Mugs" id="Mugs" width="150"
          height="19" />
    </a>
    <img src="images/interface/1px.gif" height="2" width="150" alt="" />
    <a href="products/keyrings/index.html" onmouseout="MM_swapImgRestore()"
       onmouseover="MM_swapImage('Keyrings','',
        'images/interface/nav_keyrings_on.gif',1)">
        <img src="images/interface/nav_keyrings.gif" alt="Keyrings" id="Keyrings"
            width="150" height="19" />
    </a>
    <img src="images/interface/1px.gif" height="2" width="150" alt="" />
    <a href="products/stressbusters/index.html" onmouseout="MM_swapImgRestore()"
       onmouseover="MM_swapImage('StressBusters','',
        'images/interface/nav_stress_on.gif',1)">
        <img src="images/interface/nav_stress.gif" alt="Stress busters"
            id="StressBusters" width="150" height="19" />
    </a>
    <img src="images/interface/1px.gif" height="40" width="150" alt="" />
```

After the navigation items is an image of the guaranteed delivery dates, which lived inside a `<center>` element. This `<center>` element has been removed. An `alt` attribute has also been added to this image because it lacked one previously.

```
            <img src="images/interface/guarantee.jpg" height="126" width="127"
                alt="Guaranteed delivery within 3 weeks" />
        </td>
```

The closing of this table cell brings the navigation column to a close, so it is time to move on to the central column.

Central column

The central column holds the main content of every page. On the home page, it carries two key types of information: a welcome message and some featured items. These are followed by some footer links that are common to all pages.

You start off with an opening `<td>` tag that creates the table cell that holds the central column of the page; this needs its attributes removed. Then the `<center>` element needs to be removed (and don't forget to remove the corresponding closing tag every time you remove an opening tag).

```
    <td>
```

Next is one of the single-pixel images used to position content in the page. This is no longer required now that CSS can help us with positioning; therefore, the following line is no longer required:

```
        <img src="images/interface/1px.gif" height="15" width="1">
```

The first content in this center column is a single-celled table that is used to create a box that holds the welcome text and makes it stand out from the rest of the page. The box has a gray line around the outside and a light-gray background. You no longer need this table, and you can replace it with a `<div>` element, because with CSS you will be able to add styles to this `<div>` element, rather than use a table.

Inside the single-celled table was a `<font>` element used to control the presentation of the text, which has also been removed.

There are two paragraphs of welcome text, and these have been placed inside `<p>` tags, which means you can remove the two `<br />` tags that were between the paragraphs:

```
        <div class="welcomeText">
            <p>Welcome to First Promotions, specialists in corporate gifts and
            promotional items. Our extensive range of promotional bags,
            mugs, pads and pens help your company stick in the mind of
            your customers.</p>

            <p>All of our promotional gifts can be personalized with your logo,
            name and web address. First Promotions can even help with the
            design of your promotional gifts.</p>
        </div>
```

Next are a couple of elements that were just used for positioning: a simple line break followed by a single-pixel transparent GIF. Both of these are removed.

The subsequent featured items image is left in, but is made to follow the empty element syntax of XHTML. It also has to carry the `alt` attribute, which is required in Strict XHTML. The value of the image is an alternative text description of the image, and if your image should not be explained (for example, if it is a placer or design image), then you should just leave empty double quotes (without a space between them).

```
<img src="/images/interface/featuredItems.gif" alt="Featured Items">
```

The featured items table is the second main feature of the central column. This table was inside a `<center>` element, which has been removed from the page (the closing tag for this element is after the footer links).

Next, take a look at the table that contains the featured items. You might want to refer to the screenshot of the index page shown in Figure 1-4 in Chapter 1 to see what was going on here. The table held four products spread across two columns. The table also had four rows — the first and third rows contained images of the featured items (which acted as links to the pages about those products), while the second and fourth rows contained the title of the product.

The changes that should happen here are as follows:

❑   The opening `<table>` tag should have all attributes removed.

❑   All the table cells holding the images and titles of featured items should have attributes removed.

❑   All font and `<b>` elements can be removed from the table cells holding the titles.

❑   All `<img />` elements must have their `border` attributes removed.

❑   All `<img />` elements must be given an `alt` attribute.

❑   All `<img />` elements should follow the correct syntax for empty elements.

```
<table>
  <tr>
    <td>
      <a href="products/mugs/mug2.html">
        <img src="products/mugs/images/mugs2_thumb.gif" alt="Mug" />
      </a>
    </td>
    <td>
      <a href="products/pens/pen2.hml">
        <img src="products/pens/images/pens2_thumb.gif" alt="Pen" />
      </a>
    </td>
  </tr>
  <tr>
    <td>Marrow mugs from $1.25</td>
    <td>Buggy ballpoint pens $0.25</td>
  </tr>
  <tr>
    <td>
```

```
          <a href="products/bags/bag4.html">
            <img src="products/bags/images/bags4_thumb.gif" alt="Bag" />
          </a>
        </td>
        <td>
          <a href="products/pads/pad3.html">
            <img src="products/pads/images/pad3_thumb.gif" alt="Pad" />
          </a>
        </td>
      </tr>
      <tr>
        <td>Jupiter bags $2.55</td>
        <td>A4 spiral-bound pads $1.15</td>
      </tr>
    </table>
```

The last part of the central column is the footer links that are common to each page. These links are inside `<font>` elements and are preceded by `<br>` tags, both of which have been removed and replaced with a `<div>` element whose class attribute has a value of `footer`:

```
    <div>
      <a href="/about.html">About Us</a> |
      <a href="/contact.html">Contact Us</a> |
      <a href="/terms.html">Terms and Conditions</a> |
      &copy; 2004 FirstPromotions.co.uk
    </div>
  </td>
```

Right column

The right-hand column of the home page just contains information about how to order from the site. It is common to all pages except for the individual product information pages.

First, you can remove the attributes from the opening `<td>` tag that starts this right-hand column. Then you can delete the single-pixel image and `<center>` elements used to position the first item in the column.

The first thing you see in this right-hand column should be the image with the order hotline number on it (`orderHotline.gif`); this image needs to have an `alt` attribute added to it to explain its purpose, and a closing slash before the right-angled bracket:

```
    <td>
      <img src="images/interface/orderHotline.gif" width="155" height="38"
          alt="Order Hotline telephone 8369 5972" />
```

This image was followed by a `<br>` element and another single-pixel positioning image, both of which should be removed. The subsequent opening `<table>` tag should then have its attributes removed.

```
      <table>
```

The rows of this table have only one cell. In the first row is an image that just needs converting to XML syntax by adding the now familiar closing slash character; and the `<img />` element needs an `alt` attribute added:

```
    <tr>
      <td>
        <img src="/images/interface/howToOrder.gif" width="153" height="21"
            alt="How to order" />
      </td>
    </tr>
```

On the second row of this table, you come across another cell whose attributes should be removed. It contains a single-cell table used to draw a line around the instructions about how to order. This single-cell table should be removed, too. Then the `<font>` element that was in this table should be deleted.

You should then make sure that all of the `<br />` elements use the correct syntax:

```
    <tr>
      <td>
        1) Select an item from our extensive catalog.<br /><br />
        2) Send us the logo or text you want printed on the gifts.<br />
           <br />
        3) We e-mail you a picture of the item with your design.<br /><br />
        4) Confirm the order, and we'll deliver the goods within
           21 days.<br />
      </td>
    </tr>
  </table>
</td>
```

All that is left to do now is to close up the table and the page:

```
    </tr>
  </table>
</div>
</body>
</html>
```

This page should now be significantly shorter than the original version. In fact, it has decreased in size from 8,511 characters to 6,142, which will add up to a great deal more across the whole site.

Of course, this page will not look anywhere near as attractive now. It has had nearly all of the presentation rules removed from it. Figure 2-9 shows you what the index.html file looks like now in a browser without any formatting. You should not, however, worry about the appearance of the page; you will soon make it look more attractive again when you start learning about CSS in Chapter 3.

Product list page

Having looked at the home page, the next page to address is the product list page. This should be much quicker to go through because the masthead, left navigation, and right column (containing the ordering information) are the same as they were on the home page (the only difference being the URLs that point to images and links to other pages). Therefore, you can start by copying the changes you made on the home page and updating these sections of the product list page to be XHTML-compliant.

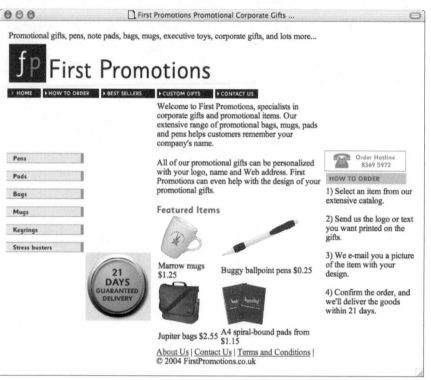

Figure 2-9

Once you have altered the first two tables on the page, and the left and right columns on the third table, you can focus on the middle cell of the third table, which contains the real content of the page — the product list. You will be looking at the list of bags in this chapter, although all the lists follow an identical structure.

First, remove all of the attributes from the `<td>` tag that forms this middle column:

```
<td>
```

The next item on the page is the title of the section of products you are looking at — in this case, Bags. The next few lines, until the word Bags, can be deleted. You should see a single-pixel transparent GIF image, a `<br>` element, a `<font>` element, and a `<b>` element, all of which can be removed. The word Bags should stay, although the line break tag that follows it can be deleted. Remember to remove the closing tags from the elements as you go. You should end up with the following:

```
<td>
Bags
```

Having seen to the section heading, the next thing on the page is the table containing the list of products. This table is contained in a `<center>` element, which should be deleted. Looking at the table, you have a few changes to make:

- ❑ Remove the attributes from the opening `<table>` tag, because these are all stylistic attributes.

- ❑ Delete the `width`, `bgcolor`, `align`, and `valign` attributes from the `<td>` element.

- ❑ Remove the `border` attribute from images.

- ❑ Add an `alt` attribute to each image, with a description of the image (because this is a required attribute on images in Strict XHTML).

- ❑ Format the `<img />` elements correctly as empty elements with their closing slash.

- ❑ Remove the `<font>` and `<b>` elements from inside the `<td>` elements that contain text.

- ❑ Format the `<br />` tags properly as empty elements with their closing slash.

The table should end up looking a lot clearer and more like this:

```
<table>
  <tr>
    <td>
      <a href="bag1.html"><img src="images/bags1_thumb.gif" alt="City bag" /></a>
    </td>
    <td>City Conference Bags<br />
      Best-selling, low-priced bags with detachable strap and interior pockets.
<br />
      From $2.49 min qty 150
    </td>
  </tr>
  <tr>
    <td>
      <a href="bag2.html"><img src="images/bags2_thumb.gif" alt="Seattle bag"
/></a>
    </td>
    <td><a href="bag2.html">Seattle Conference Bags</a><br />
      Rugged construction for added durability and a zipped front pocket. <br />
      From $3.89 min qty 50
    </td>
  </tr>
  <tr>
    <td>
      <a href="bag3.html"><img src="images/bags3_thumb.gif" alt="Cambridge bag"
/></a>
    </td>
    <td><a href="bag3.html">Cambridge Conference Bags</a><br />
      High-quality bags in polyester with many pockets and features at a
      great price. <br />
      From $3.58 min qty 100
    </td>
  </tr>
  <tr>
    <td>
```

```
        <a href="bag4.html"><img src="images/bags4_thumb.gif" alt="Jupiter bags"
/></a>
    </td>
    <td><a href="bag4.html">Jupiter Business Bags</a><br />
        Manufactured in 600D polyester in either royal blue or navy.
        Ideal for executives on the move <br />
        From $2.99 min qty 100
    </td>
  </tr>
</table>
```

This is followed by the footer links, which you have seen already on the home page:

```
    <div>
        <a href="../../about.html">About Us</a> |
        <a href="../../contact.html">Contact Us</a> |
        <a href="../../terms.html">Terms and Conditions</a> |
        &copy; 2004 FirstPromotions.co.uk
    </div>
    </td>
```

Again, you end up with a simpler, smaller page. Figure 2-10 shows you what this page will look like in the browser. Again, remember that this is without any formatting. You will start to make the page look much more attractive when you look at CSS in Chapter 3.

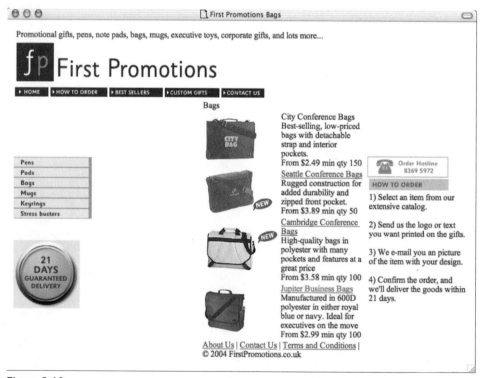

Figure 2-10

If you come across problems with the navigation column taking up twice the width it should (and making other items look out of line), you might have to add a couple of <br /> tags after some of the images in the navigation column, like so:

```
<img src="/images/interface/nav_stress.gif" alt="Stress busters"
        id="StressBusters" width="150" height="19" />
</a><br />
<img src="/images/interface/1px.gif" height="40" width="150" /><br />
```

Product details page

The final page to look at is the product details page. The first two tables containing the header and the top navigation are the same as they were for the two pages you have just looked at. Similarly, the first column of the third table, which contains the left navigation, is the same as the first two pages, so you do not need to read about those sections again here. What you do need to look at is the other cell of the third table that contains all of the details about the products.

Remember that the product details pages do not contain ordering information in a column on the right-hand side of the page, so the remaining cell of this table that you are looking at takes up the majority of the page.

To start off, you need to remove the width, bgcolor, and valign attributes that were on the opening <td> tag that started this main section of the page:

```
<td width="650" bgcolor="#FFFFFF" valign="top">
```

Following that, you can also delete the <br /> and <center> elements that follow it (remembering to remove the closing </center> tag at the same time).

The details of each item are held in two tables. The first table contains the name of the item and a link to the product list page for this section, showing all of the bags. On this table, you need to do the following:

❑ Strip the border, cellpadding, cellspacing, and width attributes from the opening <table> tag.

❑ Remove the align and valign attributes from the <td> elements.

❑ Remove the <font> and <b> elements from within the <td> elements.

You should end up with a simple table like the following:

```
<table>
 <tr>
  <td>Jupiter Business Bags</td>
  <td>
    <a href="../../products/bags/index.html">
    View All Bags</a>
  </td>
 </tr>
</table>
```

Following this table is a `<br />` element, which can go. The next table is a one-celled table used to draw a line around the table that controls the layout of the product details. As with all of these single-celled tables used to create outlines, it can be replaced with a `<div>` element. While you are at it, you can remove the attributes from the `<table>` tag:

```
<div>
   <table>
     <tr>
```

In the next cell, which holds the image of the product, you must do four things:

- ❑ Remove the attributes from the `<td>` tag.
- ❑ Remove the `border` attribute from the `<img />` element.
- ❑ Add an `alt` attribute to the `<img />` element.
- ❑ Add the closing slash to the `<img />` element.

```
<td><img src="images/bags4.jpg" alt="Jupiter Bag" /></td>
```

In the following table cell, you can do the following:

- ❑ Remove the attributes from the `<td>` tag.
- ❑ Delete the `<font>` and `<b>` elements.
- ❑ Add a `<p>` element to contain the paragraph describing the product.

```
<td><p>Manufactured in high quality 600D polyester in either black or navy
   and featuring 2 plastic turn locks and underneath the flap additional
   pen holders.</p>
```

You can leave the `<b>` elements that are used to tell the readers about the product specifications, but you do need to make sure that the `<br />` tags are written correctly with their closing slashes:

```
<b>PRODUCT SPECIFICATIONS</b><br />
<b>Product size:</b> 32 x 9 x 36 cm<br />
<b>Print area:</b> 200 x 120 mm<br />
<b>Product colors:</b> black, navy<br />
<b>Leadtime:</b> 3-4 weeks <br /><br />
</td>
</tr>
```

In the next row, the first cell you come across contains tables that hold the pricing details. You should remove all attributes from the `<td>` and `<table>` elements on the way:

```
<tr>
   <td>
      <table>
         <tr>
```

The first row of this table indicates the quantities of items to be ordered, and the second row provides the prices. For the items in each row, you should remove the bgcolor attributes and the <font> elements. You should also make all of the heading cells into <th> elements, not <td> elements:

```
                <th>Quantity</th>
                <th>100</th>
                <th>250</th>
                <th>500</th>
                <th>1000</th>
            </tr>
            <tr>
                <th>Unit price</th>
                <td>$4.25</td>
                <td>$3.66</td>
                <td>$3.44</td>
                <td>$3.22</td>
            </tr>
            <tr>
                <th>Additional colors (each)</th>
                <td>$0.50</td>
                <td>$0.45</td>
                <td>$0.45</td>
                <td>$0.45</td>
            </tr>
        </table>
    </td>
```

The final cell contains information about printing of the products. It needs the following changes:

❑   Remove the attributes from the <td> tag.

❑   Delete the <font>, <b>, and <br> elements.

❑   Place the text inside two <p> elements.

```
        <td><p>Price is inclusive of single color print in one position.</p>
            <p>Screens are charged at $35 per color per position.</p>
        </td>
    </tr>
</table>
</div>
```

The final change is to update the footer links just as you did on both of the other pages you looked at, making exactly the same changes:

```
    <div>
        <a href="../../about.html">About Us</a> |
        <a href="../../contact.html">Contact Us</a> |
        <a href="../../terms.html">Terms and Conditions</a> |
        &copy; 2004 FirstPromotions.co.uk
    </div>
</td>
```

Again, the page will look rather odd in a browser until you add more style rules using CSS, but you should end up with something similar to what is shown in Figure 2-11.

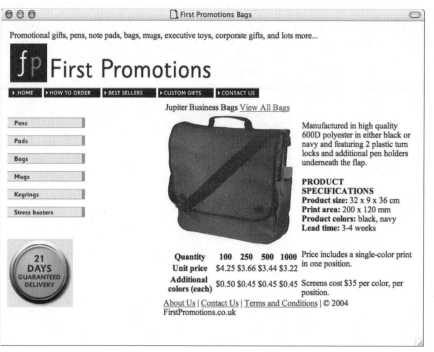

Figure 2-11

Validation

Now that you have looked at the three pages upon which all of the others are based, it is time to check them using a validation tool. This will indicate whether you have any syntax errors, such as missing closing elements, incorrectly nested elements, disallowed attributes, or values without quotes.

Remember that it is always sensible to validate one page before changing every page that uses that template. If you find an error in the template document, you will not repeat it in all of the files.

The three files you have met — the home page, the product lists for the bags, and the product details page for the Jupiter bag — have all been validated to ensure that they meet the Strict XHTML 1.0 guidelines, and have been validated in both the W3C online validator and Macromedia Dreamweaver.

Summary

In this chapter, you have learned all about the differences between writing HTML and XHTML documents. You have examined the three variations of XHTML — Strict, Transitional, and Frameset. Each of these versions is written in XML, so your syntax has to obey the same rules that any language written in XML must obey. This use of XML syntax is one of the biggest differences between HTML and XHTML.

The other big difference is that XHTML aims to take the rules that control the style and presentation of a page out of the document that contains the markup and content. Strict XHTML, therefore, does not contain any of the elements and attributes that control the presentation of a document. Nor does it contain any of the elements that enable you to create frames. Many of the elements also have stricter constraints upon which elements are allowed to appear as their children.

In recreating HTML using the syntax of XML, the W3C helped create a language that is much stricter (and better defined), which in turn allows for smaller browsers, stronger validation of documents, programmatic creation and access of documents, and the capability for the language to evolve in the future.

Once you have made the sample site compliant with the rules of strict XHTML and have removed all of the presentational rules, you will find that it looks nothing like the first version; it looks rather sparse and some of the items seem poorly placed. Not to worry; in the Chapter 3, you will start to add a bit more style using CSS.

Using CSS to Style Documents

In this chapter, you will start to learn all about *Cascading Style Sheets* (or *CSS*, for short). You will see how CSS enables you to control the presentation of an HTML or XHTML document using rules that reside in a separate document known as a *style sheet*. You will also learn how using CSS style sheets has several advantages over using stylistic markup in HTML.

CSS is a language that enables you to write rules that indicate how the content of an element should appear. You will therefore have to learn not only what properties of the document you can affect (such as colors and widths of lines and boxes, fonts, and so on), but also how to associate these rules with the elements you want the properties to affect.

CSS is quite a large topic, so it is not possible to learn everything in one chapter. Nonetheless, by the end of this chapter, you will have learned the following:

❑   How to link an XHTML document to a style sheet

❑   How to write CSS style sheets and CSS rules

❑   How CSS uses properties and values to control the presentation of different elements within your document

❑   How to control the presentation of text using CSS

❑   How CSS is based on a box model and how you set different properties for these boxes (such as width and styles of borders)

❑   How to control colors and backgrounds in CSS

❑   The advantages of using CSS to style documents

That's a lot to cover, but by the end of the chapter you should be able to write your own style sheets.

Problem

You have embarked on a journey to update a site that was written in HTML 4 and rebuild the site using the current the Web standards XHTML and CSS. This involves separating the styling rules from the content and putting them in a separate document. In the last chapter, you learned how to make the site compliant with the rules of Strict XHTML 1.0, and in doing so you saw how removing the stylistic markup left the site looking nothing like the original version. The pages looked very plain, the layout was disjointed, text and images were not in the right position, and there was a lack of color.

Now it's time to learn all about CSS so that you can make the site look attractive again. Therefore, you need to learn what CSS is, how CSS rules work, what properties of the document you can alter, and how to use CSS to make the site more attractive.

Design

As indicated at the start of the chapter, CSS is a language that enables you to write rules that indicate how the content of an element should appear. There are actually two versions of CSS — CSS1 and CSS2. CSS1 was originally released as a W3C recommendation in December 1996, while CSS2 came along in May 1998 and expanded upon the existing CSS1 recommendation, adding new features to those in CSS1. In this chapter, you will look at the main properties from both versions that are supported by the major browsers.

Once you have learned the basics of creating a style sheet, you should find it very easy to learn how new properties affect presentation of the document.

In this chapter, you will focus on learning how CSS works and then look at how it can be used to control the most fundamental aspects of styling a document. Once you have a good grounding in this chapter, the following chapter will present many of the other aspects of a document that you can control with CSS.

How CSS works

CSS works by enabling you to write *rules* that you can associate with elements in the HTML or XHTML document. These rules control how the content of that element should be displayed. For example, you might create a rule specifying that all <h1> elements should be displayed in a black, 28-point, Arial font. Or you might create a rule specifying that the background color of everything inside the <body> element should be white (which is the equivalent of using the bgccolor attribute on the <body> element).

Every CSS rule is made up of two parts:

❑ The **selector**, which indicates the element or elements to which the rule applies. (If the same rule applies to more than one element, you can use a comma-separated list of several elements.)

❑ The **declaration**, which indicates how you want to style the content of the element specified in the selector

Figure 3-1 shows a rule that applies to all <h1> elements and indicates that they should appear in the Arial typeface.

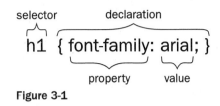

Figure 3-1

As Figure 3-1 shows, the declaration is also split into two parts, each separated by a colon:

❑   A **property**, which is the aspect of the selected element(s) that you want to affect; in this case, it is the font-family property, which controls the typeface used

❑   A **value**, which is a setting for this property; in this case, it is the Arial typeface

Properties and their values in CSS are very similar to the stylistic attributes and their values that you know from HTML. For example, the CSS font-family property is just like the face attribute on the <font> element, and the CSS font-size property is just like the size attribute on the <font> element.

The rule in Figure 3-1 illustrates how one CSS rule can control the presentation of all <h1> elements in any document associated with this style sheet, rather than having to add a <font> element to control the presentation of each individual <h1> element.

You can indicate that a rule should apply to several elements by adding each element name to the selector, separated by a comma. For example, the following CSS rule would apply to all <h1>, <h2>, and <h3> elements. Each CSS rule can also contain several properties and values; they all reside inside the same set of curly braces and should be separated by a semicolon. For example, the following rule specifies the color, typeface, and font weight that should be used with the <h1>, <h2>, and <h3> elements:

```
h1, h2, h3 {
   color:#000000;
   font-family:arial, verdana, sans-serif;
   font-weight:bold;}
```

This should be fairly straightforward; the content of each heading element will be written in a bold, black, Arial font (unless the computer does not have Arial installed, in which case it will look for Verdana and then its default sans-serif font).

A sans-serif font does not have the curls or tails (known as serifs) on the tops and bottoms of letters that are present in a serif font. For example, an l (lowercase L) in a sans-serif font will be a straight line, whereas in a serif font it will usually have a "foot" stretching out both sides on the bottom and a little line pointing left at the top.

In addition, you can add more than one rule to apply to each element; for example, in addition to specifying the color, font-family, and font-weight properties of the <h1>, <h2>, and <h3> elements in this rule, you could have separate rules for each element to indicate their size:

```
h1, h2, h3 {
   color:#000000;
   font-family:arial, verdana, sans-serif;
   font-weight:bold;}
```

```
h1 {font-size:32pt;}
h2 {font-size:26pt;}
h3 {font-size:20pt;}
```

By creating two rules for each of the elements here, you can avoid repeating the color, font-family, and font-weight properties for each element, and therefore end up with a slightly smaller style sheet.

If you are specifying just one property in a rule, you do not need to follow it with a semicolon. However, if you are setting more than one property in the rule, you must separate each property using a semicolon. If you omit the semicolon, then all subsequent declarations in that rule will not be applied. Therefore, it is good practice to use the semicolon at the end of each rule in case you update the style sheet later and forget to check for a semicolon on the preceding line.

You do not need to put each property on a new line, as I have done here, although it makes the style sheet much easier to read.

A simple style sheet

Before you start to look at CSS in detail, it would help if you briefly examined a complete example of a CSS style sheet. Therefore, in this section you will see a very simple XHTML page being styled with a fairly basic CSS style sheet. Some of the properties used in this example will not be covered in detail until Chapter 4, but it will give you a good idea of how CSS works.

First, here is the XHTML page I will be using (ch03_eg01.html). Note a couple of points about this page:

❑   If you look inside the <head> element, you can see the <link /> element, which you will be reading about soon in this chapter; this element links the style sheet to the XHTML page.

❑   The second <p> element uses a class attribute. When you look at the CSS style sheet, you will see a rule that contains a *selector* specifying that the rule should apply only to the elements whose class attribute has a specified value (in this case, important).

```
<?xml version="1.0" encoding="iso-8859-1"?>
<!DOCTYPE html PUBLIC "-//W3C//DTD XHTML 1.0 Strict//EN"
    "http://www.w3.org/TR/xhtml1/DTD/xhtml1-strict.dtd">
<html xmlns="http://www.w3.org/1999/xhtml">
<head>
  <title>CSS Example</title>
  <meta http-equiv="Content-Type" content="text/html; charset=iso-8859-1" />
  <link rel="stylesheet" type="text/css" href="ch03_eg01.css" />
</head>

<body>
  <h1>Simple CSS Example</h1>
  <p>This simple page demonstrates how CSS can be used to control the presentation
    of an XHTML document.</p>
  <p class="important">This paragraph demonstrates the use of the
    <code>class</code> attribute.</p>
</body>
</html>
```

Next, take a look at the style sheet. Don't worry if it looks a little complicated at first; everything you see here will soon become clear. Remember that the items inside the curly braces are the properties you are setting and their values, while the names before the curly braces are the names of the elements to which the properties apply. You can see that this style sheet contains four rules: one for the <body> element, one for the <h1> element, one for the <p> element, and one for any <p> elements whose class attribute has a value of important. Here is ch03_eg01.css:

```
body {
    font-family:arial;
    background-color:#efefef;}

h1 {
    color:#666666;
    font-size:22pt;}

p {
    color:#999999;
    font-size:10pt;}

p.important {
    border:solid black 1px;
    background-color:#ffffff;
    padding:5px;
    margin:15px;
    width:40em;}
```

Take a quick look at each of these rules:

❑   The first rule applies to the <body> element; you can see the name body in the selector:

```
body {
    font-family:arial;
    background-color:#efefef;}
```

Note that many of the properties in CSS *inherit*, which means that a child element will assume the same properties as its parent elements. This is one of the reasons why CSS contains the word *cascading* it its title — because the rules cascade through the document. This point is important because this first selector indicates that the rule should apply to the <body> element, and like many other properties, the font-family and background-color properties will also apply to all elements that are children of the <body> element.

The first property is the font-family property, which indicates that the Arial typeface should be used throughout the document. The second property is called background-color and controls the background color for the page, which in this case should be a very light gray. Colors are specified in CSS using hexadecimal color codes, just as they are in HTML.

❑   The second and third rules both use the color and font-size properties, but the rules apply to different elements — the first rule applies to the <h1> elements and the second to the <p> elements. The color property affects the foreground color, just like the color attribute in HTML. The font-size property controls the size of the text. (Remember that you do not need to specify the typeface that should be used, because that was specified on the rule that applied to the <body> element.)

```
h1 {
   color:#666666;
   font-size:22pt;}

p {
   color:#999999;
   font-size:10pt;}
```

❑ The fourth and final rule controls several properties, but it is the selector that is particularly interesting in this rule. This rule also applies to <p> elements (just like the last one), but this rule is more specific: It applies only to those <p> elements that have a class attribute whose value is important. (Note the period between the element name (p) and the word important indicating this.) When you look at selectors in more detail later in this chapter, you will see that a rule can also be applied to an element with a specific value for an id attribute by using a hash, or pound, sign (#) in place of the period.

```
p.important {
   border:solid black 1px;
   width:40em;
   background-color:#ffffff;
   padding:5px;
   margin:15px;}
```

The first property in this final rule is border, which draws a thin, black line around the paragraph, while the width property indicates how wide the paragraph should be (if the width property were not used, the paragraph would take up the full width of the browser window).

Next up is the background-color property, which you may remember was used in the first rule. This demonstrates another important point. The background-color property specified in the rule for the <body> element is inherited by other elements in the document, so why not this one? The answer has nothing to do with the order in which the rules appear in the document; rather, it is because the selector in this rule is more specific to this element. A rule that has a more specific selector will take precedence over rules with less specific selectors. Because this rule applies to <p> elements whose class attribute has a value of important, the selector is more specific and the background-color property in this rule overrides the one in the first rule.

Finally, you see the padding and margin properties. The padding property creates a gap between the border of the paragraph and the text inside it, while the margin property creates a gap around the outside of the border (which in this case makes the paragraph look like it is indented).

Figure 3-2 shows a screenshot of what the page will look like.

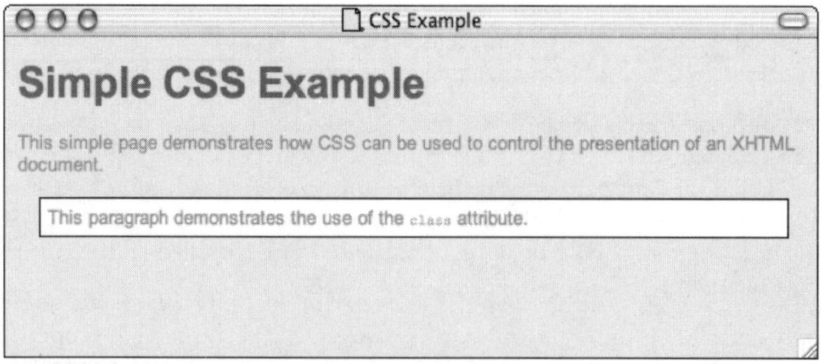

Simple CSS Example

This simple page demonstrates how CSS can be used to control the presentation of an XHTML document.

This paragraph demonstrates the use of the class attribute.

Figure 3-2

Inheritance

As you have just seen, one of the powerful features of CSS is that many of the properties that are applied to one element will be *inherited* by other elements. For example, once the `font-family` property was declared for the `<body>` element in the previous example, it applied to all of the elements inside the `<body>` element (all of the `<body>` element's child elements). If a rule is added that has a more specific selector, it will override any properties associated with the `<body>` element (the less specific selector).

The way in which some properties inherit saves you from having to write the same property-value pairs for each element, and makes for a more compact style sheet.

As you will see in Chapter 4, it is also possible for style sheets to import and include rules from other style sheets, which makes it possible for you to develop your style sheets in a modular fashion.

Adding CSS rules

The example that you saw at the beginning of this section put all of the CSS rules in a separate style sheet document known as an *external style sheet*. This involved the use of the `<link />` element in the header of the XHTML document to indicate the presence of a style sheet for the document and where it could be found.

HTML 4 also enabled you to place CSS rules in two places *within* the HTML document:

❏   Inside a special `<style>` element that resided in the `<head>` element

❏   As a value of a `style` attribute on any element that can carry the `style` attribute

Because these options were part of the HTML 4 recommendation, you can use both of these options in Transitional XHTML (although you should use external style sheets in Strict XHTML where possible). When the style sheet rules are contained inside a `<style>` element in the head of the document, as shown in the following example, they are referred to as an *internal style sheet*:

```
<head>
  <title>Internal Style sheet</title>
  <style type="text/css">
  body {
    color:#000000;
    background-color:#ffffff;
    font-family:arial, verdana, sans-serif; }
  h1 {font-size:18pt;}
  p {font-size:12pt;}
  </style>
  </head>
```

When `style` attributes are used they are known as *inline style rules*. By their very nature, inline style rules combine presentational markup with the content, which is one of the main things you are trying to avoid. Here is an example of an inline style rule:

```
<td style="font-family:courier; padding:5px; border:solid 1px #000000;">
```

You can see that this rule contains no selector or pair of curly braces; the properties and their values are simply given as a value of the `style` attribute. The selector and curly braces are not needed, because the properties apply only to this element. You must, however, still separate each property from its value using a colon, and each of the property-value pairs from each other using a semicolon.

Advantages of external CSS style sheets

In addition to completely removing stylistic markup from the document that contains the real content of the page, here are some more reasons why you would want to use an external style sheet rather than internal style rules:

❑ You can *reuse* the same style sheet with all of the Web pages in your site; you do not need to repeat the stylistic markup in each individual document.

❑ You can change the appearance of several pages by just altering the style sheet, rather than each individual page; this is particularly helpful if you want to change your company's colors, for example, or the font used for a certain type of element wherever that element appears.

❑ Because the style rules are written only once, rather than appearing on every element or in every document, the source documents are smaller. This means that once the CSS style sheet has been downloaded with the first document that uses it, subsequent documents will be quicker to download (because the browser retains a copy of the CSS style sheet and the presentation rules do not have to be downloaded for every page). This also puts less strain on the Web server.

❑ The style sheet can act as a style template, helping different authors achieve the same styles in their documents without learning all of the individual style settings (for example, each heading and paragraph could be automatically styled using the rules for those elements).

❑ Because the source document does not contain the style rules, different style sheets can be attached to the same document. Therefore, you can use the same XHTML document with one style sheet when the viewer is on a desktop computer, another style sheet when the user has a handheld device, another style sheet when the page is being printed, another style sheet when the page is being viewed on a TV, and so on. You reuse the same document with different style sheets for different visitors' needs.

❑ A style sheet can import and use styles from other style sheets, enabling you to develop style sheets in a modular fashion for better reuse.

❑ If you remove the style sheet, the site should be a lot more accessible for those with visual impairments because it does not have restrictions regarding size and color of fonts, background or link colors, and other design features that might make the site harder for some people to view.

It is fair to say, therefore, that whenever you are writing an entire site, you should use an external style sheet to control the presentation—although as you will see in the next chapter, you might use several external style sheets for different aspects of the site.

While you might be tempted to use an internal style sheet to include rules for one document that override the style sheet used with the rest of the site, you could just as easily create an external style sheet that has the rules that override the main style sheet, and then use the **@import** *rule, which you will meet in Chapter 4, to import the rules from the main style sheet.*

A closer look at adding CSS rules

Now that you know how CSS works, and you have seen an example of a simple CSS style sheet, learning CSS is largely a matter of learning all of the properties, the values each property can take, and whether that property inherits or not. Therefore, a good deal of the rest of this chapter and the next acts as a kind of reference to each of the properties and their values. To make it easy to follow, the properties have been grouped in related sections.

Before you look at the properties, however, you should take a closer look at the `<link />` element to ensure that you know the attributes it takes, and then you should have a look at the units of measurement used with properties that control aspects of a page such as font size, line height, width of lines, and size of boxes (units such as pixels, ems, and picas).

The <link> element

As you saw in the first simple example in this chapter, the `<link />` element can be used to create a link from an XHTML document to a CSS style sheet. It is always an empty element, and its purpose is to describe the relationship between two documents. It's a very different kind of link from those created with the `<a>` element because the user is not required to click on anything to activate the link; the style sheet is automatically loaded at the same time as the document.

The `<link />` element can be used in several ways for different purposes (it is also commonly used for Favorites icons in Internet Explorer 5+), but when used with CSS style sheets it must carry three attributes — `type`, `rel`, and `href` — like so:

```
<link rel="stylesheet" type="text/css" href="../style sheets/interface.css" />
```

In addition to these three core attributes, the `<link />` element can also take the following attributes:

```
charset dir href hreflang media rel rev style target type
```

The most important attributes that the `<link />` element uses are discussed in the following sections.

The rel attribute

The `rel` attribute is required and specifies the relationship between the document containing the link and the document being linked to. The key value for working with style sheets is `stylesheet` because the document being linked to is a style sheet.

```
rel="stylesheet"
```

You may also see this attribute with a value of `alternate stylesheet`, like so:

```
rel="alternate stylesheet"
```

This enables you to provide alternative style sheets, either enabling the user to see different presentations of the same page or in order to provide different versions for different devices (for example, desktop PCs, printers, TV set top boxes, and so on). You can see how this works in Chapter 8.

The type attribute

The `type` attribute specifies the MIME type of the document being linked to. MIME types are used on the Web to indicate the type of document being sent to a browser. In the case of a CSS style sheet, the MIME type is `text/css`:

```
type="text/css"
```

You can find a list of popular MIME types in Appendix E.

The href attribute

The `href` attribute specifies the URL for the document being linked to. The value of this attribute can be an absolute or relative URL:

```
href="../stylesheets/interface.css"
```

The hreflang attribute

The `hreflang` attribute uses a language code to specify the language in which the specified resource is written:

```
hreflang="en-US"
```

The media attribute

As explained in Chapter 1, the goal of separating style from content was partly set to achieve the aim of enabling the same content to be served to various devices—not just desktop computers. The `media` attribute specifies the output device that is intended for use with the document:

```
media="screen"
```

While it is not used much at present, this attribute will have increasing impact as more people access the Internet in different ways. Here are the possible values:

Value	Uses
screen	Computer screens (typically, these will scroll and will not have pages in the same way that a book or magazine has a fixed page size)
tty	Media that display fixed-width characters, such as teletypes, terminals, or portable devices with limited display capabilities
tv	TV devices with color screens that are lower resolution than computer monitors and which have limited ability to scroll down pages
print	Printed matter that displays documents in pages of fixed size (such as books and magazines) and for documents shown on a screen in print preview mode
projection	Projectors
handheld	Handheld devices, small screens, bitmapped graphics, and limited bandwidth
braille	Braille tactile feedback devices
embossed	Braille page printers
aural	Speech synthesizers
all	Suitable for all devices

The <style> element

If you are going to include the style rules in the same document as the content, you can still separate them from the actual content by placing them inside the <style> element, which itself resides within the <head> element. It is also sometimes used when a document needs to contain just a few extra rules that do not apply to other documents that share the same style sheet.

For example, here you can see a style sheet attached to the XHTML document using the <link /> element you just met, as well as a <style> element containing an additional rule:

```
<head>
  <title>
  <link rel="stylesheet" type="text/css" href="../styles/mySite.css" />
  <style type="text/css">
    h1 {color:#FF0000;}
  </style>
</head>
```

If your CSS rules contain either a < or & character, you need to place your style rules in a CDATA section as described in Chapter 2 in order for XHTML processors to read the rules properly.

The <style> element takes the following attributes:

```
dir lang media title type
```

Some browsers also support the id and src attributes, although they are not part of any W3C recommendation.

Many document authors add comment marks inside the **<style>** *elements so that all CSS rules appear between the* **<!--** *and the* **-->** *comment marks. The idea is that this will hide the code from older browsers that do not understand CSS. The drawback with this technique is that the XHTML specification provides browsers and Web servers with the capability to strip the contents of comments, so a browser might not see these rules at all — although no major browsers or Web servers do this at the time of publication. As previously mentioned, in XHTML you might need to place your CSS rules in a* **CDATA** *section, which is not understood by all older browsers.*

Units of measurement

When specifying values for many of the properties in CSS, you need to specify measurements, such as size of fonts, height of lines, widths of tables or paragraphs, and so on; all of these specify *lengths*. Lengths can be measured in one of three ways in CSS:

❑ Absolute units

❑ Relative units

❑ Percentages

Absolute units

The following table shows the *absolute units* that you can use in CSS:

Unit	Full Name
pt	A point
pc	A pica
in	An inch
cm	A centimeter
mm	A millimeter

I probably don't need to clarify inches, millimeters, or centimeters, but the other two are less common:

❑ A **point** is ½ of an inch (the same as a pixel in most computer screen resolutions).

❑ A **pica** is ½ of an inch (12 points).

Typographers tend to use points to measure font sizes and leading (the gaps between lines), whereas picas are commonly used to measure line length.

Relative units and percentages

Relative units and percentages can be very useful, but they also pose problems for two reasons:

❑ Their size can vary depending on the kind of media on which the document is shown.

❑ Users can increase and decrease the size of fonts on a Web browser, which can affect some of the units of length.

px

Many designers use pixels (px) to precisely control the positioning of elements and the layout of a document on computer screens. A *pixel* is the smallest unit of resolution, and most computer screens have a resolution of 72 dots per inch (dpi), although other devices can have different resolutions and differently sized pixels. For example, most modern laser and bubble-jet printers are set with a higher resolution, currently around 300 dpi; however, IE and Netscape tend to adjust the pixel size to make it readable when printed.

This unit of measurement has the greatest level of support in browsers, and many designers like to use it because it affords them greater control over the layout of a page.

> *The CSS recommendation suggests that user agents rescale pixel units so that reading at arms length, one pixel would correspond to about 0.28 mm or ¹⁄₉₀ₜₕ of an inch. This would, however, turn a pixel from a relative unit into an absolute unit.*

em

An *em* unit corresponds directly to the font size of the *reference* element, which will be either that element or the containing element. The term *em* is thought to be derived from the width of a lowercase m, although it is now generally considered the height of the font. (Note that an *en* is half an *em*.)

ex

The *ex* should be the height of a lowercase *x*. Because different fonts have different proportions, the ex is related to the font size and the type of font.

Percentages

Percentages provide a value in relation to another value. The value depends upon the property in question; for example, you might use the `line-height` property to control the space between two rows of text, and if it is given a value of 150 percent, the gap between lines will be half the height of the font itself (because the height of the font equates to 100 percent, and 50 percent of the font's height will be used to create the gaps between lines of text). Note that when a percentage value is inherited, it is the value that is set by the percentage that is inherited (not the percentage).

Selectors

Earlier in the chapter, you learned that selectors indicate the element or elements to which a rule applies. However, in order to get the full benefit of writing CSS style sheets, you need to learn a few more ways of indicating the element or elements to which you want your rules to apply. In addition to using element names in selectors, you can use several other ways to select elements — some of which provide you with a lot more control over the elements to which a rule applies than just by using the element name.

You will often want to display two of the same elements in different ways. Perhaps you want to show the content of the first <p> element in a document in a bold font, while the rest of the paragraphs have a normal font weight. You might want to show one <h2> element in a different color than all other <h2> elements. Different types of selectors enable you to do this.

> *Remember that because XHTML is case-sensitive, you should use all lowercase characters for element names in your selectors.*

The simple selector

A *simple selector* just uses an element's name. The rule then applies to all elements that share the name. For example, the following rule applies to all <p> elements:

```
p {font-face:arial, verdana, sans-serif;}
```

The universal selector

If you want a rule to apply to all elements, you can use the *universal selector*, which is an asterisk. It can be helpful for providing default values for properties. For example, the following rule specifies Arial as the default typeface for the whole document. If any element has a more specific selector that uses a different value for the `font-family` property (and any selector is more specific than the universal selector), it will override the universal selector because it is more specific.

```
*{font-family:arial, verdana, sans-serif}
```

Using the universal selector is slightly different from applying default styles to the <body> element, as the universal selector applies to every element and does not rely on the property being inherited.

The type selector

The *type selector* matches all of the elements specified in the comma-delimited list. It enables you to apply the same rules to several elements. For example, the following would match all <p>, <h1>, and <h2> elements:

```
p, h, h2, {font-family: geneva, helvetica, sans-serif;}
```

As you saw in the first simple example, if you have rules that apply to several elements, using this technique can result in a smaller style sheet.

Differentiating between elements with the same name

At times, you will want the content of either one or several elements to have different rules compared with other elements that share the same name. For example, you might want a summary paragraph to appear in bold, while the rest of the paragraphs are normal. Similarly, you might want to distinguish between the <a> elements that link to other pages on your site and the <a> elements that link to external sites — perhaps using different colors.

Two selectors enable you to differentiate between elements that share the same name:

❑ The **class selector** should be used when you want to change the presentation of more than one element and differentiate these elements from others that share the same name. It uses the value of the class attribute to determine the elements to which the rule applies.

❑ The **id selector** should be used when you want to make the content of just one element unique among all the others. It uses the value of the id attribute to determine the element to which the rule applies. Because the value of an id attribute must be unique within the document, this ensures that the rule applies only to that one element in the document.

The class selector

The *class selector* enables you to match a rule with an element carrying a class attribute whose value you specify in the class selector. For example, imagine you want some of the paragraphs in an article to be in an italicized font that is slightly lighter than the rest of the text because they are background notes. You could create a class called note, and each paragraph that is a background note could be given a class attribute with the value note like so:

```
<p class="note">This paragraph contains a background note.</p>
```

Then you can use the class selector as follows to indicate that all <p> elements whose class attribute has a value of note should be in bold:

```
p.note {
    font-style:italic;
    color:#666666;}
```

Of course, you can think of other elements that you might want to follow these properties, not just <p> elements. In this case, you can use the class selector on its own without the element name, simply by prefixing the class name with a period:

```
.note {
  font-style:italic;
  color:#666666;}
```

Using this second rule, any element that carries a `class` attribute that has a value of `note` would follow the rule.

The id selector

The *id selector* works just like the class selector, but selects elements with `id` attributes that match the id name given in the selector.

Rather than using a period (or full stop) before the value of the `id` attribute, you use a hash, or pound, sign (`#`). Therefore, a `<p>` element with an `id` attribute whose value is `summary` could be identified with this selector:

```
p#summary {font-weight: bold;}
```

Because the value of an `id` attribute must be unique within a document (no two elements can share the same value for the `id` attribute), this selector should apply only to the content of one element.

The child selector

The *child selector* will match an element that is a direct child of another. In the following case, it matches any `<b>` elements that are direct children of `<td>` elements:

```
td > b {font-size:12px;}
```

This would enable you to specify a different style just for those `<b>` elements that are direct children of the `<td>` element, rather than for any `<b>` elements that appear elsewhere in the document.

Because the child selector works only on elements that are direct children of an element, the following example does not make sense:

```
table > b {font-size:12px;}
```

The problem here is that the selector will be looking for `<b>` elements that are direct children of a `<table>` element, which would not make sense because there should not be any; you are likely to find only a `<tr>` or `<caption>` element as a direct child of the `<table>` element. In this case, you should use the descendent selector.

The child selector was introduced in CSS2, and unfortunately it does not work in IE 6 (or earlier versions), and was first supported in Netscape's version 6 browser.

The descendent selector

The *descendent selector* matches an element type that is a descendent of another specified element, at any level of nesting, not just a direct child. In CSS1, this type of selector was referred to as a *contextual selector*, but CSS2 changed its name to descendent selector. In the following example, the selector matches any `<b>` element that is a child of the `<table>` element, which means it would apply to `<b>` elements both in `<td>` and `<th>` elements:

```
table b {font-size:12px;}
```

This differs from the child selector because it applies to all of the children of the `<table>` element, rather than just the direct children.

This type of selector was first supported in IE 5 and Netscape 6.

The adjacent sibling selector

An *adjacent sibling selector* matches an element type that is the next sibling of another. For example, if you want to make the first paragraph after any level 1 heading a different style, you could use the adjacent sibling selector like so:

```
h1 + p {font-weight:bold;}
```

The adjacent sibling selector was introduced in CSS2, and unfortunately it does not work in IE 6 on Windows (or earlier versions), and was first supported in Netscape's version 6 browser.

Attribute selectors

Attribute selectors enable you to use the attributes that an element carries in the selector. There are several ways in which you can use attribute selectors. For example, the following paragraph carries an `id` attribute:

```
<p id="important" class=" XHTML, attributes">All attribute values must be written
in double quotes.</p>
```

The following table lists the attribute selectors and what they would match in this example. Note that none of these work in IE 6, and only the first two work in Netscape 6 and later.

Selector	Matches
p[id]	Any `<p>` element carrying an attribute called `id`
p[id="important"]	Any `<p>` element carrying an attribute called `id` whose value is `important`
p[class~="XHTML"]	Any `<p>` element carrying an attribute called `class` whose value is a list of space-separated words, and one of the words is `XHTML`
paragraph[class|="XHT"]	Any `<p>` element carrying an attribute called `class` whose value begins with `XHT`

When support for these selectors grows, they will be powerful tools for enabling you to apply a style to an element based on the presence of, or value of, an attribute.

CSS2 also introduced the capability to use regular expressions in selectors. However, the use of regular expressions in selectors is not yet supported in any of the major browsers. Furthermore, regular expressions are a quite complicated topic, and you are better off getting used to the selectors named here before you consider learning about regular expressions.

Fonts

Now that you know how to write a basic style sheet and link to it from your XHTML pages, you come to the core part of learning to work with CSS: learning the long list of properties and the values they can take. You will start looking at properties in more detail by looking at those that affect the font used.

Be aware that when fonts are installed on your computer, details of the font are added to a font database that can be accessed by all other programs in the operating system. This is why, when you install a new font, it should become available in all of the programs on your computer.

font-family

The `font-family` property indicates which typeface should be used; the value is simply the name of the typeface — for example, Times or Arial. If the font name contains spaces, it should be placed in quotes.

Just as with the HTML `<font>` element, the specified fonts will be displayed only if they are installed on the user's computer. However, you can specify a list of several typefaces in order of preference.

Any comma-separated list of fonts should end with one of the five generic font families specified in CSS. If the browser cannot find the font you have specified, it will use a font that falls into one of these five generic categories, which are `serif`, `sans-serif`, `cursive`, `fantasy`, and `monospace`. You will see examples of each of these generic font families in the next example.

To help demonstrate the font properties, following are some basic HTML pages that contain several `<p>` elements, each of which will carry class attributes with different values to which the style sheet rules can be linked. For example, here is what is in the `<body>` of `ch03_eg02.html`:

```
<p class="one">The first paragraph of text should be displayed in a
    sans-serif font.</p>
<p class="two">The second paragraph of text should be displayed in a
    serif font.</p>
<p class="three">The third paragraph of text should be displayed in a
    monospace font.</p>
<p class="four">The fourth paragraph of text should be displayed in a
    cursive font.</p>
<p class="five">The fifth paragraph of text should be displayed in
    fantasy font.</p>
```

Here is the style sheet (`ch03_eg02.css`) to be used with the preceding example; it demonstrates three rules for three different paragraph elements:

```
p.one {font-family:arial, verdana, sans-serif;}
p.two {font-family:times, "times new roman", serif;}
p.three {font-family:courier, "courier new", monospace;}
p.four {font-family: Zapf-Chancery, Santivo, cursive;}
p.five {font-family: Cottonwood, Studz, fantasy;}
```

Figure 3-3 shows you what these three paragraphs would look like in a browser; each is written in a different font.

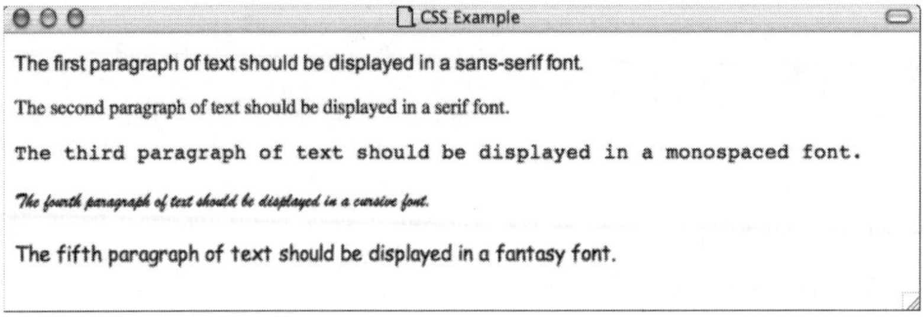

The first paragraph of text should be displayed in a sans-serif font.

The second paragraph of text should be displayed in a serif font.

The third paragraph of text should be displayed in a monospaced font.

The fourth paragraph of text should be displayed in a cursive font.

The fifth paragraph of text should be displayed in a fantasy font.

Figure 3-3

As a general rule:

- **Serif** fonts have "hats and tails" on letters
- **Sans-serif** fonts have straight edges to letters
- **Monospace** fonts have characters that are of equal size, so the letter *i* is the same width as the letter *m*
- **Cursive** fonts have strokes either like "scripts" or joined up handwriting
- **Fantasy** fonts are primarily decorative, although they can also contain representations of real letters

When specifying your preference for fonts, be aware that fonts can vary dramatically in width and height, which can dramatically affect the layout of your pages. As you can see in Figure 3-3, Courier (the third example) is a lot wider and shorter than Times (the second example).

When designers want to ensure that some text is shown in a less common typeface, they tend to use a GIF image for the text. While this practice is accepted for logos, headings, buttons, and small amounts of text, you should not use images for whole paragraphs of text. You must also remember to use the `alt` attribute on every `<img />` element to provide a text alternative for the image.

font-style

The `font-style` property can take one of the following values: `normal`, `italic`, or `oblique`. To understand the difference among these three values:

- A **normal** font is often referred to as a roman font. It is a normal upright (serif or sans-serif) font.
- An **italic** font is a version of the font designed to appear on a slant (this is created by the author of the font separately from and in addition to the normal version).
- An **oblique** font is a normal (or roman) font placed on a slant (usually of about 12 degrees) to make it look italic.

The oblique option is important because many fonts do not have a specially made italic version. If the value of `italic` is chosen and the browser cannot find an italic version of the font in the operating system's font database, it will create an oblique version (using an algorithm to place the normal font on a slant).

These three values are demonstrated in the following example (`ch03_eg03.css`):

```
p.one {font-style:normal;}
p.two {font-style:italic;}
p.three {font-style:oblique;}
```

Figure 3-4 shows you how these values appear in the browser (from `ch03_eg03.html` and `ch03_eg03.css`).

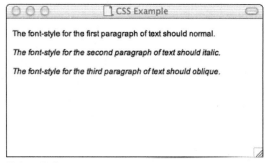

The font-style for the first paragraph of text should normal.

The font-style for the second paragraph of text should italic.

The font-style for the third paragraph of text should oblique.

Figure 3-4

font-variant

There are three possible values for the `font-variant` property: `normal`, `small-caps`, and `inherit`. A small-caps font looks like a smaller version of the font in uppercase characters. `inherit` indicates that this element should inherit the `font-variant` of its parent element.

The following example works with a simple paragraph that contains a `<span>` element whose `class` attribute has a value of `small-caps` (`ch03_eg04.html`):

```
<p class="normal">The value for font-variant in the first paragraph is normal.</p>
<p class="smallcaps">The value for font-variant in the second paragraph is small
    caps.</p>
```

Here is the corresponding style sheet (`ch03_eg04.css`):

```
p.normal {font-variant:normal;}
p.smallcaps {font-variant:small-caps;}
```

You can see the result in Figure 3-5.

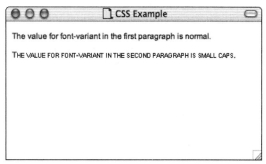

The value for font-variant in the first paragraph is normal.

THE VALUE FOR FONT-VARIANT IN THE SECOND PARAGRAPH IS SMALL CAPS.

Figure 3-5

font-weight

The `font-weight` property affects the width of the line of the font and can take the following values:

```
normal bold bolder lighter 100 200 300 400 500 600 700 800 900
```

Even though the creators of many fonts design a special bold version (just as they design a special italic version), browsers often just use an algorithm to add thickness to a text and make it appear bold. Because they use an algorithm to add weight, browsers are also able to use an algorithm to create lighter versions and other variations, too:

❑   `normal` and `bold` are the most common values, and they also have the greatest support.

❑   `bolder` and `lighter` are designed to add weight relative to the weight of the containing font.

❑   100, 200, 300, 400, 500, 600, 700, 800, and 900 are values that represent variations in line thickness, where 400 is equivalent to a value of normal and 700 is equivalent to a value of bold (currently unsupported).

Here are the examples from `ch03_eg05.css`:

```
p.normal {font-weight:normal;}
p.bold {font-weight:bold;}
p.lighter {font-weight:lighter;}
p.bolder {font-weight:bolder;}
p.onehundred {font-weight:100;}
p.seven hundred {font-weight:700;}
```

Figure 3-6 shows you how these values appear in the browser.

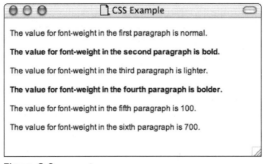

Figure 3-6

The numerical values and the keyword `lighter` do not always appear to work; the font has to be large enough for the differences to be noticeable (and small fonts cannot always be made lighter).

font-size

The `font-size` property enables you to specify a size for the font. There are several ways in which you can specify a value for this property:

❑   Absolute size

❑   Relative size

❑   Length

❑   Percentage (in relation to the parent element)

Here you can see the syntax used with the `font-size` property in the next few examples:

```
p.xx-small {font-size:xx-small;}
p.px {font-size:12px;}
p.pc {font-size:2pc;}
p.fifty {font-size:50%;}
```

An absolute size would be one of the following values:

```
xx-small x-small small medium large x-large xx-large
```

These sizes correspond to the numbers 1–7, used as values for the `size` attribute on the `<font>` element. You can see the absolute sizes in Figure 3-7, which shows `ch03_eg06.html`.

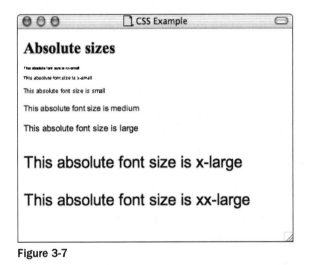

Figure 3-7

A relative size would be one of the following two values:

```
smaller larger
```

The relative size is either one size smaller or larger than the containing element. You can see examples of the relative sizes in Figure 3-8, which shows `ch03_eg07.html`.

Length can be any unit of length (each of which was described earlier in the chapter in the section entitled "Units of Measurement"):

```
px em ex pt in cm pc mm
```

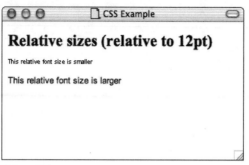

Figure 3-8

Probably the most common of these values is px, for pixels. However, Internet Explorer for Windows does not allow users to resize text that is measured in pixels (to make it larger if they have difficulty reading it or smaller if they want to fit more on the screen), so for accessibility reasons, where possible, it is recommended that designers avoid using the option of specifying text in pixels. You can see examples of lengths in Figure 3-9, which shows ch03_eg08.html.

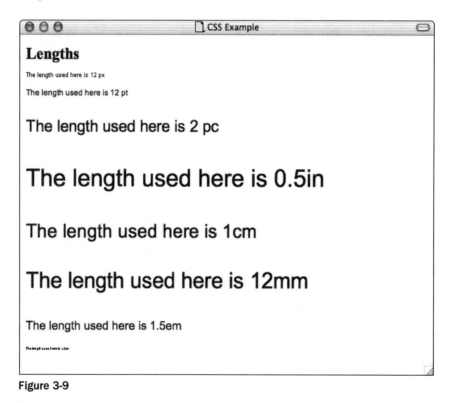

Figure 3-9

A percentage is calculated as a proportion of the element that contains the text. For example, when the text in the containing element is using a `font-size` of 12pt, if the percentage is 50 percent, it is equivalent to a `font-size` of 6pt; whereas if it is a percentage of 150 percent, it would be equivalent to 18pt.

```
2% 10% 25% 50% 100%
```

You can see examples of using percentages with the `font-size` property in Figure 3-10, which shows `ch03_eg09.html`.

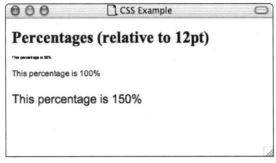

Figure 3-10

font-stretch

Some fonts have variations that use terms such as *condensed* and *expanded* to describe the width of the actual characters. The `font-stretch` property enables you to select these variations of a font using one of the following absolute keywords, stretching from the narrowest to the widest settings:

```
ultra-condensed, extra-condensed, condensed, semi-condensed, normal, semi-expanded,
expanded , extra-expanded, ultra-expanded
```

You can also use the keyword `normal` and two relative keywords that increase or decrease the value to the next above or below (they will not work beyond the limits of the absolute sizes):

```
wider, narrower
```

You can see examples of how they should be written in `ch03_eg10.css`:

```
p.normal {font-stretch:normal;}
p.wider {font-stretch:wider;}
p.narrower {font-stretch:narrower;}
p.ultra-condensed {font-stretch:ultra-condensed;}
p.condensed {font-stretch:condensed;}
p.expanded {font-stretch:expanded;}
p.ultra-expanded {font-stretch:ultra-expanded;}
```

Unfortunately, none of these work in IE 6 or Netscape 7, but they are included here for completeness.

font

The `font` property offers a shorthand way of writing all of the other font properties at one time. You can specify the following properties using the same values that are available for individual properties (you will meet the `line-height` property in the following section on text properties). While you need to specify only the properties you want, some browsers might cause errors if you do not provide them in the following order:

```
font-style font-variant font-weight font-size line-height font-family
```

Only a space should separate the values. For example, you could specify a 12pt, bold, Arial font as follows (`ch03_eg11.css`):

```
p {font:bold 12pt arial;}
```

You can see in Figure 3-11 how this one property works as a shorthand for the three separate font-related properties.

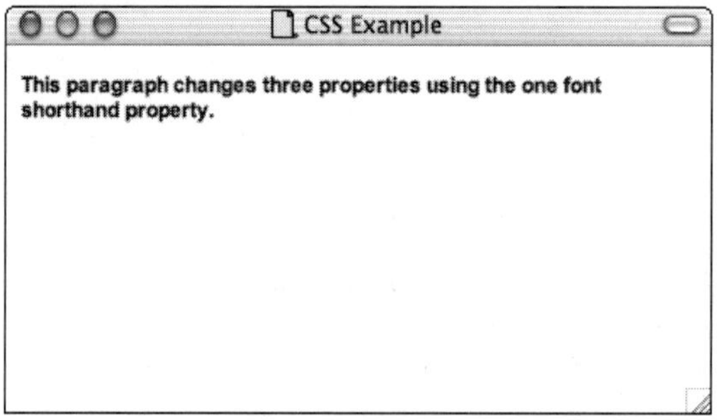

```
⊙ ⊙ ⊙            CSS Example                      ⊖

This paragraph changes three properties using the one font
shorthand property.



```

Figure 3-11

*When a value for the **line-height** property is given, it should be separated from the **font-size** with a forward slash; for example, **small/150%** for a small **font-size** whose **line-height** is 50 percent taller than the height of the font.*

Text properties

The font properties discussed in the preceding section are not the only properties that affect how text is displayed; several other properties do not affect the actual font used but affect the spacing and alignment of the text. These properties are discussed in the following sections.

word-spacing

The `word-spacing` property enables you to specify the gap between whole words. The value of this property should be a unit of length (pt, px, pc, em, ex, in, cm, mm) or the keyword `normal`. The following example shows three different word spacings — the first is `normal`, the second is wider than normal, and the third is set to be less than normal (`ch03_eg12.css`):

```
p.normal {word-spacing:normal;}
p.wide {word-spacing:3em;}
p.narrow {word-spacing:-5ex;}
```

Figure 3-12 shows you what these spacings would look like.

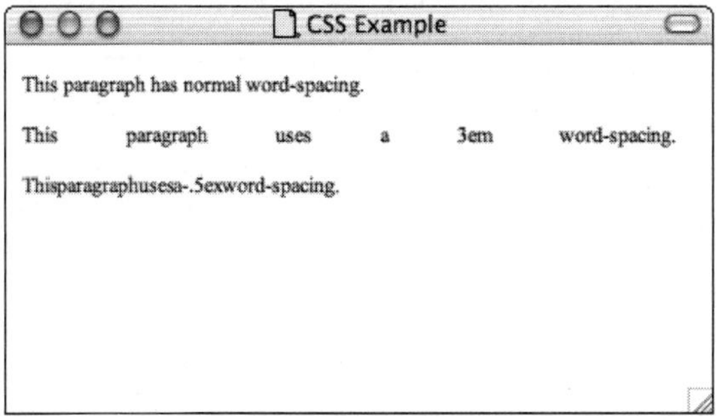

Figure 3-12

You can set the value of this property to be a negative value, although browsers are not required to display a word spacing that is any less than the normal word-spacing of the font.

Note that if the text-align property has a value of justify, this value might be affected (because justify tries to make the text spread evenly across the width of the page or the containing element).

letter-spacing

The letter-spacing property enables you to specify the gap between each character. The value for this property should be a unit of length (pt, px, pc, em, ex, in, cm, mm) or the keyword normal. Here you can see three different examples of letter spacing (ch03_eg13.css):

```
p.normal {letter-spacing:normal;}
p.wide {letter-spacing:1.5em;}
p.narrow {letter-spacing:-.2ex;}
```

Figure 3-13 gives you an indication of what this looks like.

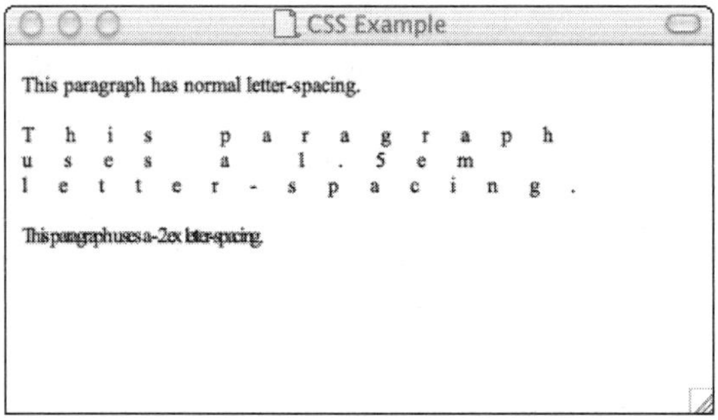

Figure 3-13

The value of this property can be a negative length, and if the spacing is anything other than normal, the browser should not use ligatures.

text-decoration

The text-decoration property enables you to change the presentation of text using the following values:

Value	Purpose
none	Prevents any decoration from being added to the text (often used in conjunction with links to prevent their being underlined, as is the default in most browsers)
underline	Adds a line under the content
overline	Adds a line over the top of the content
line-through	Like strikethrough text, with a line through the middle. This should generally be used only to indicate text that is marked for deletion.
blink	Creates blinking text (which is generally frowned upon and considered annoying)

If the element does not contain text, then this property will have no effect. You can see an example of these values for the text-decoration property in ch03_eg14.css:

```
p.underline {text-decoration:underline;}
p.overline {text-decoration:overline;}
p.line-through {text-decoration:line-through;}
p.blink {text-decoration:blink;}
```

You can see the first three of these values displayed in Figure 3-14. The value of blink does not work in IE 6; indeed, the CSS specification indicates that browsers do not need to support it, and its use is generally frowned upon (like the Netscape <blink> tag).

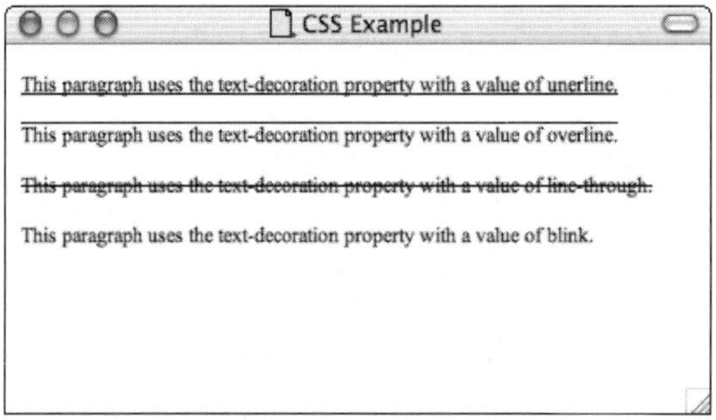

Figure 3-14

This property is commonly used with links — for example, to prevent the link from being underlined (which is the default presentation for most browsers) and to underline the link when the user hovers the mouse over the link.

text-transform

The `text-transform` property enables you to specify the case for the content of an element. The possible values are shown in the following table:

Value	Purpose
none	No change should take place
capitalize	The first letter of every word should be capitalized
uppercase	The entire content of the element should be uppercase
lowercase	The entire content of the element should be lowercase

The following four paragraphs look similar, but they actually have different values for the `class` attribute:

```
<p class="none">This paragraph has a value of none for the text-transform
    property</p>
<p class="capitalize">This paragraph has a value of capitalize for the
    text-transform
    property</p>
<p class="uppercase">This paragraph has a value of uppercase for the text-transform
    property</p>
<p class="lowercase">This paragraph has a value of lowercase for the text-transform
    property</p>
```

Here you can see the four different values for the `text-transform` property in use (`ch03_eg15.css`):

```
p.none {text-transform:none;}
p.capitalize {text-transform:capitalize;}
p.uppercase {text-transform:uppercase;}
p.lowercase {text-transform:lowercase;}
```

Figure 3-15 shows you how the paragraphs would appear in a browser with these styles applied.

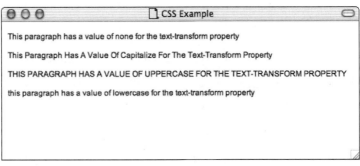

Figure 3-15

If the characters used are not part of the Latin-1 character set, the browser can choose to ignore this property.

text-align

The text-align property aligns text in a similar way to the deprecated align attribute. It aligns the text within its containing element or, if there isn't one, the browser window. Its possible values are as follows:

Value	Purpose
left	Aligns the text with the left-hand border of the containing element
right	Aligns the text with the right-hand border of the containing element
center	Centers the content in the middle of the containing element
justify	Spreads the width across the whole width of the containing element

The following example (ch03_eg16.css) works with cells of a table that are 300 pixels wide:

```
td.leftAlign {text-align:left;}
td.rightAlign {text-align:right;}
td.center {text-align:center;}
td.justify {text-align:justify;}
```

Figure 3-16 shows you how these four values work.

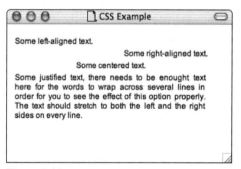

Figure 3-16

line-height

The line-height property enables you to set the distance between two parallel baselines, and therefore adjust the space between lines of text, which print designers refer to as *leading*. The possible values are a number, a length, a percentage, or the keyword normal. If the value is a number, the line height is the font size multiplied by the number given; negative numbers are not allowed.

You can see an example of the line-height property in ch03_eg17.css:

```
td.number {font-size: 12pt; line-height:1.5;}
td.length {font-size: 12pt; line-height:1.5em;}
td.percentage {font-size: 12pt; line-height:75%;}
```

The result of these values, where the line height is one and a half times the height of the font, is shown in Figure 3-17.

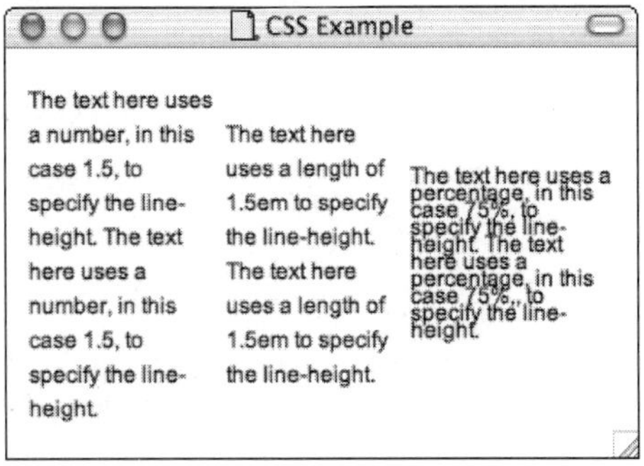

Figure 3-17

text-indent

The text-indent property enables you to specify an indent for the first line of a piece of text. The value indicates how far in from the left-hand margin the first line of the text should be indented. Possible values are a length, a percentage, or the keyword inherit.

ch03_eg18.html shows the XHTML for an example where only the second paragraph is indented:

```
<p>This paragraph should be aligned with the left-hand side of the browser. </p>
<p class="indent">The first line of this paragraph should be indented by 3em,
    although the rest of the paragraph will start in the normal position as
    you can see when the line wraps around.</p>
```

Now, here is the rule that indents the second paragraph (ch03_eg18.css):

```
p.indent {text-indent:3em;}
```

You can see what this looks like in Figure 3-18.

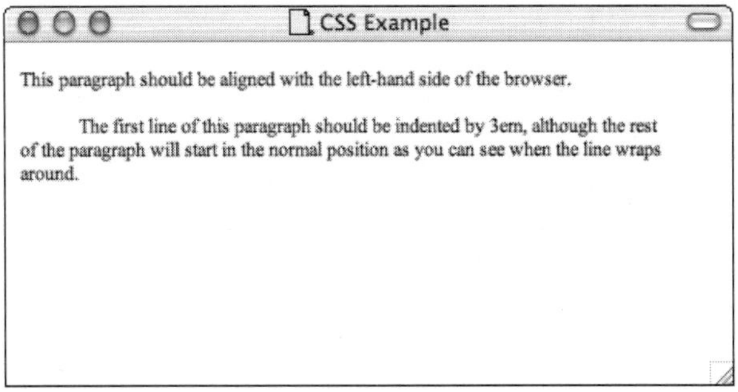

Figure 3-18

text-shadow

The `text-shadow` property is supposed to create a *drop shadow*, which is a dark and slightly offset version of the word just behind it. This effect is often used in print media, and its popularity has meant that it has gained its own CSS property in CSS2.

The value for this property is quite complicated, because it can take three lengths and an optional color:

```
.dropShadow { text-shadow: black 0.3em 0.3em 0.5em }
```

The values are as follows; only the first two values are required:

- ❏ The first value specifies the horizontal distance at which the shadow will appear to the right of the text (a negative value will move the shadow to the left).
- ❏ The second value specifies the vertical distance at which the shadow will appear to the bottom of the text (a negative value will place the shadow above the text).
- ❏ The third (optional) value specifies the radius of the blur.
- ❏ The color value may optionally come before or after the shadow effect and is used for the basis of the color for the shadow effect. If none is specified, the current color property is used.

Here is an example of a simple `text-shadow` that would be placed to the bottom right of the text at a distance of about a fifth of the height of the text (`ch03_eg19.css`):

```
h1.basic { text-shadow: 0.2em 0.2em;}
```

The next example places a shadow to the right and below the element's text. The shadow has a 5px blur radius and is red:

```
h1.blurredColor { text-shadow: 3px 3px 5px red;}
```

You can even specify multiple `text-shadows`, each separated by a comma:

```
h1.complex { text-shadow: 3px 3px red, yellow -3px 3px 2px, 3px -3px }
```

Unfortunately, this property does not work in IE 6 or Netscape 7.

Text pseudo-elements

While you are learning about text, two very helpful *pseudo-elements* can change the presentation of your text. These pseudo-elements enable you to render either the first letter or the first line of an element in a different way than the rest of that element. Both of these techniques are commonly used when laying out text in print, and have therefore been given a CSS equivalent.

You will learn more about pseudo-elements and pseudo-classes in Chapter 4.

The first-letter pseudo-element

The `first-letter` pseudo-element enables you to specify different properties for just the first letter of an element; you may have seen this technique used in magazine and newspaper articles.

Here is an example of the `first-letter` pseudo-element being applied to a `<p>` element
(`ch03_eg20.css`):

```
p:first-letter {
    font-size:32px;
    font-weight:bold;}
```

You can see the effect of this `first-letter` pseudo-element in the screenshot shown in Figure 3-19.

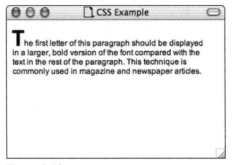

Figure 3-19

The first-line pseudo-element

The `first-line` pseudo-element enables you to specify different properties for the first line of text
compared with the rest of the element. This is typically rendered in a bold font so that the reader can see
an introduction in the case of articles, or the first line in the case of poems or hymns. The name of the
pseudo-element is separated from the element it should appear on by a colon, as you can see here in
`ch03_eg21.css`:

```
p:firstline {
    font-size:18px;
    font-weight:bold;}
```

You can see the `first-line` pseudo-element in action in Figure 3-20.

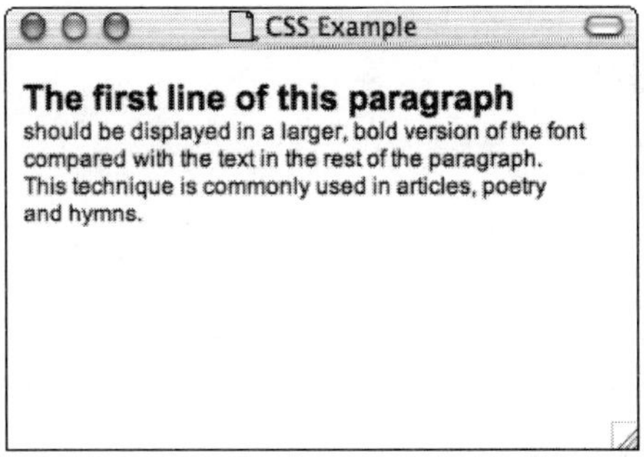

Figure 3-20

Understanding the box model

Now that you know how to write basic style sheets, and having started to learn the properties that affect the contents of our elements, you now need to consider something known as the *box model*. The visual rendering of pages using CSS is entirely based upon this box model, so learning about it now will make learning about subsequent properties much easier. The key to understanding the box model is to remember the following:

> **Every element is treated like a *box* in CSS.**

Every box has three properties:

Property	Description
border	Even if you cannot see it, every box has a border. This separates the edge of one box from all other boxes.
margin	The margin is the distance between the edge of a box and any box positioned next to it.
padding	The padding is the space between the border and what is inside the box.

You can get a better idea of these properties in Figure 3-21, which shows you a box created by a paragraph element (the black line is the border).

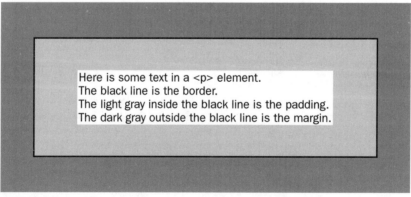

Figure 3-21

As you can see from Figure 3-21, the black line is the border (although by default the borders on most boxes are invisible), the lighter of the two grays is the padding, and the darker of the two grays is the margin.

You can use CSS to individually control the top, bottom, left, and right sides of the margin, border, and padding; and you can even specify a different color for each side of the border.

The `padding` and `margin` properties are particularly helpful in providing a sense of space to a page and preventing items from touching each other. This space, which designers refer to as *white space*, makes a page look much more attractive and easier to read.

Note, however, an interesting aspect of margins: When a bottom margin of one element meets the top margin of another, only the larger of the two margins will be displayed (and if they are both the same size, only one will be displayed). Figure 3-22 shows the vertical margins of two adjacent boxes collapsing.

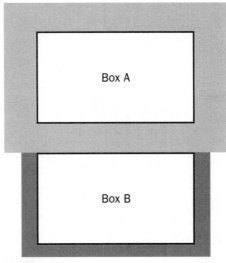

Figure 3-22

As you can see, the margin of Box A is larger than the margin of Box B; therefore, where the two boxes meet vertically, only the margin for Box A is visible. The way in which two vertical margins collapse like this (and only the larger of the two is shown) is very important to remember when you are positioning items on the page. You might expect that if one box with a margin of 20 pixels sits on top of another box with a margin of 30 pixels that there would be 50 pixels of space between them, but this is not the case; it will be only 30 pixels because only the larger of the two margins is shown.

To really understand how the box model works with elements, take a look at the example in the next section.

A demonstration of the box model

So that you can get a better idea of how the box model works, we are going to look at a very simple page, and give each item a visible border to show you where the boxes start and end. Take a look at the following XHTML (ch03_eg22.html):

```
<!DOCTYPE html PUBLIC "-//W3C//DTD XHTML 1.0 Strict//EN"
    "http://www.w3.org/TR/xhtml1/DTD/xhtml1-strict.dtd">
<html xmlns="http://www.w3.org/1999/xhtml">
<head>
<title>A Demonstration of the Box Model</title>
<meta http-equiv="Content-Type" content="text/html; charset=iso-8859-1" />
<link rel="stylesheet" type="text/css" href="ch03_eg22.css" />
</head>

<body>
  <h1>Box Model Demonstration</h1>
  <p>As you can see from this simple demonstration, each element is treated as if
     it lives in its own <b>box</b>.</p>
  <p>Every element has a border around it, and some boxes can <em>contain</em>
     other boxes. </p>
</body>
</html>
```

In the preceding example, each element involved with the body of the document is treated as if it were in a separate box. You can see this by adding border properties to each element; and to help make the lines clearer, margins and padding have also been added (ch03_eg22.css):

```
h1, p {
   border:solid 2px #000000;
   padding:5px;
   margin:4px;
   font-family:arial, verdana, sans-serif;}

b, em {
   border:solid 2px #999999;
   padding:2px;
   margin:23px;}
```

You will look at each of these properties in detail in the upcoming sections of this chapter, but notice how the borders have been drawn around all of the boxes in Figure 3-23.

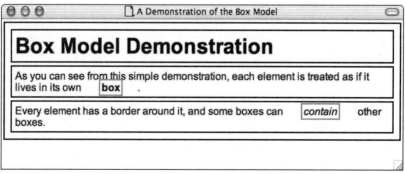

Figure 3-23

This gives you an even better idea of how styling with CSS is a matter of selecting an element and then setting different properties with appropriate values. It also highlights the difference between *block-level elements* and *inline elements;* which were introduced in Chapter 2. As you can see, block-level elements such as the <h1> and <p> elements are displayed as if they start on a new line, and anything that follows them is on a new line, whereas inline elements do not start on a new line. Rather, they flow within their containing element. You should also remember that inline elements cannot contain block-level elements.

ch03_eg22.html illustrates the point well; if you look at the <h1> element, its box takes up the full width of the browser and starts on a new line, whereas the boxes around the <b> elements sit in the middle of the rest of the paragraph and don't start on a new line.

> *You might well think that* **<img />** *elements would be block-level elements; however, they are actually inline elements. This makes sense when you consider that text can wrap around an image.*

In Strict XHTML, only block-level elements may appear as children of the <body> element, and you must place all inline elements inside a block-level element. This often trips people up when they validate their pages.

The <div> and <span> elements

Many HTML authors are not really familiar with two of HTML's most helpful elements — namely, <div> and <span>. Most of those who use them first came across them when working with layers; however, their purpose is far more general. The <div> and <span> elements are designed for grouping related elements together.

The capability to group elements together is particularly helpful when defining styles for groups of elements. For example, if you want to ensure that a group of elements use a particular font, have the same background color, or have a border around them all, you could group them together and apply a set of rules to that group of elements:

❑   The **<div>** element is designed to group block-level elements (which in turn can contain other block-level elements and inline elements).

❑   The **<span>** element is designed to group a collection of inline elements.

In the past, you may have used tables to group elements and provide them with a special set of formatting rules using borders and background colors of table cells to create a desired effect. However, a <div> would be better suited to such a task because it was designed to create a group of elements (whereas the table was designed to hold tabular data).

You can think of the <div> and <span> elements as creating new boxes around the group of elements they contain. In the case of the <div> element, it appears to be a block-level element, and in the case of a <span> element, it appears to be an inline element. While this is not a technically accurate description, this is certainly how they appear to act. The boxes they appear to create have no inherent styles of their own, but you can (as you are about to see) attach styles to the group of elements.

Before considering the code for an example that demonstrates using the <div> element, take a look at what the example will look like in the browser (see Figure 3-24).

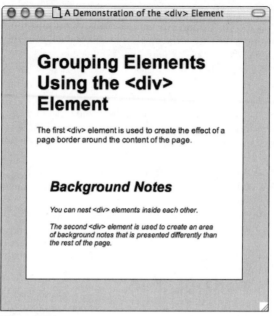

Figure 3-24

Now have a look at the body of this example. As you can see, it contains two <div> elements, both of which contain headings and paragraphs, and each has a different value for its class attribute (ch03_eg23.html):

```
<body>
<div class="page">
  <h1>Grouping Elements Using the &lt;div&gt; Element</h1>
  <p>The first &lt;div&gt; element is used to create the effect of a page border
     around the content of the page.</p>
  <div class="background">
    <h2>Background Notes</h2>
    <p>You can nest &lt;div&gt; elements inside each other.</p>
    <p>The second &lt;div&gt; element is used to create an area of background notes
       that is presented differently than the rest of the page. </p>
  </div>
</div>
</body>
```

Now take a look at the style sheet. While you have not met all of the properties yet, you should be able to get an idea of what each one does:

❑   The rule for the <body> element sets up the default font and the background color for the document.

❑   The rule for the <div> element whose class attribute has a value of page sets borders, margins, and padding for the box it creates.

❑   The rule for the <div> element whose class attribute has a value of background increases the padding (making the text appear indented) and makes the font italic.

Here is `ch03_eg23.css`:

```css
body {
    font-family:arial, verdana, sans-serif;
    font-size:14px;
    background-color:#d6d6d6;}

div.page {
    border:solid 1px #000000;
    background-color:#ffffff;
    margin:30px;
    padding:15px;}

div.background {
    padding:20px;
    font-style:italic;
    font-size:smaller;}
```

The `<span>` element works in a very similar manner but creates an inline group of elements, which means it can contain only inline elements — not block-level elements.

Box properties

Having looked at the box model, learned the difference between inline and block-level elements, and seen how the `<div>` and `<span>` elements can be used to group elements, you can now look at some of the properties that affect boxes — in particular, the `border`, `padding`, and `margin` properties.

The border properties

The `border` properties enable you to specify how the border of the box representing an element should look. You can change three properties of a border:

❑ `border-color` indicates what color a border should be.

❑ `border-style` indicates whether a border should be solid, a dashed line, a double line, or one of the other possible values.

❑ `border-width` indicates the width of the line created by the border.

The border-color property

The `border-color` property enables you to change the color of the border surrounding a box:

```css
p {border-color:#ff0000;}
```

The value can be a hex code for the color or a color name like those you use in HTML 4. It can also be expressed as values for red, green, and blue (RGB), between 0 and 255; or percentages of red, green, and blue. For example, you could use any of the four values listed in the following table to represent the same colors:

Color Name	Hex	RGB Values	RGB Percentages
red	#ff0000	rgb (255, 0, 0)	rgb (100%, 0, 0)
green	#00ff00	rgb (0, 255, 0)	rgb (0, 100%, 0)
blue	#0000ff	rgb (0, 0, 255)	rgb (0, 0, 100%)

You can individually change the color of the bottom, left, top, and right side of a box's border using the following properties:

- ❑ border-bottom-color
- ❑ border-right-color
- ❑ border-top-color
- ❑ border-left-color

The border-style property

The border-style property enables you to select the style of line used with the border:

```
p {border-style:solid;}
```

The default value for this property is none, so by default there is no visible border. The following table shows this property's permissible values:

Value	Description
none	No border (equivalent of border-width:0;)
solid	Border is a single solid line
dotted	Border is a series of dots
dashed	Border is a series of short lines
double	Border is two solid lines; the value of the border-width property creates the sum of the two lines and the space between them
groove	Border looks as though it were carved into the page
ridge	Border looks the opposite of groove
inset	Border makes the box look like it is embedded in the page
outset	Border makes the box look like it is coming out of the canvas
hidden	Same as none, except in terms of border-conflict resolution for table elements (see the section on tables in Chapter 4)

Figure 3-25 shows an example of what each of these would look like (taken from `ch03_eg24.html` and the accompanying style sheet `ch03_eg24.css`). This screenshot was taken in Netscape 7, because IE 6 does not support the last five values.

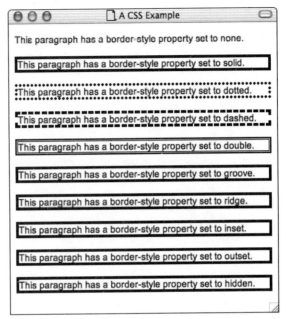

Figure 3-25

Here you can see the style sheet used to create the different border styles (`ch03_eg24css`):

```
p{border-style:solid; border-color:#000000;}

.none {border-style:none;}
.solid {border-style:solid;}
.dotted {border-style:dotted;}
.dashed {border-style:dashed;}
.double {border-style:double;}
.groove {border-style:groove;}
.ridge {border-style:ridge;}
.inset {border-style:inset;}
.outset {border-style:outset;}
.hidden {border-style:hidden;}
```

You can change the style of the bottom, left, top, and right border of a box using the following properties:

- ❏ `border-bottom-color`
- ❏ `border-right-color`
- ❏ `border-top-color`
- ❏ `border-left-color`

The border-width property

The `border-width` property enables you to set the width of your borders:

```
p {border-style:solid;}
   border-width:4px;}
```

The value of the `border-width` attribute must be a length (as discussed in the section "Units of Measurement" earlier in the chapter), but not a percentage, or it can take one of the following values:

❏   `thin`

❏   `medium`

❏   `thick`

The width of these three values is not specified in the CSS recommendation in terms of pixels; the actual width is dependent on the browser.

You can change the width of the bottom, top, left, and right border of a box using the following properties:

❏   `border-bottom-width`

❏   `border-top-width`

❏   `border-left-width`

❏   `border-right-width`

Expressing border properties using shorthand

The `border` property enables you to specify the color, style, and width of lines in one property:

```
p {border: 4px solid red;}
```

If you use this shorthand, the values should not have anything between them. You could also specify the three properties on any of the following properties in the same way:

❏   `border-bottom`

❏   `border-top`

❏   `border-left`

❏   `border-right`

> *The CSS2 recommendation also contains a set of properties for creating outlines. These are almost identical to borders, except they do not take up any space (so an outline of 3 pixels will not add 3 pixels to the size of the box); rather, outlines are placed on top of the layout as if on a new layer. The outline properties are covered in Appendix C, although they are not covered in detail in this chapter because they work just like the border properties and are not currently supported in IE 6 or Netscape 7.*

The padding property

The `padding` property enables you to specify how much space should appear between the content of an element and its border, like so:

```
td {padding:5px;}
```

The value of this attribute should be a length, a percentage, or the keyword `inherit`. By default, `padding` does not inherit, but if the value `inherit` is used, then the element will have the same padding as its parent.

If a percentage is used, it is treated as a percentage of the containing box. For example, if you had a 500-pixel square box, and there was supposed to be 10 percent padding for an element inside this box, the whole of the padding on both sides would equal 50 pixels, which translates to 25 pixels between each side of the box and the center of the page.

You can specify different amounts of padding for each side of the box using the following properties:

- ❑ `padding-bottom`
- ❑ `padding-top`
- ❑ `padding-left`
- ❑ `padding-right`

The `padding` attribute is especially helpful in creating white space between the content of an element and any border it has (even if the border is not visible, `padding` will prevent the content of two adjacent boxes from touching). Take a look at the following example of an XHTML page (without a style sheet attached) in Figure 3-26.

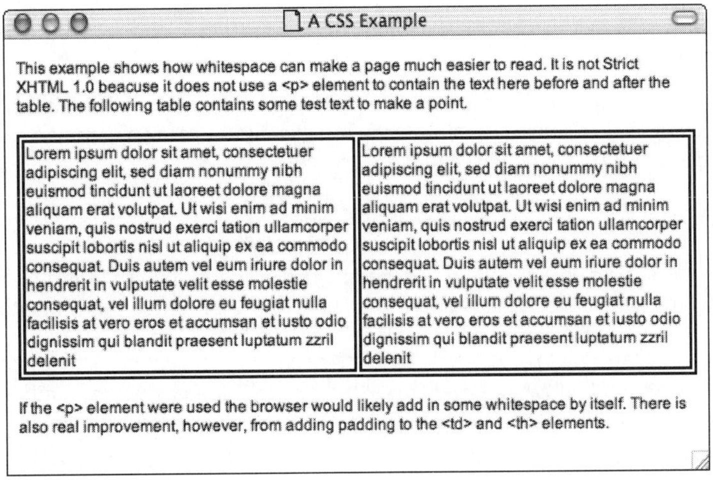

Figure 3-26

As you can see, the text looks squashed and hard to read. Simply by adding two rules, you can make the page a lot easier to read (ch03_eg25.css):

```
table{margin:15px;}
th, td{padding:20px;}
```

As you can see from Figure 3-27, the addition of this style sheet makes a big difference to the page.

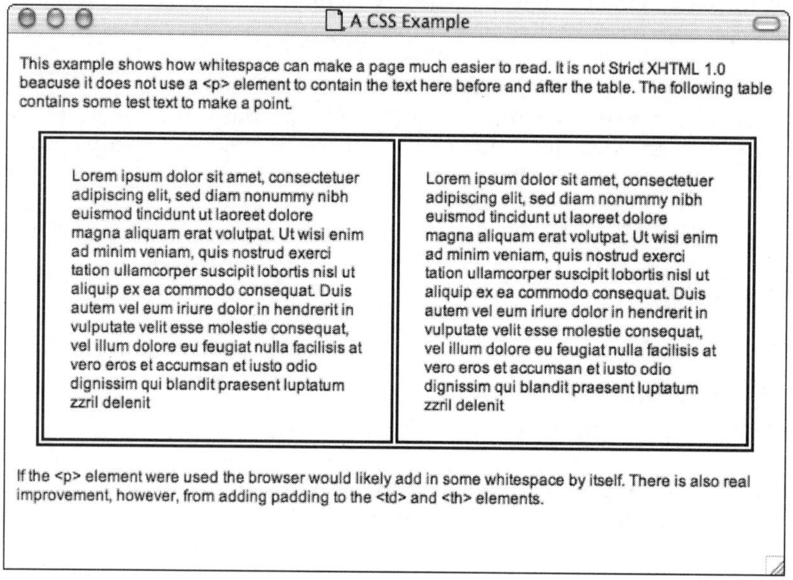

Figure 3-27

The margin property

The margin property sets the gap between a box and any surrounding boxes; its value is a length, a percentage, or the keyword inherit, each of which has exactly the same meaning as it did for the padding property described in the preceding section:

```
p {margin:20px;}
```

As with the padding property, the values of the margin property are not inherited by child elements, so using the keyword inherit means that a box will inherit the amount of padding its parent element had.

> Remember that when two boxes have adjacent vertical margins (top and bottom margins), only the larger of the two margins will be displayed.

You can set different values for the margin on each side of the box using the following properties:

- ❑   margin-bottom

- ❑   margin-top

- ❑   margin-left

- ❑   margin-right

If you look at the following example (ch03_eg26.html), you can see three paragraphs. If you look at the style sheet (or at the bottom of Figure 3-28), you can see that each paragraph has a taller margin to the top (40px) than the bottom (10px), and therefore the bottom margin is collapsed when it meets a top margin — the gap between adjoining paragraphs is not 50px.

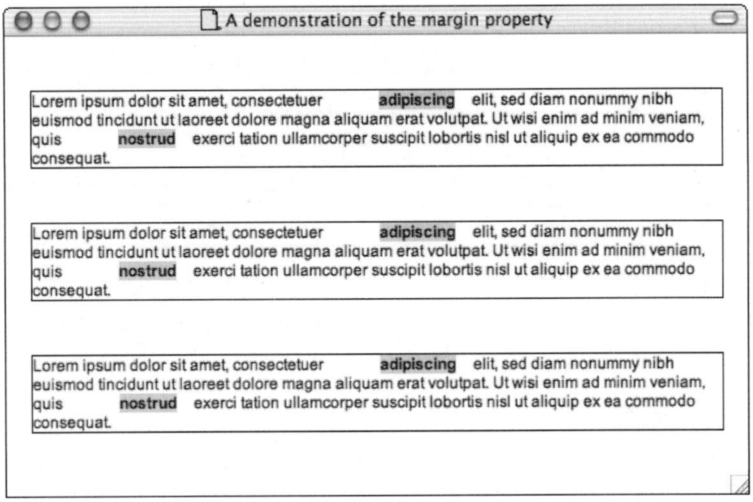

Figure 3-28

The words in the <strong> elements (bold with gray backgrounds) have margin-left and margin-right properties set, and you can see their effect from the wide gaps on either side of the words.

Here are the rules from ch03_eg26.css:

```
p {
    margin-top:40px;
    margin-bottom:10px;
    margin-left:10px;
    margin-right:10px;
    border-style:solid;
    border-width:1px;
    border-color:#000000;}

strong {
    margin-left:40px;
    margin-right:10px;
    background-color:#d6d6d6;}
```

Dimensions

Now that you have seen that CSS treats every element like a box, and that each box has a border surrounding it, padding between the border and the content, and a margin between the border and adjoining boxes, it is time to look at how you can change the dimensions of boxes.

Several properties enable you to control the dimensions of a box:

Property	Purpose
height	Sets the height of a box
width	Sets the width of a box
line-height	Sets the height of a line of text (like leading in a layout program)
max-height	Sets a maximum height that a box can be
min-height	Sets the minimum height that a box can be
max-width	Sets the maximum width that a box can be
min-width	Sets the minimum width that a box can be

Unfortunately, the last four properties dealing with the maximum and minimum sizes of a box do not work in IE 6 or Netscape 7.

The height and width properties

The height and width properties enable you to set the height and width for boxes. They can take values of a length, a percentage, or the keyword auto (the default value being auto).

In the following example, you can see the CSS rules for three paragraph elements; each paragraph has a corresponding class attribute whose value is one, two, or three. All paragraphs share the same border, margin, and padding properties, but have different settings for their height and width properties. The first two use pixels to determine lengths, while the third uses em and ex measurements, which are relative to the font size (ch03_eg27.css):

```
.one, .two, .three {
   border-style:solid 1px #000000;
   margin:20px;
   padding:10px;}

.one {
   width:300px;
   height:200px;}

.two {
   width:300px;
   height:50px;}

.three {
   width:20em;
   height:15ex;}
```

The following points are apparent from this example:

❑ The first paragraph will be 300 pixels wide and 200 pixels high. As you can see from Figure 3-29, the text settings in this browser mean that the box is too tall for the text, and there is a large gap underneath the text.

❑ The second paragraph will be 300 pixels wide and 50 pixels high. As you can see from Figure 3-29, the text settings in this browser mean that the box is not big enough for the text, and the border goes right through the text.

❑ The third paragraph will be 20em wide (remember that an em is the height of the font) and 5ex tall (an ex is the height of the *x* character). If you try to adjust the size of fonts in your browser, you will see that the box scales to fit the text. When using this technique, remember that different fonts have different heights and widths, and you must use fonts with similar aspect ratios in your font lists.

The line-height property

The `line-height` property enables you to increase or decrease the vertical space between lines of text, which print designers refer to as *leading*.

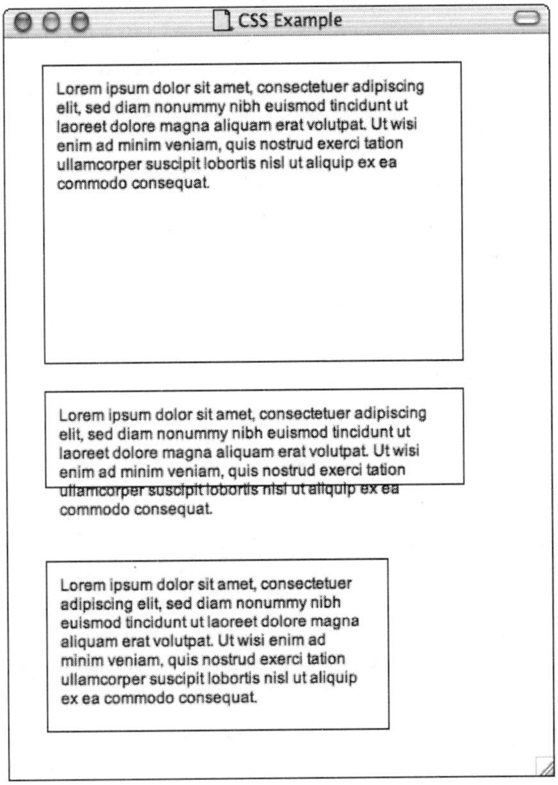

Figure 3-29

The value of the `line-height` property can be a number, a length, or a percentage. It is a good idea to specify this property in the same measurement in which you specify the size of your text.

The following example shows four rules setting different `line-height` properties using different values (ch03_eg28.css):

```
.one {line-height:normal;}
.two {line-height:18px;}
.three {line-height:1.5em;}
.four {line-height:1.9ex;}
```

You can see the result of changing the `line-height` property in Figure 3-30.

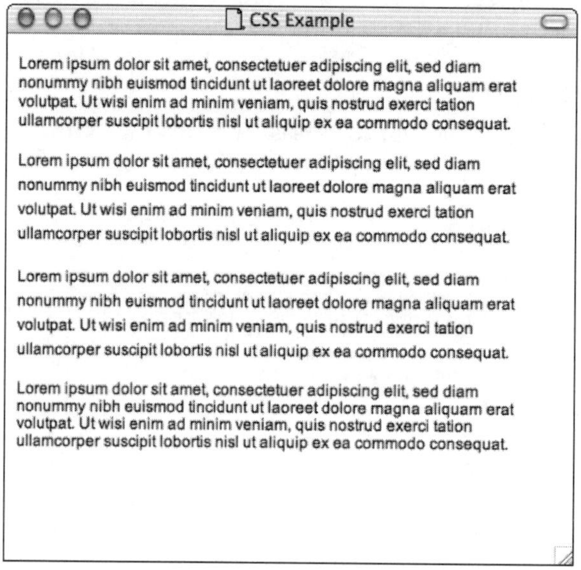

Figure 3-30

Remember that if you choose to use a pixel size for the `line-height` property, different fonts can vary in height.

The max-height and max-width properties

The `max-height` and `max-width` properties enable you to specify maximum height and width for a box. The value of these properties can be a length or a percentage:

```
p {max-height:300px; max-width:300px;}
```

These properties will be particularly useful when supported because they will enable you to specify the maximum area an element's content can occupy when you create templates for pages whose content can vary. Unfortunately, they do not work in either Netscape 7 or IE 6.

The min-width and min-height properties

The min-width and min-height properties correspond with the max-height and max-width properties, but specify a minimum width and height for the box. The value of these properties can be a length or a percentage:

```
p {min-width:100px; min-height:100px;}
```

These properties, when supported, will also be very helpful when creating style sheets that are templates for pages whose content is unknown. The min-width and max-width properties will ensure that a box occupies at least a certain space — which can be very important for aligning boxes correctly.

vertical-align

The vertical-align property controls the vertical positioning of elements. It is not only helpful for positioning text within containing boxes, but also in positioning any inline element — in particular, images. Two groups of keywords can be used with this property. The members of the first group control positioning relative to the containing element:

Value	Purpose
baseline	Everything should be aligned on the baseline of the parent element (this is the default setting).
middle	The vertical midpoint of the element should be aligned with the vertical midpoint of the parent.
sub	Make the element subscript. With images, the top of the image should be on the baseline. With text, the top of the font body should be on the baseline.
super	Makes the element superscript. With images, the bottom of the image should be on a level with the top of the font. With text, the bottom of the descender (the part of a letter such as g and p that extends beneath the line of text) should align with the top of the font body.
text-top	The top of the text and the top of the image should align with the top of the tallest text on the line.
text-bottom	The bottom of the text and the bottom of the image should align with the bottom of the lowest text on the line.

The second group of keywords controls the position of the element in relation to the line that the element is part of.

Value	Purpose
top	The top of the text and the top of the image should align with the top of the tallest element on the line.
bottom	The bottom of the text and the bottom of the image should align with the bottom of the lowest element on the line.

Values can also be a percentage, in which case the position is relative to the value of the line-height property and the baseline of the element (or the bottom of the element if there is no baseline) is raised by the specified amount. Negative values are allowed.

You can also use a length, which is relative to the baseline (in other words, if a length of 0 is given, it is the equivalent of using the keyword baseline). A positive length will raise it above the baseline, while a negative length will lower it beneath the baseline.

The example ch03_eg29.css demonstrates the use of the keywords:

```
/* positioned in relation to containing element */
img.baseline {vertical-align:baseline;}
img.middle {vertical-align:middle;}
img.sub {vertical-align:sub;}
img.super {vertical-align:super;}
img.text-top {vertical-align:text-top;}
img.text-bottom {vertical-align:text-bottom;}
/* positioned in relation to the line the element is part of */
img.top {vertical-align:top;}
img.bottom {vertical-align:bottom;}
```

Figure 3-31 shows you some of these values.

Color and background

There is one property to alter the foreground color in CSS, and six properties that enable you to change the background of either the whole page (when used with the <body> element) or any single box created by the box model (when used with any other element):

Property	Purpose
color	Specifies the foreground color of a box
background-color	Specifies a solid color for the background of the page or box
background-image	Sets an image to be in the background of the page or box
background-repeat	Indicates whether the background image should be repeated (or tiled) across the page or box
background-position	Indicates where an image should be positioned in either the window or the containing box
background-attachment	Indicates whether a background image should remain static or move with the rest of the page as the user scrolls up and down
background	A shorthand form that enables you to specify all of these properties

Note that the shorthand background property is better supported in some browsers than the individual properties, but you need to learn what values the individual properties can take before using the shorthand.

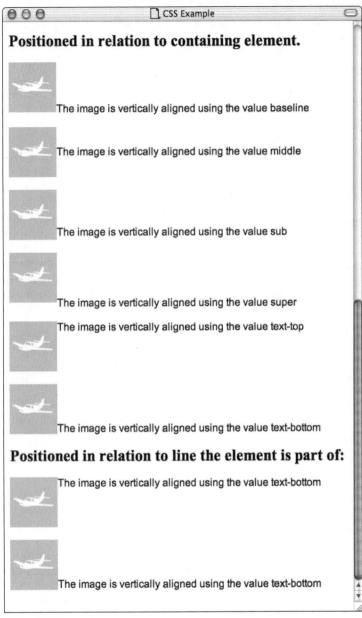

Figure 3-31

The color property

The color property enables you to specify a foreground color for a page or box (just like the color attribute in HTML). It is particularly useful to specify the color of text and lines within a box.

The possible values are a hex code or a color name (like those used in HTML 4); values for red, green, and blue between 0 and 255; or percentages of red, green, and blue (just as you saw with the `border-color` property earlier in the chapter). For example, the following all specify the same red:

```
ff0000;  red  rgb(255,0,0)  rgb(100% 0% 0%)
```

The following example (`ch03_eg30.css`) makes the text and the border around the paragraph red:

```
p {
    color:#ff0000;
    width:200px;
    border-style:solid;}
```

The background-color property

The `background-color` property enables you to specify a single solid color for the background of your pages and the inside of any box created by CSS (it is just like the `bgcolor` attribute that was available in HTML).

The value of this property can be a hex code, a color name, or an RGB value (this is the same as the `border-color` property). Here is an example that uses the `background-color` property on three different elements (`ch03_eg31.css`):

```
body {
    background-color:#cccccc;
    font:12pt arial;}

p {
    background-color: rgb(255,255,255);
    padding:10px;}

code {
    background-color:black;
    color:#FFFFFF; }
```

When the `background-color` property is set for the `<body>` element, it affects the whole document, and when it is used on any other element, it will just change the background of that box, as shown in Figure 3-32.

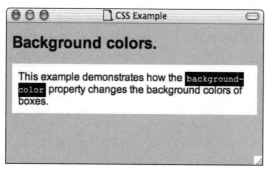

Figure 3-32

*It is a good idea to set a **background-color** property for the **<body>** element in any page you create because some users set a different background color for all windows by default.*

The background-image property

As its name suggests, the `background-image` property enables you to add an image to the background of any block-level box in CSS (it is just like the `background` attribute in HTML).

The value of the `background-image` property is as follows, starting with the letters `url` and then holding the URL for the image in brackets:

```
body {background-image: url(images/background.gif); }
```

The `background-image` property overrides the `background-color` property; however, it is a good idea to supply a `background-color` property in addition to the `background-image` property, giving it a value that is similar to the main color in the image in case the specified background image does not load for any reason.

Here is an example of using a background image. The image is only 200 pixels wide and 150 pixels high, and the `background-color` property is given the same value as the background color of this image in case the image does not load (`ch03_eg32.css`):

```
body {
    background-image:url(images/background.gif);
    background-color:#cccccc;
    font-family:Arial, verdana, sans-serif;}
```

Figure 3-33 shows you an image used for a background; by default, this image is repeated across the entire page.

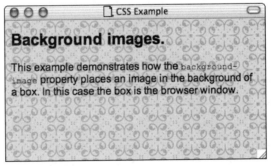

Figure 3-33

This is not a great example of a background image, but it highlights an important point. There isn't enough contrast between the colors used in the background image and the text that appears on top of it, which makes the text too hard to read. You must make ensure that there is sufficient contrast between any background image and the writing that appears on top of it. This means that your background image itself must have low contrast (use similar colors), while the text that appears on it must contrast highly with the background so that it can be read.

Figure 3-34 shows an improved example of the background image. With its lighter colors and bolder text, it should be much easier to read.

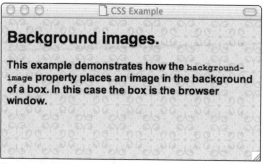

Figure 3-34

*With a background image, you cannot specify the size of the image or give it an **alt** attribute. Therefore, you should never use it to convey important information; it should be used only for decoration. You should also be wary of using large files as background images because they can be slow to load.*

The background-image property works well with most block-level elements, although older browsers have difficulty using background images in tables.

The background-repeat property

By default, the background-image property repeats to fill the whole page, as you saw in ch03_eg32 .html. This is often referred to as *wallpaper*. When wallpaper images are designed well, you will not see the edges where the image repeats; therefore, it is important that any patterns should tessellate well. Wallpaper is often made up of textures such as paper, marble, or abstract surfaces, rather than photos or logos.

If you do not want your image to repeat over the entire background of the page, you should use the background-repeat property, which has four helpful values:

Value	Purpose
repeat	Image will repeat to cover the whole page (the default)
repeat-x	Image will be repeat horizontally across the page (not down the whole page vertically)
repeat-y	Image will be repeat vertically down the page (not across horizontally)
no-repeat	Image is displayed only once

These different properties can have interesting effects. It is worth looking at each in turn. You have already seen the effect of the repeat value, so the next one to look at is repeat-x, which creates a horizontal bar following the browser's *x* axis (ch03_eg33.css):

```
body {
    background-image: url(images/background2.gif);
    background-repeat: repeat-x;
    background-color: #ffffff;}
```

You can see the result of this property in Figure 3-35.

Figure 3-35

The repeat-y value works just like repeat-x but in the other direction — vertically following the browser's *y* axis (ch03_eg34.css):

```
body {
    background-image: url(images/background2.gif);
    background-repeat: repeat-y;
    background-color: #ffffff;}
```

In Figure 3-36, you can see the result, with the images creating a sidebar along the left side.

Figure 3-36

The final value is no-repeat, leaving one instance of the image that by default will be in the top left-hand corner of the browser window (ch03_eg35.css):

```
body {
    background-image: url(images/background2.gif);
    background-repeat: no-repeat;
    background-color: #ffffff;
    font-family:arial;}
```

You can see the result in Figure 3-37.

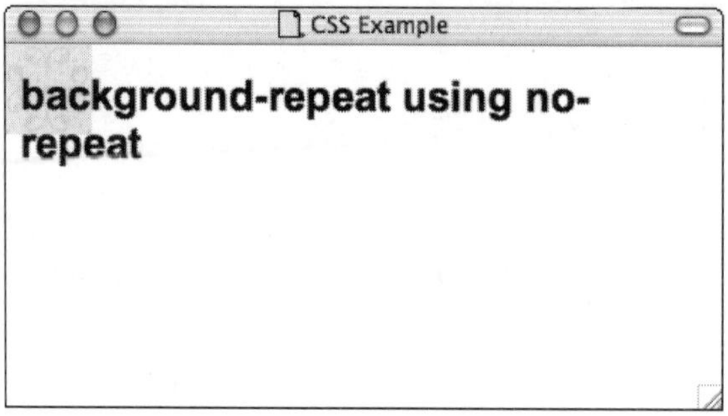

Figure 3-37

The background-position property

The `background-position` property enables you to specify where a background image should appear within the containing box (when used with the `<body>` element, the browser window is the containing element). You can specify the position using lengths or percentages from the top and left corners of the containing box. For example, `0% 0%` would position the image in the top left-hand corner of the box, `100% 100%` would place it in the bottom right, and `30% 60%` would place it 30 percent down the box and 60 percent in from the left.

There are also a number of keywords you can use with this property. In the left-hand column of the following table, you can see the keywords, and in the right-hand column, you can see the percentages that correspond to these keywords. The keywords `top`, `top-center`, and `center-top`, for example, all position the item 50 percent in on the *x* (horizontal) axis and 0 percent down on the *y* (vertical) axis.

Keywords	Corresponding Percentages
`top left` and `left top`	0% 0%
`top`, `top center`, and `center top`	50% 0%
`right top` and `top right`	100% 0%
`left`, `left center`, and `center left`	0% 50%
`center` and `center center`	50% 50%
`right`, `right center`, and `center right`	100% 50%
`bottom left` and `left bottom`	0% 100%
`bottom`, `bottom center`, and `center bottom`	50% 100%
`bottom right` and `right bottom`	100% 100%

The following example (ch03_eg36.css) demonstrates fixing the position of two background images:

❑   On the <body> element, the image is positioned in the top left using absolute positioning.

❑   On the <div> element, the image is positioned using the keyword center.

```
body {
  background-image: url(images/background2.gif);
  background-repeat: no-repeat;
  background-position:0 0;
  background-color: #ffffff;
  font-family:arial;}

div {
  background-image: url(images/background2.gif);
  background-repeat: no-repeat;
  background-position:center;
  width:500px;
  height: 100px;
  border:solid 1px black;}
```

You can see the result in Figure 3-38, which illustrates how the image is positioned within its containing box.

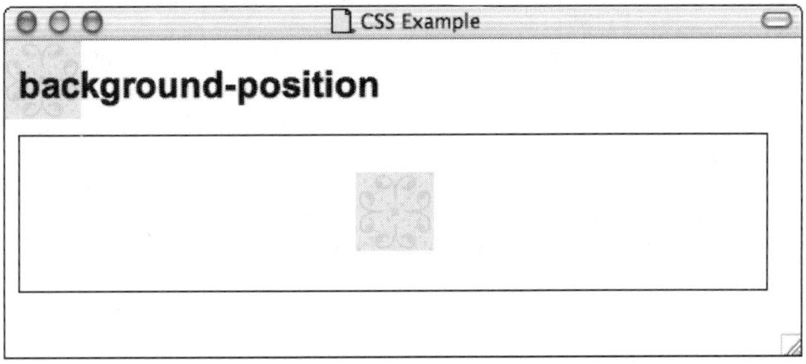

Figure 3-38

The background-attachment property (for watermarks)

The background-attachment property enables you to specify a background image, sometimes referred to as a *watermark,* that must stay in the same place even if the user scrolls up and down the page. The background-attachment property can take two values:

Value	Purpose
fixed	The image will not move if the user scrolls up and down the page.
scroll	The image stays in the same place on the background of the page. If the user scrolls up or down the page, the image moves, too.

141

In the following example, the image will stay in the middle of the page even when the user scrolls further down (ch03_eg37.css):

```
body {
    background-image: url(images/background.gif);
    background-attachment: fixed;
    background-position: center;
    background-repeat: no-repeat;
    background-color: #ffffff; }
```

Figure 3-39 shows that the image sits in the center of the page, where it remains when the user scrolls.

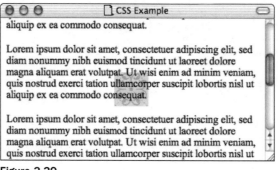

Figure 3-39

The background property

The background property enables you to specify all five of the background properties at once. If you do not supply one of the values, the default value will be used. The values can be given in any order:

❑   background-color

❑   background-image

❑   background-repeat

❑   background-attachment

❑   background-position

For example, you can just write the following:

```
body {background: #ffffff; url(images/background_small.gif) fixed no-repeat
center;}
```

This will create exactly the same effect as the example shown in Figure 3-39.

Solution

At this point, you have already learned the key skills required to write basic CSS style sheets, including the following:

- ❑ How CSS affects the properties of one or more elements that make up each CSS rule

- ❑ How to write a simple style sheet and link it to the source document

- ❑ How CSS is based upon a box model

- ❑ How to select the element to which a rule applies

- ❑ What units of measurement you can use

- ❑ What properties are available to change the appearance of text; borders, padding, and margins of boxes; dimensions; colors; and backgrounds.

There are still three key topics you need to learn — namely, how to use some additional key CSS properties, how to create modular style sheets, and how to use CSS for positioning elements. However, you have already learned plenty to start making a real difference to the site.

In this section, you will be revisiting the XHTML pages developed for the sample site in the last chapter and adding CSS style rules. This will give you a chance to see how all of the things you have learned in this chapter apply to a real site, which will help fulfill the aim of controlling presentation of the site using CSS.

As with the last chapter, you will be dealing with the three types of pages (home page, product list pages, and product details pages) used in the site one at a time.

The home page

When we left the home page at the end of the last chapter, it did not look like we might have hoped; it certainly didn't look very attractive (see Figure 3-40).

The process of creating a style sheet involves deciding which elements you want to make look different and what properties you need to change to get the look you are after. Because it will take quite a few pages to develop this style sheet, I have split the page up into sections, each with separate headings in order to make it easier to follow. As with other chapters, the home page takes the longest because other pages share parts in common with the home page, enabling you to reuse the code without duplicating your efforts.

> As you look at adding the CSS styles to the example, you might find it helpful to open two browser windows, one holding the examples from the Solution section of Chapter 2, the other holding the solution examples from this chapter. This will enable you to compare the versions of the pages as you go along. You could even have the original HTML version open as well if you wish.

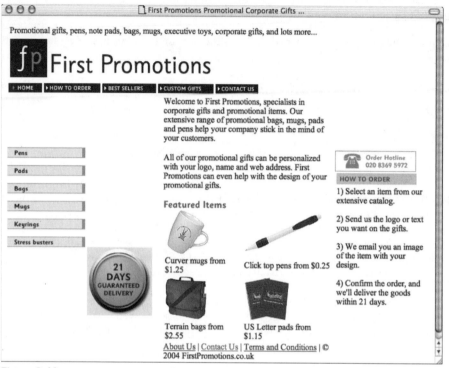

Figure 3-40

Top of page — masthead

You can begin by setting a couple of properties you want to apply to the whole document:

- ❑ You want to ensure that the background of the page is white (even if the user's default settings are a different color), so you will use the `background-color` property with a value of `#ffffff;`.

- ❑ You want the typeface to be Arial. To do this, you use the `font-family` property, and just in case the user does not have Arial (which is, admittedly, unlikely), you will offer two other options in order of preference. You might remember that the last option should simply be a generic font family (in this case, `sans-serif`) indicating that the default sans-serif font for the computer should be used if no other properties can be found.

To make these rules apply to the whole document, the selector for this rule will indicate that the properties you are altering belong to the `<body>` element. Here is the first rule for this document:

```
body {
   background-color:#FFFFFF;
   font-family:Arial, Helvetica, sans-serif;}
```

In the original HTML version of the site, the whole page was contained within a single-celled table; the purpose of this table was to add a one-pixel, black border around the page. When you created the XHTML version of the site in Chapter 2, rather than using a single-celled table to contain the page, you used a `<div>` element. This `<div>` element was given a `class` attribute whose value was `page` (indicating that it contained the whole page). You can therefore recreate the single-pixel black border around the page by attaching a rule to this particular `<div>` element, identifying it using a class selector (which has a period between the element name and the value of the `class` attribute). This rule will then use the shorthand `border` property to create the single-pixel black border:

```
div.page {border: solid 1px #000000;}
```

In the HTML version of the document, this table also served the purpose of controlling the size of the page, making sure it was 800 pixels wide. You can control the width of the page in CSS using the `width` property on this `<div>` element in the same rule:

```
div.page {
   border: solid 1px #000000;
   width:800px;}
```

You might remember that inside this `<div>` element, the page layout is created using three tables, vertically stacked on top of each other. The top table holds the masthead (or logo), the second table holds the navigation, and the third table holds the main part of the page (side navigation, details of products, and details for how to order). Start then by turning your attention to the masthead for the page, which consists of a tagline, followed by a logo. Here is the first table that holds this information:

```
<table>
  <tr>
    <td> Promotional gifts, pens, note pads, bags, mugs,
        executive toys, corporate gifts, and lots more...</td>
  </tr>
  <tr>
    <td><img src="/images/branding/logo_400x80.gif" alt="logo" /></td>
  </tr>
</table>
```

The first thing you might notice that you want to do here is make the descriptive line (the line that indicates what the site offers) look more like it did in the original version. In the old HTML site, this line of text was in white writing on a blue background, and it had some padding to keep the text away from the edges of the box (which makes it look more attractive and more readable).

Therefore, you want to associate a rule with the table cell that holds this site description, and in order to do so, you need to give this table cell an `id` attribute whose value is `siteDescription` in order to uniquely identify it among all the other table cells in the page:

```
<td id="siteDescription"> Promotional gifts, pens, note pads, bags, mugs...
```

Over in the CSS style sheet, you can create a rule to apply to this element. The first thing you want to do is create a selector to identify the element, so your rules apply only to the content of this table cell. To do this, you use the `id` selector, which uses a hash to separate the element name from the value of the `id` attribute:

```
td#tagline {
```

Next you can set the foreground and background colors using the `color` and `background-color` properties:

```
td#tagline {
    color:#FFFFFF;
    background-color:#000066;}
```

You also need to ensure that the width of the cell stretches across the full width of the containing <div> element that holds the page, so you set the width attribute to a value of 800px. You can also give the cell 5 pixels of padding to create space around the text:

```
td#tagline {
    color:#FFFFFF;
    background-color:#000066;
    width:800px;
    padding:5px;}
```

Finally, you want to set the font-size and font-weight properties to make the text in this table cell small and bold. Your final rule should look like this:

```
td#tagline {
    color:#FFFFFF;
    background-color:#000066;
    width:800px;
    padding:5px;
    font-size:x-small;
    font-weight:bold; }
```

Navigation

The navigation resides in the second table, underneath the table that holds the masthead. The navigation is made up of several images with JavaScript rollovers. If you are looking at the site in Internet Explorer, you might have noticed the blue lines around all of the images that are links in the navigation; this is because IE gives images that are links a blue border by default. You can easily override this by creating a rule for all images that gives the border property a value of none:

```
img {border-none;}
```

In the original design, each navigation item resided in its own table cell, and each cell was given the same background color as the background color of the images (a dark blue). There was also a lighter blue one-pixel line between each navigation item. This was created by giving the table's cellpadding attribute a value of 1 and making the background color of the table different from the background color of the table cells containing the navigation items.

Here is the start of that original HTML table to remind you of all the stylistic attributes used in it:

```
<table border="0" cellpadding="0" cellspacing="1" width="800" bgcolor="6699FF">
  <tr>
    <td width="150" bgcolor="#000066"></td>
    <td bgcolor="#000066"><a href="/FirstPromotions/index.html"
```

In addition, the navigation items were aligned with the main content of the page, looking as if they had been centered, although it was actually because there were table cells to the left and right of the navigation that were as wide as the columns to the left and right on the main page.

Therefore, you need to define styles for the following elements:

❑ **The table holding the navigation** — Set a background color of light blue and a give it a fixed width.

❑ **All of the table cells that hold navigation items** — Set a dark blue background color and a 1-pixel margin (this margin will allow the lighter blue background to show through the table).

❑ **The table cell on the left of the navigation** — Ensure that it is 150 pixels wide (the same width as the left column on the main page).

❑ **The table cell on the right of the navigation** — Ensure that it is 180 pixels wide (the same width as the right column on the main page).

Start by adding the necessary id attribute to the table that holds the navigation. So you can associate the rules just with this one table, give this ID attribute a value of navigation. You should also add class attributes to the first table cell in the navigation (and give it a value of leftColumn) and the right-most table cell (give this a value of rightColumn). Note that you are using class attributes for the left and right table cells because you will reuse the rules that specify their widths in the main page. The structure of the table that holds the navigation will, therefore, look like this (the lines that have changed are highlighted and the rollover images have been removed to save space):

```
<table id="navigation">
  <tr>
    <td class="leftColumn"></td>
    <td>  <!-- navigation item goes here -->  </td>
    <td>  <!-- navigation item goes here -->  </td>
    <td>  <!-- navigation item goes here -->  </td>
    <td>  <!-- navigation item goes here -->  </td>
    <td class="rightColumn"></td>
  </tr>
</table>
```

Over in the style sheet, the rule for this <table> element will look like the following. As you can see, I have set the background-color property to light blue (this color will show up between table cells) and specified the width of the table to ensure that it stretches 800 pixels across the page:

```
table#navigation {
  background-color:#6699FF;
  width:800px; }
```

The next rule applies to all of the cells in this table; it uses the descendent selector to indicate that the properties being changed apply to any table cells that are children of the <table> element whose id attribute has a value of navigation — and therefore the rules apply only to the cells in this table. (Because no two elements in one document should have the same value for the id attribute, it is not strictly necessary to have the table element in the selector, but I find it helps remind me which element the rule applies to.)

The properties being set for each cell are the darker blue background-color that matches the background color of the images and a one-pixel margin to ensure that you can see the lighter blue of the table behind:

```
table#navigation td {
  background-color:#000066;
  margin:19px; }
```

Finally, you just have to specify the width of the table cells to the left and right of the navigation items. These have already been given class attributes that have the values leftColumn and rightColumn (the class attribute was used with these elements rather than the id attribute because, as you will see shortly, these rules will be used again on elements in the third table, which contains the main body of the page).

```
.leftColumn {width:150px;}
.rightColumn {width:180px;}
```

Main page

Now you come to the main part of the page, which is held in the third of the tables (underneath the masthead and navigation). This table is made up of three cells: the first cell holds the left navigation in the left column; the second cell holds the main page content; and the third cell holds the ordering details in the right column.

In order to make the left and right columns the correct width, you just add the class attributes with the values leftColumn and rightColumn to the table in the XHTML page. After all, you just added the CSS rules to the style sheet at the end of the last section to deal with these classes. You also add a class attribute with a value of middleColumn to the middle table cell.

Although you already have rules defined in the style sheet to control the width of the left and right columns, you want to add a few properties to these rules:

❑ First, you might have noticed that the content of both columns is halfway down the page, and you want it to be right at the top, so you can use the vertical-align property, which you met in the section called "Dimensions" earlier in this chapter. This property should be given a value of top.

❑ Second, you want the content of these columns to be centered, so you add the text-align property with a value of center.

❑ Third, you want to give them their correct background colors; light blue for the left column and gray for the right column.

When you have finished, the rules for the leftColumn and rightColumn classes should look like this:

```
.leftColumn {
  width:150px;
  vertical-align:top;
  text-align:center;
  background-color:#D9ECFF;}

.rightColumn {
  width:180px;
  vertical-align:top;
  text-align:center;
  background-color:#efefef;}
```

While you are looking at the columns, you can add the width, vertical-align, and background-color properties to the middle column, like so:

```
.middleColumn {
  width:470px;
  vertical-align:top;
  background-color:#FFFFFF;}
```

The changes made in this section of the chapter to the left column of the table are the only changes you need to make to that part of the page. In the next section of the chapter, you can continue with the main part of the page.

Center column — main content

In the center column of the page, you have the main content, which consists of the following:

❑ Two welcome paragraphs held inside a <div> element

❑ A table of featured items

❑ Some footer links for the site and a copyright notice

In the original HTML site, the welcome paragraphs used to be in a single-celled table, which controlled the width of the lines and gave the text a border. However, in Chapter 2, the table was replaced with a <div> element. The <div> element has an id attribute whose value is welcomeText. Without styling, this element takes up the full width of the center column and has no border, so you can add rules to control the width and border properties of this <div> element:

```
div#welcomeText {
   width:400px;
   border:solid 2px #666666;}
```

These rules are not quite enough to make the page look correct. The box that has been created is in the top left of the column, rather than having space all around it. A margin property will cure this problem and reposition the <div> element, because the margin controls the gap between the border of a box and any adjoining boxes.

You should also add a padding property to keep the text away from the edge of the box — remember that this white space makes the page more readable and attractive. Finally, you can control the size of the text for this element by giving the font-size property a value of medium. The final rule looks like this:

```
div#welcomeText {
   width:400px;
   border:solid 2px #999999;
   margin:25px;
   padding:10px;
   font-size:medium;}
```

Underneath the welcome text is the image that says "Featured Items." You need to inset this image from the left, and the obvious way to do this would be with a margin-left property. However, the margin properties work only with block-level elements, and the <img /> element is an inline element. Therefore, you need to put the image inside a <div> element, give that <div> element an id attribute so you can write a selector that identifies it, and then use the margin-left property on the <div> element. Here is the <img> element inside the <div> in the XHTML page:

```
<div  id="FeaturedItemsImage"><img src="images/interface/featuredItems.gif"
      alt="Featured Items" /></div>
```

Here is the rule you will add to the CSS style sheet to inset the <div> holding the image:

```
div#FeaturedItemsImage {left-margin:25px;}
```

The featured items themselves are held in a table, which has two columns and four rows. This table will need `class` attributes that can be used to associate style rules. Three classes will be added to the table:

❑ A `productsTable` class for the table as a whole

❑ A `productImage` class for table cells that hold product images

❑ A `productDescription` class for table cells that hold descriptions of the items

When you look at the product list pages, you will see these classes used again.

```
<table class="productsTable">
  <tr>
    <td class="productImage">
      <a href="products/mugs/mug2.html">
        <img src="products/mugs/images/mugs2_thumb.gif" alt="mug" />
      </a>
    </td>
    <td class="productImage">
      <a href="products/pens/pen2.hml">
        <img src="products/pens/images/pens2_thumb.gif" alt="pen" />
      </a>
    </td>
  </tr>
  <tr>
    <td class="productDescription">Curver mugs from $1.25</td>
    <td class="productDescription">Click top pens from $0.25</td>
  </tr>
  <tr>
    <td class="productImage">
      <a href="products/bags/bag4.html">
        <img src="products/bags/images/bags4_thumb.gif" alt="bag" />
      </a>
    </td>
    <td class="productImage">
      <a href="products/pads/pad3.html">
        <img src="products/pads/images/pad3_thumb.gif" alt="pad" />
      </a>
    </td>
  </tr>
  <tr>
    <td class="productDescription">Terrain bags from $2.55</td>
    <td class="productDescription">US Letter pads from $1.15</td>
  </tr>
</table>
```

First look at the `productsTable` class. The CSS rule associated with this class needs to do the following:

❑ Set a `margin-left` property to indent the table 25 pixels from the edge of the left column.

❑ Set the `width` of the table to be 400 pixels.

❑ Set the `background-color` property to be gray. (Just as you did with the navigation, setting this property enables you to create the look of lines between each item in the table, which, in the HTML version of the site, was created using the `border` attribute.)

```
table.productsTable {
  margin-left:25px;
  width:400px;
  background-color:#999999;}
```

The properties for the `productImage` and `productDescription` classes are both the same, so you only need to create one rule for the pair of them. This rule has to do the following:

❑　　Set the `width` of the cells to be 199 pixels.

❑　　Set the `background-color` property of the cells to be white.

❑　　Set the `font-size` property to be `medium`.

❑　　Give the cells some padding so that the text and images do not touch the borders — again, a matter of adding white space to make the page more attractive.

Here is the resulting rule:

```
td.productImage, td.productDescription {
  width:199px;
  background-color:#ffffff;
  font-size:medium;
  padding:4px;}
```

Now you have only one thing left to deal with on this table — centering the product images — and this is simple using the `text-align` property like so:

```
td.productImage {text-align:center;}
```

This rule has to be separate from the one you just created for both the `productImage` and `productDescription` class because you do not want to center the text in the cells that contain the `productDescription` class.

Just before you finish dealing with the center column, you need to look at the links in the footer. Links are something you have not yet learned to style in CSS — you will come to them in Chapter 4. However, you should just position the links correctly. You can do that by adding some simple rules to the `<div>` element that contains these footer links; it has a `class` attribute whose value is `footer`. Here is the CSS rule that sets the width of the footer and gives it a margin to separate it from other elements:

```
div.footer {
  margin:25px;
  width:400px;}
```

You could also make those links smaller using the `font-size` property and align them in the center of the box using the `text-align` property like so:

```
div.footer {
  margin:25px;
  width:400px;
  font-size:x-small;
  text-align:center;}
```

151

Right column

In the right column, which holds the ordering information, you are already off to a good start because you have the correct background color and the items are centered. The next thing you need to do is position the image that contains the order hotline telephone number. Therefore, give the `<img />` element an id attribute whose value is `orderHotline` and create the following rule in the style sheet to add some space above and below it:

```
img#orderHotline {
    margin-top:10px;
    margin-bottom:10px;}
```

Right under this image is a table containing information about how to order, and you do need to improve the presentation of this text. Here is the table to remind you (you have to add a couple of id attributes first to the `<table>` element and then to the `<td>` element containing the text so you can associate rules with these elements:

```
<table id="orderInfo">
    <tr>
        <td>
            <img src="images/interface/howToOrder.gif" width="153" height="21"
                alt="How to order" />
        </td>
    </tr>
    <tr>
        <td id="orderInstructions">
            1) Select an item from our extensive catalog.<br /><br />
            2) Send us the logo or text you want on the gifts.<br /><br />
            3) We email you an image of the item with your design.<br /><br />
            4) Confirm the order, and we'll deliver the goods within 21 days.<br />
        </td>
    </tr>
</table>
```

The table itself had a single-pixel border; to recreate this, you will use the same technique you have already seen in the navigation and featured items tables. Namely, you will make the background color for the table the color you want the border to be. Then, when the background color of the table cells is changed, this will make it look like there is a border around the table. You also have to set the width of the table and give it a margin so that it stays in the middle of the column:

```
table#orderInfo {
    background-color:#FF9900;
    width:130px;
    margin:2px;}
```

The table cell containing the instructions has a `background-color` property set to give the cell a white background and a `color` property to make the text the same color as it was in the HTML version. Next up is the `font-size` property used to make the text smaller than the default text and the `padding` property to prevent the text from touching the edge of the cells:

```
td#orderInstructions {
  background-color:#ffffff;
  color:#904C2D;
  font-size:small;
  padding:10px; }
```

That brings you to the end of the home page and the CSS rules you will be creating for it at the moment. You will extend upon this in the next chapter, but as you can see from Figure 3-41, you have come a long way in making the page look like it did in the original HTML version.

The product list pages

Using the same style sheet you created for the home page, you are already well on the way to making the XHTML product list pages look more like their HTML counterparts. After all, large portions of the page are identical. In order to use this style sheet, you just need to perform two tasks:

❑   Add a link to the style sheet.

❑   Give all the elements that the product list pages have in common with the home page the id and class attributes that were added in this chapter.

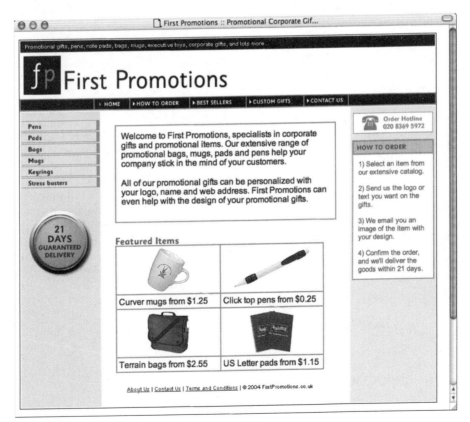

Figure 3-41

Once you have done these two tasks, the page should look more like the one shown in Figure 3-42.

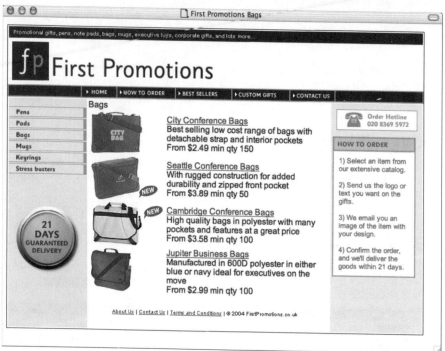

Figure 3-42

Looking at Figure 3-42, you can see that the only part of the page that needs work is the center column of the third table (which is the only part of the page that is different from the home page).

Looking at this column, if you simply add `class` attributes to the table that holds the details of the products and ensure that these `class` attributes match the `class` attributes on the featured items table that was in a similar position on the home page, your product list should be formatted for you:

```
<table class="productsTable">
   <tr>
     <td class="productImage">
       <a href="bag1.html"><img src="images/bags1_thumb.gif" alt="City bag" /></a>
     </td>
     <td class="productDescription">
       <a href="bag1.html">City Conference Bags</a><br />
         Best selling low cost range of bags with detachable strap and
         interior pockets<br />
         <strong>From $2.49 min qty 150</strong>
     </td>
   </tr>
   ...
</table>
```

Now you have to address only the title, which for this page is Bags. You will put the text inside an <h1>
element and then control its color and positioning using a CSS rule, like so:

```
h1 {
   margin-left:25px;
   margin-top:10px;
   margin-bottom:10px;
   color:#000066;}
```

You can see the result in Figure 3-43.

You still have to deal with the links, but you will come back to them in the next chapter.

The product details pages

The third and final page template is the product details page. As with the product list page, you can
make sure that the product details page has the link to the same style sheet and uses the class and id
attributes that the home page does (after all, much of the page is identical).

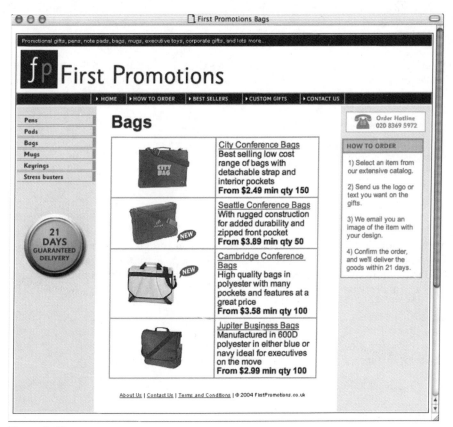

Figure 3-43

The first two tables and the navigation will already be styled using the same rules you met in the previous two pages. However, there is one key difference with this page: There is no right column in the third table, which means more space for the product details. It is just this one cell that you have to deal with now. You begin by giving the second table cell in this third table an id attribute whose value is productDetail:

```
<td id="productDetail">
```

You can associate a style with this table cell to indicate that it should have 20 pixels of padding, creating white space around the items:

```
td#productDetail {padding:20px;}
```

In this cell are two tables:

- ❏ The first holds the name of the product and a link to the product list for this type of product.
- ❏ The second holds the details of the product.

Both of these are going to be the same width, so you can add a class attribute with a value of productInfo to each of these <table> elements and then create the following CSS rule in the style sheet:

```
table.productInfo {width:550px;}
```

Taking a closer look at the first table (which contains the product title and a link to the product list page for this category), you begin by adding some id and class attributes. This enables you to associate styles with the elements. While you are at it, you can put the title for the product in an <h3> element:

```
<table class="productInfo">
  <tr>
    <td id="productTitle"><h3>Jupiter Business Bags</h3></td>
    <td id="productListLink">
      <a href="../products/bags/index.html">View All Bags</a>
    </td>
  </tr>
</table>
```

The rule for the product title sets the width of the table cell and gives it some white space using the padding property. The rule for the link to the product list page for this category sets the width of the table cell, adds white space using the padding property, and aligns the text to the right of the cell using the text-align property:

```
td#productTitle {width:225px; padding:10px;}
td#productListLink {width:225px; text-align:right; padding:10px;}
```

There is also a rule for the <h3> element, which sets the color of the text:

```
h3 {color:#000066;}
```

The second table, which contains the details of the product, contains four table cells (two rows and two columns).

- ❑ The top left cell holds an image of the product and has an `id` attribute whose value is `productInfoImage`.

- ❑ The top right cell holds a description of the product and has an `id` attribute whose value is `productInfoDescription`.

- ❑ The bottom left cell holds pricing details for the product and has an `id` attribute whose value is `productInfoPrice`.

- ❑ The bottom right cell holds printing information specific to the product, and gives information on lead times; it has an `id` attribute whose value is `productPrintInfo`.

Each of the cells is the same width, using the same size text and the same padding, so you can create one rule to set all of these properties (avoiding having to repeat the properties for each element):

```
td#productInfoImage, td#productInfoDescription, td#productInfoPrice,
td#productPrintInfo {
   width:215px;
   padding:10px;
   font-size:small;}
```

The image needs to be centered, so you add a special rule just for that cell:

```
td#productInfoImage {text-align:center;}
```

You also need to make the background colors of the top right and bottom left cells a light gray, so you use another rule that just selects these two cells:

```
td#productInfoDescription, td#productInfoPrice {background-color:#efefef;}
```

Inside the bottom left cell is another table, which holds the details for prices of the products. You have to set the width of this table, the font size, as well as different colors for the table headings compared to the other table cells:

```
table#priceTable{
   width:200px;
   font-size:small;}

table#priceTable  th {
   background-color:#000000;
   color:#ffffff;
   padding:2px;}

table#priceTable td {
   background-color:#eeeeee;
   padding:2px;}
```

With that, the product page is done; you can see the final result in Figure 3-44.

Of course, you can still do more to the presentation of these pages, which is exactly what we will be looking at in Chapter 4.

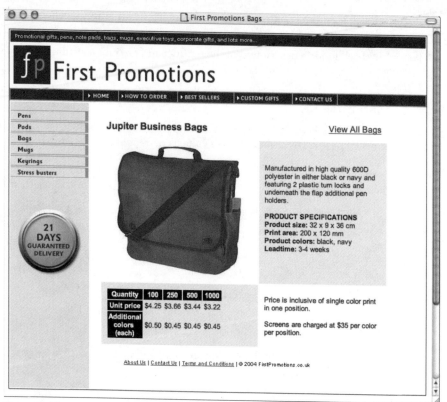

Figure 3-44

Summary

In this chapter, you have seen how CSS can be used to control stylistic aspects of pages using an external document called a style sheet. You have seen how its rendering model is based upon boxes, with a box being created for each element in your markup. The CSS style sheet then enables you to change the properties of these boxes.

You have already seen how properties can affect the following:

❑   Typeface, fonts, and text properties

❑   Borders, margins and padding of boxes

❑   Dimensions of boxes

❑   Colors and backgrounds

You have seen examples of each of these properties and have learned how they fit together to create style sheets for our sample site. In Chapter 4, you will continue to look at CSS style sheets, and explore some of their more advanced properties.

4

Adding More Style with CSS

In this chapter, you are going to continue to look at CSS and how it can be used to style XHTML documents. In Chapter 3, you learned how a CSS style sheet is made up of rules that apply to the content of one or more elements in your XHTML document and how each element is treated as a separate box by CSS. In addition, you also met many of the properties that can be used to control the presentation of documents. In this chapter, you will mainly focus on other properties that can be used to style your documents, and some of the more advanced features of CSS. As you will see in this chapter, some of these advanced properties are not yet fully supported by the major browsers, although they will provide some exciting new possibilities when they are widely available for use (and it is anticipated that these features will be supported in future releases).

In this chapter, you will learn about:

- ❑ Pseudo-classes that enable you to attach styles to specific parts of documents, even if no corresponding element is present
- ❑ Pseudo-elements that insert text into pages
- ❑ Properties that affect the presentation of links, tables, and lists
- ❑ Rules of precedence, including which rules take priority over others
- ❑ Modular style sheets and how to include rules from one style sheet in other style sheets
- ❑ Validating style sheets

By the end of the chapter, you will have learned many of the more advanced ways in which you can use CSS to control the presentation of a document.

Problem

Because stylistic markup has been removed from Strict XHTML, and because there are many good reasons to separate style from content, you will now want to use CSS to style your XHTML documents. As you already know, CSS is a powerful language that enables you to control the presentation of many aspects of a page, and you have made a good start toward learning how to use CSS properties to control the presentation of documents in Chapter 3.

In the example site, however, some parts of the pages still need improving. For example, you have not yet learned how to control the presentation of links. While HTML offered you the link, vlink, and alink attributes that you could use on the opening <body> tag to control the color of links, you have not yet seen the best ways of presenting them using CSS. You also need to learn how CSS enables you to control the presentation of lists and tables. Once you have written your CSS style sheets, it is also a good idea to validate your markup, so you need to learn how to validate CSS style sheets.

Therefore, to have full control over the appearance of pages without relying upon presentational markup, you need to look at and learn several more CSS properties.

Design

You have yet to learn about a wide range of CSS properties that will help you gain full control over the presentation of your XHTML documents, including properties that affect the presentation of links, lists, and tables. In addition to these properties, other features known as *pseudo-classes* and *pseudo-elements* enable you to control the presentation of parts of an element, and to display content that does not even exist in the source document.

Therefore, before you can continue with the design of the First Promotions site, you need to learn about more of the features of CSS. Once you have learned more about the ways you can control the presentation of your documents, you can finish styling the site and make use of the advanced features CSS has to offer.

Pseudo-classes and pseudo-elements

In Chapter 3, you saw how most CSS rules are applied to an element in the XHTML (or HTML) file. Pseudo-classes and pseudo-elements are designed to offer something different:

❑ **Pseudo-classes** create new classes of elements to which styles can be applied, but they do not use element names, attributes, or content to define the class.

❑ **Pseudo-elements** act as if they were creating new elements in the document where they do not exist.

Both of these features help you to achieve a number of tasks, some of which were available in HTML and some of which are completely new functionality.

Pseudo-classes

Pseudo-classes can affect how elements behave in different conditions. In this section, you will meet the following pseudo-classes:

Pseudo-class	Purpose
:first-child	Enables you to specify styles for just the first child element within a specified element
:link	Enables you to specify styles to be used with links in general
:visited	Enables you to specify styles to be used with links that have been visited
:hover	Enables you to specify styles to be used when an item is selected (for example, hovered over) but not activated (which would require the user to click on the element)
:active	Enables you to specify styles to be used when the item is activated by the user (for example, by clicking and releasing a mouse button)
:focus	Enables you to specify styles to be used when an element gains focus

:first-child pseudo-class

The :first-child pseudo-class enables you to create a separate set of styles for the first element that appears as a child of the element specified in the selector. For example, imagine you were writing an article, and that the body of the article resided within a <div> element. This article contains several <p> elements. If you wanted the first paragraph to look slightly different from the rest of the text (perhaps by putting it in a bold font), you could use the :first-child pseudo-class to create a rule that would apply only to the first child element of the <div> element.

In the following snippet of XHTML code, you can see the structure of an article (ch04_eg01.html):

```
<h1>Learning to Use Pseudo-Elements</h1>
<div class="ArticleBody">
   <p>Here is the first paragraph</p>
   <p>Here is the second paragraph</p>
   <p>Here is the third paragraph</p>
</div>
```

Now, look at the following CSS rule, which uses the :first-child pseudo-class. The pseudo-class is written in the selector after the part that indicates the element to which this rule applies (ch04_eg01.css):

```
div.ArticleBody p:first-child {font-weight:bold;}
```

This rule indicates that the first child of the <div> element that has a class attribute whose value is ArticleBody should be displayed in a bold font. Figure 4-1 shows you what this page would look like in Netscape 6+; unfortunately, it is not supported in Internet Explorer 6 (IE 6).

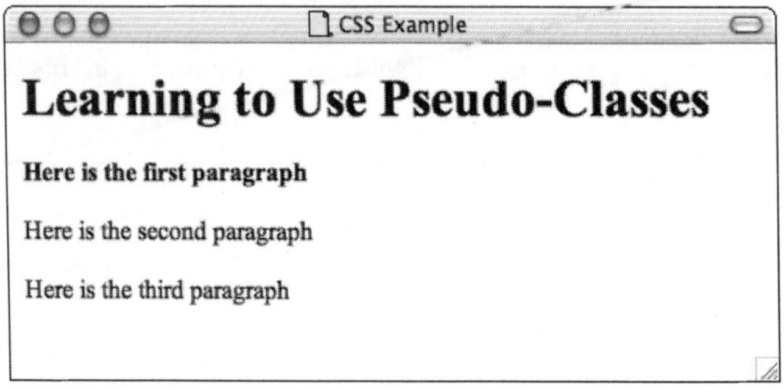

Figure 4-1

:link and :visited pseudo-classes

You probably have noticed many Web sites where links change color when you have visited them. In HTML, you could specify the colors in which links should appear before and after they have been visited using the `link` and `vlink` attributes on the `<body>` element. In CSS, these are replaced with the `:link` and `:visited` pseudo-classes:

❑ `:link` enables you to define styles to be used for links in general throughout the document.

❑ `:visited` enables you to define styles to be used for links that have already been visited.

Differentiating between the colors of links that have and have not been visited helps users navigate a site because they can see where they have been. The length of time that a link retains its visited state depends upon the browser, and after a while, links return to their unvisited state.

The main properties you are likely to want to use with these pseudo-classes are as follows:

❑ `color` changes the color of the links (using a slightly different color for links that have already been visited enables users to see at a glance where they have been).

❑ `text-decoration` controls whether the link is underlined or not. By default, most browsers will underline links, so you can use this property to prevent links from being underlined.

In the following example, normal links are a slightly darker shade of blue than those that have been visited, and this example also prevents the links from being underlined. Again, the pseudo-class appears in the selector directly after the element being selected (`ch04_eg2.css`):

```
a:link {
  color:#003399;
  text-decoration:none;}
a:visited {
  color:#006699;
  text-decoration:none;}
```

Figure 4-2 shows you a couple of links that use this style sheet in the browser. You can see from this figure that neither link is underlined, although it may be hard to tell the difference between the colors in print. In this screenshot, the second link has not yet been visited.

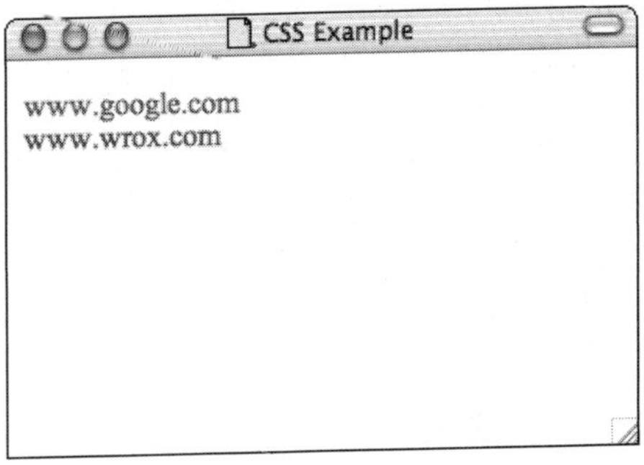

Figure 4-2

:hover pseudo-class

The :hover pseudo-class enables you to specify different styles for when a user hovers over a control, but has not clicked on it. The two properties most commonly used with the :hover pseudo-class are as follows:

❑ text-decoration is often used when links are not underlined in their normal state and is used to underline text links when the user hovers over them.

❑ background-color is occasionally used to highlight the link (in a manner similar to how a highlighter pen can be used). The color should be very similar to the background color to ensure that the text of the link is still easy to read.

The following rule could be added to the preceding example to highlight links when users run their mouse over the link and to underline the text (ch04_eg03.css):

```
a:hover {
    text-decoration:underline;
    background-color:#ccffff;}
```

You can see what a link would look like when the user is hovering over it in Figure 4-3.

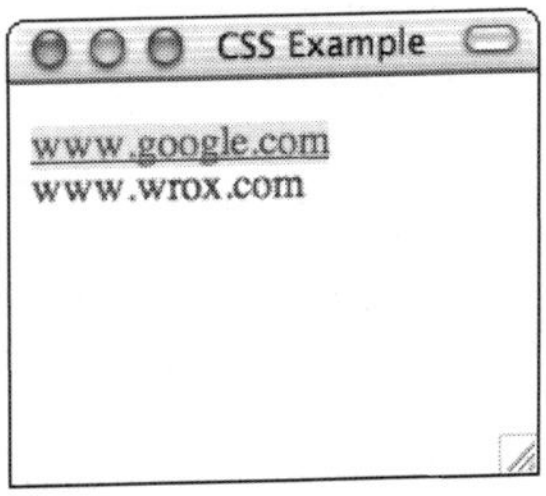

Figure 4-3

:active pseudo-class

The active pseudo-class enables you to associate styles with the content of a link when the user activates it — usually by pressing the mouse button and releasing it. This pseudo-class is not as common as others because users do not tend to hold onto the mouse button for a long period of time, and therefore its effects are harder to notice.

The following rule shows a change of colors for when the user clicks on the link (ch04_eg04.css):

```
a:active {color:#ff0000;}
```

You should be able to discern that the color of the link is different in the screenshot in Figure 4-4.

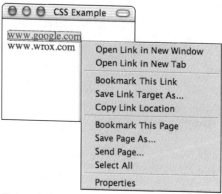

Figure 4-4

:focus pseudo-class

Any item that the user can interact with is capable of having *focus*, which means all links and all form controls are able to gain focus. You can navigate between the items on a Web page that can attain focus by pressing the Tab key on your keyboard; and each time you press the Tab key, you should be taken to the next item on the page that is capable of receiving focus (the last item to gain focus is often the address bar). If you look very carefully at the edge of links and form fields as they gain focus, you can usually see a faint line.

The :focus pseudo-class enables you to add styles to any element as it gains focus, and it is commonly used with form controls to highlight the current input. For example, you might have seen text inputs whose background or border colors change when you are entering data into that field.

The following XHTML code features a set of links and a form (ch04_eg05.html):

```
<a href="index.html">Home</a> | Login | <a href="help.html">Help</a><br /><br />
<form action="login.asp" method="post" name="frmLogin">
  Username <input type="text" size="15" name="txtUsername" /><br />
  Password <input type="password" size="15" name="pwdPassword" />
  <input type="submit" value="Log In" />
</form>
```

Now take a look at the following style sheet rule that is designed to highlight the form controls that have focus. When an input element gains focus, the background color will change, and a border will appear around the control (ch04_eg05.css):

```
input:focus {
  background-color:#ffffcc;
  border-width:3px;
  border-color:#ff0000;}
```

You can see what the active form control looks like in Figure 4-5.

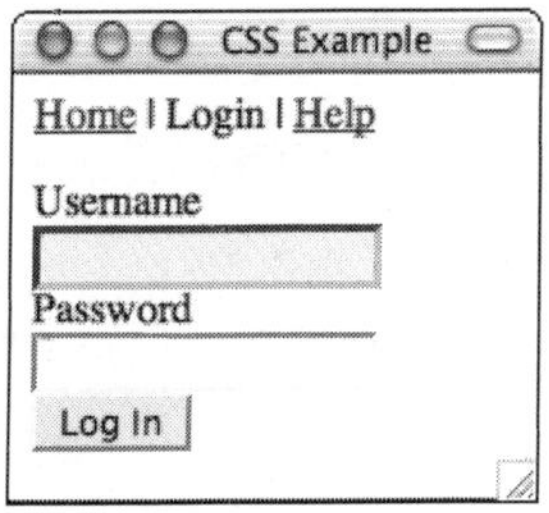

Figure 4-5

When you change the colors of active form elements, make sure that doing so does not affect the ease with which users can read the form; visitors need to be able to clearly see what they are entering.

Pseudo-elements

Pseudo-elements create the illusion of an element where it does not really exist in the source (XHTML or HTML) document. In this section, you are going to meet four pseudo-elements.

Pseudo-element	Purpose
:first-letter	Enables you to specify styles to be used with the first letter of an element specified in the selector
:first-line	Enables you to specify styles to be used with the first line of an element specified in the selector
:before	Enables you to insert content before the element(s) named in the selector
:after	Enables you to insert content after the element(s) named in the selector

Changing the first letter or line of an element

The first two pseudo-elements you will be looking at enable you to change the presentation of the first letter or first line of an element. They act as if they are creating a <span> element around the first letter or line of the element so that styles can be attached to that element.

:first-letter pseudo-element

The :first-letter pseudo-element enables you to create a different set of styles for the first letter of a selected element. For example, you might wan to make the first letter of a paragraph larger than all of the others. The following example shows how you can use the `:first-letter` pseudo-element to make the first letter of a `<p>` element larger than all of the other characters in the paragraph (`ch04_eg06.css`):

```
p{font-size:12px;}
p:first-letter{font-size:32px;}
```

You can see the result of this in Figure 4-6. The `:first-letter` pseudo-element works in IE 5.5+ and Netscape 6+.

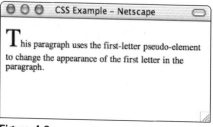

Figure 4-6

You might also want to change the typeface or color of this first letter or make it bold or italic.

:first-line pseudo-element

The `:first-line` pseudo-element enables you to create a different set of styles for the first line of a selected element. For example, you might want to make the first line of a normal paragraph bold. Even if the width of the pages varies, the first line of text displayed will use these properties.

In the following example, you can see how the `:first-line` pseudo-element can be used to make just the first line of a paragraph bold (`ch04_eg07.css`):

```
p{font-weight:normal;}
p:first-line{font-weight:bold;}
```

If you try this example in the browser, you can resize the window of your browser and the amount of text in bold will change so that only the first line of text will follow this style (see Figure 4-7). The `:first-line` pseudo-element works in IE 5.5+ and Netscape 6+.

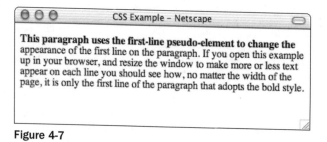

Figure 4-7

Generated content — adding content before or after an element

Sometimes you will want to include content in a document that did not actually appear in the source (XHTML or HTML) document. For example, you might want to include section numbers before paragraphs of a document or images before certain classes of element. This is referred to in CSS as *generated content*.

There are two ways to generate content in CSS:

❑ Using the content property, which you are about to meet, with the :before and :after pseudo-elements

❑ Giving the display property a value of list-item, as you will see later in the chapter

You will start by looking at the :before and :after pseudo elements.

:before pseudo-element

The :before pseudo-element enables you to add content to a document before the element specified in the selector. The content you want to add is specified using the content property. If you just want to add text to the document, you should specify the words in quotes as the value of this property. For example, if you wanted to add the words Quick Tip: before every <p> element whose class attribute had a value of QuickTip, you could use the following rule (ch04_eg08.css):

```
p.QuickTip:before {content: "Quick Tip: "}
```

You can see this result of this example in Figure 4-8 (in Netscape). Unfortunately, while the :before pseudo-element works in Netscape 6+, it is not yet supported in IE.

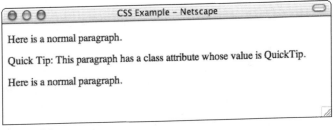

Figure 4-8

The content property can also take a number of other values, as you will see in a moment.

:after pseudo-element

The :after pseudo-element works just like the :before pseudo-element you just met, but it enables you to add content to a document after the element specified in the selector, rather than before it. The following example shows a rule that adds the text Postage and packaging included after a <span> element whose class attribute has a value of price (ch04_eg09.css):

```
p.price:after {content: " Postage and packaging included"}
```

You can see the result of this example in Figure 4-9, again in Netscape. The :after pseudo-element works in Netscape 6+, but it is not yet supported in IE.

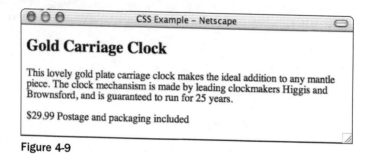

Figure 4-9

The content property

In addition to using a string as shown in the last two examples, the content property can also take a number of other values, as shown in the following table.

Remember that generated content is not added to the source XHTML or HTML document; it affects only what is displayed in the browsers that use this style sheet to display the document.

> *If you want to change the actual source of the document, you could use a different style sheet language called Extensible Stylesheet Language Transformations (XSLT).*

Type of Content	Purpose
a string	Text content that you want to appear in the document specified in quotes
a URI	A link to an external file that should be used. For example, the URI may point to an image that you want to include, although the processing application must support the type of file to which you are pointing.
a counter	These are used to automatically number the occurrences of an element in a document.
open-quote and close-quote	Opening and closing quotes are added to the representation of the document, using the appropriate string from the quotes property.
no-open-quote and no-close-quote	Using this, no quotes will appear, but it can help keep count of the indentation of quotes (whether they should be single or double).
attr(attributeName)	Adds the value of the attribute contained in the parentheses

You have already seen examples of a string being added using quotes. The following sections describe some of the other types of generated content you can include in your documents.

Generated content and URIs

You can insert an external file in the document before or after an element by providing a URI to the document's location. The browser will have to be able to support the MIME type of the file in order for it to be included, but this is an ideal mechanism for adding images before certain content.

The following example is a rule that adds an image of a pencil before any <p> element whose class attribute has a value of note (ch04_eg10.css):

```
p.note:before {content: url(images/pencil.gif);}
```

As you can see, the syntax for including the file is the same syntax you learned in Chapter 3 for working with background images. The URL is given in brackets following the keyword url. You can see the result of this example in Figure 4-10 (because this example uses the :before pseudo-element, it will work in Netscape 6+ but not IE).

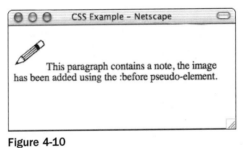

Figure 4-10

Generated content and counters

CSS2 introduced the capability to automatically number the occurrence of elements. This enables you not only to create numbered lists but also to number sections of documents, figures, or any occurrence of a specified element.

The capability to add counters is particularly powerful when creating numbered parts of a document because if you need to insert new sections or delete old ones, the style sheet will automatically renumber the remaining elements, saving you from manually updating all subsequent section numbers (which you would have to do if the numbers were hard-coded into the page).

Two functions enable you to add counters to your documents:

❑   counter(name, style), where name corresponds to a name used for the counter, and style is the way of indicating the style of counter you want (the default is decimal, and other options are shown in the table that follows). You do not have to specify a style.

❑   counters(name, style, string), where name corresponds to the name of the counter; style indicates the style of counter you want (the default is decimal, and other options are given in the table that follows); and string is used to separate counters when more than one are used. You do not have to specify a style. You will learn more about this type of counter a bit later.

The available styles for counters are the same as those for the `list-style-type` property that you will meet later in the chapter; the possible values that are widely supported are described in the following table:

Value	Description
disc	A solid-black, circular bullet point
circle	An empty circular bullet point
square	A square bullet point
decimal	Decimal numbers, beginning with 1
lower-roman	Lowercase roman numerals (i, ii, iii, iv, v)
upper-roman	Uppercase roman numerals (I, II, III, IV, V)

The following example should give you a better idea of how counters work. If you wanted to number each paragraph under a heading, with the numbering starting from 1 again after each <h1> element, you could use the following rule (c04_eg11.css):

```
p:before {content: counter(paragraphNumber, upper-roman) ": ";}
h1 {counter-reset: paragraphNumber;}
p {counter-increment: paragraphNumber;}
```

Let's take a closer look at this example. In the first line, you use the `:before` pseudo-element to add the counter before the <p> element:

```
p:before {content: counter(paragraphNumber, upper-roman) ": ";}
```

In this rule, you have the `content` property, whose value is the `counter()` function. The `counter()` function has two parameters—first up is the counter's name, which in this case is `paragraphNumber`; and this is followed by the type of numbering you want to use, in this example uppercase roman numerals.

The second line uses the special `counter-reset` property to indicate that the paragraph numbers should be reset every time you come across a new <h1> element. The value of this property is the counter that you want to reset when you come across the element specified in the selector:

```
h1 {counter-reset: paragraphNumber;}
```

The third line indicates when the counter should be incremented using the special `counter-increment` property. The value of this property is the name of the counter you want to increment, and the selector indicates when the counter should be incremented (every time an element specified by the selector is met, 1 will be added to the counter).

In this case, you can see that every time a new <p> element is encountered, the `paragraphNumber` counter should be incremented by 1.

Unfortunately, counters are not currently supported by either Netscape or IE, but Figure 4-11 shows what this looks like in a browser called Opera.

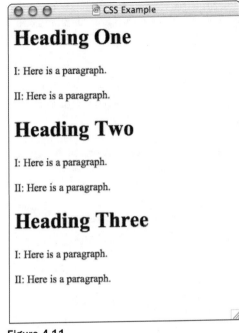

Figure 4-11

Generated content and nested counters

If you reuse a counter in a child element, it automatically creates a new instance of that counter; hence, the counters in CSS are referred to as *self-nesting*.

This is especially helpful in XHTML, where lists can be nested to arbitrary depths. For example, if you have nested ordered lists, they might follow a structure like this (ch04_eg12.html):

```
<ol>
  <li>List Item</li>
  <li>List Item
    <ol>
      <li>List Item</li>
      <li>List Item
        <ol>
          <li>List Item</li>
          <li>List Item</li>
        </ol>
      </li>
      <li>List Item</li>
    </ol>
  </li>
  <li>List Item</li>
</ol>
```

Self-nesting is based upon the principle that every element that has a `counter-reset` property for the named counter creates a new counter of the same name, and its scope is for only that element and its descendents or siblings.

Therefore, the following rule indicates that the `counter-reset` property should be called each time the `<ol>` element is encountered (ch04_eg12.css):

```
ol {counter-reset: Item;}
```

The next rule indicates that before each `<li>` element, the counter called `Item` should be added to the view of the document, and the counter should be incremented. Where the `content` property has double quotes at the end with a space between them, this adds a space between the counter and the content of the element:

```
li:before {
    content:counter(Item) " ";
    counter-increment(Item);}
```

You can see the result in Opera in Figure 4-12.

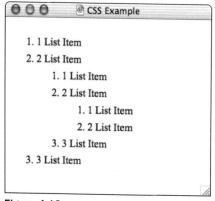

Figure 4-12

If the `counters()` function were used, then the values of all counters would be added, separated by the given string. For this to work, you need to indicate that each `<li>` element should be displayed as a block-level element, as shown in the following example:

```
li:before {
    content:counters(listItem) " ";
    counter-increment(listItem);}
li {display:block;}
```

You can see the result in Opera in Figure 4-13.

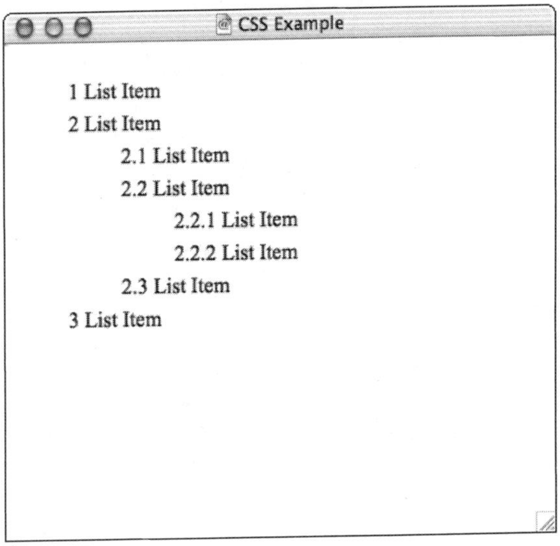

Figure 4-13

Generated content and quotes

You can use the `open-quote` and `close-quote` values with the `content` property to automatically insert quotation marks in a document. The following rules insert opening quotes before each <q> element, insert closing quotes after every <q> element (`ch04_eg14.css`), and indicate the type of quotation marks that should be used:

```
q:before {content:open-quote;}
q:after  {content:close-quote;}
q {quotes:'"' '"';}
```

In the last line of this example, you can see the `quotes` property; which enables you to specify which quotes should be used. You can even specify different types of quotes for different depths of quotations when you have nested quotations. CSS will automatically use the correct type of quote based upon the level of nesting. It even enables you to use different types of quotations for different languages.

The first pair of quotes in the value represent the outermost level of quotation, while the second pair are for use with the first level of embedding, and so on. The following two rules set the quotes for <q> elements depending upon the language of the document:

```
q:lang(en) {quotes: '"' '"' '"' '"';}
q:lang(no) {quotes: '<<' '>>' '"' '"';}
```

Quotes work in Netscape 6+, but not in IE. You can see an example of nested quotes in Figure 4-14.

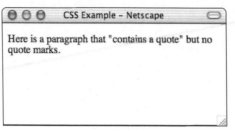

Figure 4-14

Generated content and attribute values

You can use the `attr()` function to display the value of an attribute in the browser before or after the element that carries it. The name of the attribute whose value you want to display in the document should be given in parentheses. For example, take a look at the following XHTML:

```
<p class="Note">Here is a note.</p>
<p class="Reference">Here is a reference.</p>
<p class="Explanation">Here is an explanation.</p>
```

If you wanted to display the value of the `class` attribute before each `<p>` element, and follow it with a colon and a space, you could use the following rule (`ch04_eg15.css`):

```
p:before {content:attr(class) ": ";}
```

This will work in Netscape 6+, but unfortunately it is not yet supported in IE. You can see the result in Figure 4-15.

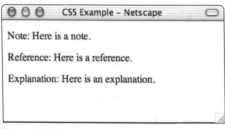

Figure 4-15

Because XHTML is case-sensitive, you should ensure that you use the correct case for the attribute whose value you want to print to the document. If there is no attribute of that name, a blank string will be returned.

Generated content and line breaks

If you want to insert a line break in a string of generated content, you can use the escape sequence `\A`. For example, imagine you wanted to add the following text, with line breaks:

```
Styled using the interface.css style sheet
Created by John Doe
Last updated 18/10/2004
```

If you wanted to add this after a `<p>` element whose `class` attribute had a value of `footer`, you would use the following rule:

```
p.footer:after {"Styled using the interface.css style sheet \A Created by John
Doe\A Last updated 18/10/2004"}
```

Unfortunately, browser support for the line break is poor. It does not work in IE or Netscape 7, and Opera inserts only a line-break character, as shown in Figure 4-16.

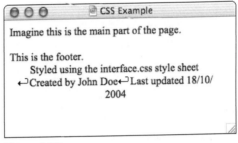

Figure 4-16

Generated content and marker-offsets

When you use the `:before` or `:after` pseudo-elements, you can specify that the generated content should appear in its own box, known as a *marker box*, while the content of the element remains in what is referred to as a *principle box*. You specify that the generated content should have its own box by using the `display` property and giving it a value of `marker`. Once you have done this, you can then specify the distance from which the marker box is offset from the principle box, thereby enabling you to control the space between the generated content and the element content.

The following example adds a counter before the item, and the counter is given a marker-offset of 6em, so the counter should have a larger offset from the principle box than it would by default (`ch04_eg16.css`):

```
li:before {
   display: marker;
   marker-offset: 10em;
   content: counter(item, lower-roman) ".";
   counter-increment: item; }
```

Unfortunately, however, the `marker-offset` property is not supported in Netscape 7 or IE 6.

Lists

Several properties enable you to control the presentation of lists. Some of these offer new capabilities, while others replace attributes that were deprecated from list elements in HTML 4.

list-style-type

HTML 4 enabled you to use the `type` attribute with numbered lists to indicate the type of numbering you wanted to use; you could choose between Arabic numerals (1, 2, 3), capital or lowercase letters, or large and small roman numerals.

The effects of the deprecated `type` attribute can be achieved using the `list-style-type` attribute in CSS. The following table describes some of the more popular values the `list-style-type` property can take. The first three values in this table are for use with an unordered list, while the second three create different types of numbered lists (these are the same values as those you met earlier in this chapter in the section "Generated Content and Counters").

Value	Description
disc	A solid-black, circular bullet point
circle	An empty circular bullet point
square	A square bullet point
decimal	Decimal numbers, beginning with 1
lower-roman	Lowercase roman numerals (i, ii, iii, iv, v)
upper-roman	Uppercase roman numerals (I, II, III, IV, V)

The following rule indicates that an unordered list should use hollow bullets (`ch04_eg17.css`):

```
ul {list-style-type: circle;}
```

Similarly, the following rule indicates that an ordered list should use small roman numerals:

```
ol {list-style-type: lower-roman;}
```

While the selectors in this example specify the `<ul>` and `<ol>` elements, rather than the `<li>` elements, you could use the `<li>` element in the selector. You can see the result in Figure 4-17.

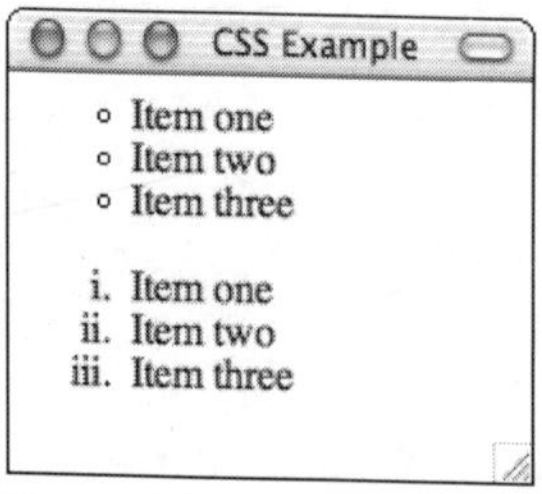

Figure 4-17

list-style-image

The `list-style-image` property enables you to use an image for a bullet point. This is perfect if you want to use a type of bullet that is not supported by CSS — for example, if you wanted to use a miniature version of your company logo as a bullet point. The following example uses the Wrox triangle as a mini-bullet (ch04_eg18.css):

```
ul { list-style-image: url("images/wroxBullet.gif")}
```

The images are specified using the same syntax that you saw when specifying background images in Chapter 3. The value given must be the letters url, followed by the URL to the image given in quotes within brackets.

You can see an example of the list image in Figure 4-18.

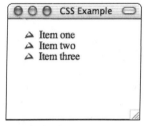

Figure 4-18

list-style-position

The list-style-position property specifies where the marker appears within the box that is created for a list item. It can take one of the following two values:

Value	Purpose
outside	The marker appears outside the box (to the left of the text).
inside	The marker appears within the first line of the text, and subsequent lines of text flow underneath the marker.

To get a good idea of how this works, take a look at the following example. Here are the style rules for two classes of unordered lists (ch04_eg19.css):

```
ul.inside { list-style-position:inside;}
ul.outside {list-style-position:outside;}
ul {width:170px;}
```

You can see the difference between the two positions in Figure 4-19. Note how the second line of text in the first set of bullet points wraps underneath the actual bullet point; however, in the second set of bullets, the marker is set to the left of the text.

list-style

list-style is a shorthand property that enables you to specify values for the following properties in one property. When given, they must be presented in the following order:

```
list-style-type   list-style-position   list-style-image
```

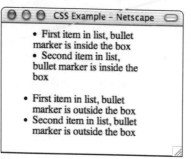

Figure 4-19

This shorthand property can also take the value `inherit` to indicate that the value given must inherit properties of the containing elements, which is particularly useful with nested lists.

To demonstrate this shorthand, the following rule indicates that the list should use uppercase roman numerals, and that the marker should be within the box created for the list item, which means that any text wrapping onto more than one line will continue underneath the bullet marker (`ch04_eg20.css`):

```
li { list-style: lower-roman inside }
```

You can see the result in Figure 4-20.

```
○ ○ ○                    ☐ CSS Example                         ○
     i.  Item one using the shorthand list-style property to control
     the list-type and list-position properties
     ii. Item two using the shorthand list-style property to control
     the list-type and list-position properties
     iii. Item three using the shorthand list-style property to
     control the list-type and list-position properties
```

Figure 4-20

Table properties

This section describes five CSS properties that affect the presentation of tables. You will first learn how to deal with borders that meet each other, including borders of cells that have no content. Then you will learn how to position a caption on a table.

border-collapse

You have two ways to set borders for table cells:

❑ **Separated borders model** — A gap is preserved between the borders of each table cell.

❑ **Collapsed borders model** — Adjacent table cells have their borders collapsed into each other.

The `border-collapse` property indicates which of these methods should be used, and therefore whether borders should be collapsed into each other. The possible values for this property are as follows:

Value	Description
collapse	The collapsed borders model should be used to render tables.
separate	The separated borders model should be used to render tables.
inherit	The table should use the same border model as the parent element.

You will see the effects of this property and the two different models over the next three sections.

border-spacing

In the separated borders model, each cell has its own border, and the `border-spacing` property can be used to specify the distance between the borders of adjacent cells. (The space between the cells will be filled by the background of the table.)

If one value is given for the `border-spacing` property, it specifies both horizontal and vertical distance between table cells, whereas if two values are given, then the first indicates the horizontal spacing value and the second is the vertical spacing value.

The following rule sets a gap of 20 pixels between each table cell (`ch04_eg21.css`):

```
table {
   border-collapse: separate;
   border-spacing: 20px;}

td {border:1px solid black;}
```

You can see how this looks in Figure 4-21.

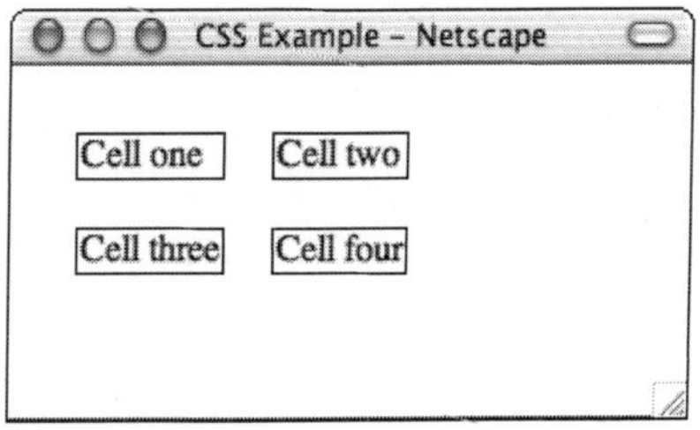

Figure 4-21

Collapsed borders model

In the collapsed borders model of table layouts, some rules govern how the borders of adjacent table cells should be displayed.

Even when you use the collapsed borders model, you can specify different borders for each of the sides of a cell, row, row group, column, or column group. Borders are centered on the lines between cells.

The rules of which borders are shown when two cells adjoin are quite complex. The general rule of thumb is that the most "eye-catching" border style will be chosen:

❑ Any border with a border-style attribute of hidden takes precedence over all other borders.

❑ Borders with a value of none have lowest priority, and all adjacent borders have to be none for the style to be used.

❑ If no border is hidden, and at least one does not have a value of none, the widest border will be used. If the adjacent borders have the same style, the preferred order is double, solid, dashed, dotted, ridge, outset, groove, and finally lowest.

❑ If border styles only differ in color, a style for a cell takes priority over a row, which takes priority over a row group, column, column group, and then table.

The display property (which you will learn more about later in the chapter) can be given a value of collapse. If used with any elements other than the table, row, row-group, column, or column group elements, it is treated as if it means hidden.

empty-cells

If a table cell is supposed to have borders, but it actually has no content, then the empty-cells property can be used to determine whether the borders of the cells are shown. The empty-cells property can take three values:

Value	Description
show	Borders are drawn around any cell that is empty.
hide	Borders are not drawn around empty cells, and if a whole row has empty cells, the whole row is hidden.
inherit	Inherits from parent elements

In the following example, the empty cells in the first table are shown, while the empty cells in the second table are hidden (ch04_eg22.css):

```
table.show {empty-cells:show;}
table.hide {empty-cells:hide;}
td {border-style:solid; border-width:1px; width:30px;}
```

You can see the result in Figure 4-22.

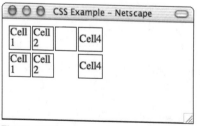

Figure 4-22

caption-side

Although few people use it, the opening `<table>` tag can be immediately followed by a `<caption>` element. The `<caption>` is intended to provide a caption to describe the content of the table. The purpose of the `caption-side` property is to indicate the side of the table on which a caption should appear, and it can take the following properties:

Value	Description
top	The caption is at the top of the table.
bottom	The caption is at the bottom of the table.
left	The caption is to the left of the table.
right	The caption is to the right of the table.

Unfortunately, Netscape 6+ is the only browser to support this property (version 6 supports only the values `top` and `bottom`, while version 7 supports all four values).

The box created by the `<caption>` element inherits the same box properties as the `<table>` element, and the `text-align` and `vertical-align` properties can be used to control the position of the text within the caption box.

By default, the caption appears at the top of the table; however, the following rule places the caption at the bottom (`ch04_eg23.css`):

```
caption {
    caption-side: bottom;
    text-align: right;
    vertical-align: top;}
```

You can see this in Netscape in Figure 4-23. 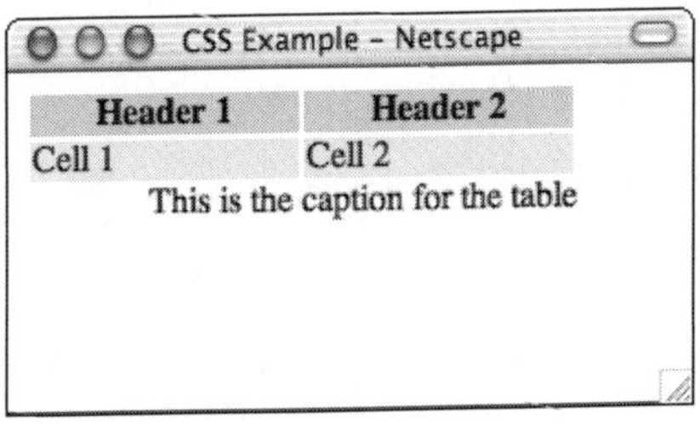

Figure 4-23

table-layout

Tables can be slow to load, especially if they contain a lot of data. Therefore, the `table-layout` property enables you to indicate to a browser how it should render the table. It can have two values, `fixed` or `auto`, both of which require a little explanation:

❑ The **fixed** table layout is the faster of the two algorithms. The horizontal layout of the table does not depend on the content of all the cells; it depends only on the table and column width and the borders and spacing between cells.

The table starts to render after the first row has been received; it does not wait for the entire content of the table. If the width property of any column has been set, that will determine the width of the column. Other columns will then share the remaining width equally. If the width for the `<table>` element is wider than the sum of the columns, the extra space will be divided equally between the columns.

❑ With the **automatic** table layout, the width of the table is governed by the width of its columns (and their borders). This requires the whole table to load before rendering can commence, and is the primary method used by most browsers.

The minimum width of each cell is calculated. The content may run across several lines, but may not overflow the cell box. If a width property has been specified for a column and it is greater than the minimum width of the cell, this will be used. The maximum width of the cell is also calculated, making each cell as wide as possible — with the content breaking, except for places marked with explicit line breaks.

From the minimum and maximum cell widths, the minimum and maximum widths of the column are calculated — the minimum being the cell with the largest minimum cell width, and the maximum being the largest maximum cell width.

If a cell in the column has a width property, then that is used if it is larger than the minimum width for the column (otherwise, the minimum width for the column is used).

If the table has a width property, and this is larger than the sum of the minimum width properties for each column, this value will be used for the width of the table, and the extra width is shared between all columns. Otherwise, the width of the table will be the sum of the minimum column widths.

If the table does not have a width property, then the maximum width available in the containing box will be used, unless this is more than the total of the maximum widths for the columns.

Visibility of elements

Two properties can affect the visibility of element content:

❑ visibility will hide a property from view, but the element will still take up space in the layout.

❑ display will have the effect of the element never having appeared in the first place.

Remember that the content of the elements will still be visible in the source code. They are just not displayed on screen; therefore, you should not use these properties to hide sensitive information such as passwords.

The visibility property

The visibility property indicates whether the boxes created by an element are shown to the user. Even if a box is invisible, it will still take up the necessary space; it just won't be seen by the user. (Giving the display property — which you meet next — a value of none prevents the box from being created at all.)

The possible values are as follows:

Value	Meaning
visible	The box is visible.
hidden	The box is invisible, or transparent, although the box still affects the layout of the page. Child elements will be visible only if they specifically have their visibility property set with a value of visible.
collapse	This has special meaning for use with tables (as explained at the end of this section).

The following example shows three paragraphs, the middle of which will be invisible (ch04_eg24.html):

```
<p>You can see this paragraph.</p>
<p class="invisible">You cannot see this paragraph.</p>
<p>You can see this paragraph.</p>
```

The following rule prevents the middle paragraph from being shown to the user (ch04_eg24.css):

```
p.invisible {visibility:hidden;}
```

As you can see from Figure 4-24, the middle paragraph still occupies space in the browser window even though you cannot see it.

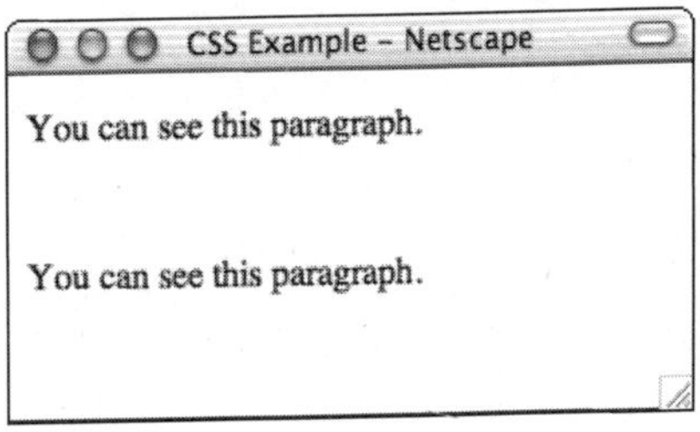

Figure 4-24

This property can be used in conjunction with scripts to create dynamic effects, although it is important to remember that if the user's browser does not support JavaScript, the effect will not work.

Any row, row group, column, or column group element can use the visibility property with a special value of collapse. This value will prevent the entire row or column from being displayed, and the space normally occupied by that row or column will be available to other content (the space will not be preserved as it is when the visibility property is given a value of hidden). This can help create dynamic effects that remove table rows or columns. If a column or row spans cells, the content will be clipped to reflect the width of the visible columns or rows.

display property

The display property enables you to change the way in which a box is displayed. For example, you can force an inline element to become a block-level element and vice-versa. The possible values the display property can take are as follows:

Value	Description
block	Each element creates a block-level box.
inline	Each element creates an inline box.
list-item	Each element creates a principal box like those created by an <li> element.
none	The box is not generated, and therefore the element has no effect on the layout of the rest of the page — it is like it does not exist.

*There are two other possible values (**run-in** and **inline-block**), although these are for use with languages other than XHTML, in which the browser does not already know how the element should be formatted.*

Using a similar example to the one just presented for the visibility property, in the following example the middle of three paragraphs will not be displayed (ch04_eg25.html):

```
<p>You can see this paragraph.</p>
<p class="notDisplayed">You cannot see this paragraph.</p>
<p>You can see this paragraph.</p>
```

The following rule prevents the middle paragraph from being shown or affecting the layout (ch04_eg25.css):

```
p.notDisplayed {display:none;}
```

As you can see from Figure 4-25, the middle paragraph does not take up any space in the browser window and you cannot see it.

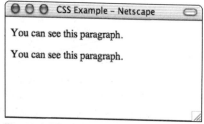

Figure 4-25

Usually, `<code>` elements are treated as inline elements. The following paragraph contains two `<code>` elements (ch04_eg26.html):

```
<p>You can write content to a page using the <code>write()</code> function. You can
force it to be written when the document loads using the <code>onload</code>
event.</p>
```

Here is the CSS rule that will force these inline elements to be displayed as a block-level element (ch04_eg26.css):

```
code {display:block;}
```

You can see the result in Figure 4-26.

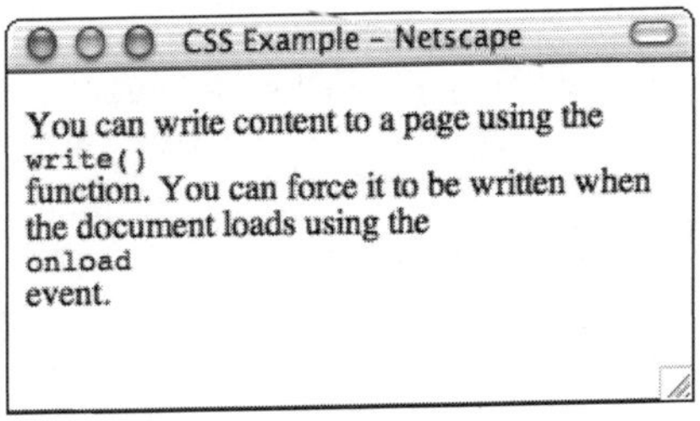

Figure 4-26

Multiple style sheets and @import

If you are working on large sites, you may well have different styles for different sections of the site, or you might have common styles that you want to use across several sites. CSS enables you to create modular sets of style sheets and import rules from one style sheet into another.

To import a style sheet into another CSS document, you use the `@import` rule. It must appear before any rules in the style sheet, and you can use either of the following syntax options:

```
@import "codeStyles.css";
```

or

```
@import url("codeStyles.css");
```

Note also that you must include the semicolon after this rule; otherwise, the style sheet will not be imported.

You can also specify the resource for which the style sheet is intended, in order to prevent browsers from retrieving resources that are not intended. The following example shows a style sheet called `lowRes.css` designed for use with TV sets:

```
@import url("lowRes.css") tv;
```

The capability to import rules from one style sheet into another means that you can create modularized style sheets and reuse common rules in several style sheets, rather than having to repeat them. For example, I often use code styles in documents, such as these:

```
code {font-family:courier;}
code.foreground {
   display:block;
   font-size:smaller;
   background-color:#d6d6d6;
   padding:2px;
   margin:5px;}
code.background {
   display:block;
   padding:2px;
   margin:5px; }
```

I keep styles such as these in a CSS document called `codeStyles.css` and can import them whenever I am creating a page that uses code. For example, if I am writing an article, I might have a style sheet that contains the rules for displaying the article, but I import the code styles rather than repeat them in each document I write. For example, here is a style sheet called `article.css` that uses these rules:

```
@import "codeStyles.css"

body {
   font-family:arial, verdana, sans-serif;
   background-color:#ffffff;}

p.abstract {font-weight:bold;}

div.figure {
   font-weight:bold;
   padding-bottom:12px;
   padding-left:12px;}
```

Similarly, if you are working on a site that uses different styles for different sections of the site, you can use the main styles for the site in an include file and use it in any of the section style sheets. For example, the main styles for the site might be in a file called `mainStyles.css`, while each section has its own rules.

Here is some sample XHTML that uses the `article.css` style sheet, which in turn imports the `codeStyles.css` style sheet (`ch04_eg27.html`):

```
<h1>Modularized Style Sheets</h1>
<p class="abstract">You can use the <code>@import</code> rule to help develop
   modular style sheets that enable re-use and save bandwidth.</p>
<p>In order to include rules from a different style sheet, you have to
   import the whole other style sheet into the one you are writing. Therefore
   smaller style sheets make for more reusable chunks.</p>
<p>The following line imports a style sheet called codeStyles.css</p>
<div><code class="foreground">@import "codeStyles.css"</code></div>
```

You can see the result in Figure 4-27.

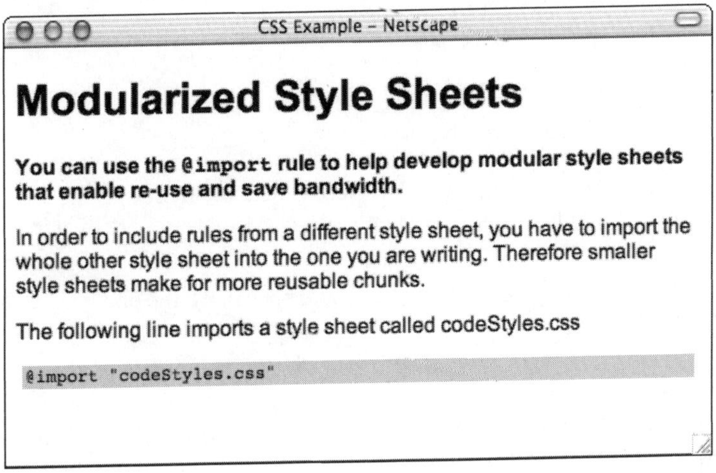

Modularized Style Sheets

You can use the @import rule to help develop modular style sheets that enable re-use and save bandwidth.

In order to include rules from a different style sheet, you have to import the whole other style sheet into the one you are writing. Therefore smaller style sheets make for more reusable chunks.

The following line imports a style sheet called codeStyles.css

```
@import "codeStyles.css"
```

Figure 4-27

Precedence of rules

Style sheets can come from any of the following three sources:

❑ The Web page author, who specifies the style sheet for a source document as you have been doing in this book; these are often referred to as *author style sheets*.

❑ The user, who may specify preferred default styles for themselves; these are often referred to as *user style sheets*.

❑ The user agent, which must display the content of a file as you would expect for that language (for example, all XHTML heading, paragraph, emphasis, and list elements should be formatted as intended, although not all XML languages can be expected to be supported visually to the same level); these are often referred to as *user agent style sheets*.

Indeed, within any of these sources, you might find that more than one selector applies to any given element. Therefore, it is important to understand how a browser will decide which rule should take priority over the other rules. Browsers should adhere to the following guidelines:

❑ All declarations that apply to the element and property in question must be found for that target media type (for example screen, projector, tv). Declarations are applied if the associated selector matches the element.

❑ The rules are sorted by order of importance. All author and user rules take precedence over the browser's default style sheet (which is used when no style rules are applied for a particular element), and the author's style sheets take precedence over other rules in user style sheets, unless an !important rule has been used (as you will see in the next section). Therefore, the following list shows the order of precedence of style rules:

5. User agent style sheets

4. User normal style sheets

3. Author normal style sheets

2. Author important style sheets

1. User important style sheets

❑ The rules are sorted by specificity of a selector, with the more specific selectors overriding the more general ones (any pseudo-elements and pseudo-classes are treated as normal elements and classes).

❑ If two rules have the same weight, origin, and specificity, the one added last in the style sheet will be applied.

!important rules

By default, rules created by a document author in his or her suggested style sheet take precedence over rules in a user's style sheet. However, the use of an !important rule allows users to override the authors settings. This is particularly helpful when users have vision impairments and need to be able to make the text of a site larger or control the color combinations.

For example, if the author's style sheet contained the following rule:

```
body {background-color:#d6d6d6;}
```

and the user's style sheet had this rule:

```
body {background-color:#ffffff !important;}
```

the user's style sheet would take precedence.

Validating CSS

Just as there are tools to validate XHTML documents, you also have tools available that help you validate your CSS documents, and it is good practice to run any style sheet through a validator before you use it on your site in order to help ensure that you have followed the correct syntax and used permitted values for the properties. The W3C offer a free CSS validation service on their Web site at http://jig saw.w3.org/css-validator/.

The W3C validator enables you to check your CSS documents in one of three ways:

❑ By entering a URL to the CSS document

❑ By uploading a CSS file from your local computer

❑ By entering the style rules into a `<textarea>` form field

The validator not only provides error notices if your code does not follow the syntax of CSS or does not use an allowed value for any property, it also provides warning notices if you do not follow some suggested practices. In Figure 4-28, for example, the W3C CSS validator indicates that you should be using a generic font name as a last alternative when a font-family property is specified; this is under the heading Warnings because it is not a requirement, just a recommendation.

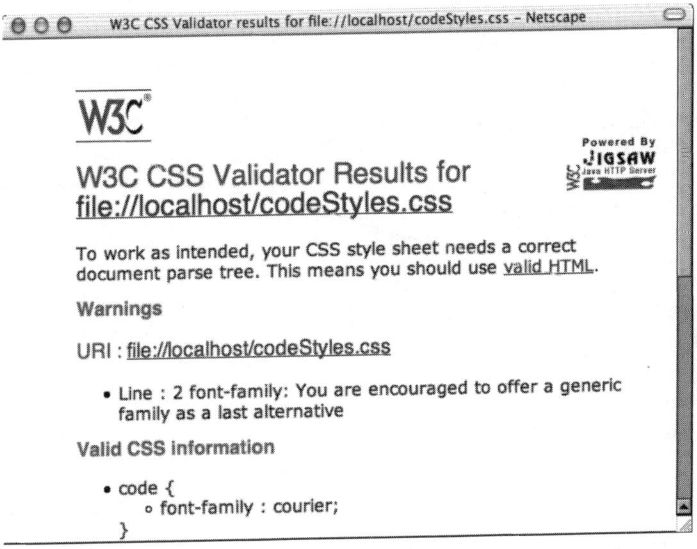

Figure 4-28

Solution

Now that you have learned several of the more advanced features of CSS, you can return to the sample site and look at how you can improve it using the new techniques you learned in this chapter.

Improving the look of links

Because all of the pages of this site use the same style sheet, you do not need to look at links on every page. The product list page contains the most links, so you can just look at how to improve the look of the links on that page, and the rest of the pages will adopt the same styles.

In the HTML version of the site, the opening <body> tag carried the following attributes for controlling the appearance of links:

```
<body alink="#0000CC" vlink="#003366" link="#0066CC"
```

Of course, these are stylistic attributes, and you can no longer use them in strict XHTML. However, you learned at the beginning of the chapter that several pseudo-classes help you control the presentation of links. The following table summarizes which pseudo-class helps with each task related to links:

Type of Link	Pseudo-class	HTML Equivalent
Unvisited links	a:link	link
Visited links	a:visited	vlink
User hovering over link	a:hover	n/a
User clicking on link	a:active	alink

You can add three corresponding pseudo-classes to the style sheet, plus a new one for situations in which users are hovering over the link. First you have the link pseudo-class for unvisited links, which corresponds to the old link attribute in HTML. You want to change the color of the links to #0066CC. You can also use the trick of using the text-decoration property to prevent links from being underlined, which you also met in this chapter:

```
a:link {
    color:#0066cc;
    text-decoration:none;}
```

Next, you have to change the color of visited links; this pseudo-class corresponds with the vlink attribute in HTML:

```
a:visited {color:#003366;}
```

There was no HTML equivalent for the pseudo-class that enables you to change the styles when a user hovers over a link, but you should add one in the style sheet here. You should also make sure that the link is underlined when the user hovers over it to reinforce the fact that it is a link:

```
a:hover {
    color:#9966CC;
    text-decoration:underline;}
```

Finally, you come to the pseudo-class that controls how a link should appear when it is clicked, which corresponds with the alink attribute in HTML:

```
a:active {color:#0000cc;}
```

Having added these four pseudo-classes to the style sheet, you have finished the transformation of the HTML version to the XHTML and CSS version of the site. You can see the new links in Figure 4-29.

Product pages table borders

On the product details pages in the original version of the site, the tables that held details about the individual products did not have a border between each of the cells. It would be nice to be able to add a single-pixel line between each cell in a table (between the image of the product, the details about it, its price, and related printing information).

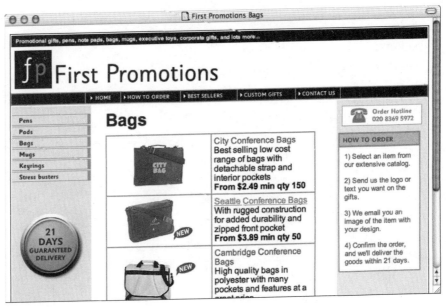

Figure 4-29

You already know how to create a single-pixel line between each table cell by setting the `background-color` property of a table and then leaving a single-pixel space between the cells. However, having learned some of the more advanced features of CSS used to deal with tables in this chapter, you can also now use the `border` property on the table cells to draw the borders between each cell, and use the `border-collapse` property to ensure that adjacent cells do not take up twice the width of outer cells.

The only changes you need to make to the style sheet are as follows. First, you need to add the `border-collapse` property to the tables whose `class` attribute have a value of `productInfo`. Then, you need to add a rule to indicate that all of the cells on these tables have a single-pixel black border:

```
table.productInfo {
    width:550px;
    border-collapse:collapse;}
```

```
table.productInfo td {border: solid 1px black;}
```

You can see the result in Figure 4-30.

However, these changes introduce a couple of problems:

❑ Two tables share the same class: The table holding the title of the product and the link back to the product list and the table holding the details of the product share the same value for the `class` attribute. Therefore, the top of the two tables (holding the title and product list link) has lines where they are not necessary. There is also no gap between the two tables, so the second of these tables should really have a different class name.

❑ The pricing details have inherited the table borders in the bottom left cell, which you do not want.

191

Figure 4-30

Here is the XHTML to remind you. The first of these two tables needs to have a different value for the class attribute than the second one, and the table whose class attribute has a value of priceTable needs to have no border for each cell:

```
<table class="productInfo">
  <tr>
    <td id="productTitle"><h3>Jupiter Business Bags</h3></td>
    <td id="productListLink">
      <a href="/FirstPromotions/products/bags/index.html">View All Bags</a>
    </td>
  </tr>
</table>

<div>
  <table class="productInfo">
    <tr>
      <td id="productInfoImage"><img src="images/bags4.jpg" alt="Jupiter Bag" />
      </td>
      <td id="productInfoDescription">
        <p>Manufactured in high quality 600D polyester in either black or navy
            and featuring 2 plastic turn locks and underneath the flap additional
            pen holders.</p>
```

```
            <b>PRODUCT SPECIFICATIONS</b><br />
            <b>Product size:</b> 32 x 9 x 36 cm<br />
            <b>Print area:</b> 200 x 120 mm<br />
            <b>Product colors:</b> black, navy<br />
            <b>Leadtime:</b> 3-4 weeks <br /><br />
        </td>
    </tr>
    <tr>
        <td id="productInfoPrice">
            <table id="priceTable">
              <tr>
                <th>Quantity</th>
                <th>100</th><th>250</th><th>500</th><th>1000</th>
              </tr>
              <tr>
                <th>Unit price</th>
                <td>$4.25</td><td>$3.66</td><td>$3.44</td><td>$3.22</td>
              </tr>
              <tr>
                <th>Additional colors (each)</th>
                <td>$0.50</td><td>$0.45</td><td>$0.45</td><td>$0.45</td>
              </tr>
            </table>
        </td>
        <td id="productPrintInfo"><p>Price is inclusive of single color print
            in one position.</p>
            <p>Screens are charged at $35 per color per position.</p>
        </td>
    </tr>
  </table>
```

To correct these problems, you first need to give the top table a different value for its `class` attribute; here I have changed it to `productTitle`:

```
<table class="productTitle">
```

Then you need to make sure that this table has a style that will match with the element:

```
table.productTitle {border: solid 1px black;}
```

Next, you need to clear the border on the cells in the table whose `class` attribute has a value of `priceTable`, like so:

```
table#priceTable {border:none;}
```

This should solve the problems, and the page should now look like the one shown in Figure 4-31. Unfortunately, the `border-collapse` property does not work as it should in IE, but this highlights the problems you face when working with some of the more advanced features of CSS — fewer browsers support them at the current time (although it is hoped that this will improve with subsequent versions).

Figure 4-31

Summary

In this chapter, you learned a lot more about how to use CSS to control the presentation of your documents. Not only can you control what is actually in the document, you can also add new content into the representation of your document using pseudo-elements, and you can control the presentation of links and the first child element of a container with pseudo-classes. You also learned some properties that affect the presentation of lists and tables and how to control the visibility of any boxes.

This chapter also described how you can use the @import rule to import rules from one style sheet into another, and how CSS determines which rule takes precedence over other rules if more than one rule applies to an element. Finally, you learned how you can validate your CSS style sheets, which will help you find and avoid errors in your CSS documents.

As you have seen, many of the features you have learned about in this chapter do not yet work in all browsers. To help you keep track of which ones are supported by different versions of browsers, Appendix C contains a reference of all CSS properties covered in the book, including which version of IE and which version of Netscape first supported the property or feature.

In Chapter 5, you take your final look at CSS and learn how it can be used to control the layout of documents.

5

Using CSS for Layout

Most HTML designers use tables to control the layout of their Web pages. The cells of the table form grids that can be used to divide a page into sections and position items where the designer wants them. By setting the width and height of tables, rows, and cells, these items can be positioned accurately to the pixel. However, tables are not the only way you can control the layout of your pages. After all, using tables for layout purposes does, strictly speaking, mix presentational markup with the structural and semantic markup, which is something that XHTML and CSS are designed to prevent.

Therefore, it is preferable, where possible, to use CSS to control the layout of your pages. In this chapter, you will learn how CSS enables you to control where items appear on a page and how to recreate some common layouts.

Because this chapter deals with layout, the end of the chapter includes a brief discussion of when you might still want to use tables or frames to control layouts.

In this chapter, you will:

❑   Learn about the differences between fixed and liquid layouts

❑   Become familiar with the different methods of positioning in CSS

❑   Look at some common page layouts using CSS

❑   Briefly look at the use of frames in XHTML

By the end of the chapter, you should be comfortable with the different ways of laying out pages using CSS.

Problem

Tables were originally designed for displaying tabular data, not as a layout technique. However, it did not take Web page authors long to figure out that tables would be very good for controlling the position of elements on the pages. As a result, the real content of pages can become buried within complex structures of nested tables. While Strict XHTML does not explicitly state that tables cannot be used for layout, you ideally want to use CSS positioning, not tables, for layout purposes. Furthermore, using tables in design can seriously affect the accessibility of a page (as you will see in Chapter 7).

In this chapter, therefore, you will redesign the First Promotions site using CSS to control positioning, rather than tables.

Design

You have already seen how CSS renders documents based upon a box model, whereby the content of each element is treated as though it were in its own box. CSS enables you to position these boxes on the page using various *positioning schemes*, which means you can create complex layouts using CSS. In this section, you will learn the various ways in which CSS enables you to position items on the page.

By default, the order in which elements appear in the document, and the type of box they are (block or inline), will control the way in which the elements are laid out on the page. This is commonly referred to as *normal flow*, and boxes appear on the page in the same order that they appear in the source document. However, you can use several techniques to position boxes in places other than where they would appear in normal flow, placing them elsewhere on your pages.

CSS positioning schemes

In this section, you will learn the three positioning schemes CSS uses to control the position of items on a page:

- ❑ **Normal flow** — The default positioning scheme
- ❑ **Floating** — Whereby a box is taken out of the flow and shifted as far to the left or right as possible, while the rest of the content flows around that block
- ❑ **Absolute positioning** — Whereby boxes are removed from normal flow and assigned a position relative to their containing block

You will also be introduced to two subsets of theses positioning schemes in this chapter:

- ❑ **Relative positioning** — Enables you to position items using offsets from normal flow
- ❑ **Fixed positioning** — Ensures that items remain in a fixed position on the page even if the user scrolls

You will then learn how each of these techniques can be used to create effective layouts.

The position property

You select which positioning scheme to use with the position property. It can take one of the following values:

Value	Description
static	A normal box laid out according to normal flow (because normal flow is the default positioning scheme, you will rarely have to specify this value).
relative	The box is positioned according to the rules of normal flow and is then offset relative to the normal position (any subsequent boxes are calculated as if the box were not offset).
absolute	The box's position is determined using offsets from the top, left, bottom, or right of the containing block. These boxes are removed from normal flow, and while child elements will be positioned within this containing box, there is no impact on the layout of sibling elements.
fixed	The box's position follows the same model as absolute positioning, but it will be fixed to some point within the page or screen, and will not move when the user scrolls the page.

You will learn more about each of these values as you look at each of the positioning schemes.

You might have noticed that the description of the absolute value mentioned a *containing block*. It is important to remember that a containing block is a block (or box) in which this box lives, not the one it generates. Therefore, in the following example the box created by the <p> element would be the containing box for the box created by the <strong> element:

```
<p>It is important to remember that the <strong>containing box</strong> is the
block this box lives in.</p>
```

Before learning about the positioning schemes, you should take a look at the *box offset properties*, because these will be used with all of the positioning schemes except normal flow.

Box offset properties

Whenever you use relative, absolute, or fixed as the values of the position property, you need to specify positions for the offsets of the boxes. These are given using the following properties:

Property	Purpose
top	How far the top of a box is offset below the top of the containing block
right	How far the right-hand side of the box is offset from the right edge of the containing block
bottom	How far the bottom of a box is offset above the bottom of the containing block
left	How far the left-hand side of the box is offset from the left edge of the containing block

You should specify only a left or right offset and a top or bottom offset. If you specify both left and right or both top and bottom, one must be the absolute negative of the other (for example, top:3px; bottom:3px;). If you have top and bottom or left and right that do not have absolute negative values of each other, the right or bottom offset will be ignored.

The values for these properties will usually be a length (a fixed distance from the edge) or a percentage (a percentage of the containing block's width for the left and right properties and the boxes height for the top and bottom properties).

By way of example, take a look at the following `top` and `left` properties:

```
top:10px;
left:10px;
```

Using these values, the top left-hand corner of this box would be positioned 10 pixels from the top and 10 pixels in from the left of its containing box.

Normal flow

You should already be familiar with how normal flow affects the layout of the page; this is how a page would be laid out if a page contained no tables, and no hacks such as using single-pixel GIFs for positioning of elements. Because it is the default way in which pages are laid out, you do not need to use the CSS `position` property to make your elements obey normal flow.

In normal flow, block-level boxes are stacked vertically from top to bottom of the containing block. The distance between the boxes is set by the margin properties (remember that vertical margins between adjacent boxes collapse). The outer edge of the box (which includes any margin around the border) will usually touch the left-hand side of the containing block.

For example, Figure 5-1 shows a page consisting of five block-level boxes. There is one `<div>` element, which contains one `<h1>` and three `<p>` elements. The edges of the `<div>` element touch the containing block (which in this case is the browser window), while the other elements' boxes are stacked on top of each other, touching the left margin of the containing block (in this case, the `<div>` element).

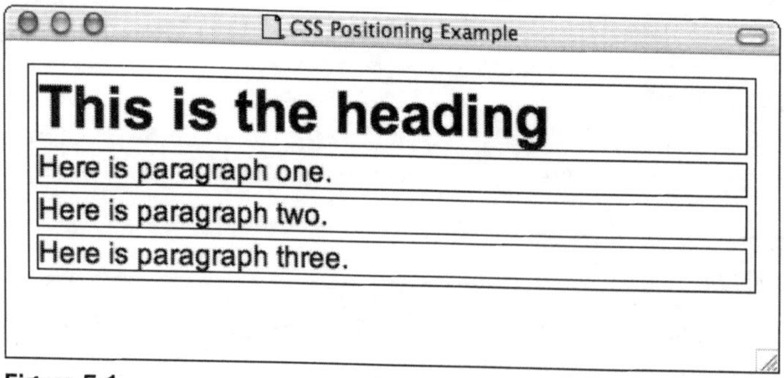

Figure 5-1

Here is the XHTML for this example (`ch05_eg01.html`):

```
<body>
  <div id="page">
    <h1>This is the heading</h1>
    <p>Here is paragraph one.</p>
```

```
      <p>Here is paragraph two.</p>
      <p>Here is paragraph three.</p>
   </div>
</body>
```

And here is the simple CSS for this example (ch05_eg01.css). Single-pixel borders have been given to each box in this example so you can see their edges and how they are positioned; each box also has a 5-pixel margin to separate it from the other boxes and the browser window:

```
div, h1, p {
   font-family:arial, verdana, sans-serif;
   border:1px solid #000000;
   margin:5px;}
```

Remember that you do not need to specify the position property, because you are looking at the default layout position — normal flow.

Now that you know how block boxes are displayed in normal flow, you may be wondering about inline boxes. Inline boxes are laid out horizontally one after the other starting at the top of the containing block. Every line in a containing box is treated as a separate *line box*. The width of the box is determined by the containing block. However, the height of line boxes can vary because each line can contain more than one inline box, which may have differently sized content or different values for the vertical-align property.

The following example (ch05_eg02.html) shows an inline box (created by the <span> element), which in turn contains other inline boxes created by the <code> and <strong> elements:

```
<body>
   <div class="page">
      <span class="explanation">The <code>span</code> element creates an inline box.
      Each line of text in this box generates a new line box, although you cannot
      specify properties for each of the individual line boxes; rather the
      properties of the <code>span</code> element will determine font, text and
      line height properties. The <strong>inline</strong> elements will also
      generate boxes that flow within the <code>span</code> element.</span>
   </div>
</body>
```

Figure 5-2 shows how the <div> element acts as a block-level container, and how the text in the <span> element wraps onto several lines. This example also illustrates how line boxes can vary depending on the properties of the child elements.

Let's take a look at the style sheet for this example (ch05_eg02.css). The <span> element has been given a single-pixel black border so you can see the edges of each of the line boxes (note that the properties for the <span> element affect all the line boxes; you cannot change each line individually). Meanwhile, the <code> and <strong> elements have been given larger font sizes. The font-size of these child elements does not affect the line height itself, so you can see an overlap in the line boxes that contain <code> elements. Meanwhile, the line-height property does affect the size of the line boxes and this has been set for the <strong> elements.

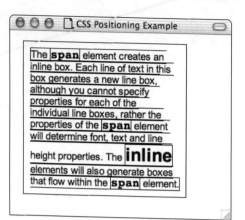

Figure 5-2

```
div.page {
    border:1px solid #000000;
    margin:10px;
    padding:10px;
    width:250px;}

span.explanation {
    font-family:arial, verdana, sans-serif;
    font-size:10px;
    border:1px solid #000000;}

strong {
    font-weight:bold;
    font-size:18px;
    line-height:22px;
    border:1px solid #000000;}

code {
    font-family:courier, monospace;
    font-size:12px;
    font-weight:bold;
    border:1px solid #000000;}
```

Usually, the left edge of a line box will touch the left edge of the containing block, and the right edge will touch the right edge of the box; in this example, the `padding` property of the `<div>` element creates space between the two. When you look at floating elements, however, the floated elements may come between the container and the edges of the line box, and this can affect the width of the line box.

Relative positioning

Relative positioning lays out a page according to normal flow, but then offsets any element whose `position` property has a value of `relative` from its position in normal flow according to the offset properties. It can be offset to the top, right, bottom, or left of where it would normally appear using the box offset properties you read about earlier in the section "Box Offset Properties."

When relative positioning is used, the size of the boxes in relative flow remains the same as it would in normal flow, line breaks remain in the same place, and subsequent elements are not affected, although a relatively positioned box does create a new containing block for any child elements.

To understand how relative positioning works, you can revisit the first example you looked at in this chapter, which was a `<div>` element that contained a heading and three paragraphs. Here I simply repeat the `<div>` element in this example and give each `<div>` a different value for its id attribute to distinguish them (ch05_eg03.html):

```
<body>
  <div id="page1">
    <h1>This is the heading</h1>
    <p>Here is paragraph one.</p>
    <p>Here is paragraph two.</p>
    <p>Here is paragraph three.</p>
  </div>
  <div id="page2">
    <h1>This is the heading</h1>
    <p>Here is paragraph one.</p>
    <p>Here is paragraph two.</p>
    <p>Here is paragraph three.</p>
  </div>
</body>
```

Figure 5-3 shows you what this example would look like using the same style sheet that was used in the first example.

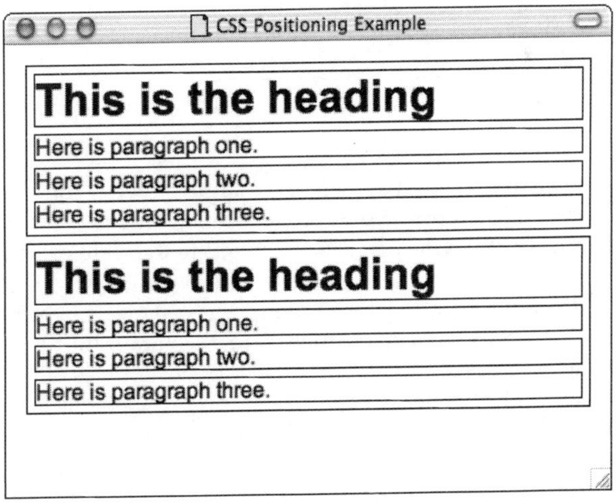

Figure 5-3

Now use the `position` property with the second `<div>` element, whose id attribute has a value of page2, and give it some offsets. Because the current boxes take up the full width of the window, if you use offsets, they might disappear off the edge of the browser window, so you limit the width of the boxes using a `width` property (ch05_eg03.css):

```
div, h1, p {
    font-family:arial, verdana, sans-serif;
    width:300px;
    border:1px solid #000000;
    margin:5px;}

div#page2 {
    position:relative;
    top:20px;
    left:20px;}
```

You can see what this would look like in Figure 5-4.

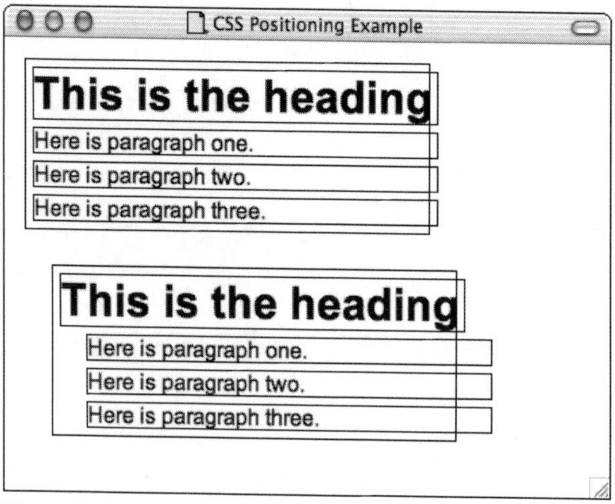

Figure 5-4

In the first set of elements, you can see that there is a margin between the edge of the browser and the border of the `<div>` element. However, in the second set of elements, the `<div>` element has been offset and appears 20 pixels further down the page and 20 pixels to the right of where it did in Figure 5-3.

You might have noticed that the width of the paragraphs is 300 pixels, whereas in Figure 5-3 they were kept within the box for the `<div>` element. Furthermore, the paragraphs have inherited the offset of 20 pixels and have been moved 20 pixels to the right. This screenshot was taken in IE 5.5 on a Mac, and is a good demonstration of how different browsers can interpret style sheets in different ways. On IE 6 on a PC, the paragraph boxes would be kept inside the confines of the `<div>` element (as they were in Figure 5-3), but the `<div>` and the individual `<p>` elements would not be offset to the right. In Netscape 7 on both a PC and a Mac, the `<p>` elements spread outside their containing `<div>`, retaining their 300–pixel width. However, on Netscape 7 on a PC, the right-hand edges of the `<p>` element are cut off at the edge of the `<div>` element. Therefore, you should always test your style sheets on as many browsers as you can; and if you get differing results, you can specify rules for each of the elements to prevent conflicts like this.

Now let's change this example a little. In this case, we'll give the value of one of the offsets a negative value, the `top` property. This example also specifies widths for the <p> and <div> elements (ch05_eg04.css):

```
div, h1, p {
    font-family:arial, verdana, sans-serif;
    border:1px solid #000000;
    margin:5px;}
```

```
div {width:350px;}
p {width:300px;}
```

```
div#page2 {
    position:relative;
    top:-100px;
    left:20px;}
```

As the result in Figure 5-5 shows, this can cause a bit of a problem; boxes are transparent by default, so when elements overlap, it can be very hard to read their contents.

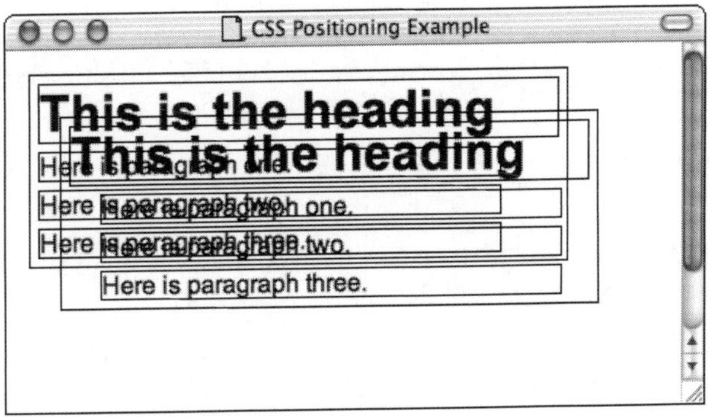

Figure 5-5

If you add a simple `background-color` property, or a background image, this problem is fixed:

```
div, h1, p {
    background-color:#ffffff;
    font-family:arial, verdana, sans-serif;
    border:1px solid #000000;
    margin:5px;}
```

You can see the fixed version of ch05_eg04b.css in Figure 5-6.

Note that the CSS recommendation does not indicate which element should appear on the top when two relatively positioned elements overlap. Therefore, you should use the `z-index` property (which is discussed later in the chapter) to control which element should appear on the top.

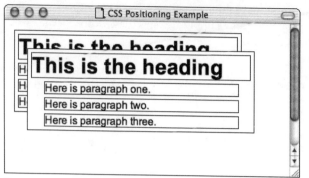

Figure 5-6

Float

A *float* (also referred to as a *floated* or *floating box*) is a box that is taken out of normal flow and moved to the far left or right of the containing box, yet still allows content to flow alongside it (although you can prevent text from flowing alongside it using the `clear` property).

You can specify that the box which an element creates should be a floating box using the `float` property, which can take one of the following values:

Value	Purpose
left	The box is floated to the left of the containing element, and the content of the containing element will flow to the right of it.
right	The box is floated to the right of the containing element, and the content of the containing element will flow to the left of it.
none	The box is not floated and remains where it would have been positioned in normal flow.
inherit	The box takes the same value for this property as its containing element.

> You *must* specify the width for a floating box (using the `width` property); otherwise, it will automatically take up the full width of the containing box.

Because the floated box is taken out of normal flow, the remaining surrounding elements flow around it. When a box is floated to the left, other page content flows to the right of it, while a box floated to the right allows the remaining page content to flow to its left. The line boxes created by surrounding elements that are next to the float are shortened so that they can fit alongside the float.

Vertically, the floated box is aligned with the top of the containing box or the current line box. If there isn't enough horizontal room on the current line for the float, it is moved down the page until there is a line that has space for it.

Take a look at the following XHTML. This time, the first `<p>` element in the `<div>` element contains a pull quote, not part of the text for the page (ch05_eg05.html):

```
<div id="page">
  <h1>Heading One</h1>
  <p id="pullQuote">Here is a pull-quote with a summary of the article.</p>
  <p>Lorem ipsum dolor sit amet, consectetuer adipiscing elit. Curabitur in neque.
    Etiam condimentum, dui sed sodales tristique, libero tellus bibendum felis, vel
    malesuada lacus mauris eget dui. </p>
  <p>Lorem ipsum dolor sit amet, consectetuer adipiscing elit. Curabitur in neque.
    Etiam condimentum, dui sed sodales tristique, libero tellus bibendum felis, vel
    malesuada lacus mauris eget dui. Quisque condimentum volutpat sem. Nunc dictum.
    Morbi elit lacus, ultricies faucibus, adipiscing non, sollicitudin ut, arcu.
    Curabitur cursus odio eu felis. </p>
</div>
```

Now take a look at the CSS for this example (ch05_eg05.css):

```
div {width:400px;}

div, h1, p {
  font-family:arial, verdana, sans-serif;
  border:1px solid #000000;
  margin:5px;}

p#pullQuote {
  float:right;
  width:100px;}
```

You can see the result in Figure 5-7. If you look at the borders of these boxes, you will notice that the pull quote is moved right to the edge of the containing box — the right-hand side margin is ignored. However, the 5-pixel margin at the top of the box is preserved.

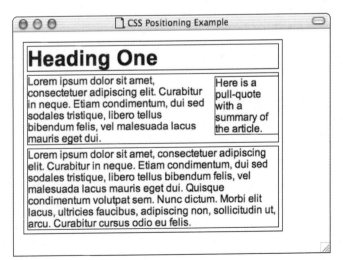

Figure 5-7

It is worth noting that if the pull quote had been an inline element (such as a <span> element) within the paragraph, the result would have looked the same.

You can position more than one float on the same line. For example, the following rule indicates that the three paragraphs should be shown next to one another (ch05_eg06.css):

```
p {
    float:left;
    width:150px; }
```

You can see the rather interesting result in Figure 5-8.

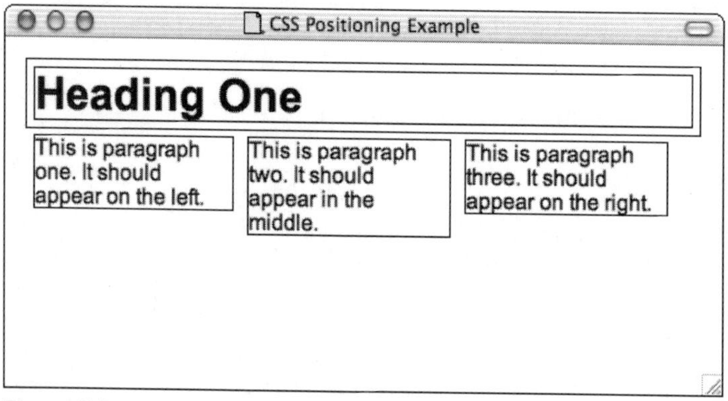

Figure 5-8

Because the floated boxes are taken out of the normal flow, the containing <div> element holds only the heading, not the floated boxes. If there were some other content in the containing <div> element after the floats, or if it had a height property set, they would appear within the box; but without any other content following them, they are taken outside. Again, there is a peculiarity with IE 6 on Windows, which will display the floated elements inside the box.

The capability to float an element is commonly used with images, because this enables text to flow around the image. You will see an example of this when you meet the clear property in the next section.

> *If the display property has a value of **none**, any values for **position** and **float** should be ignored (as no box is generated).*

The clear property

Sometimes you will want to float an element to the left or right, but not have any text wrap around the floated item. You can prevent anything from appearing next to a floated box using the clear property.

This property is used on any box that appears after the floated element, and indicates which sides may not touch the floated box. For example, giving the box following a float a clear property whose value is left means that the box cannot touch the left-hand side of the floated element. The values for the clear property are as follows:

Value	Purpose
none	There are no constraints on the box's position with respect to floats.
left	The top margin of the generated box is increased so that the box is below the bottom outer edge of any left-floating boxes preceding this element.
right	The top margin of the generated box is increased so that the box is below the bottom outer edge of any right-floating boxes preceding this element.
both	The top margin of the generated box is increased so that the box is below the bottom outer edge of any left- or right-floating boxes preceding this element.
inherit	The box takes the same property as its containing element.

To understand the use of the `clear` property better, consider the following example in which an image is used before a paragraph:

```
<div id="page">
    <img src="images/plane.gif" height="100" width="175" alt="A sample image" />
    <p>Here is some text that would normally appear to the left of the floated
        image. When the clear property is given a value of right, the text will not
        be allowed to touch the image that is floated to the right, and will instead
        appear beneath that image.</p>
</div>
```

Normally, the text in the paragraph would wrap around the image, displaying on the left-hand side of the image. However, when the `clear` property is used on the `<p>` element and given a value of `right`, the content cannot touch any right-floating boxes—such as the image. Here is the CSS for this example (`ch05_eg07.css`):

```
div {
    font-family:arial, verdana, sans-serif;
    border:1px solid #000000;
    padding:3px;
    margin:5px;
    width:300px;}

img {
    float:right;
    margin:5px;
    width:175px;}

p {clear:right;}
```

You can see the result in Figure 5-9, which shows the text appearing beneath the image.

Absolute positioning

Absolute positioning enables you to position a box using offsets from the top, right, bottom, and left of the containing block. An absolutely positioned box is removed from normal flow and forms a new containing block for any children.

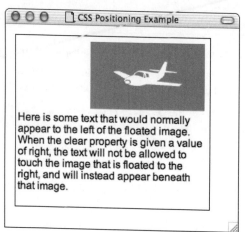

Figure 5-9

Absolutely positioned elements do not flow around other boxes, so they may obscure the contents of another box. To control which element appears on top, you need to look at stacking levels, which are described in the section on the z-index property later in the chapter.

Take again the example of two pages (using different values for the id attributes on each <div>). I will position each page using absolute positioning. By adding class attributes to the <p> elements, I can also position the paragraphs within the <div> elements (which are the containing elements). Here is ch05_eg08.html:

```
<body>
  <div id="page1">
    <h1>Heading One</h1>
    <p class="para1">This is paragraph one.</p>
    <p class="para2">This is paragraph two.</p>
  </div>
  <div id="page2">
    <h1>Heading One</h1>
    <p class="para1">This is paragraph one.</p>
    <p class="para2">This is paragraph two.</p>
  </div>
</body>
```

Now look at the style sheet to see how you control the positioning of the items on the page (ch05_eg08 .css). In this example, you use absolute positioning to position the two pages next to each other. Before you do, however, you can set the fonts, borders, and margins for the <div>, <h1> and <p> elements:

```
div, h1, p {
  font-family:arial, verdana, sans-serif;
  border:1px solid #000000;
  margin:5px;
  background-color:#ffffff;}
```

You also fix the height and width of the pages and the width of the paragraphs:

```
div {width:300px; height:120px;}
p {width:250px;}
```

Now you want to position the first page, whose id attribute has a value of page1. You want the page to be positioned 20 pixels from the top and the left of the browser window, so you give the position property a value of absolute and set the top and left offset properties:

```
div#page1 {
    position:absolute;
    top:20px;
    left:20px;}
```

Because you know the width of the page, you can position the second page to the right of the first one. You just give this one a larger offset from the left:

```
div#page2 {
    position:absolute;
    top:20px;
    left:350px;}
```

Inside the pages are the paragraphs, and these can be absolutely positioned, too. Just position the paragraphs under each other. You can see that each page has been taken out of flow and given its own containing box by looking at the content of the <h1> elements, but the reason why you are absolutely positioning the <p> elements is to demonstrate how they are positioned in terms of the containing element:

```
p.para1 {
    position:absolute;
    top:50px;
    left:20px;}

p.para2 {
    position:absolute;
    top:80px;
    left:20px;}
```

You can see the result of this example in Figure 5-10.

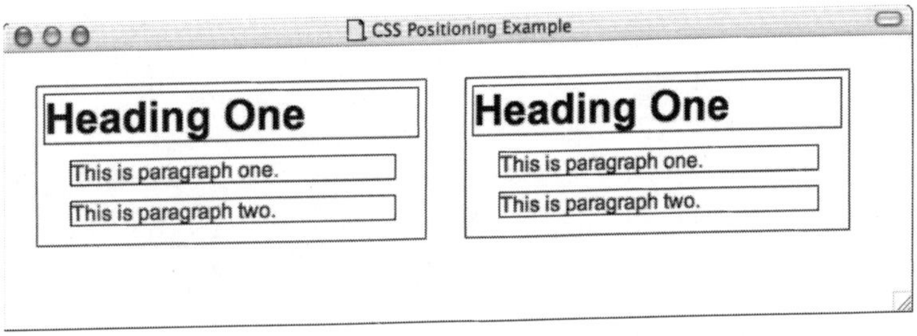

Figure 5-10

Remember that overlapping boxes may obscure other content, and the `z-index` property helps you control which box appears on top. As with the overlapping of relatively positioned boxes you saw earlier in the chapter, if no `background-color` property is set on the boxes, the result may be unreadable because the boxes are, by default, transparent.

Fixed positioning

Fixed positioning is like absolute positioning, except the containing box for any element that has fixed positioning is the browser window, or the top left-hand corner of every page for printed material.

Fixed positioning can create layouts that are similar to frames. In this example, you will see a masthead that is in a fixed position and a left-hand navigation pane that is also fixed. The rest of the page on the right-hand side will scroll. Unfortunately, fixed positioning is not properly implemented in IE 6 on Windows or in IE 5 on the Mac, so you have to look at the example in Netscape.

Before you look at the code for the page, you can see what it looks like in Figure 5-11. It is also worth trying this example out for yourself in a browser so that you can see how this page would scroll.

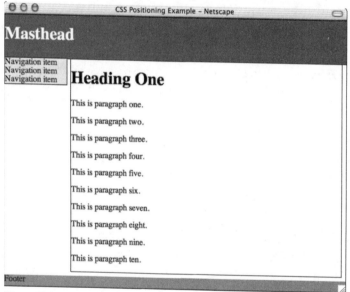

Figure 5-11

First, take a look at the XHTML for the example (ch05_eg09.html):

```
<body>
  <div id="heading"><h1>Masthead</h1></div>
  <div id="nav">
    Navigation item<br />
    Navigation item<br />
    Navigation item<br />
  </div>
```

```
   <div id="page">
     <h1>Heading One</h1>
     <p>This is paragraph one.</p>
     <p>This is paragraph two.</p>
     <p>This is paragraph three.</p>
     <p>This is paragraph four.</p>
     <p>This is paragraph five.</p>
     <p>This is paragraph six.</p>
     <p>This is paragraph seven.</p>
     <p>This is paragraph eight.</p>
     <p>This is paragraph nine.</p>
     <p>This is paragraph ten.</p>
   </div>
   <div id="footer">
     Footer>
   </div>
 </body>
```

The following code shows the CSS to control the positioning of elements (ch05_eg09.css). To begin, the <div> element whose id attribute has a value of heading will be fixed at the top of the screen. As with any fixed-position box, in addition to giving the position property a value of fixed and giving the offsets for the box, you should also specify the height and width properties for the box.

You want the heading to appear at the top-left of the browser window, so you give the top and left offsets values of 0. You also want the heading to stretch across the full width of the browser, so you give it a width property with a value of 100%, and you set its height property to have a value of 80 pixels:

```
div#heading {
    position:fixed;
    top:0px;
    left:0px;
    width:100%;
    height:80px;
    color:#ffffff;
    background-color:#666666;
    border:1px solid #000000;}
```

Next, you want to position the <div> element containing the navigation items along the left of the page, and beneath the heading. Therefore, the top offset must be set to 80 pixels; if this property were not set, you would not see the first 80 pixels. You must also set the width property:

```
div#nav {
    position:fixed;
    top:80px;
    left:0px;
    width:120px;
    background-color:#efefef;
    border:1px solid #000000;}
```

Because you want the main part of the page to scroll, you do not use fixed positioning. Nor do you have to give this element a height or width property, but you have to remember that fixed positioning elements are taken out of normal flow, so the top and left parts of the page are going to be hidden by the header and the navigation if you do not correct this. The solution in this case is to set the `margin-top` property of the `<div>` containing the rest of the page to the height of the heading, and the `margin-left` property to the width of the `<div>` containing the navigation:

```
div#page {
  margin-top:80px;
  margin-left:120px;
  background-color:#ffffff;
  border:1px solid #000000;}
```

The last thing you need to do is position the `footer` element at the bottom of the page using fixed positioning. Because you want this element to go at the bottom of the page, you will use the `bottom` offset this time; this ensures that the footer appears at the bottom of the page regardless of how large the user has set his or her browser window:

```
div#footer {
  position:fixed;
  bottom:0px;
  left:0px;
  background-color:#999999;
  width:100%;
  height:20px;}

p {width:250px;}
```

Overlapping layers

As you have seen in earlier examples, sometimes boxes overlap. The CSS `z-index` property enables you to control which box appears on top of other boxes when layers do overlap, and which layers are underneath (and therefore hidden by the top layer).

Therefore, in addition to being able to position boxes from the left and right of the containing box (on what is commonly known as the *x* axis) and the top and bottom (known as the *y* axis), you can also position items on this *z* axis, from the front to the back of the screen. This creates a function similar to the "bring to front" and "send to back" options common in desktop publishing packages.

The order from the front to the back of the layers is known as the *stacking context*, and elements inherit their parent element's stacking context.

> Remember that you usually have to set the **background-color** property of any boxes that overlap, or give them a background image, so that the background of the box is not transparent, which could cause an unreadable mess.

The z-index property

To indicate an element's stacking context, you need to use the `z-index` property. The higher the number given as the value of the `z-index` property, the nearer to the top the box will appear on the page.

Take a look at the following simple example that has three `<div>` elements (ch05_eg10.html):

```
<body>
  <div id="layer1"><h1>Layer One</h1></div>
  <div id="layer2"><h1>Layer Two</h1></div>
  <div id="layer3"><h1>Layer Three</h1></div>
</body>
```

To illustrate stacking context and the z-index property, the style sheet is going to use absolute positioning to ensure that each <div> element overlaps. In this style sheet, the first <div> element is going to appear on the top, the second in the middle, and the third on the bottom; therefore, the first <div> element must be given the highest value for the z-index property, the second <div> element should be lower than this first one but higher than the third, and the third <div> element should have the lowest value for the z-index property (ch05_eg10.css):

```
div#layer1 {
    z-index:3;
    position:absolute;
    top:10px;
    left:10px;
    width:200px;
    height:100px;
    background-color:#ffffff;
    border:1px solid #000000;
    padding:5px;}
```

The rules for each of the <div> elements are very similar; only the z-index and the top and left offset properties need to change:

```
div#layer2 {
    z-index:2;
    position:absolute;
    top:20px;
    left:20px;
    width:200px;
    height:100px;
    background-color:#ffffff;
    border:1px solid #000000;
    padding:5px;}
```

```
div#layer3 {
    z-index:1;
    position:absolute;
    top:30px;
    left:30px;
    width:200px;
    height:100px;
    background-color:#ffffff;
    border:1px solid #000000;
    padding:5px;}
```

You can see the result in Figure 5-12.

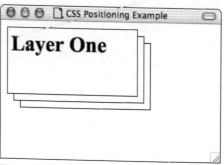

Figure 5-12

Now change the values of the z-index property around (ch05_eg11.css):

```css
div#layer1 {
  z-index:1;
  position:absolute;
  top:10px;
  left:10px;
  width:200px;
  height:100px;
  background-color:#ffffff;
  border:1px solid #000000;
  padding:5px;}

div#layer2 {
  z-index:2;
  position:absolute;
  top:20px;
  left:20px;
  width:200px;
  height:100px;
  background-color:#ffffff;
  border:1px solid #000000;
  padding:5px;}

div#layer3 {
  z-index:3;
  position:absolute;
  top:30px;
  left:30px;
  width:200px;
  height:100px;
  background-color:#ffffff;
  border:1px solid #000000;
  padding:5px;}
```

You can see the result in Figure 5-13, where the order of the <div> elements has been reversed.

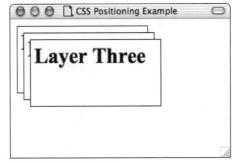

Figure 5-13

Common layouts

Now that you understand how CSS can be used to control the position of elements on a page, it's time to look at how you can recreate some common layouts that you might have seen on the Web. Instead of relying upon tables to position content, you will use <div> elements to group sections of a page, and CSS to position these <div> elements where you want them on the page.

Vertical panels

In this section, you will learn how to create pages that have a series of vertical panels. The layout you are trying to achieve is shown in Figure 5-14.

Figure 5-14

As you can see from Figure 5-14, this page has one box to hold the masthead at the top, followed by a second box underneath it, which contains the top navigation, and then a third box that contains the main content of the page. First you'll look at how the XHTML is structured.

The page starts out just like any other page, but in the <body> you will notice some differences: three <div> elements, each with different values for their id attributes that hold the content of the page (ch05_eg12.html):

```
<!DOCTYPE HTML PUBLIC "-//W3C//DTD HTML 4.01 Transitional//EN">
<html>
<head>
  <title>CSS Positioning Example</title>
  <meta http-equiv="Content-Type" content="text/html; charset=iso-8859-1">
  <link rel="stylesheet" type="text/css" href="ch05_eg12.css" />
</head>

<body>
  <div id="masthead"><h1>Masthead</h1></div>
  <div id="navigation">
    <span class="navItem">Navigation item 1</span> |
    <span class="navItem">Navigation item 2</span> |
    <span class="navItem">Navigation item 3</span> |
    <span class="navItem">Navigation item 4</span>
  </div>
  <div id="body"><h1>Headline</h1><p>Article goes here</p></div>
</body>

</html>
```

As you can see from Figure 5-14, the three <div> elements correspond to the three boxes on the page, each of which has a single-pixel black border:

❑   The first <div> element has an id attribute whose value is masthead, and this element would contain the logo or title for the site.

❑   The second <div> element has an id attribute whose value is navigation, and this element would contain the main navigation items for the site.

❑   The third <div> element has an id attribute whose value is body, and this element would contain the body or content of the page.

Now look at the CSS for this page. There are five rules: one for general page settings, one for rules common to each <div> element, and then a rule for each of the three <div> elements. Here is the first rule from ch05_eg12.css, which simply sets a background-color property for the page and the font-family used on the page:

```
body {
  background-color:#efefef;
  font-family:arial, verdana, sans-serif;}
```

Next up is the rule that controls the appearance of all of the boxes:

- ❏ The width of the page has been set to 800 pixels, so the width property of each of these <div> elements can be set at the same time.

- ❏ They all have a single-pixel black border, so you can see the outlines of the boxes.

- ❏ Each has been given a margin of 1px, to separate the boxes.

- ❏ Each box has been given 5 pixels of padding so that the content does not touch the edges of the boxes.

```
div {
   width:800px;
   border:1px solid #000000;
   margin:1px;
   padding:5px;}
```

The masthead is the first box on the page, and the <div> for the masthead has a height property to control the height of the box and a background-color property to make it stand out from the other boxes:

```
div#masthead {
   height:100px;
   background-color:#d6d6d6;}
```

The navigation items are in a box that is only 40 pixels high, so it has a height property set, too. There is also a background-color property to make the links stand out, and because this background color is so dark, the links are made in a lighter color using the color property:

```
div#navigation {
   height:40px;
   background-color:#666666;
   color:#ffffff;}
```

The final <div> element contains the main part of the page. This has a white background, and the height has been set to 100% so that it fills a good portion of the screen:

```
div#body {
   height:100%;
   background-color:#ffffff;}
```

That was quite simple, but you may be wondering where the positioning rules are. There does not seem to be anything in this example to control where the boxes appear on the page. The answer is that there are no positioning rules; they are not required. Normal flow dictates that block-level elements should appear one on top of each other in the containing element (which is the browser window). Therefore, as long as these <div> elements appear in the correct order, you do not need to control the position of these elements.

Two columns

Many layouts have more than one column, so in this section you will look at an example of a layout that uses two columns on the page and looks something like what is shown in Figure 5-15.

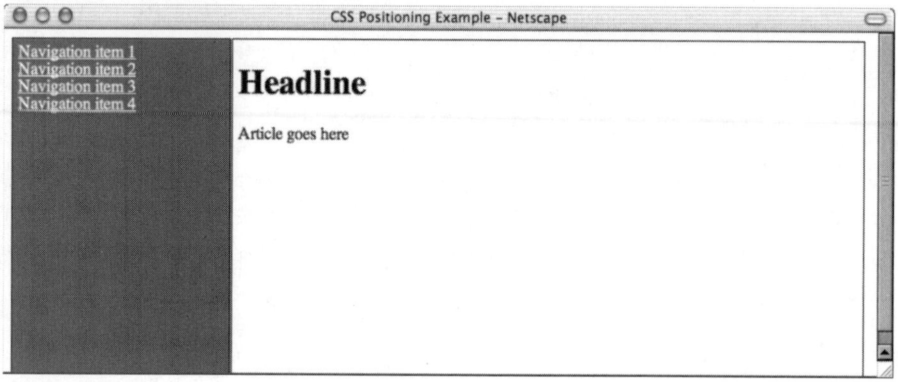

Figure 5-15

As before, begin by taking a look at the XHTML for this example. As you can see, it contains two `<div>` elements, each with different values for their `id` attributes. The first `<div>` element contains the navigation for the page, while the second contains the main content of the page (ch05_eg13.html):

```
<html>
<head>
  <title>CSS Positioning Example</title>
  <meta http-equiv="Content-Type" content="text/html; charset=iso-8859-1">
  <link rel="stylesheet" type="text/css" href="ch05_eg13.css" />
</head>

<body>
  <div id="navigation">
    <a href="#">Navigation item 1</a>
    <a href="#">Navigation item 2</a>
    <a href="#">Navigation item 3</a>
    <a href="#">Navigation item 4</a>
  </div>
  <div id="content"><h1>Headline</h1><p>Article goes here</p></div>
</body>

</html>
```

To create a two-column layout from this page, you float the first `<div>` to the left, and then leave the second one so it appears next to the navigation. Here is the first rule that positions the navigation (ch05_eg13.css):

❑   First, the `float` property is set to `left` so that the element appears to the left of the page.

❑   The `width` of the float must be set; otherwise, it will take up the full width of the containing element.

❑   The `height` property has been set so that it takes up the same size as the main part of the page.

❑   The `background-color` property sets the background color to make the links stand out, and a border is drawn around the box to indicate its edges.

❑   Finally, padding is added so that there is a gap between the border and the links.

```
div#navigation {
  float:left;
  width:200px;
  height:100%;
  color:#ffffff;
  background-color:#666666;
  border:1px solid #000000;
  padding:5px;}
```

The second `<div>` element contains the main part of the page, and the following properties are set:

❑ The `margin-left` property ensures that the content is to the right of the navigation. It is there-fore set 1 pixel further from the edge of the containing box (in this case, the browser window) than the width of the navigation box. (Remember that padding, border, and margin widths are added to the `width` property to determine the width of the box, so the real width of the naviga-tion box is 212 pixels.)

❑ The `width` property controls the width of the block that will appear next to the navigation; in this case, it will be 600px wide.

❑ The `height` property ensures that the page is at least the size of the browser window.

❑ The `background-color` property is set to be white, and a single-pixel black border is drawn around the box to show its border.

❑ Padding has been added so that there is a gap between the border and the content of the box.

```
div#content {
  margin-left:213px;
  width:600px;
  height:100%;
  background-color:#ffffff;
  border:1px solid #000000;
  padding:5px;}
```

Finally, there are a couple of rules for the links. The first sets their color:

```
a:link, a:visited {color:#ffffff;}
```

The second rule ensures that each link appears on a new line. To do this, you indicate that the links should be rendered in block-level boxes (rather than the inline boxes that are created by default for links) by giving the `display` property a value of `block`:

```
a {display:block;}
```

This example should work fine in most browsers; however, you will encounter some problems if you try it in IE 5, which is still a very common browser. The next section looks at a couple of the IE bugs.

IE hacks

If you look at `ch05_eg13.html` in IE on Windows, you will notice a problem: There is quite a large gap between the two columns, as shown in Figure 5-16.

This gap arises because of the way in which IE interprets the box model.

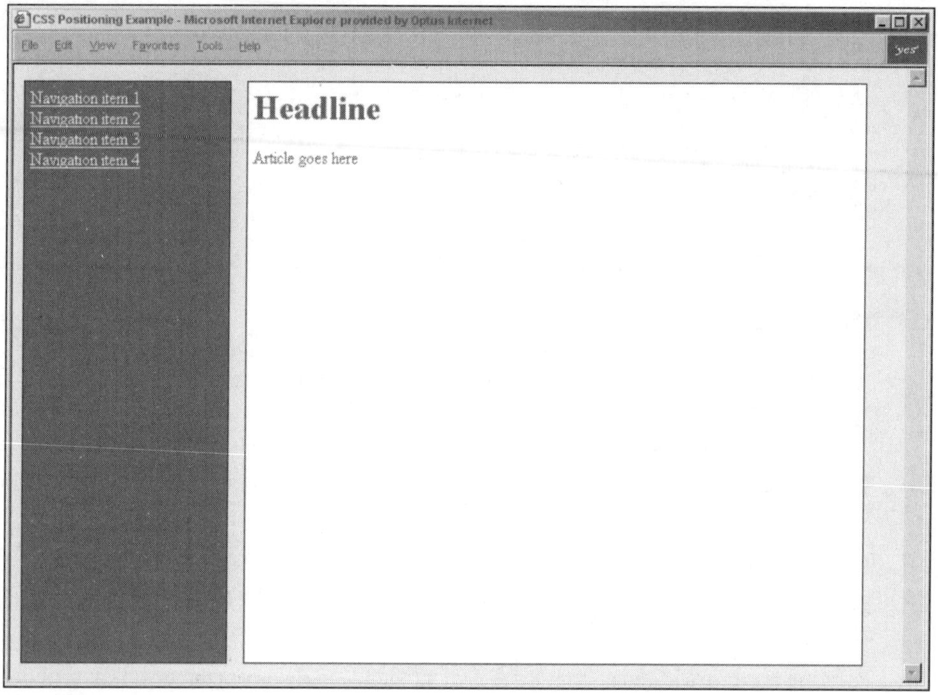

Figure 5-16

In version 5 of IE for Windows, Microsoft decided that any padding and borders are part of the width of the box, rather than an addition to the width of the box. Therefore, a box that is 100 pixels wide and has a border of 20 pixels should be 140 pixels wide according to the W3C and standards-compliant browsers; however, IE 5 for Windows includes the border in the size of the box, so the internal dimensions of the box itself, not including the border, given the same 100 pixels of width and a border of 20 pixels, would be only 60 pixels.

When IE 6 was released, and in IE 5 for Mac, Microsoft moved closer to the box model proposed by the W3C; however, they still wanted to support their older interpretation of the box model. As a result, IE 6 for Windows and IE 5 for Mac can run in two modes:

❑ **Standards mode** tries to emulate the W3C standards.

❑ **Quirks mode** tries to emulate older IE5 implementations.

Therefore, if you want IE 6 for Windows and IE 5 for Mac to run as the W3C recommend, you need to ensure that the browser is running in standards mode. To do this, you can simply add a !DOCTYPE declaration (any of the W3C HTML !DOCTYPE declarations since HTML 4 will force the browser to run in standards mode); for example, here is the !DOCTYPE declaration for Strict XHTML 1.0:

```
<!DOCTYPE html PUBLIC
"-//W3C//DTD XHTML 1.0 Strict//EN"
"http://www.w3.org/TR/xhtml1/DTD/xhtml1-strict.dtd">
```

If you do not use a `!DOCTYPE` declaration and the `<html>` element is the root element, IE will run in quirks mode. Adding this `!DOCTYPE` declaration to the example is the first step in curing this gap problem.

However, IE 5 for Windows is still a very popular browser, and you will likely want to support it. Therefore, you should set a different `width` property that will apply only to IE 5 on Windows.

Several hacks have been created to solve the problems with IE5's interpretation of the box model, but the one that I use is the Tan hack, which was discovered by Edwardson Tan (and is documented on the very useful Position Is Everything site at `www.positioniseverything.net/articles/box-model.html`). To fix the problem using the Tan hack, you just add one new rule (which you can see in `ch05_eg14.css`) with two `width` properties (one of which contains a backslash character):

```
* html div#navigation {
  width:212px;
  w\idth: 200px; }
```

The secret behind this hack is the way in which IE interprets the `<html>` element. Most browsers understand that the `<html>` is the root element, and therefore think that the asterisk (the universal selector) cannot refer to any real element; as a result, they will ignore the rule.

However, IE seems to think that there is a wrapper element around the `<html>` element, and that the `* html div#navigation` selector refers to a real `<html>` element inside this imaginary wrapper. Therefore, IE will follow this rule, rather than the rule that used the selector `div#navigation`.

The reason why there are two properties in this rule (the `width` and `w\idth` properties) is that all versions of IE are now following the rule, and you want only IE 5 on Windows to have a different value for the `width` property.

IE 5 on Windows uses the first `width` property, which is given a value of 212 pixels.

The second `w\idth` property with the backslash is ignored by IE 5 on Windows, but is recognized by IE 6 on Windows and IE 5 on Mac, so this can be given the original value of 200 pixels now that the browser is running in standards (as opposed to quirks) mode.

As you can see, this new rule that uses the Tan hack applies only to IE, and because IE 5 on Windows does not understand the `w\idth` property (which contains the backslash character), it is possible to set a different `width` that works only with IE 5 on Windows.

As you can see from Figure 5-17, adding this rule creates a vast improvement.

Unfortunately, this is still not quite right; the gap between the boxes is still slightly bigger than you would hope. This is due to something commonly referred to as the *IE 3px bug*. IE applies a 3px space to the side of floats. At the time of writing, there was not a hack to get around this problem, so you just have to be aware of it, particularly if you were hoping to design pages with pixel accuracy.

You can come across quite a lot of bugs when working with CSS, and the Position Is Everything site at `www.positioniseverything.net` is a very helpful resource that documents problems found in major browsers' implementation of CSS. If you find something that does not behave as you would hope, this is a good first stop.

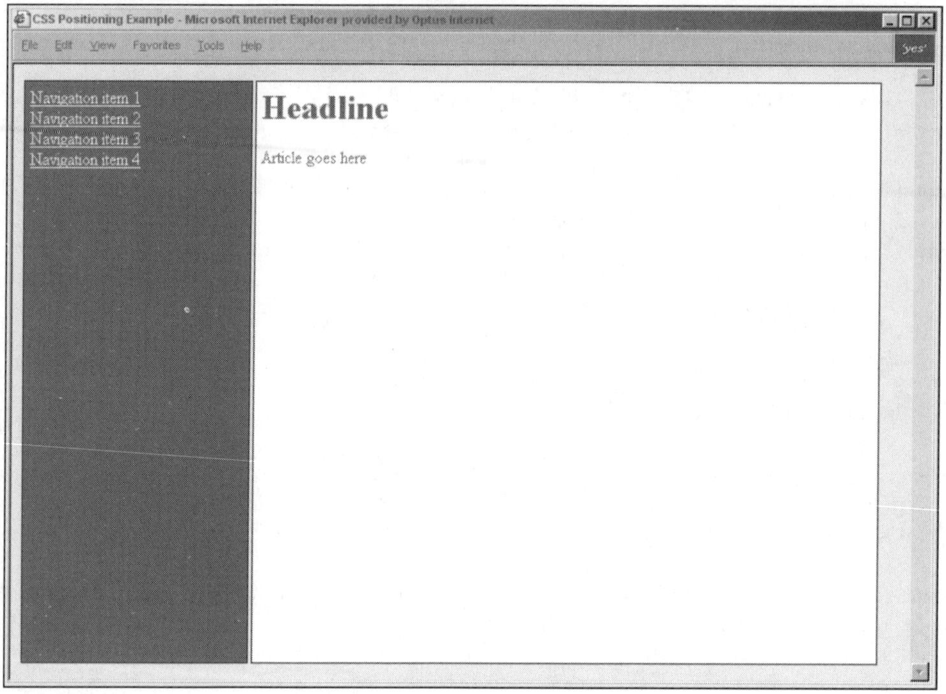

Figure 5-17

Vertical panels and two columns

You have learned how to create vertical panels (or rows) and how to create column layouts, but you are likely to want to mix these techniques. Therefore, this section takes a look at a layout containing a mast-head that stretches across the page, then two columns of content, and finally a footer at the bottom of the page. You can see the page in Figure 5-18.

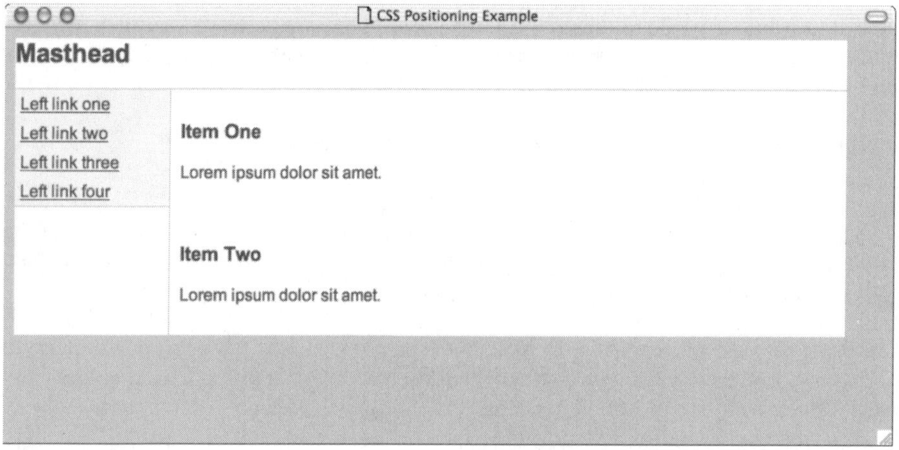

Figure 5-18

First, take a look at the XHTML for this page (ch05_eg15.html):

```
<!DOCTYPE HTML PUBLIC "-//W3C//DTD HTML 4.01 Transitional//EN">
<html>
<head>
  <title>CSS Positioning Example</title>
  <link rel="stylesheet" href="ch05_eg12.css" type="text/css">
</head>
<body>
<div id="page">
  <div id="masthead">
    <h2>Masthead</h2>
  </div>
  <div id="sideNav">
    <a href="#">Left link one</a>
    <a href="#">Left link two</a>
    <a href="#">Left link three</a>
    <a href="#">Left link four</a>
  </div>
  <div id="content">
    <div class="item">
      <h3>Item One</h3>
      <p>
       Lorem ipsum dolor sit amet.
      </p>
    </div>
    <div class="item">
      <h3>Item Two</h3>
      <p>
       Lorem ipsum dolor sit amet.
      </p>
    </div>
  </div>
</div>
</body>
</html>
```

As you can see, the whole page is contained inside a <div> element whose id attribute has a value of page. Inside this containing element are three more <div> elements:

❑   The <div> element whose id attribute has a value of masthead would contain the logo and branding for the site.

❑   The <div> element whose id attribute has a value of sideNav would contain the left navigation.

❑   The <div> element whose id attribute has a value of content would contain the main content of the page.

You can also see that the <div> element whose id attribute has a value of content contains two other <div> elements whose class attributes have a value of item, because they each contain an item in the main part of the page.

Now on to the interesting part: the style sheet (ch05_eg15.css). You start off with a few rules that just control the look of the page as a whole:

```
body{
    font-family:arial, verdana, sans-serif;
    color:#333333;
    margin:0px;
    padding:0px;
    background-color:#cccccc;}
```

This is followed by the rule that controls the layout of the <div> element that contains the rest of the page. The page is fixed to have a width of 800px using the width property. It is positioned 10 pixels from the top and left edges of the browser using absolute positioning. The background-color property of the page is also set so that it is distinct from the rest of the page:

```
#page{
    width:800px;
    position:absolute;
    top:10px;
    left:10px;
    background-color:#ffffff;}
```

The first thing in this container is the <div> element whose id attribute has a value of masthead. Following the rules of normal flow, this will appear at the top of the page. The only thing you want to change about the appearance of this block is to give it a border-bottom property to create a line underneath the box, separating it from the navigation and content:

```
#masthead{border-bottom:1px solid #cccccc;}
```

Next up is the navigation, which is floated to the left using the technique you saw in example eg05_13.html. Because it is a float, it needs a width property set (otherwise, it would take up the full 800 pixels of the containing element). This element is also given a background-color property and a border-bottom property to set it apart from other content on the page:

```
#sideNav{
    float: left;
    width:150px;
    background-color: #F5f7f7;
    border-bottom:1px solid #cccccc;}
```

The main part of the page is held in the <div> element whose id attribute has a value of content. This element needs its left margin set to 150px so that the content is not hidden behind the float to the left of it. It is also given a border-left property to draw a line between the main content and the navigation:

```
#content{
    margin:0px 0px 0px 150px;
    border-left:1px solid #cccccc;}
```

That is it for the main rules for the layout. All that is left is to control the properties for the items on the page and the links. Here is the rule for the <div> elements that have a class attribute whose value is item, which gives them padding and height properties:

```
.item{
    padding:10px;
    min-height:75px;
    height:75px;}
```

Finally, you deal with the navigation links. These are given a `display` property whose value is `block` to make them appear on a new line, a `padding` property to space them out, and a special rule to change the color of the background of the links when users hover over them:

```
#sideNav a:link, #sideNav a:visited {
    display:block;
    padding:5px;}
```

```
#sideNav a:hover {background-color:#d6d6d6;}
```

Three-column layouts

In the First Promotions site, you use a three-column layout with a masthead that runs across the width of the page. It is quite easy to add a third column to the example presented in the last section by adding another float like the one that held the navigation, this time floating it to the right. You can see what the page will look like in Figure 5-19.

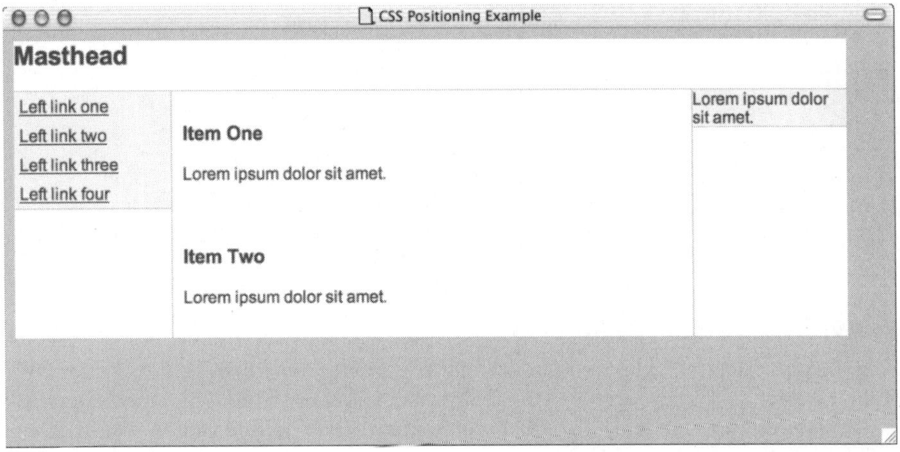

Figure 5-19

First, here is the XHTML that will add the third column. This is held within a `<div>` element whose `id` attribute has a value of `sideRight`. This `<div>` needs to appear before the nonfloated element that holds the main content for the page (this is in the `<div>` element whose `id` attribute has a value of `content`). Here you can see the element that has been added to the previous example to create `ch05_eg16.html`:

```
<div id="sideNav">
    <a href="#">Left link one</a>
    <a href="#">Left link two</a>
    <a href="#">Left link three</a>
```

```
        <a href="#">Left link four</a>
    </div>
    <div id="sideRight">
        Lorem ipsum dolor sit amet.
    </div>
    <div id="content">
```

You need to make a couple of changes to the style sheet to handle this extra column (ch05_eg16.css). First, you can add the styles that deal directly with this element. This time, the box to be floated has a float property that has a value of right to push it to the right-hand side of the containing element. Again, you must set the width property; otherwise, it will take up the full width of the containing element:

```
#sideRight{
    float:right;
    width:150px;
    padding:0px;
    background-color: #F5f7f7;
    border-bottom:1px solid #cccccc;}
```

You also need to change the values for the padding on the rule for the <div> element that holds the main content of the page; it needs to have a 150px margin on the right now in addition to the margin to the left so that it does not overlap with this new column. You also add a border-right property to draw a line between the content and this side panel:

```
#content{
    margin:0px 150px 0px 150px;
    border-left:1px solid #cccccc;
    border-right:1px solid #cccccc;}
```

In this and the preceding example, the borders have been added to the content because it is assumed that these sections of the page will be longer than the side columns. If this were not the case, the line separating the content from the side panel would not reach the bottom of the page.

Adding more features to the layout

The example presented in the last section was starting to look more like the designs for Web pages that you might expect to come across in the real world, and indeed more like the design for the First Promotions site, but you can make the page even more realistic. In this section, you'll enhance the three-column example with the following features:

❑   Top navigation underneath the masthead (in addition to the navigation in the left column)

❑   A footer at the bottom of the page

❑   A search box in the top right-hand corner

When you have finished, the page should look like the one shown in Figure 5-20.

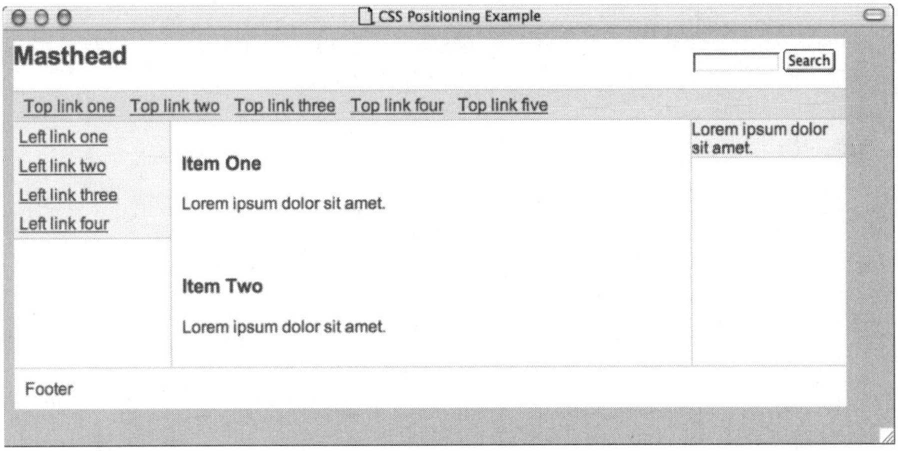

Figure 5-20

The following example shows the XHTML you need to add to create a top navigation bar; it sits between the containers for the masthead and the side navigation. This is in ch05_eg17.html:

```
<div id="masthead">
  <h2>Masthead</h2>
</div>
<div id="topNav">
  <a href="#">Top link one</a>
  <a href="#">Top link two</a>
  <a href="#">Top link three</a>
  <a href="#">Top link four</a>
  <a href="#">Top link five</a>
</div>
<div id="sideNav">
```

Just as with the masthead, the top navigation bar will follow normal flow and sit underneath the masthead without any positioning. Here are the rules you need to add to the style sheet that correspond with these new elements, the first controlling the styles for the box, the second controlling the presentation of the links (ch05_eg17.css):

```
#topNav {
  border-bottom:1px solid #ccd2d2;
  padding:5px;
  background-color:#e7e7e7;}

#topNav a:link, #topNav a:visited{
  padding:0px 5px 0px 5px;}
```

Adding the footer is a similar process. In ch05_eg17.html, the <div> element containing the footer appears just before the closing </div> tag for the whole page:

```
          </div>
          <div id="footer">
            Footer
          </div>
        </div>
      </body>
```

Here you can see the extra rule added to the style sheet for the footer (shown in ch05_eg17.css):

```
#footer{
    clear:both;
    border-top:1px solid #cccccc;
    padding:10px;}
```

This rule must start with a clear property set to both to ensure that it appears at the bottom of the page. If the left or right columns are longer than the main content of the page, and you had not added this clear property, then the footer could appear underneath the main content of the page next to one (or both) of the columns.

Finally, you come to the search box. The search box is going to be absolutely positioned, and you want it to be positioned using offsets from the <div> element that holds the entire page. Therefore, it must appear within the <div> element that contains the page. Because this box is going to be absolutely positioned, it will be removed from normal flow, so this element can appear as a sibling of any of the other major <div> elements that contain the masthead, content, or left and right columns. I have chosen to place it at the end of the page, between the footer and the last closing </div> tag (again, see ch05_eg17.html):

```
        <form id="search" action="">
          <input type="text" name="txtSearch" size="12">
          <input type="submit" name="submit" value="Search">
        </form>
```

The form will be located at the top right-hand corner of the page and is absolutely positioned using offsets that place it 10 pixels from the top and 10 pixels in from the right of the page (shown in ch05_eg17.css):

```
#search{
    position:absolute;
    top:10px;
    right:10px;
    z-index:100;}
```

To ensure that the search box is not hidden behind the masthead, you also give it a z-index property with a value of 100. Finally, because some browsers add a margin around any <form> element, you specifically set the margin property of the <form> element to 0px:

```
form {margin:0px;}
```

And there you have it — a Web page that completely relies upon CSS for positioning and layout, rather than tables.

Image rollovers

It is not uncommon to see image rollovers used on the navigation of a site. In this section, you will learn how to create image rollovers using CSS, rather than JavaScript. As you might imagine, this involves using the :link, :visited, and :hover pseudo-classes.

The rollover you are going to create is for a top navigation bar. It is demonstrated in Figure 5-21.

Figure 5-21

First, look at the XHTML for this example (ch05_eg18.html). The box that contains the navigation bar is contained inside a <div> element whose id attribute has a value of topNav. You can see this stretching across the width of the page. Inside this <div> element is another <div> element, which acts as a container for all of the other links; it will be used to position the links within the navigation box. Note that the <a> elements must not have any spaces between one another; otherwise, in some browsers, you will get unwanted spaces between the image and the dividers.

```
<!DOCTYPE HTML PUBLIC "-//W3C//DTD HTML 4.01 Transitional//EN"
   "http://www.w3.org/TR/html4/loose.dtd">
<html>
<head>
  <title>Nav Bar Example</title>
  <link rel="stylesheet" href="ch05_eg18.css" type="text/css">
</head>
<body>
  <div id="topNav">
     <div id="linkContainer"><a href="#" class="topNavLink">Home</a><a href="#"
class="topNavLink">Products</a><a href="#" class="topNavLink">Services</a><a
href="#" class="topNavLink">About Us</a><a href="#" id="lastItem"
class="topNavLink">Contact Us</a></div>
  </div>
</body>
</html>
```

Now you can look at the CSS that is doing the work here (ch05_eg18.css). First, you have a rule that sets the font and background color for the page:

```
body{
   font-family: Arial, Verdana, sans-serif;
   background-color: #ffffff;}
```

Next, you set the `text-decoration` and `font-weight` properties for all of the links in the document (if you just wanted these rules to apply to the top navigation bar, you could have used the selectors `#linkContainer a:link` and `#linkContainer a:visited`):

```
a:link, a:visited{
    text-decoration: none;
    font-size: 12px;
    font-weight: bold;
    color: #000000;}
```

The `<div>` element that contains the whole navigation bar had an `id` attribute whose value was `topNav`. Like the previous examples in this section, you want the page to be 800 pixels wide, so you set a `width` property on this box. To position this example away from the edges of the page, you use relative positioning and give the box `top` and `left` offset properties, both with a value of 10 pixels.

Essentially, the rollovers work as follows: This element containing the entire navigation bar has a background image, while the `:hover` pseudo-class for each individual link has a second background image that is visible only when the user hovers the mouse over the link. Therefore, the background image for this element remains visible most of the time, and the background image for the links, specified using the `:hover` pseudo-class, shows up only when the link is rolled over. The `height` property for this element is set at the same height as the background image for the top navigation. The image needs to be only 1 pixel wide, and it should stretch across the full width of the `<div>`:

```
#topNav{
    width:800px;
    position:relative;
    top:10px;
    left:10px;
    background-image:url("topNavBackground.gif");
    height:32px;
    color:#cccccc;
    padding:0px;
    margin:0px;}
```

The next task is the container that holds the links. The container positions the links within the box for the navigation using absolute positioning. The `z-index` property is set on this element to explicitly indicate that these items should be kept on top of the box that creates the navigation bar, in case any browser wants to hide the links behind the parent `<div>`:

```
#linkContainer{
    position:absolute;
    top:10px;
    left:10px;
    height:16px;
    padding:0px;
    margin:0px;
    z-index:1;}
```

Finally, you come to the rules for the links themselves. These links are given padding to separate them from one another. They are also given a line to the right, to separate them from one another using the `border-right` property to draw a single-pixel link:

```
a.topNavLink, a.topNavLink:visited{
    padding: 0px 5px 0px 5px;
    border-right: 1px solid #666666;}
```

As it is, this would create a line to the right of the last image; however, the last link carries an id attribute whose value is lastItem, so you can create a more specific rule for just this item, setting its border-right property to none and preventing the last item from drawing a line to its right:

```
a#lastItem {border-right:none;}
```

To finish, here is the rule that creates the rollover effect when the user hovers the mouse over this option, changing the background image for the link:

```
a.topNavLink:hover{background-image:url("topNavRollover.gif");}
```

This image is again only 1 pixel wide; it will then stretch to the full width of the link, no matter how much text the link contains.

Choices for layout

This chapter has shown you how CSS offers a powerful way of controlling the layout of your pages without relying on the two techniques that prevailed in the 1990s — tables and frames. Unfortunately, CSS layout was not really supported until IE 5 and Netscape 6, and their support is still far from perfect, particularly Internet Explorer, which has several well-documented bugs and cannot always offer pixel-accurate layouts (as mentioned earlier in this chapter, the site www.positioniseverything.net is an excellent resource that covers bugs related to CSS positioning).

If you want to create complex layouts for version 4 browsers, it is unlikely that you will be relying upon CSS to control layout, although it is likely that the vast majority of visitors to your site will be using more recent browsers (and the number of Web users who still rely on these technologies decreases constantly). Furthermore, as you will see in the next chapter, separating style from content is an important aspect of creating accessible sites, so this is definitely the direction in which Web page layout is heading.

The techniques and sample layouts that you have met in this chapter should enable you to create some complex layouts that use CSS for positioning, and you will see more examples in the "Solution" section later in the chapter.

Before updating the sample site, however, it would be a good idea to look briefly at situations in which you might still want to use tables or frames (the two other alternatives for controlling Web page layout).

When to use tables for layout

The simple answer for when to use tables for layout is that they should be used only for tabular data — timetables, sports results, and so on. In such cases, a table is not only the correct way of marking up such data, but it can also make the data more accessible to those with disabilities.

However, you may encounter other scenarios in which you might need to rely on tables — for example, when you need pixel-perfect accuracy in layout (and the Internet Explorer bugs prevent you from achieving this in all browsers). This is especially likely if you have very complicated layouts that rely on numerous images that have been cut up to create a complex design, or, indeed, when you need to control layout in version 4 browsers.

As you will see in Chapter 7, the use of tables can seriously affect the accessibility of a Web page, although you will also learn in that chapter some techniques that can ensure that even if you do use tables for layout, your site will remain accessible.

When to use frames for layout

In the 1990s, it was not uncommon to see sites that used frames to control the layout of parts of a page, and some sites still use them. However, you should generally avoid using frames as a way of controlling the layout of a page (splitting it into panes). Ideally, you should use CSS to control layout, or, failing that, you should use well-designed tables.

Two exceptions to this, where you might still want to consider using frames, are as follows:

❑　When you have a large amount of content that remains the same for each page that would otherwise take a long time to download for each page. Such a case might be a photography site containing thumbnails for numerous images in one frame, and the user can click on a thumbnail to see an enlargement of that image in the main frame. Putting the thumbnails in a navigation frame would save them having to be reloaded each time a user wanted to see an enlarged image.

❑　When you have a very long document, and you want to provide an index or annotations in a frame without users having to reload the document each time they want to move to a different section of a document or read an annotation

You should certainly avoid using them to position mastheads or standard navigation links. Remember, too, that if you want to use frames in XHTML, there is a special XHTML Frameset DTD that uses the `<frameset>` element instead of the `<body>` element.

Solution

Having learned how to create some quite complex layouts using CSS, it is time to convert the First Promotions home page to use CSS for layout, rather than tables. You might have noticed that the examples you have been developing in the second half of the chapter bear a strong resemblance to the structure of the site, so it should not be too hard to adapt these examples to house your promotional goodies.

You may remember from the beginning of the book that I said you would be updating the site to make it look a little more modern. To achieve that end, the solution section of this chapter not only addresses using CSS to control layout of the site, but also features a more modern design. This chapter focuses on the home page, but you can see the completely rebuilt and modernized site in Appendix A.

You can see what the home page will look like when you have finished in Figure 5-22.

The structure of the page is very similar to how it looked when we started. There is a masthead at the top, followed by navigation that runs the width of the page. The main part of the page is divided into three sections: the left-hand navigation, the main content, and ordering information. One difference you might notice with this design is that the footer links run the width of the bottom of the page. In addition, only two featured items are present on this version of the home page.

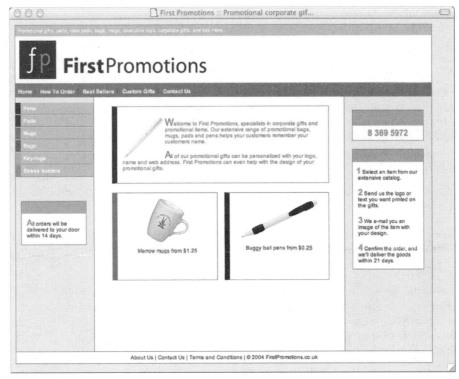

Figure 5-22

To begin, take a look at the XHTML for the page. Note how all of the tables (except for the featured items) have been replaced with `<div>` elements, each with different values for the id attributes.

The whole page is held within a `<div>` element whose id attribute has a value of page. Next are the child `<div>`s for the byline, masthead, and top navigation:

```
<?xml version="1.0" encoding="iso-8859-1"?>
<!DOCTYPE html PUBLIC "-//W3C//DTD XHTML 1.0 Strict//EN"
    "http://www.w3.org/TR/xhtml1/DTD/xhtml1-strict.dtd">
<html>

<head>
  <title>First Promotions :: Promotional corporate gifts (pens, notepads, mugs,
    and bags)</title>
  <link rel="stylesheet" href="interface.css" type="text/css" />
  <meta http-equiv="Content-Type" content="text/html; charset=iso-8859-1" />
</head>

<body>

<div id="page">
  <div id="byline">Promotional gifts, pens, note pads, bags, mugs, executive toys,
    corporate gifts, and lots more... </div>
```

```
<div id="masthead">
  <img src="images/interface/logo.gif" alt="logo" width="364" height="77" />
</div>
<div id="topNav">
  <div id="linkContainer"> <a href="index.html" class="topNavLink">Home</a><a
href="howToOrder.html" class="topNavLink">How To Order</a><a
href="bestSellers.html" class="topNavLink">Best Sellers</a><a
href="customerGifts.html" class="topNavLink">Custom Gifts</a><a
href="contactUs.html" id="lastItem" class="topNavLink">Contact Us</a></div>
</div>
```

Still within the `<div>` holding the page, you have the side panels, which must appear before the main content in the central column because they are floated. You might notice that the left navigation items now have divider images between them, and the ordering information on the right is no longer contained within a table.

Both side panels also contain child `<div>` elements; on the left they hold the guarantee information and on the right they show the ordering information (even the table that used to hold the four steps for ordering have been replaced with `<div>` elements):

```
<div id="sideLeft"><a href="products/pens/index.html" class="pens">Pens</a>
  <img src="images/interface/nav_divider.gif" alt="" width="149" height="2" />
  <a href="products/pads/index.html" class="pads">Pads</a>
    <img src="images/interface/nav_divider.gif" alt="" width="149" height="2" />
  <a href="products/mugs/index.html" class="mugs">Mugs</a>
    <img src="images/interface/nav_divider.gif" alt="" width="149" height="2" />
  <a href="products/bags/index.html" class="bags">Bags</a>
    <img src="images/interface/nav_divider.gif" alt="" width="149" height="2" />
  <a href="products/keyrings/index.html" class="keyrings">Keyrings</a>
    <img src="images/interface/nav_divider.gif" alt="" width="149" height="2" />
  <a href="products/stressbusters/index.html" class="stessbusters">
    Stress busters</a>
    <img src="images/interface/nav_divider.gif" alt="" width="149" height="2" />
  <br /><br />

  <div class="leftPanel">
    <img src="images/interface/guarantee.gif" alt="our guarantee"
      width="124" height="22" />
    <div class="point">All orders will be delivered to your door within
      21 days.</div>
  </div>
</div>

<div id="sideRight">
  <div class="rightPanel">
    <img src="images/interface/orderHotline.gif" width="138" height="28"
      alt="Order hotline 8 369 5972" />
    <div class="orderNumber">8 369 5972</div>
  </div>

  <div class="rightPanel">
    <img src="images/interface/howToOrder.gif" width="137" height="23"
      alt="How to order" />
```

```
        <div class="point">1 Select an item from our extensive catalog.</div>
        <div class="point">2 Send us the logo or text you want printed on the
          gifts.</div>
        <div class="point">3 We e-mail you an image of the item with your
          design.</div>
        <div class="point">4 Confirm the order, and we'll deliver the goods within
          21 days.</div>
      </div>
    </div>
```

Following the <div> elements that hold the left and right columns is the <div> element that contains the main central column of the page, which starts off with a box containing some text:

```
<div id="content"><br />
  <div class="item">
    <img src="images/interface/photo_pen.jpg" alt="Photograph of silver pen"
      width="75" height="75" id="homePenImage" />
    <p>Welcome to First Promotions, specialists in corporate gifts and
      promotional items. Our extensive range of promotional bags, mugs, pads
      and pens helps your customers remember your customers name.</p>
    <p>All of our promotional gifts can be personalized with your logo, name
      and Web address. First Promotions can even help with the design of your
      promotional gifts.</p>
  </div>

  <br/>
```

In the same central column is a table containing the featured items. As you might notice, the table that held these items has been removed:

```
<div class="featuredRow">
  <p id="left" class="mugs"><a href="#">
    <img src="products/mugs/images/mugs2_thumb.gif" alt="Marrow mug"
      width="88" height="80" /><br /><br />
    Marrow mugs from $1.25</a></p>
  <p id="right" class="pens"><a href="#">
    <img src="products/pens/images/pens2_thumb.gif" alt="Buggy Pen"
      width="150" height="75"  /><br /><br />
    Buggy ball pens from $0.25</a></p>
  </div>
</div>
```

Finally, there is the <div> element containing the footer:

```
<div id="footer">
  <a href="#">About Us</a> |
  <a href="#">Contact Us</a> |
  <a href="#">Terms and Conditions</a> | &copy; 2004 FirstPromotions.co.uk
</div>

</div>
</body>
</html>
```

Now have a look at the style sheet for this example. You can begin with a few general rules, first indicating some rules for the whole document, then for the images (remember that if you do not specify that images should not have a border, then any images that are links will have a border around them), and finally a rule for links:

```
body{
    font-family: arial, verdana, sans-serif;
    color: #333333;
    margin: 0px;
    padding: 0px;
    background-color: #f1f1f1;}

img {border:none;}

a {text-decoration:none; color:#990000;}
```

The next rules control the positioning of the main <div> elements that contain the sections of the page, starting with the one that contains the whole page. The <div> element that holds the content of the whole page is absolutely positioned 10 pixels from the top left-hand corner of the page and is given a width of 800px:

```
#page{
    position:absolute;
    padding:0px;
    margin:0px;
    top:10px;
    left:10px;
    width:800px;
    border: 1px solid #888888;
    background-color:#ffffff;}
```

Next up are the rules for the <div> elements that hold the byline, the masthead, and the top navigation:

```
#byline{
    color:#ffffff;
    background-color:#cbcbcb;
    font-size:xx-small;
    padding:5px;}

#masthead{
    border-bottom:1px solid #888888;
    padding:5px;}

#topNav {
    border-bottom:1px solid #888888;
    padding:5px;
    background-color:#999999;}
```

Following next are the rules for the left and right columns, which are similar to those described in the section that introduced a three-column layout. This involves floating one element to the left and another to the right, while leaving the space in the middle for the third column. The left column has been given a 1-pixel border to the right to separate it from the middle column, and the right column has been given a 1-pixel border to the left to separate it from the middle column:

```
#sideLeft{
  float: left;
  width:150px;
  height:450px;
  border-right:1px solid #888888;
  background-color: #efefef;
  padding:10px 0px 10px 0px; }

#sideRight{
  float: right;
  width:165px;
  height:450px;
  border-left:1px solid #888888;
  background-color: #efefef;
  text-align:center;
  padding:10px 0px 10px 0px; }
```

The rule for the middle column needs the left and right margin properties to be set so that the content of the middle column does not overlap with the left and right floats:

```
#content{
  margin:0px 165px 0px 150px;}
```

The footer, as you saw in the section "Adding More Features to the Layout" earlier in the chapter, requires a clear property whose value is both to ensure that it clears the floats and appears on its own line:

```
#footer{
  clear: both;
  border-top: 1px solid #888888;
  padding:5px;
  font-size:x-small;
  text-align:center;}
```

The item class holds the text that introduces the site, which lives in the middle column in a gray box. The margins to the left and the right of this element make the box look like it is centered; it is given padding to add white space and make the text more readable; and the borders are set individually so that the left-hand side can have a 10-pixel colored border, while all others are single-pixel gray borders (you will see this technique used on all of the links and the featured items boxes, too):

```
.item{
  margin:0px 35px 0px 35px;
  padding:10px;
  font-size:x-small;
  color:#888888;
  border-left:10px solid #990000;
  border-right:1px solid #888888;
  border-top:1px solid #888888;
  border-bottom:1px solid #888888;}
```

A special rule controls the appearance of the image of the pen in this box; the image is floated to the left of the text and given a 10-pixel margin at the top to align it with the text:

```
#homePenImage {
   float:left;
   margin-top:10px;}
```

For each paragraph in this box containing the introductory text, the first letter is made a lot larger using the `first-letter` pseudo-class:

```
.item p:first-letter {font-size:large;}
```

Now look at the CSS for the featured items. These are no longer kept inside a table; rather, they reside in a `<div>` whose `class` attribute has a value of `featuredRow`. Inside this `<div>` are two `<p>` elements that hold the picture, description, and link for the featured items. The featured row has margins set just like the box containing the introductory text:

```
div.featuredRow {
   margin: 0px 35px 0px 35px;}
```

Then the paragraph elements contained within this element are floated, one to the left and one to the right:

```
div.featuredRow p#left {float:left;}
div.featuredRow p#right {float:right;}
```

Each of these featured items shares some common rules. As with all floated elements, you must specify a width for these boxes; otherwise, they will take up the full width of the containing box.

*You might also notice that this rule does not contain a property for **border-left**, although the top, right, and bottom borders are set. This is because each section of the site is color-coded — if you look at the links to each section in the left-hand column, different colors identify each section. The left-hand border of the featured items matches the color for the section in which the item belongs. The **border-left** property is set using a CSS rule that corresponds with the value for the **class** attribute that is used on both the featured items boxes and the side navigation items.*

```
div.featuredRow p#left, div.featuredRow p#right {
   margin:0px;
   width:170px;
   height:150px;
   padding:10px;
   text-align:center;
   font-size:x-small;
   border-right: 1px solid #888888;
   border-top: 1px solid #888888;
   border-bottom: 1px solid #888888;}
```

There is one problem with this layout: It contains a bug that shows up only on IE 5/IE 6 on Windows (not on IE 5 for Mac). As it is, this rule will leave a large gap between the featured items on IE for Windows, which requires that you assign a different width for the featured items boxes that can be seen only by IE on Windows. Therefore, you have to resort to a hack that is based upon the Tan hack, but works only for IE on Windows. As you can see, there is a comment at the beginning of the rule that carries a backslash before it is closed, which will hide this rule from IE on a Mac, and the * html in the selector will prevent the rule from showing in browsers other than IE:

```
/* hide from IE/Mac \*/
* html div.featuredRow p#left, * html div.featuredRow p#right {
  width:200px;}
/* end hiding */
```

That fixes the problem for all browsers.

Next in the style sheet are the rules for the navigation, which are just like the ones described in the section entitled "Adding More Features to the Layout" earlier in the chapter, except this time no background image is displayed when the user's mouse is not hovering over the links—just a background color:

```
#topNav a:link, #topNav a:visited{
  padding:0px 5px 0px 5px;
  font-size:x-small;
  font-weight:bold;}

#topNav{
  width:100%;
  background-color:#888888;
  height:24px;
  padding:0px;
  margin:0px;}

#linkContainer{
  position:relative;
  top:4px;
  height:16px;
  padding:0px;
  margin:0px;
  z-index:1;}

a.topNavLink, a.topNavLink:visited{
  padding: 0px 5px 0px 5px;
  border-right: 1px solid #666666;
  color:#ffffff;
  font-size:small;}

a.topNavLink:hover{background-image:url("images/interface/topNavRollover.gif");
  color:#990000;}

a#lastItem {border-right:none;}
```

You also need to add special rules for the side navigation items. The first rule ensures that each link is displayed as a block box and sets some colors for the box:

```
#sideLeft a:link, #sideLeft a:visited{
  display:block;
  color:#ffffff;
  font-size:x-small;
  font-weight:bold;
  padding:5px;
  background-color:#cbcbcb;}
```

If you look at the XHTML for this part of the page, the links are separated by images that are 2 pixels high, and the following rule is another hack that prevents gaps from appearing between the navigation items and the divider images in Netscape and Firefox:

```
#sideLeft img {display:block;vertical-align:top;}
```

Each section of the site has been color-coded, and the `class` attributes on the `<a>` elements that create the side navigation correspond with `border-left` properties that show the relevant colors:

```
.pens {border-left:10px solid #003366;}
.pads {border-left:10px solid #990000;}
.mugs {border-left:10px solid #996699;}
.bags {border-left:10px solid #669900;}
.keyrings {border-left:10px solid #ffcc00;}
.stessbusters {border-left:10px solid #ff9900;}
```

The final rule for the side navigation changes the background color of the links when the user's mouse hovers over them, creating a similar effect to a rollover navigation image:

```
#sideLeft a:hover {background-color:#999999;}
```

In the left-hand column of the main part of the page is a `<div>` element that holds the guarantee information. This `<div>` element has a `class` attribute whose value is `leftPanel`. The following rule controls the presentation of that box (to center the box in the middle of the column, the `margin` property has been set):

```
.leftPanel {
    width:124px;
    margin:10px;
    border: 1px solid #888888;
    background-color:#ffffff;
    text-align:left;
    font-size:x-small;}
```

A similar rule is used for panels on the two panels on the right-hand column of the page:

```
.rightPanel {
    width:137px;
    margin:15px;
    border: 1px solid #888888;
      background-color:#ffffff;
    text-align:left;
    font-size:x-small;}
```

Separate rules control the presentation of the phone number for orders and for each of the four points that tell customers how to order:

```
.orderNumber {
      text-align:center;
      padding:5px;
      font-size:medium;
```

```
        font-weight:bold;
        color:#ff9900;}

    .point {
     padding:5px;
     color:#333333;
        margin:5px;}

   .point:first-letter {
        color:#ff9900;
        font-size:medium;
        font-weight:bold;}
```

That completes the version of the home page written solely in XHTML and CSS, and without a single table. You can see a complete version of the entire site using this approach and incorporating the accessibility techniques you will be learning in the next two chapters in Appendix A. There you will find some additional CSS techniques that will be of interest, as neither the product list pages nor the product details pages use tables for layout.

Summary

In this chapter, you have seen how CSS can be used to control the layout of pages. You examined the three main layout models (normal flow, floats, and absolute positioning) used in CSS to position boxes on a page. Having learned about the CSS layout models, you then looked at some common examples of page designs and how they can be recreated in XHTML and CSS without using tables. You saw vertical panels, multiple columns, and a mix of the two approaches.

At the end of the chapter, you used the techniques you learned to create a new home page for the First Promotions site that relied upon CSS for layout, rather than tables.

That wraps up the section of this book that covers CSS. In Chapters 6 and 7, you will learn how to ensure that your site meets accessibility requirements.

Understanding Accessibility

The topic of accessibility has been highlighted a lot in the news lately. Laws have been passed in many countries around the world that now require Web sites to be accessible to those with disabilities; and if a site does not meet accessibility guidelines, its owners can be forced to redesign the site. If the owner of the site fails to redesign the site within a given time frame, they can face a heavy fine. This does not mean that you should wait until you are told to redesign a site before you make it accessible. As you will see in this chapter, making a site accessible not only ensures that visitors with disabilities can access the site; it can also offer several other advantages.

Furthermore, as a designer or programmer, you may find it hard to get another job unless you understand the accessibility requirements, because many employers require a good understanding of accessibility as part of the key skills required for Web-related positions.

In this chapter, you will learn:

❑   What it means to make a site accessible

❑   The advantages of making a site accessible

❑   Different ways in which users might access Web sites — in particular, using screen readers to read the content of the screen to the user

❑   What the W3C Web Content Accessibility Guidelines (or WCAG) are, how they are structured, and what some of the specific guidelines govern

❑   What the U.S. Government Section 508 guidelines are, how they are structured, and what some of the specific guidelines govern

❑   Several techniques to help make your Web pages accessible — in particular, issues relating to structure, text, images, audio, color, contrast, and navigation

Chapter 7 will then proceed to look at some additional specific details regarding accessibility (such as tables, forms, and frames) and describe how to test your site for accessibility requirements.

Problem

As the Internet has grown in popularity, and is now being used to offer a huge range of services from online shopping/banking/bill paying to electronic voting, it is important that those with disabilities are able to access these services. Laws and job requirements have forced Web designers and developers to learn how to create Web sites that are accessible to those with disabilities, much in the same way that architects now have to design public buildings so that they can be accessed by visitors in wheelchairs.

Therefore, you need to make sure that the First Promotions site meets accessibility requirements—in particular, the W3C Web Content Accessibility Guidelines and the U.S. Government Section 508 guidelines.

To help you learn these two sets of guidelines, this chapter looks at different aspects of a site (such as its structure, how text is marked up, use of color, and navigation) and explains how you can improve the accessibility of each of these aspects.

To give you an idea of the kinds of problems Web users face, consider a couple of examples:

❑   If a user has severe vision impairment, he or she will probably use a program called a *screen reader* to read the text on a page. However, if a designer uses images with words in them and does not provide a text equivalent for the image, the program will not be able to read this content. These images could represent anything from the company name in the logo at the top of the page to the main navigation links on a site. In addition, those using devices to read the content of a screen often have to listen to the same header information and links at the start of every page before they get to the real content of the page, whereas sighted users can scan the page to find the information they are looking for with a lot greater ease; therefore, it is important to enable users of screen readers to skip content that is repeated on every page. In addressing the problems faced by people with disabilities who use screen readers, you will also be preparing your site for other visitors who might want to access it without looking at the screen—maybe when they are driving or jogging.

❑   Many Web users have difficulty using a mouse or other pointing devices, so you need to ensure that people can navigate your site without relying upon precise positioning of a cursor. For example, many users would have difficulties with drop-down menus that are overreactive. Therefore, it is important to enable users to navigate a site one step at a time. In helping users with motor control, or hand-eye coordination, difficulties, you are also helping any users who might have a "sticky" mouse, or who might navigate using a keyboard, rather than a pointing device.

In short, by addressing the challenges of those with disabilities, you not only help those who might have had difficulty accessing your site; you also make your site available to a wide range of other Web users, and generally easier to use. In particular, you will learn how accessible content can be made available to people who do not have physical disabilities, but who may be limited by the situations in which they find themselves—for example, if they are not able to read or do not have their hands free to navigate because they are driving or jogging.

Design

Accessibility is all about enabling people to get to (or access) the content of a Web site and ensuring that they can navigate (get around) the site to find the information or perform the task they want.

Designing sites that are accessible requires a combination of adding some new elements and attributes to your documents that help increase accessibility and slightly changing existing techniques you are already familiar with from other parts of your Web pages.

As I have already indicated, most of this chapter will be spent looking at different aspects of site design, such as the structure of pages, text markup, nontext items (such as images, video, objects, and applets), and navigation, addressing each in turn and examining how you can make these aspects of the site accessible. This chapter covers the following main topics:

❑   Assistive technologies are technologies that make it easier for users with disabilities to access and navigate a site. Reviewing these can help you understand how those with disabilities access Web sites.

❑   Accessibility does not just affect those with disabilities, and as you will see in the following sections, many additional benefits are gained by developing accessible sites.

❑   Two key sets of guidelines offer advice about how to make Web sites accessible; it's worth finding and reviewing them.

Assistive technology

Many Web users with disabilities rely on what is known as *assistive technology* to help them use the Web and computers in general. There are several types of assistive technology, but the most common type used on the Web is the *screen reader*, which is a program used by those with visual impairments in order to access information on the screen.

Modern screen readers are quite complex tools; they do not simply read the content of the screen from left to right and top to bottom as you might imagine. Such an approach would not work because many Web pages have different sections of a page on the same level. For example, in a three-column layout (such as the First Promotions site), you may have left navigation, a central column of text, and an advertisement on the right. If all of this content were read across the same horizontal line, it would make little sense (the reader might end up hearing one item from the navigation in the left column, a line of content from the middle column, and a line of the advertisement from the right column). Therefore, screen readers need to *linearize* a page, reading the boxes in an order that will make sense to the user. (You will learn more about linearization in Chapter 7.)

It is also important to remember that sighted Web users can scan a page to quickly find the information they want, looking up and down the page as well as from left and right and vice versa; and this information will usually be clearly defined (either by using different levels of headings or by creating boxes that hold sections of a page). However, users with visual impairments cannot easily scan a page; they cannot see the visual clues that sighted users can, and they can hear only one set of words (and therefore one section of content) at a time.

Rather than wait for the entire page to be read to them from start to finish, blind readers usually use keyboard shortcuts to navigate the page and find the content or links they are seeking. This is possible because most modern screen readers can look at the markup of the document and skip blocks of text, or find headings and links (this is achieved because modern screen readers work with the Document Object Model, or DOM, which you may be familiar with if you have written any JavaScript).

The three most common pieces of screen-reading software are as follows:

❑ **JAWS for Windows (JFW)** — which is made by Freedom Scientific (`www.FreedomScientific.com`). At the time of writing, it cost $895 for the standard version and $1,095 for the professional version. This is the most popular software.

❑ **Home Page Reader (HPR)** — which is made by IBM (`www.IBM.com/able`). It cost $142 at the time of writing. This is possibly the easiest of the three tools for Web developers to learn (as well as the cheapest).

❑ **Windows-Eyes** — which is made by GW Micro (`www.gwmicro.com`). It currently costs $299 for a single-user license.

Even if the price does not deter you from acquiring one of these programs, using it might. Screen readers use complex keyboard combinations so that they do not conflict with shortcuts offered by other programs; and unless you regularly use one, it can be very difficult to get the hang of navigating a site using one. (It would be a good idea to download a demo version before buying one of these programs.) However, the best way to learn how a page will sound when read by a screen reader is to use one, and if you are going to develop accessible Web sites, you should invest in one and take time to learn the basics of navigating pages and having content read to you.

Other examples of assistive technologies include the following:

❑ Braille readers, which create a Braille equivalent of what a screen reader might read out on an electronic Braille pad

❑ Screen magnifiers, which increase the magnification of content on a screen to help those who have trouble reading a screen with text at normal sizes

❑ Custom CSS style sheets that increase the size of text on pages

❑ Alternatives to mice, including trackballs, touch screens, foot control mice, eye or head movement tracking systems, and joysticks

Additional accessibility benefits

While one of the main focuses of work on accessibility has been providing access to those who have disabilities, this work has also produced many benefits for those who do not have any disabilities but who are trying to access the Web when they are not at their desk and are using devices other than a PC. It is helpful, therefore, to make a distinction between two types of limitations that people face when attempting to access to the Web:

❑ **Functional limitations** refer to disabilities such as blindness or limited control over a keyboard or pointing device (such as a mouse). Functional limitations can be visual, auditory, physical, or cognitive. (Cognitive limitations could include language or learning disabilities.)

❑ **Situational difficulties** refer to the way in which devices are used in certain circumstances, such as driving or running (when the use of hands and eyes are limited), and by types of device (which can have differently sized screens, different control or input methods, and different amounts of memory and power available to them — for example, mobile phones typically have small screens, no mouse, less memory, and a limited power supply).

Therefore, you have several reasons why you should create sites that comply with accessibility regulations. In addition to regulations and legal requirements that force you to comply (or redesign your site), the following reasons also point to the benefits of compliance:

❏ Accessible sites separate design from content, and therefore carry all the benefits associated with keeping presentational markup and rules out of the document; these issues have been addressed throughout the book.

❏ You make your site accessible on more devices and in more situations, saving you from re-writing your site in the future.

❏ An accessible site gives you a bigger audience, not only expanding your potential visitors to users with functional limitations but also to users on devices other than desktop PCs operating in a range of situations.

❏ Designing a site with accessibility in mind from the start is far cheaper than going back and redesigning it just because it did not meet accessibility requirements.

❏ A site designed with accessibility in mind is often a lot easier to use for many people (not just those with disabilities).

Clearly, the benefits of accessible designs stretch far beyond helping those with disabilities. In creating an accessible site, you ensure that your site is available to more people, at more times, and in more situations.

Introducing the guidelines

You need to be aware of two key sets of guidelines when creating accessible Web sites:

❏ The **Web Content Accessibility Guidelines 1.0** published by the W3C's Web Accessibility Initiative. These were released in May 1999 and have been adopted by many countries. These are referred to throughout the chapter as the *WCAG guidelines*.

❏ The **Electronic and Information Technology Accessibility Standards** published by the U.S. Access Board in December 2000 following a U.S. rule-making process that was required by Section 508 of the Rehabilitation Act Amendments of 1998. These are referred to throughout the chapter as the *Section 508 guidelines*.

No matter where you live, you should be looking at, and following, both sets of guidelines. The more points you meet, the more visitors will be able to access your site (and the less likely you are to fall afoul of the law).

WCAG guidelines

The WCAG contain a set of 65 checkpoints (grouped together under a set of 14 general guidelines) that a site must meet in order to be considered accessible. You can find a copy of the WCAG guidelines at `www.w3.org/TR/WCAG10`. The W3C also publishes examples showing how you should implement the guidelines in HTML (and XHTML) at `www.w3.org/TR/WCAG10-HTML-TECHS`.

There are three different priority levels for the checkpoints in the WCAG guidelines:

❏ **Priority 1** — A Web content developer *must* satisfy this checkpoint. Otherwise, one or more groups will find it impossible to access information in the document. Satisfying this checkpoint is a basic requirement in order for some groups of people to be able to use Web documents.

247

❑   **Priority 2** — A Web content developer *should* satisfy this checkpoint. Otherwise, one or more groups will find it difficult to access information in the document. Satisfying this checkpoint will remove significant barriers to accessing Web documents.

❑   **Priority 3** — A Web content developer *may* address this checkpoint. Otherwise, one or more groups will find it somewhat difficult to access information in the document. Satisfying this checkpoint will improve access to Web documents.

Of the 65 checkpoints, there are 16 priority 1 checkpoints, 30 priority 2 checkpoints, and 19 priority 3 checkpoints. When you follow these guidelines, your site is likely to conform to the WCAG, which designates three corresponding levels of conformance:

❑   **Conformance Level "A"** — All priority 1 checkpoints are satisfied.

❑   **Conformance Level "Double-A"** — All priority 1 and 2 checkpoints are satisfied.

❑   **Conformance Level "Triple-A"** — All priority 1, 2, and 3 checkpoints are satisfied.

If your site conforms to the guidelines, you may wish to indicate it on each page in one of the two following ways:

❑   You can use one of the icons provided by the W3C, which link to the W3C explanation of the claim. You can find the logos and information on how to use them at `www.w3.org/WAI/WCAG1-Conformance.html`.

❑   You can specify the conformance information in text, in which case you should supply the following:

> ❑   **Title of the guidelines** — "Web Content Accessibility Guidelines 1.0"
>
> ❑   **URL for the guidelines** — `www.w3.org/TR/1999/WAI-WEBCONTENT-19990505`
>
> ❑   **Level of conformance reached** — "A," "Double-A," or "Triple-A" (note that this should be spelled out as shown here for screen readers)
>
> ❑   **Scope covered by the claim** — For example, the page, site, or section of the site

For example, you might add the following to your page:

```
This page conforms to W3C's "Web Content Accessibility Guidelines 1.0", available
at http://www.w3.org/TR/1999/WAI-WEBCONTENT-19990505, level Double-A.
```

At the time of writing, the W3C was also working on the Web Content Accessibility Guidelines version 2. In early 2005, these guidelines were at the working draft *status, which means that there was still potential for a lot of change. However, some key points of that draft have been added as background notes in this and the following chapter, so you can consider these points when developing sites in the future.*

Section 508 guidelines

The Section 508 guidelines were based upon the W3C WCAG 1.0, but they contain some additional rules particular to U.S. law. Two important differences to keep in mind are the following:

❑ Unlike the WCAG guidelines, the Section 508 guidelines do not contain different levels of conformance; you must obey all of the rules in Section 508 to comply with the guidelines.

❑ The Section 508 guidelines are part of a much larger effort, not just focused on the Web but on all electronic and information technology resources.

You can find a copy of the Section 508 guidelines at `www.section508.gov/index.cfm?FuseAction=Content&ID=12`. You can find more information about Section 508 at `http://usability.gov/accessibility/508.html`.

The section of specific interest to Web developers is Section 1194.22, entitled "Web-based Intranet and Internet Information and Applications," which contains sixteen guidelines — 1194.22 (a) to 1194.22 (p).

Creating accessible Web pages

Now that you are familiar with the two sets of guidelines you need to follow and have learned a little about how users with disabilities access Web pages, it is time to learn how to make specific aspects of your Web pages accessible.

To learn how to make a site accessible, you will look at particular aspects of a site or page design and address how to make each aspect comply with the necessary accessibility guidelines. Specifically, you will be looking at the following:

❑ Using W3C standards where possible

❑ Controlling presentation with CSS

❑ Structuring content and correctly using markup

❑ Dealing with nontext content, including images, audio, video, applets, and objects

❑ Controlling dynamic content such as scripts and pop-up windows, and refreshing pages

❑ Color and contrast

❑ Creating accessible navigation

As you look at each topic, you will see which WCAG and Section 508 guidelines apply to each topic or aspect of the site.

Using the W3C standards

You have actually already learned a lot about making your site accessible in this book, even if you did not realize it. You have learned about using XHTML and CSS to create Web pages, which are a far stronger foundation for creating accessible pages than using older versions of HTML:

❑ The combination of XHTML and CSS separates the content and the markup that describes the structure of a document from the rules that control how the document is presented.

❑ XHTML uses a stricter structure, which makes it easier for accessibility tools to process, and makes it easier to display the same content on different devices.

❑ You can use CSS to control the layout of a document, rather than use tables to create layout grids (which can cause problems for assistive technologies, as you will see in Chapter 7).

The checkpoints in this section refer to creating documents as a whole (rather than specific sections of a Web page), and the first guideline you are going to meet is a WCAG checkpoint that specifically indicates you should use W3C technologies where appropriate for a task and to use the most recent versions where possible:

> **OWCAG 11.1 Use W3C technologies when they are available and appropriate for a task and use the latest versions when supported. [Priority 2]**

The following point in the WCAG guidelines indicates that you should avoid deprecated features; for example, you should use CSS to control the presentation of text, rather than the `<font>` element:

> **WCAG 11.2 Avoid deprecated features of W3C technologies. [Priority 2]**

When a user requests a page, information about the browser is sent to the server that hosts the page. This includes information such as the type of browser you are using, the type of files it can accept, and the default language to which you have it set. You should therefore try to specify information in your documents that will help users receive documents according to their preferences (and their browsers capabilities):

> **WCAG 11.3 Provide information so that users may receive documents according to their preferences (e.g., language, content type, etc.) [Priority 3]**

Practically speaking, this means the following:

❑ When including or linking to a resource such as a style sheet, Flash movie, or MP3, you should use the `type` attribute to indicate the MIME type of the resource (for example, a Braille reader is unlikely to be able to play MP3 files).

❑ If you have versions of the same content in more than one language, you should try to offer the page in the user's chosen language, and you should provide links to other versions of the document. This involves using the `lang` or `xml:lang` attributes in your documents and will usually require that some work is done on the server to determine the user's language and send the appropriate version.

❑ You should make it clear if you provide alternate presentations of the same page using alternative style sheets.

It is also important to use `!DOCTYPE` declarations to indicate the language in which your documents are written and to validate the documents that you have written before putting them on your site:

> **WCAG 3.2 Create documents that validate to published formal grammars. [Priority 2]**

The WCAG also recommends that you provide metadata about the document, such as its author, the type of content, keywords, and so on. Ways of adding this information include using <meta> tags in the <head> of the document or using RDF:

> **WCAG 13.2 Provide metadata to add semantic information to pages and sites. [Priority 2]**

It also helps users navigate a site if you create a site map that describes the structure of the site and its content. This is a helpful first entry point for anyone who wants to know the general content of the site and where information can be found:

> **WCAG 13.3 Provide information about the general layout of a site (e.g., a site map or table of contents). [Priority 2]**

It is also a good idea to explicitly describe any particular accessibility features of the site that the user might find helpful in the site map document.

Here is the start of a page that incorporates many of the points in this section by providing the following:

- ❑ The markup language used to create the page

- ❑ A lot of metadata about the page such as the author, copyright, date created, a description, and keywords

- ❑ The content type, character set, and language used

- ❑ The MIME type of included and linked resources (in this case, the MIME type of the style sheet)

```
<?xml version="1.0" encoding="iso-8859-1"?>
<!DOCTYPE html PUBLIC "-//W3C//DTD XHTML 1.0 Strict//EN"
          "http://www.w3.org/TR/xhtml1/DTD/xhtml1-strict.dtd">

<html xmlns="http://www.w3.org/1999/xhtml">
  <head>
    <meta name="author" content="Jon Duckett" />
    <meta name="copyright" content="&copy; 2005 Wrox Press" />
    <meta name="date" content="2005-02-02T12:24:37+00:00" />
    <meta name="description" lang="en" content="Learn to create Web sites that
          meet WCAG and Section 508 accessibility guidelines" />
    <meta name="keywords" lang="en" content="accessibility accessible Web
          sites WCAG section 508 guidelines" />
    <meta http-equiv="Content-Type" content="text/html; charset=iso-8859-1" />
    <link rel="stylesheet" type="text/css" href="interface.css" />
  </head>
  <body xml:lang="en">
...
```

While it might seem a nuisance to add all of this information into every page, it provides more information to all manner of processing applications, from users' browsers to search engines.

After you have prepared this information once, you can often copy and paste most of it from a template, rather than having to rewrite it again for each document you create.

Controlling the presentation of documents

As you have already seen in this book, when it comes to styling a document, you should be using CSS to control the presentation of your pages:

> **WCAG 3.3 Use style sheets to control layout and presentation. [Priority 2]**

You might want to note that this is a priority 2 checkpoint, because (as you saw in Chapter 5) even though CSS offers some very powerful layout capabilities, at times you might still need to rely upon tables to position content. In an ideal world you would design pages to work with CSS layouts, but because significant numbers of Web users have browsers that do not fully support CSS, you might need to resort to tables. (If you do use tables, you must ensure that they linearize correctly, which is something you will learn more about in Chapter 7.)

As you learned in Chapter 3, you should try to use relative units of measurement where possible in CSS (and any other languages), rather than absolute units of measurement, because it is important for those with visual impairments to be able to resize the content of a Web page so that they can read it:

> **WCAG 3.4 Use relative rather than absolute units in markup language attribute values and style sheet property values. [Priority 2]**

The use of relative units particularly affects the use of pixels as a unit of measurement, which is a very popular unit of length. The problem with using pixels is that IE for Windows does not enable the user to resize text and other content that is measured in pixels (although other browsers do).

Though I have stressed that your site should use CSS to control presentation (and where possible layout, too), you should also make sure that your site makes sense when the style sheet is not used (i.e., that the information is presented in a logical order). This situation could arise because the user has turned off style sheets, because they have their own style rules that take preference over rules in your style sheet, or even because it simply did not load:

> **WCAG 6.1 Organize documents so they may be read without style sheets. For example, when an HTML document is rendered without associated style sheets, it must still be possible to read the document. [Priority 1]**

A corresponding rule in the Section 508 guidelines makes a very similar point:

> **Section 508 §1194.22(d) Documents shall be organized so they are readable without requiring an associated style sheet.**

In designing your site, you should aim to create consistency in the design of the pages, because placing like parts of a page in familiar places makes it a lot easier for visitors to use the site. For example, if you are designing a site with two levels of navigation (global navigation and subnavigation for individual sections), users should find the global navigation and the subnavigation in the same place on each page:

> **WCAG 14.3 Create a style of presentation that is consistent across pages. [Priority 3]**

Structuring content

As you learned in Chapter 1, in their efforts to control the layout of Web pages and create attractive Web pages, Web designers frequently used HTML elements to create visual effects, rather than describe the structure of their Web pages. For example, they would use the `<font>` element to control the presentation of text that was a heading, rather than use the correct heading elements; this just gave an illusion of structure. Similarly, elements were used for the visual effects they created even when the content did not correspond with the purpose of the element; for example, tables were used to control positioning of elements on pages even when they did not contain tabular data.

In Chapter 2, you learned that one of the aims of XHTML was to ensure that markup was used for its original purpose (describing the structure of documents) and how presentational rules should be kept separate from the content.

Because XHTML is designed to describe the structure and semantics of a document, it is important that your markup be used in a manner that describes the structure of your Web pages. This enables assistive technologies to interpret the structure of documents and help visitors that rely on these technologies to find the information they want on the page — for example, by enabling them to jump from one heading to the next, skipping the text between them.

In this section, you will address the correct way to add markup to the following types of content:

- ❏ Headings, so that they describe the structure of the document
- ❏ Emphasis, which is usually displayed in a bold or italic font
- ❏ Acronyms and abbreviations to ensure that users understand their meaning
- ❏ Lists, including ordered and unordered lists
- ❏ Quotation marks, without relying upon escape characters
- ❏ References and citations so that the source can be given
- ❏ Computer-related content such as variables, key strokes, and sample code
- ❏ Mathematical and chemical equations

The content of many of the elements in XHTML are, by default, rendered in different ways; for example, headings are larger than standard text, `<blockquote>` elements can indent text, and `<th>` elements usually make the content of a table cell bold and centered. However, it is very important that you do not use markup simply to control the presentation of the document; it must be used to describe the structure or semantics of the document.

Correct use of headings

Headings are commonly used to create structure in all kinds of document, from newspaper articles to company reports, and you should use the heading elements in your XHTML documents to give them structure. For example, the <h1> element should be used to create primary headings, the <h2> element to create subheadings, the <h3> to create further subsections within the <h2> elements, and so on. Each heading would then consist of paragraphs and other elements.

If you describe the structure of a document in this way, assistive technologies are able to help users scan the page quicker; for example, screen readers enable users to skip between the headings on a page. The WCAG specifies that you should use the correct heading elements to convey the structure of your documents:

> **WCAG 3.5 Use header elements to convey document structure and use them according to specification. [Priority 2]**

This is particularly useful because sighted visitors to your site can scan a page quickly, looking at headings for more information; and without this feature, visitors relying on screen readers would have to wait for the whole page to be read to them.

The second part of this checkpoint, indicating that you should "use them according to specification," is important because you should never use *any* markup simply to change the presentation of the content; for example, you should not use heading elements just to create larger text. Using CSS, it is still possible to affect the presentation of these elements and to make them appear just as the designer wants, but the structure of the document should always be preserved in the markup.

A second WCAG checkpoint also addresses headings:

> **WCAG 13.8 Place distinguishing information at the beginning of headings, paragraphs, lists, etc. [Priority 3]**

The use of distinguishing information at the beginning of headings, paragraphs, and other content is commonly referred to as *front-loading*. It helps the user get the gist of the section without reading it all, which is especially helpful when the content is being read to the user (which takes longer than scanning an entire section of text).

Adding emphasis

You'll find no guidelines in either the WCAG or Section 508 guidelines that specifically deal with adding emphasis to documents; however, it is worth noting two particular elements that can be used for this purpose.

When you want to add emphasis to a document, you should use the <strong> and <em> elements, rather than the <b> and <i> elements. This is because the <b> and <i> elements affect only the visual presentation of a document, whereas the <strong> element (whose content is usually rendered in a bold font) and the <em> element (whose content is usually rendered in an italic font) indicate strong emphasis and emphasis, respectively, so a screen reader could actually interpret these elements and add the correct inflection to a voice.

For example, take a look at the following two paragraphs (ch06_eg01.html):

```
<p>This sentence contains <em>emphasis</em>, displayed in an italic font.</p>
<p>This sentence contains <strong>strong emphasis</strong>, which is displayed
    in a bold font.</p>
```

You can see how these two elements add the same formatting effects to the <b> and <i> elements in Figure 6-1, but they also add extra meaning to the document, which can also be of use to assistive technologies.

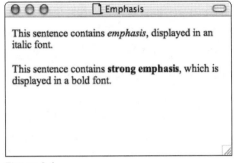

Figure 6-1

Acronyms and abbreviations

The WCAG specify that you should use the <abbr> and <acronym> elements whenever you first add an abbreviation or acronym to your documents:

> **WCAG 4.2 Specify the expansion of each abbreviation or acronym in a document where it first occurs. [Priority 3]**

The title attribute of the <abbr> and <acronym> elements should describe the full version of the abbreviation or acronym, as shown in the following example:

```
This document is marked up using <acronym title="Extensible Hypertext Markup
    Language">XHTML</acronym>.
```

By default, these elements will not change the presentation of the document, unless the mouse is hovered over the word, in which case some browsers will show the value of the title attribute in a tooltip. You could, however, change the style of these elements (perhaps putting them in bold or italic fonts) using CSS.

Lists

Checkpoint 3.6 of the WCAG specify that you should mark up all lists using <dl>, <ol>, and <ul> elements to create types of list, that <li> elements should contain each list item, and that you must not use these elements for their visual effects. Furthermore, you should also use CSS to control the numbering of lists or to control the type and appearance of bullets, rather than add numbers or images to your XHTML document (as you saw in Chapter 4):

> **WCAG 3.6 Mark up lists and list items properly. [Priority 2]**

Because this is a priority 2 checkpoint, if you have to target older browsers that do not support CSS, you can still use the type attribute to control the type of bullet mark.

Quotations

You should use the `<q>` and `<blockquote>` elements to mark up quotations, not the escape characters:

> **WCAG 3.7 Mark up quotations. Do not use quotation markup for formatting effects such as indentation. [Priority 2]**

As you saw in Chapter 4, you can use CSS to add the quotation marks to a document, but due to the lack of support for this feature in current browsers, you will probably have to continue to use escape characters to add the quotation marks until browser support for this aspect of CSS improves.

Structural elements

This section contains some additional elements that you may or may not be familiar with and that should be used to help describe the structure of a document. These elements are not specifically addressed in any guidelines, but they are covered here because they are not as widely known among Web developers as other markup.

The following structural elements should be used only with corresponding content, and they should not be used for visual formatting effects:

❑ `<cite>` for any citations or references

❑ `<dfn>` for a defining instance of a term

❑ `<code>` for code fragments

❑ `<samp>` for sample output from programs

❑ `<kbd>` for things users are supposed to enter using a keyboard

❑ `<var>` for any variables in programs

❑ `<ins>` for text inserted into a document

❑ `<del>` for text deleted from a document

Using markup instead than images

Since the late 1990s, several XML-based languages have been developed for marking up information pertaining to math (MathML) and chemistry (CML), as well as a language for creating vector graphics

(SVG). The W3C, as noted in the WCAG, would like document authors to use these languages where appropriate, rather than using images. For example, if you want to include a mathematical equation in a document, the W3C wants you to use MathML to do so.

> **WCAG 3.1 When an appropriate markup language exists, use markup rather than images to convey information. [Priority 2]**

There are two key advantages to using markup rather than images:

- ❏ Any text can be magnified or made available to assistive technologies as text.
- ❏ Search engines can access the information.

You will learn more about how to mix these new markup languages with XHTML in Chapter 8.

In the real world, however, until these languages are better supported by browsers and users are not required to download extra plug-ins, Web developers are likely to continue to use images to convey such information. After all, without the browser support, most users would not be able to access the information.

Clearly identifying the language used

You should identify the main language in which your document is written using the `lang` attribute in HTML or the `xml:lang` attribute in Strict XHTML.

> **WCAG 4.3 Identify the primary natural language of a document. [Priority 3]**

Furthermore, you should also specify any changes to the primary language of your document (for example, if it contains sections in another language). You should indicate changes to the language used with either the `lang` or `xml:lang` attributes.

> **WCAG 4.1 Clearly identify changes in the natural language of a document's text and any text equivalents (e.g., captions). [Priority 1]**

Here is an example of part of a document that correctly highlights the languages used:

```
<body lang="en" xml:lang="en-us">
  <h1>Learning French</h1>
  <p>You can say your favorite color is yellow like so:</p>
  <p lang="fr" xml:lang="fr">Mon couleur favorite est juane.</p>
```

As you can see, the default language in this example is U.S. English, but the paragraph written in French uses the `lang` and `xml:lang` attributes to indicate that it is written in French.

Carefully using language

With any text content, it is important that you try to use language that your readers will understand. If you are creating a specialty site, you may choose to use jargon; however, it would be unwise to use technical terms if you are expecting nontechnical visitors to your site:

> **WCAG 14.1 Use the clearest and simplest language appropriate for a site's content. [Priority 1]**

You should also consider the most helpful way to present information. You can often make use of photographs, information graphics, audio, or video to help understanding:

> **WCAG 14.2 Supplement text with graphic or auditory presentations where they will facilitate comprehension of the page. [Priority 3]**

The following sections elaborate on the preceding guideline, outlining the ways in which you can offer a text equivalent for any nontext content.

Text equivalents for nontext content

Most Web pages do not consist solely of marked-up text; they also contain nontext content, such as images, objects, applets, audio, and video. This section describes how you can deal with nontext content.

Readers with disabilities generally have a way of accessing text, even if they cannot read the text from the screen themselves. However, any kind of nontext content — such as images, video, and audio — can pose serious problems for some users.

Unfortunately, no technology can interpret the content of an image or video and automatically describe its contents to a user. Therefore, when creating pages, it is important to add text equivalents for any nontext content that assistive technologies can then present to the user so that they are not excluded.

Both the WCAG and Section 508 guidelines indicate that you should provide a text equivalent for any nontext content. Indeed, the first point of the WCAG refers to this very topic. This is a priority 1 checkpoint and must therefore be adhered to in order for ensure compliance with the guidelines.

> **WCAG 1.1 Provide a text equivalent for every nontext element (e.g., via "alt", "longdesc", or in element content). This includes: images, graphical representations of text (including symbols), image map regions, animations (e.g., animated GIFs), applets and programmatic objects, ascii art, frames, scripts, images used as list bullets, spacers, graphical buttons, sounds (played with or without user interaction), stand-alone audio files, audio tracks of video, and video. [Priority 1]**

As you can see, this list covers a lot more than just images. The following point from the Section 508 guidelines is very similar:

> **Section 508 §1194.22(a) A text equivalent for every nontext element shall be provided (e.g., via "alt", "longdesc", or in element content).**

The following sections take a closer look at how you deal with each of these nontext types of content. In learning how to create text alternatives for both visual and auditory content; you will be looking at dealing with the following:

❑ Images

❑ Objects and applets

❑ Audio and video

Text equivalents for images

A typical Web page features many images, both images that convey some kind of meaning and images that are just used to control the presentation of a page, such as those used for backgrounds or for positioning items correctly on a page. To make such content accessible, you must provide a text alternative for any image used to convey some information to the user, using the `alt` attribute on the `<img>` element:

```
<img src="images/logo.gif" width="180" height="50" alt="Acme Company Logo" />
```

This is commonly referred to as *alt text*, and it should describe what someone would need to know if they could not see the image.

Any image that conveys information should carry the `alt` attribute; for example, here is a button on a form that uses an image:

```
<input type="image" src="images/sendMail.gif" alt="Click button to send message"
       name="Send message" width="80" height="20" />
```

If someone were using a screen reader with this example, he or she would hear the words "Click button to send message."

If an image is not supposed to convey any meaning — for example, if it is just used to control the presentation of a page — then the `<img>` element must still carry the `alt` attribute, but it should not have anything between the quotes (not even a space), as shown here:

```
<img src="images/texture.gif" alt="" width="8" height="5" />
```

If you want to use acronyms in alt text, remember to write them in capital letters and add either a space or period between each character.

Remember that alt text also helps sighted users see what the image will represent while the page is loading and can benefit users who cannot load the images (perhaps because they have a slow connection, because they have turned images off, or because the device they are using does not support that type of image).

A graph or chart that carries a lot of information should not only use the `alt` attribute to indicate what the graph contains, it should also use the `longdesc` attribute, which links to a full text description for what is shown in the graph; for example, the following image links to a page called `12_04_webTraffic.html`, which would contain a text description of the December 2004 Web site statistics (`ch06_eg02.html`):

```
<img src="images/12_2004_stats.gif" alt=" December 2004 Traffic on AcmeSales.com"
    width="500" height="350" longdesc="text/12_04_webTraffic.html" />
```

Unfortunately, not all assistive technologies support the `longdesc` attribute, so you can use something called a *D-link*, or *description link*, which is the letter D inside square brackets, linked to a description. For example, here is the chart again (again, from `ch06_eg02.html`):

```
<img src="images/1204stats.gif" alt="December 2004 Traffic on AcmeSales"
    width="349" height="335" longdesc="12_04_webTraffic.html" /><br />
<a href="/text/December_04_statistics.html">[D]</a>
```

You can see the letter D in the square brackets underneath the image in Figure 6-2.

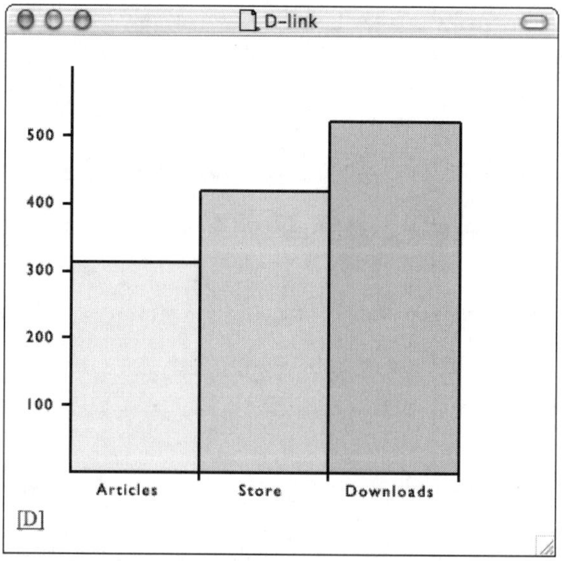

Figure 6-2

Figure 6-3 shows you the long description of the information in the graph. Long descriptions for images do not have to be in separate files; they can also be provided next to the image or at the end of the page.

You could even use CSS to hide the long description from most users by setting the `display` property for the element containing the long description to `none`, while still enabling assistive technologies to access the information.

An alternate way of creating description links, instead of using a letter D in square brackets, is to use a single-pixel, transparent GIF inside a link to the long description. This image will be invisible to sighted users (as long as a CSS rule is used to set the `border` property of images to 0 or none). The `alt` attribute of this image is usually `D-link` or `D`, although some designers use it to describe the purpose of the link so that users with screen readers will be able to access the long description. However, this approach has been deprecated in favor of the `longdesc` attribute.

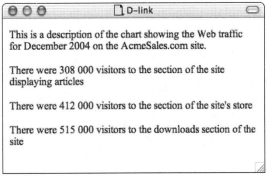

Figure 6-3

Text equivalents for objects and applets

Whenever you use the `<object>` element, you can provide a text equivalent inside it. In the following example, an `<object>` element is used to place a Flash movie on the page. Inside the object element is the content to be shown if the object is not supported:

```
<object classid="clsid:D27CDB6E-AE6D-11cf-96B8-444553540000"
    width="598" height="164"
    codebase="http://download.macromedia.com/pub/shockwave/cabs/flash/swflash.cab">
<param name="movie" value="motion/homePageAnimation.swf">
<param name="play" value="true">
<param name="loop" value="false">
<param name="quality" value="best">
<param name="menu" value="false">
    Content to be shown if the object is not supported goes here
</object>
```

Some objects, such as Flash movies, can be made accessible to assistive technologies, but you still need to supply a text alternative to the movie for those whose browsers do not support the Flash plug-in.

While use of the `<object>` element is preferred over use of the deprecated `<applet>` element, if the `<applet>` element is used, a text equivalent should be provided in both of the following two ways (because different browsers show text alternatives in different ways):

❑   Using the `alt` attribute

❑   Between the opening `<applet>` and closing `</applet>` tags

```
<applet code="ticker.class" width="400" height="40"
        alt="Java applet: text to show if applet is not supported">
  Text to show if applet is not supported...
</applet>
```

Text equivalents for audio and video

It is increasingly common to see sites that feature audio and video on them (commonly using Flash, QuickTime, Windows Media, Real, MP3s, and WAV files). The WCAG and Section 508 guidelines apply just as much to audio and video as they do to images. Therefore, if you supply any content as audio or video, a text equivalent should be provided if possible.

As far as the images on a video are concerned, you should provide a text equivalent for any instructional images that a user might not be able to see.

Meanwhile, the rules for audio (whether standalone or accompanying a video) specify that audio files should have a corresponding text version. If this audio is played alongside a video, you should provide synchronized captions. If it is just audio content, you should provide a transcript.

This obviously helps those with hearing difficulties, although not all audio translates to written word on the Web. For example, if you use sounds as decorations, as when someone moves their mouse over links, this need not be translated.

Here you can see the WCAG guidelines requiring that captions be provided to represent any graphic information in a video or multimedia presentation:

> **WCAG 1.3 Until user agents can automatically read aloud the text equivalent of a visual track, provide an auditory description of the important information of the visual track of a multimedia presentation. [Priority 1]**

Any captions or audio descriptions of information that are used with multimedia presentations should, where possible, be synchronized with the visual track:

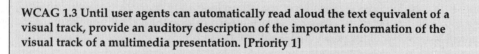

> **WCAG 1.4 For any time-based multimedia presentation (e.g., a movie or animation), synchronize equivalent alternatives (e.g., captions or auditory descriptions of the visual track) with the presentation. [Priority 1]**

And this is the Section 508 equivalent:

> **Section 508 §1194.22(b) Equivalent alternatives for any multimedia presentation shall be synchronized with the presentation.**

If you have looked at much video on the Web, you can probably understand that because of its quality, even those visitors capable of lip-reading would have trouble telling what someone is saying on the Web.

ASCII art

While ASCII art is rarely used in modern designs, specific reference has been made to it in the WCAG guidelines:

> **WCAG 13.10 Provide a means to skip over multi-line ASCII art. [Priority 3]**

As you can imagine, ASCII art will make little sense (and could prove very frustrating) to someone visiting a site who uses a screen reader, because the picture would be read to them one line at a time. The WCAG indicate that you should try to use images, rather than ASCII art, as you can easily provide a text alternative. However, if you do use ASCII art, you should provide a link to jump over it. The target of the link can be the caption underneath the art, as shown here:

```
<p><a href="#ASCIIend">skip ASCII art</a>
 * * * * * * * * * * * * * * * * * *
  * * * * * * * * * * * * * * * * * *
 * * * * * * * * * * * * * * * * * *
<a name="ASCIIend">Caption goes here</a>
</p>
```

It is more likely that you would use ASCII art in the form of emoticons — in which case, you can use the `<abbr>` element and put the description in a `title` attribute, like so:

```
<abbr title="smiley">:-)</abbr>
```

Dynamic content

Having dealt with text content and nontext content, it is time to take a look at dynamic content. Two very different types of content are often referred to as dynamic content:

- ❑ Text content that is generated dynamically (based upon things such as user input, database content, scripts, or other feeds)

- ❑ Animated/moving content (such as Flash, SVG, animated GIFs, or DHTML)

However, the two types overlap over because scripts can be used to animate content, and animated content (such as Flash movies or animated GIFs) can contain text. The WCAG checkpoint 6.5 applies equally to all types of dynamic content:

> **WCAG 6.5 Ensure that dynamic content is accessible or provide an alternative presentation or page. [Priority 2]**

Whenever the dynamic content of the page is updated, it is important to also update the text equivalent (although the updated content need not be on the same page as long as the user has access to it):

> **WCAG 6.2 Ensure that equivalents for dynamic content are updated when the dynamic content changes. [Priority 1]**

Any programmatic elements must be compatible with assistive technologies. As you will see in the following section, this means that you have to ensure that users can interact with your pages using different types of devices (not just mice or keyboards), which in turn means you have to make any event handlers device-independent:

> **WCAG 8.1 Make programmatic elements such as scripts and applets directly accessible or compatible with assistive technologies. [Priority 1 if functionality is important and not presented elsewhere; otherwise, Priority 2.]**

In addition to the preceding general rules, the following sections describe some additional, more specific points. In particular, you will need to do the following:

- ❑ Ensure that all users can interact with scripts, objects, and applets
- ❑ Ensure that pages work without scripts, objects, and applets
- ❑ Control motion and flicker
- ❑ Handle pages that automatically refresh, submit, or redirect
- ❑ Handle pop-up windows

Ensuring that all users can interact with scripts, objects, and applets

When you are using scripts, objects, and applets in your pages, it is easy to assume that visitors to your site will be using them in the same way that you do. However, they must be written so that they will work with all kinds of device, and so that the way in which the user interacts with them is device independent. After all, someone who is blind is more likely to use a keyboard to navigate a site than a mouse, so any features that respond only to `onclick` events will not be available to those relying on a keyboard.

In this vein, if you use scripts, objects, or applets within your pages that create their own interfaces, then it is your responsibility to ensure that the interface will work with a variety of devices (not just a mouse or a keyboard). Examples of elements that have their own interface range from elements used in JavaScript drop-down menus to `<object>` elements used to include things such as ActiveX or Java multimedia players in a page, which in turn have transport controls such as play, stop, rewind, and fast-forward.

> **WCAG 9.2 Ensure that any element that has its own interface can be operated in a device-independent manner. [Priority 2]**

The subsequent WCAG guideline extends upon the previous point and suggests that when you write scripts with event handlers, you use logical event handlers rather than device-dependent event handlers:

> **WCAG 9.3 For scripts, specify logical event handlers rather than device-dependent event handlers. [Priority 2]**

The Section 508 guidelines make a similar point, stating that when a script is used to generate text or interface elements, the generated text should be available to assistive technologies:

> **Section 508 §1194.22(l) When pages utilize scripting languages to display content, or to create interface elements, the information provided by the script shall be identified with functional text that can be read by assistive technology.**

Meeting guidelines such as these will also help ensure that your site works on a wider range of devices; not only those aimed at users with functional limitations, but also devices for those with situational limitations (for example, a voice browser that could be used when driving).

Another WCAG rule makes a very similar point. This one encourages you to enable users to enter information in different ways that do not rely upon a specific device:

> **WCAG 6.4 For scripts and applets, ensure that event handlers are input device-independent. [Priority 2]**

This means that whenever an event handler is used for anything other than a decorative effect, you should obey the following rules:

❑ The event handler should use application-level event triggers, rather than user interaction-level triggers. For example, application-level event attributes are `onfocus`, `onblur`, and `onsubmit`, whereas interaction-level triggers include `onclick` or `onmouseover`.

❑ If you must use device-dependent attributes, you should always provide redundant input mechanisms, which means you must specify two handlers for that element; for example, for each `onmousedown`, you must provide an `onkeydown` with the corresponding effect, and for each `onclick` event, you must provide an equivalent `onkeypress` for those who are using keys rather than mice.

❑ You should avoid writing event handlers that rely on mouse coordinates because these are device-dependent.

Here are some general rules that you can follow when considering how accessible a script is:

❑ Avoid content that is written using client-side scripts — because if the browser does not support scripts, the content will not be displayed.

❑ If content is displayed or hidden using scripts and style sheets, the default action should be to display the content (and then hide it using a script); and the page must make sense with all of the information showing. For example, if you use JavaScript to create drop-down menus for navigation, the top item must provide a link to a page containing all of the items in the drop-down menu (for those whose browsers do not display the navigation items when the user hovers the mouse over them).

❑ Avoid using links that contain JavaScript in the URI, because the links will not work in browsers that do not support JavaScript.

❑ In accordance with the rules you will meet later in this section, you should also avoid scripts that cause flickering, moving, or blinking.

For more information on developing accessible applets, check out the following pages:

❑ **Java Accessibility and Usability** — `http://trace.wisc.edu/world/java/java.htm`

❑ **IBM Guidelines for Writing Accessible Applications Using 100% Pure Java** — `www.ibm.com/able/guidelines/java/snsjavag.html`

Ensuring that pages work without scripts, objects, or applets

Whenever you do use scripts, objects, or applets, pages must be designed so that they can still be used if these technologies are not supported, even if the reason they are not supported is because the user has turned them off:

> **WCAG 6.3 Ensure that pages are usable when scripts, applets, or other program-matic objects are turned off or not supported. If this is not possible, provide equivalent information on an alternative accessible page. [Priority 1]**

This means that you cannot use scripts, applets, or objects to play any vital role in a Web page. Rather, they can be used only to enhance a page.

You have the following options for showing content if a script, object, or applet does not load:

❑ For scripts, you can use the `<noscript>` element.

❑ For objects, you can put alternative content between the opening `<object>` and closing `</object>` tag.

❑ For applets, you can put alternative content in the `alt` attribute on the opening `<applet>` tag or between the opening `<applet>` and closing `</applet>` tags.

You should really be aiming to create pages that will offer the same information and functionality whether these features are available or not. For example, one popular use of JavaScript is to create drop-down menus; in this case, it would be important that the top item in each menu item (indicating the section of the site to which the menu items belong) is a link to a page that will offer the user the same options that the drop-down menu would have offered.

In Figure 6-4, the word `Products` should be a link to a page that enables users to select books, CDs, or magazines without having to use the drop-down menu.

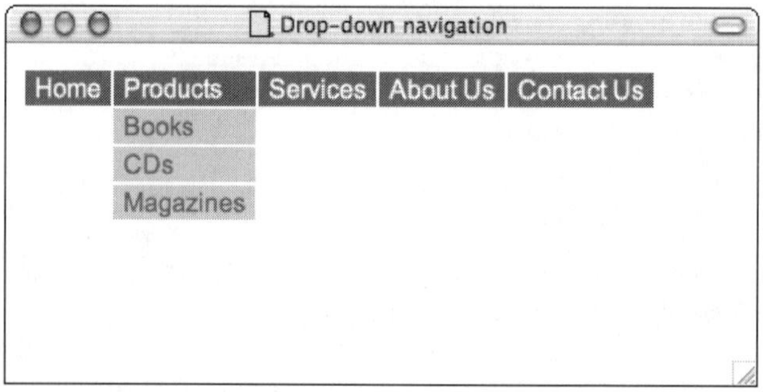

Figure 6-4

The Section 508 guidelines also indicate that whenever an applet, plug-in, or other application is used, it must comply with 508 guidelines §1194.21 (a) through (l) and that a link must be provided to download it:

> **Section 508 §1194.21(m) When a Web page requires that an applet, plug-in, or other application be present on the client system to interpret page content, the page must provide a link to a plug-in or applet that complies with §1194.21(a) through (l).**

Controlling motion and flicker

Many people can be sensitive to flashing or blinking objects and to rapidly changing visuals. Such images can cause photosensitive epileptic fits (not only in those who have a history of epilepsy, but also others who could be predisposed to such attacks, including those who have suffered from stroke). The WCAG indicate that Web developers should avoid flicker over which users have no control:

> **WCAG 7.1 Until user agents allow users to control flickering, avoid causing the screen to flicker. [Priority 1]**

Meanwhile, the Section 508 guidelines specify the maximum rate of flicker that should be allowed:

> **Section 508 §1194.22(j) Pages shall be designed to avoid causing the screen to flicker with a frequency greater than 2 Hz and lower than 55 Hz.**

The WCAG also have a separate point regarding blinking content:

> **WCAG 7.2 Until user agents allow users to control blinking, avoid causing content to blink (i.e, change presentation at a regular rate, such as turning on and off). [Priority 2]**

In addition is a point about general movement in pages:

> **WCAG 7.3 Until user agents allow users to freeze moving content, avoid movement in pages. [Priority 2]**

Both Internet Explorer and Netscape Navigator allow you to freeze animated GIFs by pressing the escape key, but animated GIFs are not the only way in which flicker, blinking, and movement can occur on a page. There are also Flash animations and SVG animations (although SVG is still quite rare), and movie files (such as .mov, QuickTime, Real, and Windows Media Files). If you are going to use any of these forms of content, you should ensure that they are accessible, and can easily be stopped; or better still, you should enable the user to choose to start them (warning the user first of any flashing, flickering, or movement).

You may also be aware of the `<blink>` and `<marquee>` elements, neither of which can be controlled by the escape key. Because these elements are both proprietary (`<blink>` works only in Netscape, and `<marquee>` works only in Internet Explorer, and neither are part of the XHTML recommendations), you should avoid using either of them.

Pages that refresh, submit, or redirect automatically

Compared to someone with normal vision, visitors who rely upon any assistive technology can take a lot longer to read a page, so you should avoid automatically refreshing the content of any page, redirecting users after a specified amount of time, or automatically submitting forms. This is important because the user may not be able to access the whole page before it refreshes itself.

> **WCAG 7.4 Until user agents provide the ability to stop the refresh, do not create periodically auto-refreshing pages. [Priority 2]**

A similar point covers automatic redirection from one page to another:

> **WCAG 7.5 Until user agents provide the ability to stop auto-redirect, do not use markup to redirect pages automatically. Instead, configure the server to perform redirects. [Priority 2]**

You will look at rules that apply to forms that offer timed submission in Chapter 7.

Pop-up windows

The WCAG contain a specific point about the use of pop-up or spawned windows, indicating that you should not use them until user agents allow a way for users to prevent new windows from opening. As you can imagine, if you have difficulty seeing the open windows, it could be very difficult to determine which window should be active.

> **WCAG 10.1 Until user agents allow users to turn off spawned windows, do not cause pop-ups or other windows to appear and do not change the current window without informing the user.**

In practical terms, you should also avoid relying on pop-up windows because several pieces of software now offer facilities to block pop-up windows, which can prevent you from seeing the content you had intended to be displayed.

Color and contrast

Color is a very important tool for designers because it can help users understand a site much better. However, you must be careful in your use of color, or you could find that you are making your site less accessible. Remember one key rule when you are working with color:

Never use color alone to convey information. All information should be provided in at least one other way.

For example, if you are going to create a form and want to indicate that certain fields are required, you should never just use color to indicate this (for example, you should not just write the form control's label in a different color). Rather, you should use a symbol such as an asterisk, which may be in a color. The form in Figure 6-5 uses a red asterisk to indicate which fields are required, although you can't see the red color in the black-and-white screenshot.

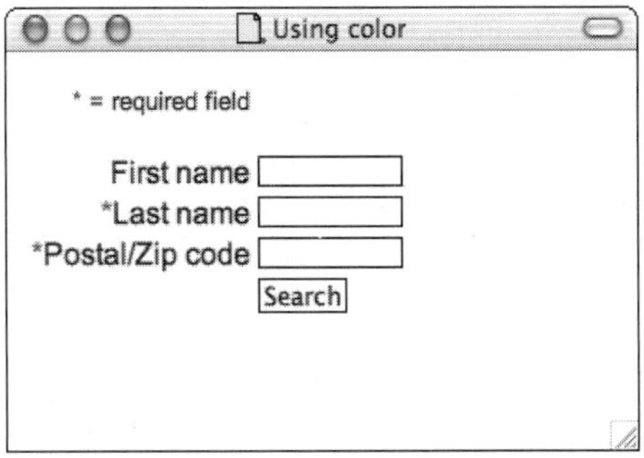

Figure 6-5

Note how the key (indicating that items with an asterisk are required) comes before the form. If it is after the form, users with a screen reader will not know what the asterisks meant until after they have had the form read to them. In addition, the "required" asterisks should come before the label for the form control.

When you are choosing colors, it is important to ensure that you use sufficient contrast so that users can understand their intention. In particular, you need to ensure that any text on your pages stands out sufficiently from the background color or image. If the background color and foreground color are too close to the same hue, people with color deficits or those on monochrome monitors might have difficulty reading the page.

Section 508 indicates the following guideline:

> **Section 508 §1194.22(c) Web pages shall be designed so that all information conveyed with color is also available without color, for example from context or markup.**

This is very similar to the WCAG checkpoint 2.1, which is a priority 1 checkpoint:

> **WCAG 2.1 Ensure that all information conveyed with color is also available without color, for example from context or markup. [Priority 1]**

The WCAG also make the following point regarding contrast (priority 2 for images, priority 3 for text):

> **WCAG 2.2 Ensure that foreground and background color combinations provide sufficient contrast when viewed by someone having color deficits or when viewed on a black and white screen. [Images Priority 2, Text Priority 3]**

The Section 508 guidelines do not refer to contrast, but it is a very important point for accessibility.

Accessible navigation

It is vital for users to be able to navigate around your site, and this section describes how you can ensure that the various ways in which users navigate your site remain accessible. In particular, you will be looking at the following:

❑ Creating accessible links

❑ Using images for links

❑ Rules that govern navigation bars and how layout can affect navigation

❑ How users should be enabled to skip navigation links

❑ Image maps

❑ Accessible searches and multiple-page documents

Accessible links

Any text between an opening `<a>` and closing `</a>` tag is known as *link text*. It is important that the link text clearly indicates to the user where the link will take them. A link like the following one, which says "click here,'" does not tell visitors where they will be taken if they click on the link:

```
<a href="contact.html">Click here</a> to contact us.
```

Rather, the link should be more descriptive; for example, it could have included the following entire sentence:

```
<a href="contact.html">Click here to contact us</a>.
```

Similarly, when using images as links, the alt text for the image should tell the user where the link will take them. Furthermore, because most screen readers say the word *link* before the image, there is no need to use the word *link* in the alt text.

The WCAG include the following checkpoint about link information:

> **WCAG 13.1 Clearly identify the target of each link. [Priority 2]**

Images for links

When using images for links it is important to indicate the kind of information users will access if they click on the image. For example:

❏ If you have an image of an envelope indicating an e-mail link, you should use alt text such as `"Click here to send us an email"`, rather than something that describes what is in the picture, such as `"envelope"`.

❏ Similarly, if you have a forward arrow that is a link to the next 10 results in a search, you should use alt text such as `"Next 10 results"`, rather than something like `"right arrow"`.

To understand just how important adding helpful alt text is, consider what happens if you do not have any. In the absence of alt text, most screen readers try to tell the reader something else—usually the URL of the link—which often makes little sense. The following link is supposed to be used on a search results page to link to the next 10 results:

```
<a href="store/products/showResults.php?from=11&to=20">
  <img src="nav/rightArrow.gif" width="50" height="20" />
</a>
```

Some screen readers, not finding any alt text on this image, would read the link to the user in full (`store/products/showResults.php?from=11&to=20`), while others would read anything following the last forward slash character (`showResults.php?from=11&to=20`); neither of these links makes a lot of sense. Other programs would read the name of the image (`nav/rightArrow.gif`), which again could leave users confused.

Instead, the image should look something like this:

```
<a href="/store/products/showResults.php?from=11&to=20">
  <img src="/nav/rightArrow.gif" width="50" height="20" alt="Next 10 results" />
</a>
```

With this code and the alt text in place, the screen reader can read out `"Next 10 results"`, which gives users a clear understanding of what's on the screen.

Navigation bars

In the same way that the WCAG checkpoint 14.3 suggests that the pages of your site have a consistent design, you should also ensure that your navigation is consistent—the global and local navigation on a site should always be in the same place on each page:

> **WCAG 13.4 Use navigation mechanisms in a consistent manner. [Priority 2]**

To do this, it helps to create navigation bars, which consist of groups of links that are presented in a different manner from the surrounding content (for example, they might have a different background color):

> **WCAG 13.5 Provide navigation bars to highlight and give access to the navigation mechanism. [Priority 3]**

To help users clearly identify different links, you should also ensure that you provide a printable character between each link. Common examples of characters include the pipestem symbol and square brackets.

> **WACG 10.5 Until user agents (including assistive technologies) render adjacent links distinctly, include non-link, printable characters (surrounded by spaces) between adjacent links. [Priority 3]**

The following example illustrates some links with the pipestem character between them to clearly separate the links:

```
<a href="http://www.Google.com/">Google</a> |
<a href="http://www.ask.com">Ask Jeeves</a> |
<a href="http://www.Yahoo.com">Yahoo</a>
```

You can see what this looks like in Figure 6-6.

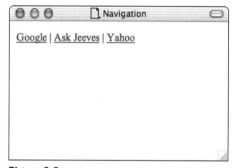

Figure 6-6

Skipping navigation links

It is very easy for someone with normal vision to scan a page to find the main content or part of the page they are looking for. However, visitors to your site who use assistive technology, such as a screen reader, will not necessarily be able to find the part of the page they want so quickly. Figure 6-7 shows a page that has several links across the top, which would be read to the user before they could read an article.

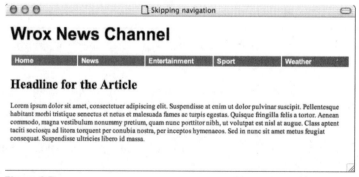

Figure 6-7

Without the addition of any extra markup, users with screen readers would either have to listen to the masthead and links before they got to the part of the page they came to look at, or they would have to use shortcuts on their assistive device to look for headings further down the page. As you can imagine, this could quickly become tedious if it happened on every page.

Therefore, it is quite simple to offer the user a massive accessibility boost by making the first item on each page a simple link to skip repetitive parts of the page such as the masthead and navigation. This idea is specified in both sets of guidelines, as shown here in the WCAG guideline:

> **WCAG 13.6 Group related links, identify the group (for user agents), and, until user agents do so, provide a way to bypass the group. [Priority 3]**

Section 508 also requires that the page should offer a function to skip repetitive navigation:

> **Section 508 §1194.22(o) A method shall be provided that permits users to skip repetitive navigation links.**

As you will see in a moment, the link does not need to be visible to everyone; it can just be made available to those with assistive devices by either of the following methods:

❑ Placing a single-pixel, transparent GIF image inside the link, which will not be visible to users looking at the screen, but whose alt text will be read to users with screen readers

❑ Making the text the same color as the background of the page

You have probably come across some longer pages on the Web that contain links to other parts of the same page or links back to the top from the bottom of the page; the capability to skip repetitive navigation is based upon the same principle. These links rely on a *target anchor* placed somewhere in the page, to which you can then create a link. A target anchor is an <a> element without an href attribute, so it does not link to anywhere itself; rather, it has a name and/or an id attribute so it can be linked *to*:

```
<a id="content" name="content"><h1>This Is the primary heading for the main content
of the page</h1></a>
```

Note how the target anchor contains some content—in this case, the headline for the article. Without the content, it will not work on all browsers. You can also see that the <a> element has both an id and a name attribute. The id attribute is the preferred method in XHTML, while the name attribute is there for backward compatibility with older browsers.

If you do not want to use any text content in the target anchor—for example, if it does not suit the template for your pages—you could use a single-pixel GIF image as the content of this target anchor.

Now that there is a target to link to, you can add the link to the beginning of the page. The link will be the first thing on the page, and it will contain a single-pixel, transparent GIF. The alt text for this image will explain the purpose of the link to users with screen readers, while users without screen readers will simply not see the image or link:

```
<a href="#content">
  <img src="images/1px.gif" alt="Skip navigation"
      height="1" width="1" />
</a>
```

The page shown in Figure 6-7 actually contained a link like this, but you could not see it. Remember that the default behaviour of Internet Explorer is to draw a blue border around images that are links, so if you do not want the border, you should add a CSS rule to indicate that the border property of images is 0 or none.

You could also put the link in normal plaintext, and prevent sighted users from seeing the link by using CSS either to make the text the same color as the background color for the page or to give the display property a value of none. The following example uses a CSS class to ensure that the text is white (the same color as the background of the body of the page):

```
<a href="#content" class="skipNav">Skip navigation</a>
```

Here is the associated CSS rule (specifying the same foreground and background colors, and using a small font):

```
a.skipNav {color:#ffffff; background-color:#ffffff; font-size:20%}
```

Some sites even offer several skip options, so that users can skip to the main content, the subnavigation options, the latest news headlines, and other parts of the page they think would be helpful.

The idea of multiple skip links is especially important for larger sites that contain several levels of navigation. Looking back at the example presented earlier in this section, each section of the site has subsections; for example, the entertainment section has Film, TV, Music, and Arts sections (see Figure 6-8).

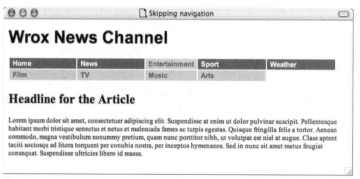

Figure 6-8

With sites like this, the main set of links is usually referred to as *global navigation* because it is the same on every page (or global) across the entire site. Meanwhile, the subnavigation or secondary navigation will change for each section. Users of a site like this might like to be able to access the secondary navigation options of each section without having to listen to the global navigation. Therefore, the start of the page might look something like this, whereby a single-pixel, transparent GIF enables users to skip the global navigation and go directly to the subnavigation, and a second link enables them to skip the subnavigation:

```
<a href="#subnav">
  <img src="images/1px.gif" alt="Skip global navigation"
      height="1" width="1" />
</a>
<div class="globalNav"
  <a href="index.html">Home</a> |
  <a href="News/index.html">News</a> |
  <a href="Entertainment/index.html">Entertainment</a> |
  <a href="Sport/index.html">Sport</a> |
</div>
  <a href="#content">
    <img src="images/1px.gif" alt="Skip sub navigation"
      height="1" width="1" />
  </a>
<div class="subNav">
  <a href="Entertainment/Film/index.html">Film</a> |
  <a href="Entertainment/TV/index.html">TV</a> |
  <a href="Entertainment/Music/index.html">Music</a> |
  <a href="Entertainment/Arts/index.html">Arts</a>
</div>

<a name="content" id="content"><h1>Entertainment</h1></a>
Lorem ipsum dollar sit amit...
```

As you can see in this example, I have also grouped all of the global navigation in one `<div>` element and the subnavigation in a second `<div>` element. Not only does this `<div>` element group the elements, but it also enables you to easily associate the navigation items with a CSS rule that will make them stand out from the rest of the page — therefore highlighting the navigation as recommended in WCAG guideline 13.5 (which you met in the preceding section).

Image maps

Image maps are another way in which visitors can navigate a site, with different sections of an image providing links to different pages; both the WCAG and Section 508 guidelines contain points that are specific to image maps.

If you are working with a client-side image map, you should not only use the `alt` attribute on the image used for the map, but also on each `<area>` element, as shown in `ch06_eg03.html` (as you will see, there is a reason why this is quite a complicated example):

```
<img src="images/UKRegions.gif" alt="UK Regions Image Map" width="206" height="349"
    border="0" usemap="#Regions">
  <map name="Regions">
  <area shape="poly" coords="6,156,21,150,34,166,42,185,29,197,16,195,8,186,0,
        188,0,161" href="NIreland.html" alt="Northern Ireland">
  <area shape="poly" coords="88,4,83,28,24,34,4,67,25,116,57,102,78,123,82,143,
        92,156,111,132,95,118,117,70,75,59,104,13" href="EScotland.html"
        alt="East of Scotland">
  <area shape="poly" coords="56,104,39,112,24,134,51,167,72,168,84,163,90,157,
        80,143,78,127" href="WScotland.html" alt="West of Scotland">
```

```
    <area shape="poly" coords="111,133,78,171,89,191,103,186,105,178,135,174"
        href="North.html" alt="North">
    <area shape="poly" coords="114,215,100,189,89,200,86,217,95,230,106,226"
        href="NWest.html" alt="North West">
    <area shape="poly" coords="100,190,116,214,127,222,134,213,121,179,109,180"
        href="WYorkshire.html" alt="West Yorkshire">
    <area shape="poly" coords="123,177,136,214,149,243,164,229,160,203,140,177"
        href="Yorkshire.html" alt="Yorkshire &amp; Lincolshire">
    <area shape="poly" coords="115,216,123,224,128,224,136,216,145,242,131,252,
        113,215" href="EMidlands.html" alt="East Midlands">
    <area shape="poly" coords="91,229,101,233,94,233,91,248,90,268,99,276,114,270,
        122,268,122,279,108,282,95,289,73,286,59,280,51,285,42,274,68,255,66,
        239,56,236,58,221,72,225,86,218" href="Wales.html" alt="Wales">
    <area shape="poly" coords="106,283,107,299,95,315,85,321,80,336,64,332,47,342,
        34, 339,60,304,68,298,89,298" href="SWest.html" alt="South West">
    <area shape="poly" coords="112,224,96,233,92,266,99,273,123,266,128,252"
        href="WMids.html" alt="West Midlands">
    <area shape="poly" coords="131,253,124,268,122,279,127,291,142,290,154,278,159,
        268,148,257,148,247" href="CSouth.html" alt="Central South">
    <area shape="poly" coords="151,248,162,236,175,231,188,234,197,246,194,261,
        189,273,181,279,176,284,157,277,163,269,151,255" href="Anglia.html"
        alt="Anglia">
    <area shape="poly" coords="110,282,120,281,125,293,141,292,139,312,135,319,123,
        318,115,319,105,319,98,316,108,301" href="Wessex.html" alt="Wessex">
    <area shape="poly" coords="158,280,183,288,192,289,190,298,175,307,164,311,
        142,313,145,293" href="South.html" alt="Southern">
</map>
```

Each <area> element needs to have the alt attribute because each of the <area> elements represents a specific part of a map. Without having alt text for each of the sections of the map, the user would not know which of the areas he or she should be selecting. The order in which elements are read using screen readers tends to reflect the order in which the <area> elements are presented inside the <map> element.

You can see the image map created using the preceding code in Figure 6-9.

It is worth noting here that client-side image maps are far easier to deal with in terms of accessibility than server-side image maps. Indeed, the guidelines recommend that you use only server-side image maps if you cannot create the shape required using a client-side map. Here is the WCAG guideline on this point:

> **WCAG 9.1 Provide client-side image maps instead of server-side image maps except where the regions cannot be defined with an available geometric shape. [Priority 1]**

The Section 508 guideline is virtually identical:

> **Section 508 §1194.22(f) Client-side image maps shall be provided instead of server-side image maps except where the regions cannot be defined with an available geometric shape.**

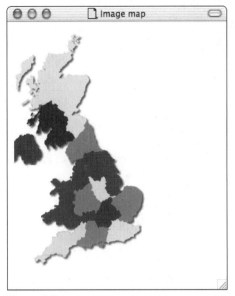

Figure 6-9

Of course, because you can create very complex shapes using client-side maps, it is unlikely that you would ever have to use a server-side image map again. Figure 6-9 showed a very complex image map indicating the regions of the U.K.

Server-side image maps create a different problem because they contain a single image, and the coordinates of the location at which the user clicked are then sent to the server. The map on the server then determines where the user clicked on the image using the coordinates it receives and decides which page to send the user to based on that information. Apart from what is visually shown in the image, nothing tells the user which part of the image links to where, so assistive devices cannot inform the user as to which part of the image should be clicked (even if they could click on the appropriate part of the image). Therefore, if you are going to use a server-side image map, you should always provide text alternatives to the links in the image map (often referred to as *redundant text links*). You can see an example of these text links in Figure 6-10.

Note how a pipestem (vertical bar) symbol is used between the links to each section of the map. It is important to ensure that each link is clearly separated either like this or using some other symbol, such as brackets, to clearly demarcate each link.

The WCAG provide a Priority 1 guideline indicating that any server-side image maps should also have corresponding redundant text links:

> **WCAG 1.2 Provide redundant text links for each active region of a server-side image map. [Priority 1]**

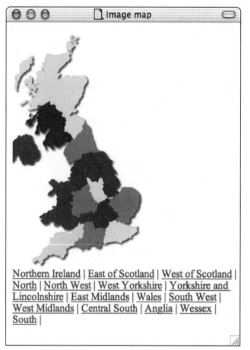

Northern Ireland | East of Scotland | West of Scotland | North | North West | West Yorkshire | Yorkshire and Lincolnshire | East Midlands | Wales | South West | West Midlands | Central South | Anglia | Wessex | South |

Figure 6-10

Section 508 contains a similar guideline for server-side image maps:

> **Section 508 §1194.22(e) Redundant text links shall be provided for each region of a server-side image map.**

The WCAG go as far as suggesting that designers also provide redundant text links for client-side image maps, in order to service user agents that cannot render text equivalents of image map links. While this is not a high priority (probably because modern screen readers can cope with the alt text on client-side image maps), redundant text links could still help those using technologies such as screen magnifiers (who might not be able to see the image as easily); therefore, they are worth considering.

> **WCAG 1.5 Until user agents render text equivalents for client-side image map links, provide redundant text links for each active region of a client-side image map. [Priority 3]**

Accessible search

In addition to links that enable visitors to navigate pages, many sites also offer a search facility. If you enable users to search your site, rather than simply offer a free text search, the WCAG suggest that you offer a more advanced set of search options to those who are trying to find something specific on your site. This may include the date when an article was published, the name of the person who wrote it, whether the search should look for any/all of the keywords entered or the exact phrase, and so on.

> **WCAG 13.7 If search functions are provided, enable different types of searches for different skill levels and preferences. [Priority 3]**

Documents spread over multiple pages

When a single document (such as a long article) is spread over several pages, you should provide information that clearly indicates it is part of a collection of documents:

> **WCAG 13.9 Provide information about document collections (i.e., documents comprising multiple pages). [Priority 3]**

You could make this information clear in two ways:

❑   Using the `<link>` element with the `rel` and `rev` attributes to indicate the relationships between pages

❑   Offering the whole set in an archive format, such as a zip, tar, gzip or stuffit file

As you have seen so far in this chapter, creating an accessible site does not mean that you have to write your sites in a completely different way, nor does it drastically increase the amount of work required to write a page. Rather, to create an accessible Web page, you just have to employ some simple additions to the familiar markup you are already using, and approach some other aspects of your design in a slightly different way.

Solution

In this section, you will take another look at the design of the First Promotions site and see what improvements you can make to increase the accessibility of the site. You will also see how you can apply several of the checkpoints you encountered in this chapter to the site to ensure that it meets the WCAG and Section 508 accessibility guidelines.

You may remember that by the end of Chapter 5, the site was written in XHTML, using `<div>` elements to hold related sections of a page, rather than table cells; and both the presentation and layout were controlled with the aid of a CSS style sheet. Therefore, the first requirements for making the site accessible have already been met: It was built using the latest W3C standards, using XHTML to structure the document and CSS to control its presentation and layout. The XHTML is also readable without the CSS style sheet, which was another one of the requirements you encountered earlier in this chapter.

In the rest of this section, you will perform the following tasks for three particular aspects of the site to ensure that it meets the WCAG and Section 508 guidelines:

- ❏ Ensure that text equivalents have been provided for nontext items
- ❏ Check for dynamic content, color, and contrast
- ❏ Add links to skip repetitive navigation items

Providing nontext items with text equivalents

The first substantial changes you have to make to the site in order to satisfy the WCAG and Section 508 guidelines are to ensure that all nontext content has a text equivalent. While you do not have any objects, applets, audio, video, image maps, or ASCII art on the First Promotions site, you have plenty of images, and the purpose of these images needs to be clearly defined in the text.

When creating an XHTML version of the site, all images were given `alt` attributes (because the `alt` attribute is required on any `<img />` element in XHTML). Furthermore, several of the images that were used for navigation in the first versions of the site have been removed, such as the JavaScript rollover images, which were replaced with CSS rollovers that made use of the `:hover` pseudo-class.

However, a couple of images could use a slightly better description for their alt text. For example, the main logo at the top of the page simply says `logo`:

```
<div id="masthead">
  <img src="images/interface/logo.gif" alt="logo" width="364" height="77">
</div>
```

Whereas it would be better to have something like this:

```
<div id="masthead">
  <img src="images/interface/logo.gif" alt="First Promotions logo" width="364"
       height="77">
</div>
```

Other than this minor change, the other images on the page already carry clear alt text describing their purpose. For example, the image that contains the words "our guarantee" looks like this:

```
<img src="images/interface/guarantee.gif" alt="our guarantee"
     width="124" height="22" />
```

Even if ensuring that the alt text on each image is self-explanatory seems rather simple, it can greatly help someone who cannot see the image to understand your site. As you will see in Chapter 7, tools are available that help you check whether your site meets the WCAG and Section 508 guidelines. However, these tools are not able to check whether the alt text accurately describes what is in the image, so it is important to go through each one and check it individually.

Checking for dynamic content, color, and contrast issues

The only dynamic content on the First Promotions site were scripts used for image rollovers in earlier versions, and these have been replaced with CSS rollovers created using the `:hover` pseudo-classes. Because these scripts were purely for visual effects, and the page would function fine without them, they could have remained unchanged. Furthermore, because there were no pop-ups, refreshing pages, motion, or flicker, you do not need to make any changes to accommodate dynamic content.

The next topic covered in this chapter was ensuring that visitors with visual disabilities would still be able to access all of the content if they had problems with color and contrast. Regarding the first point, no information on these pages is shown using color only; and regarding the second point, the best test for checking the contrast is to turn off the color on your monitor. However, because you have already seen the page in black and white printed in this book, you do not need to do that. As long as you can see these screenshots clearly, the contrast of the content does not need changing.

Adding links to skip repetitive navigation

The final point in this chapter covered accessible navigation. The key change covered here was to group related links and enable users to skip over any repetitive links. Remember that the issue here is that visitors using screen readers would not necessarily want to listen to the same content on every page before they get to the main content of that page. Therefore, the principle of skipping navigation can also be applied to any repetitive text/advertisements on pages.

To address this issue on the First Promotions site, you will be adding four links for users to skip content on this page:

1. Start by enabling users to immediately skip to the main content of the page. This involves putting an invisible link at the top of the page, linking to the main content of the page.

2. The second link would be just before the main navigation, which is grouped together using the `<div>` element whose id attribute has a value of topNav. It would enable users to skip the main navigation.

3. The third link enables users to skip the left-hand navigation; this link will take them to the end of that section (after the guarantee).

4. The fourth and final link enables users to skip the ordering information in the right-hand column because when you look at the XHTML source for the pages, this comes before the main content. It looks like it comes after the main content because it is floated to the right of the page.

Take a look at the home page and see how these skip links fit in. The highlighted lines contain the new code. Note how the target links also contain single-pixel GIF images with no alt text. This is because some browsers require target links to have some content in order for them to work, and a single-pixel GIF will have the least effect upon layout.

```
<body>
<p><a href="#mainContent"><img src="images/interface/1px.gif"
    alt="Skip to main content of page" width="1" height="1" /></a></p>

<div id="page">
   <div id="byline">Promotional gifts, pens, note pads, bags, mugs, executive toys,
corporate gifts, and lots more... </div>
   <div id="masthead"><img src="images/interface/logo.gif"
        alt="First Promotions logo" width="364" height="77" />
     <a href="#endMainNav"><img src="images/interface/1px.gif"
     alt="Skip main navigation" width="1" height="1" /></a>
   </div>
   <div id="topNav">
```

```
<div id="linkContainer"> <a href="index.html" class="topNavLink">Home</a>
    <a href="howToOrder.html" class="topNavLink">How To Order</a>
    <a href="bestSellers.html" class="topNavLink">Best Sellers</a>
    <a href="customerGifts.html" class="topNavLink">Custom Gifts</a>
    <a href="contactUs.html" id="lastItem" class="topNavLink">Contact Us</a>
    <a id="endMainNav"><img src="images/interface/1px.gif" alt=""
        width="1" height="1" /></a>
    <a href="#endSideNav"><img src="images/interface/1px.gif"
        alt="Skip side navigation" width="1" height="1" /></a>
</div>
    </div>
    <div id="sideLeft"><a href="products/pens/index.html" class="pens">Pens</a><img
src="images/interface/nav_divider.gif" alt="" width="149" height="2" /><a
href="products/pads/index.html" class="pads">Pads</a><img
src="images/interface/nav_divider.gif" alt="" width="149" height="2" /><a
href="products/mugs/index.html" class="mugs">Mugs</a><img
src="images/interface/nav_divider.gif" alt="" width="149" height="2" /><a
href="products/bags/index.html" class="bags">Bags</a><img
src="images/interface/nav_divider.gif" alt="" width="149" height="2" /><a
href="products/keyrings/index.html" class="keyrings">Keyrings</a><img
src="images/interface/nav_divider.gif" alt="" width="149" height="2" /><a
href="products/stressbusters/index.html" class="stressbusters">Stress
busters</a><img src="images/interface/nav_divider.gif" alt="" width="149"
height="2" /><br /><br />
    <div class="leftPanel">
        <img src="images/interface/guarantee.gif" alt="our guarantee"
            width="124" height="22" />
        <div class="point">
          All orders will be delivered to your door within 21 days.
        </div>

        <a id="endSideNav"><img src="images/interface/1px.gif" alt=""
            width="1" height="1" /></a>
    </div>
    </div>


    <div id="sideRight">
        <a href="#endSideRight"><img src="images/interface/1px.gif"
          alt="Skip ordering information" width="1" height="1" /></a>
        <div class="rightPanel">
          <img src="images/interface/orderHotline.gif" width="138" height="28"
alt="Order hotline 8 369 5972" />
          <div class="orderNumber">8 369 5972</div>
        </div>
        <div class="rightPanel">
          <img src="images/interface/howToOrder.gif" width="137" height="23" alt="How
to order" />
          <div class="point">1 Select an item from our extensive catalog.</div>
          <div class="point">2 Send us the logo or text you want printed on the
              gifts.</div>
          <div class="point">3 We e-mail you an image of the item with your
              design.</div>
          <div class="point">4 Confirm the order, and we'll deliver the goods within
              21 days.</div>
```

```
    </div>
      <a id="endSideRight"><img src="images/interface/1px.gif" alt=""
        width="1" height="1" /></a>
    </div>

    <div id="content"><br />
      <a id="mainContent"><img src="images/interface/1px.gif" alt=""
        width="1" height="1" /></a>
    <div class="item">
      <img src="images/interface/photo_pen.jpg" alt="Photograph of silver pen"
        width="75" height="75" id="homePenImage" />
      <p>Welcome to First Promotions, specialists in corporate gifts and
        promotional items. Our extensive range of promotional bags, mugs, pads
        and pens helps your customers remember your customers name.</p>
```

These four new links (and their targets) represent the biggest change you have had to make to the site in order to meet the accessibility requirements addressed in this chapter. They enable users to skip repetitive content and groups of navigation items, particularly if they are using a screen reader to read the content of every page to them. As the "Solution" section of this chapter has shown, your grounding in XHTML and CSS has already led you a long way down the path of creating accessible sites.

Summary

In this chapter, you have learned a lot about how to improve the accessibility of your site. You have been introduced to some of the assistive technologies that Web users with disabilities rely upon to enable them to access the Web, and you were introduced to the two sets of guidelines designed to help and protect this group of Web users.

While the U.S. regulations are based upon the Section 508 guidelines and most of the rest of the world follows the W3C WCAG, it is a good idea to implement both sets of guidelines. This will improve the accessibility of your site to all users. Furthermore, remember that it is not just those with disabilities who can benefit from you making your Web site accessible — plenty of Web users with situational limitations could find the site easier to use too!

Once you were introduced to the accessibility guidelines, the rest of the chapter focused on applying these guidelines to issues relating to structure, text, images, audio, dynamic content, color, contrast, and navigation all in turn, and all in pursuit of the creation of a more accessible Web site, a site available to more people in more situations.

This has brought you a long way toward creating Web pages that are accessible, and in Chapter 7 you will learn how to make tables, forms, and frames accessible, and how to test whether your pages meet the accessibility recommendations.

7

Creating Accessible Tables and Forms and Testing Your Site

In this chapter, you build on what you learned about accessibility in Chapter 6 and look at the remaining guidelines to ensure that you meet both the requirements of the W3C Web Contact Accessibility Guidelines and the U.S. Government Section 508 guidelines.

The focus is on methods to ensure that tables, forms, and frames can be made accessible. Tables and forms, in particular, are used on many Web sites, and both require that you learn new techniques to ensure that they are available to those with disabilities. It is very important to know how programs such as screen readers deal with tables, because they can read the content of a table in an order very different from the order in which you intend it to be read. Meanwhile, almost any Web site that wants to get information from its users will need to use forms; and unless a user is comfortable that they are entering the correct information, they will not be inclined to use the forms.

This chapter also describes some issues that can affect deaf users who come to your site and shows you how to ensure that any framesets you use in your Web pages are accessible.

Finally, you will learn how you can confirm that your pages meet the W3C and Section 508 guidelines for accessibility. Several tools can help you do this, although these are no substitute for knowing what your responsibilities are and the principles behind creating accessible pages.

By the end of this chapter, you will have learned the following:

- ❏   How a screen reader deals with tables that are used to control layout of a page
- ❏   How a screen reader deals with tables that are used for data
- ❏   How to help users understand the content of a table
- ❏   How to make forms accessible
- ❏   How to label form elements correctly

❑   Issues that might affect deaf visitors to your site

❑   How to make sure framesets are accessible

❑   Available tools to help you test whether you have met your accessibility obligations

❑   How to use some of the accessibility testing tools

Problem

To meet the legal obligations of ensuring that your Web pages are accessible, you need to ensure that any tables, forms, and frames are accessible. As you saw in Chapter 6, creating accessible designs is not just a question of meeting legal requirements, it can also significantly increase the effectiveness of sites, and can make them available to a host of new Internet-enabled devices (which have different capabilities than traditional browsers, and are used in different situations):

❑   Tables, for example, are used not only for displaying tabular data but also for layout purposes. However, the way in which programs such as screen readers access and read the content of tables can be very different from the way in which you scan a page when reading it. Furthermore, screen readers often deal with tables used to display tabular data in a different manner than those used for layout, and if you are dealing with large amounts of data in a table, you need to ensure that users can follow the content of large tables without being expected to remember the column and row headings (indeed, as you will see, you can employ certain techniques to provide information to screen readers that will assist users with this challenge).

❑   Forms, meanwhile, are used whenever you need to obtain data from a user on a Web page. Now that you can now bank, shop, and even vote using computers, it is very important that the way in which you communicate with your visitors does not exclude those who have disabilities.

❑   Finally, if you are dealing with frames, you need to incorporate markup in your design that will help users navigate between the frames on a page, which are essentially different Web pages. While those looking at a screen can see all pages in a frameset simultaneously, visitors with visual impairments will not be able to tell the relationship between each window of a frameset so easily.

Once you have learned all of these techniques, you then need to ensure that you have implemented them correctly. Luckily, tools are available that can help you test whether your pages meet the requirements and whether you have fulfilled your obligations.

Having looked at each of these problems in turn, you will then look at how the techniques you have learned apply to the First Promotions site.

Design

To familiarize yourself with the issues involved in making tables, forms, and frames accessible, you will be looking at each topic separately. Because you are covering each of these aspects of a site separately, I introduce the guidelines in a slightly different way from the last chapter. First you look at the issues that relate to a topic; and after looking at that topic, you examine the WCAG and Section 508 guidelines that apply to it.

Tables

Originally, HTML tables were supposed to be used to display tabular data. Tabular data is anything that uses rows and columns to display data (rather like a spreadsheet); for example, information such as timetables, sales figures, and sports scores can all be represented in rows and columns. However, it did not take long for Web designers to figure out that they could use tables for another purpose — to control layout. They found that tables could be used to create a *layout grid* that would enable them to position items on the page with the same level of control that print designers enjoy. This practice soon became very popular, and as a result the majority of tables used on the Web these days are used for layout purposes.

When creating accessible tables, you have to remain aware of the fact that screen readers and some other assistive technologies provide a one-dimensional view of a Web page that is very different from the two dimensional image created on a screen. By this I mean that the screen reader reads the content to the user one line at a time (a voice cannot read up and down a page at the same time as it reads from left to right in the way that a sighted user can scan a page).

Therefore, when a screen reader comes across a table, it reads out the content to the visitor, usually cell by cell, from left to right, one row at a time. This is a process known as *linearizing* a table. As a result, it is not as easy for visitors who use screen readers to scan the data in the table as it is for visitors with normal sight who can quickly check the table for the information they want (while ignoring the other information).

It is important to highlight a distinction between tables used for layout and tables used to contain tabular data. When tables are used for layout, users are not generally required to keep track of which row and column they are currently in for the page to make sense. However, when tables are used to contain tabular data, the row and column headings are vital to understanding the table, and knowing which row and column you are in is the only way of making sense of each cell in the table. As you can imagine, it could get quite confusing if you are being read the contents of a table that has several columns and rows and you have heard the column headings only once at the beginning of the table.

In fact, because users have to interact with tables that contain tabular data in a very different manner from the way in which they interact with tables used for layout purposes, most assistive technologies have different modes for dealing with the two types of table. Because layout tables are used far more widely than tables containing tabular data, the default setting for most screen readers is to treat tables as if they were used for layout, requiring users to switch modes when they come across tabular data. Therefore, to truly understand the challenges that tables create, you need to look at some examples of how tables linearize.

How tables linearize

As already mentioned, most screen readers linearize a table in order to read information to users one cell at a time, from left to right, one row after the other. This can have serious effects on the way a page sounds as it is presented. For example, consider the table shown in Figure 7-1.

Row 1 Cell 1	Row 1 Cell 2
Row 2 Cell 1	Row 2 Cell 2

Figure 7-1

The cells in this table would be read in the following order:

1. Row 1 Cell 1
2. Row 1 Cell 2
3. Row 2 Cell 1
4. Row 2 Cell 2

This simple example seems to make sense. However, designers often use very complicated configurations of tables, often with tables nested inside of tables and cells spanning rows or columns. Figure 7-2 shows a more complex layout. You have probably seen many sites with a similar structure.

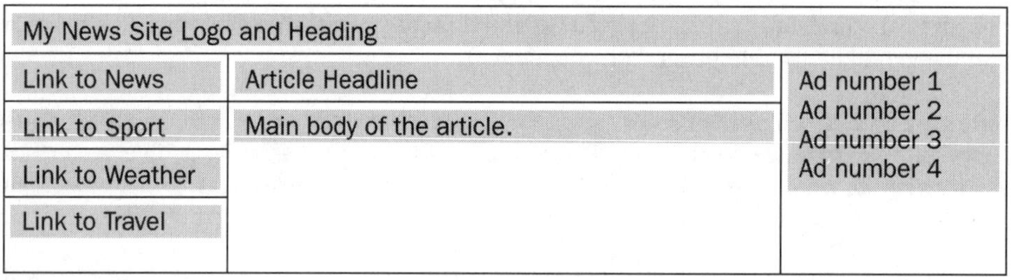

My News Site Logo and Heading		
Link to News	Article Headline	Ad number 1
Link to Sport	Main body of the article.	Ad number 2 Ad number 3
Link to Weather		Ad number 4
Link to Travel		

Figure 7-2

In Figure 7-2, the table would be linearized so that the items are read in the following order:

1. My News Site Logo and Heading
2. Link to News
3. Article Headline
4. Advertisement number 1
5. Advertisement number 2
6. Advertisement number 3
7. Advertisement number 4
8. Link to Sport
9. Main body of the article
10. Link to Weather
11. Link to Travel

You can probably imagine how confusing it would be if you could not see the layout and the site were read to you with the content appearing in this order. The first real problem appears when the headline for the article is followed by a set of advertisements (for example, these may be text ads taken from a third-party site to help generate revenue).

The next problem is that the navigation links do not follow each other and will not be read out together. For example, there is a headline and set of advertisements between the first and second navigation items, and the body of the article is between the second and third navigation items (this second issue could be solved using the rowspan attribute to merge the navigation items into one cell).

Even if you used the techniques covered in Chapter 6 for skipping navigation, the headline is in a separate cell from the main body of the article, which is another source of confusion.

This example highlights the benefits of using CSS to control layout as discussed in Chapter 5, as you can put the content in a logical order in the XHTML document. The following sections, however, will help you understand how to create more accessible designs for cases when tables are required and when you are dealing with real tabular data.

Guidelines for tables used for layout

Two checkpoints (both priority 2 checkpoints) contained in the WCAG relate to table linearization. The first says you should not use tables unless they make sense when linearized:

> **WCAG 5.3 Do not use tables for layout unless the table makes sense when linearized. Otherwise, if the table does not make sense, provide an alternative equivalent (which may be a linearized version). [Priority 2]**

The second checkpoint recommends that you not use structural markup just to achieve a visual effect inside a table:

> **WCAG 5.4 If a table is used for layout, do not use any structural markup for the purpose of visual formatting. [Priority 2]**

This second checkpoint highlights the fact that you should not use markup just to change the appearance of the page. For example, you should not use a <th> element in order to make the text in a cell appear bold and centered (which is the default appearance of <th> elements in most browsers). You should use the <th> element only if the content of the element is a table heading; if you just want bold, centered text, you should assign the appropriate cell an id or class attribute and then use a CSS rule to alter its presentation.

One additional WCAG priority 3 checkpoint relates to the way in which screen readers read the page:

> **WCAG 10.3 Until user agents (including assistive technologies) render side-by-side text correctly, provide a linear text alternative (on the current page or some other) for all tables that lay out text in parallel, word-wrapped columns. [Priority 3]**

Despite the presence of this checkpoint in the guidelines, most assistive technology will linearize tables reasonably well, as long as you create the table using the principles discussed in this section. Furthermore, if you were using CSS to create your layout (using the principles discussed in Chapter 5), the text would already be linear.

Section 508 does not say anything specific about the use of tables in presenting pages, so this completes your introduction to the issues relating to the presentation of tables, and you should do you best to design with these issues in mind.

Note that if you have a complex table layout and have trouble working out how they would be linearized, two tools can help you. First, the IBM Home Page Reader (which was introduced in Chapter 6) can be used to create a text view of the page for you; this will list the content of the cells in the order in which they would be read (www.IBM.com/able/). Second, you might check out a tool from the W3C called Tablin (www.w3.org/WAI/Resources/Tablin).

Working with tables containing data

While tables are not as widely used to hold tabular data — that is what the <table> element was designed for — many types of tabular data still need to be displayed on the Web, such as train and school timetables, TV and event listings, and scientific and sporting results; even lists of products in a catalog generated by a database sometimes require rows and columns to present their information. In fact, any data that relies on rows and columns to convey information is known as a *data table*.

As I have already hinted, if you were just read a set of times, figures, or results, it would be easy to lose track of where you were in the table. However, assistive technologies can help users understand the structure of the data table — in particular, by reading headings to the user when they move from cell to cell. (This assistance is not usually required in layout tables because they rarely have meaningful headers.) When users come across a table that contains data, they tend to have to switch modes in their assistive technology or software, from the default mode that deals with layout tables to the mode that deals with data tables.

To understand how assistive technologies work with data tables, consider the table shown in Figure 7-3. 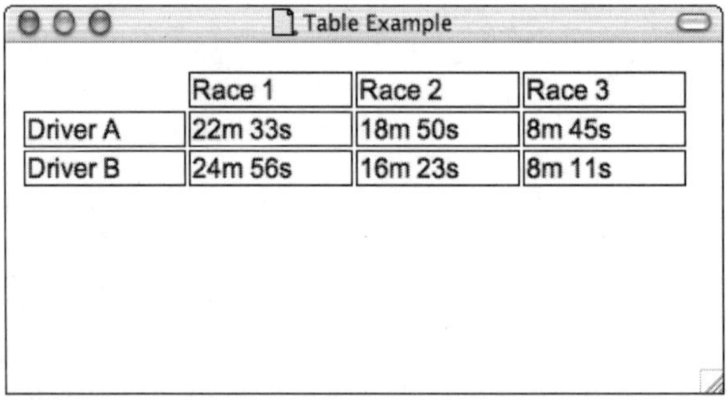

	Race 1	Race 2	Race 3
Driver A	22m 33s	18m 50s	8m 45s
Driver B	24m 56s	16m 23s	8m 11s

Figure 7-3

Here is what that table looks like in XHTML (ch07_eg01.html):

```
<table>
  <tr>
    <td></td>
    <td>Race 1</td>
    <td>Race 2</td>
    <td>Race 3</td>
```

```
   </tr>
   <tr>
     <td>Driver A</td>
     <td>22m 33s</td>
     <td>18m 50s</td>
     <td>8m 45s</td>
   </tr>
   <tr>
     <td>Driver B</td>
     <td>24m 56s</td>
     <td>16m 23s</td>
     <td>8m 11s</td>
   </tr>
 </table>
```

While this table does not contain any `<th>` table heading cells, when the screen reader knows it is dealing with tabular data, it should treat the first row as column headings, and the first column as row headings. This is important because what will be read to the user with a screen reader depends on which cell the user is moving from and which cell they are moving to:

❑　When the column changes, the program should read out the heading from the first row.

❑　When the row changes, the program should read out the heading from the first column.

To understand this properly, here are some examples of what the screen reader would speak to the user when they move between cells:

Moving from	Moving to	What You Will Hear
Row 2 column 2 (which says 22m 33s)	Row 2 column 3 (which says 18m 50s)	**Race 2 18m 50s** (the column has changed, so the heading for the new column is read out before the content of the new cell)
Row 2 column 2 (which says 22m 33s)	Row 3 column 2 (which says 24m 56s)	**Driver B 24m 56s** (the row has changed, so the heading for the new row is read out before the content of the new cell)
Row 3 column 4 (which says 8m 11s)	Row 2 column 4 (which says 8m 45s)	**Driver A 8m 45s** (the row has changed, so the heading for the new row is read out before the content of the new cell)
Row 3 column 4 (which says 8m 11s)	Row 3 column 3 (which says 16m 23s)	**Race 2 16m 23s** (the column has changed, so the heading for the new column is read out before the content of the new cell)

This first table works okay despite the lack of the `<th>` elements to indicate to the screen reader which cells contain the headings. However, a table will often include a heading or caption across the top or side of the table. Figure 7-4 illustrates an example of such a table.

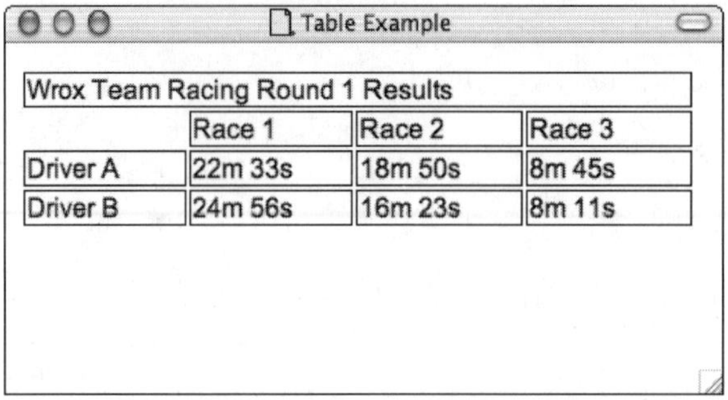

Figure 7-4

A new row has been added to the top of the table, and the first cell contains a `colspan` attribute to indicate that the cell should span the width of the table (in XHTML, you should not really be using this attribute for this purpose, but you will see an alternative later in the chapter). Here is what that row looks like (`ch07_eg02.html`):

```
<tr>
   <td colspan="4">Wrox Team Racing Round 1 Results</td>
</tr>
```

Because the first row of this table now contains the heading, some screen readers will no longer be able to read the same sort of useful information it did to the user in the previous example. Therefore, you should avoid using the first row of a table as a caption for the table.

*Although some programs have rules indicating that spanned cells should be ignored, you are better off using text before the table to describe its purpose, or even better, the **<caption>** element covered later in this chapter.*

Using <th> elements to indicate table headers

Strictly speaking, you should not use <td> elements for cells of tables that contain headings (after all, td is supposed to stand for table data). Rather, you should be using the <th> element (the th here stands for table heading).

By default, browsers will usually display the content of a <th> element centered within the cell and in a bold font (although you can override this presentation using CSS). Unfortunately, many HTML and XHTML authors do not know about the <th> element, and it is very underused. The following table shows an example of this element and how this table should really be marked up (`ch07_eg03.html`):

```
<table>
  <tr>
     <td></td>
     <th>Race 1</th>
     <th>Race 2</th>
     <th>Race 3</th>
  </tr>
  <tr>
     <th>Driver A</th>
```

```
        <td>22m 33s</td>
        <td>18m 50s</td>
        <td>8m 45s</td>
      </tr>
      <tr>
        <th>Driver B</th>
        <td>24m 56s</td>
        <td>16m 23s</td>
        <td>8m 11s</td>
      </tr>
    </table>
```

Both the row and column headings in this code have been placed inside a `<th>` element, but note how the top-left cell has been left as an empty `<td>` element. This is because it is not a header.

The `<th>` element is supported only in more recent versions of the most popular screen readers (including JAWS for Windows 4.1 and Windows-Eyes 4.5); however, earlier versions of these programs should still be able to provide helpful information to the user because the first row and first column both contain the headers (unlike the previous example, ch07_eg02.html, which contained a title for the first cell).

If your table header cells contain long descriptions, you should also consider adding an `abbr` attribute to provide an abbreviated version of the header. This technique was recommended by the W3C in the hope that it would be adopted by future versions of screen readers, because reading an abbreviated version of the heading would enable them to read headings much faster. While assistive technologies have not yet adopted this technique, it is hoped that they will in the future.

Using the scope attribute

The `scope` attribute can be used as an alternative way of indicating that a cell is a header cell (it is even less well known or used than the `<th>` element). The cell that represents the heading uses the `scope` attribute with a value of either `row` or `col` to indicate whether that cell is a heading for that row or column.

The advantage of using this attribute is that the cells are not formatted differently from the rest of the body of the table (although you could get a similar effect even if you use `<th>` elements, by attaching the same CSS formatting rules to the `<th>` element as to the `<td>` element). The following example uses this technique (ch07_eg04.html):

```
    <table>
      <tr>
        <td></td>
        <td scope="col">Race 1</td>
        <td scope="col">Race 2</td>
        <td scope="col">Race 3</td>
      </tr>
      <tr>
        <td scope="row">Driver A</td>
        <td>22m 33s</td>
        <td>18m 50s</td>
        <td>8m 45s</td>
      </tr>
      <tr>
        <td scope="row">Driver B</td>
```

```
      <td>24m 56s</td>
      <td>16m 23s</td>
      <td>8m 11s</td>
    </tr>
  </table>
```

As with the `<th>` element, this attribute has only recently been supported by major screen readers.

Using the `<caption>` element to provide a caption or title

When it comes to captioning a table, rather than use a cell that spans the width of the table, you should use an element that was introduced for this very purpose: the `<caption>` element. The `<caption>` element was introduced in HTML 3.2 and works in IE 3+ and Netscape 3+. The following code shows how the `<caption>` element should be used; it appears directly after the opening `<table>` tag and before the first `<tr>` tag (ch07_eg05.html):

```
<table>
  <caption>Wrox Team Racing Round 1 Results</caption>
  <tr>
    <td></td>
    <td scope="col">Race 1</td>
    <td scope="col">Race 2</td>
    <td scope="col">Race 3</td>
  </tr>
  ...
</table>
```

As with the `<th>` element and `scope` attribute, use of the `<caption>` element is not widespread; however, it is a very useful element (and using CSS, you can control the position of it in relation to the table).

If you do not want to use this element, you should preferably describe the purpose of the table in one of the following ways:

❑ Add the caption before the table in plaintext (a caption in text that appears after the table will not be helpful to someone about to hear its content).

❑ Use the `title` attribute on the `<table>` element.

❑ Provide a summary of the content in the table using the `summary` attribute on the `<table>` element. The `summary` attribute should describe the relationship between the cells and the rest of the document.

You could even combine two or more techniques, like so:

```
<table summary="Results of Wrox Team Racing, Round 1, 20th January 2005.
      Column 1 shows the race numbers, column 2 shows the times
      for driver 1, column 3 shows the times for driver 2.">
  <caption>Wrox Team Racing Round 1 Results</caption>
  <tr>
  ...
```

Guidelines for table headings

Table headings are required for data tables by both the Section 508 guidelines and the WCAG. Section 508 requires that row and column headings be identified in data tables (remember that the Section 508 guidelines can be found at `www.section508.gov/index.cfm?FuseAction=Content&ID=12`):

Section 508 §1194.22(g) Row and column headers shall be identified for data tables.

The WCAG checkpoint 5.1 is very similar and is a priority 1 checkpoint (remember that the WCAG can be found at `www.w3.org/TR/WCAG10/`):

WCAG 5.1 For data tables, identify row and column headers. [Priority 1]

The W3C also want to encourage the use of abbreviations for `<th>` elements using the `abbr` attribute, which they hope assistive devices will implement to save time in reading the content of tables to users.

WCAG 5.6 Provide abbreviations for header labels. [Priority 3]

Finally, you should provide summaries for tables:

WCAG 5.5 Provide summaries for tables. [Priority 3]

There are three ways in which you can do this:

- ❑ You should first aim to use the `<caption>` element to provide a caption for the table.

- ❑ If you do not use the `<caption>` element, you should use the `title` attribute on the `<table>` element to add a short description of the table.

- ❑ You can also provide a summary of the content in the table using the `summary` attribute on the `<table>` element. The `summary` attribute should describe the relationship between the cells and the rest of the document. This is especially important if you do not provide a `<caption>` element.

This is good enough for simple tables, but some tables contain cells that span rows or columns. The following section describes the additional rules that apply to these so-called *complex tables*.

Using the headers attribute in complex tables

Sometimes you will have tables that contain more than one logical level of rows or columns. This might sound complicated, but you have to remember that tables are two-dimensional—they work on *x* and *y* axes. However, some data tables cannot simply be represented on these two axes, so you might have what are effectively subsections within tables. These are sometimes referred to as *complex tables*. For example, you might have one table that contains financial reports not only for the year, but also for the four quarters of the year, resulting in what you might call subtables.

The example shown in Figure 7-5 illustrates this type of complex table.

	Receipts	Sales tax (17.5%)	Costs	Balance
Quarter 1				
Store A	12,585	2,202	4,155	6,228
Store B	15,221	2,663	5,320	7,238
Sub Total	42,806	4,865	9,475	13,466
Quarter 2				
Store A	14,682	2,569	4,650	7,463
Store B	21,166	6,704	6,240	11,222
Sub Total	35,848	6,273	10,890	18,685
Quarter 3				
Store A	16,284	2,849	4,840	8,595
Store B	24,374	4,265	6,990	13,199
Sub Total	40,658	7,114	11,830	21,794
Quarter 4				
Store A	19,454	3,404	5,520	10,530
Store B	27,366	4,789	7,360	15,217
Sub Total	46,820	8,193	12,880	25,747
Totals	111,172	26,445	45,075	79,692

Figure 7-5

HTML 4.0 introduced the `headers` attribute specifically to deal with tables such as these, and it enables authors to indicate which headers belong to which cell. To use the `header` attribute, each heading cell needs to carry an `id` attribute. This `id` attribute must have a unique value that is used to identify that header. For example, the `<th>` element for the `receipts` header might look like the following:

```
<th id="receipts">Receipts</th>
```

It is especially important to remember that the values for the `id` attributes must be unique in examples like this. The table shown in Figure 7-5 contains four instances of both the Store A and Store B headings, one for each quarter. The value of the `id` attribute must also start with a letter (not a number) but not contain any spaces. Therefore, the Store A heading for quarter 1 might look as follows:

```
<th id="StoreAQ1">Store A</th>
```

The headings for the quarters (despite doing the job of the headings for the subtables) are written the same way:

```
<th id="Q1">Quarter 1</th>
```

Now look at the `headers` attribute, which must occur on every cell that is not a header and is not empty. The value of the `headers` attribute should be a list of the values of the `id` attributes for the cells that contain the corresponding headings. Each value should be separated by a space. For example, the cell that shows the receipts for Store A in Quarter 1 should look like this:

```
<td headers="Q1 receipts StoreAQ1">12,585</td>
```

Here you can see that the values of the id attributes (both of which you just saw above) are provided with a space in between them.

The whole table would look like the following (ch07_eg06.html):

```
<table>
  <tr>
    <td></td>
    <th id="receipts">Receipts</th>
    <th id="salestax">Sales tax (17.5%)</th>
    <th id="costs">Costs</th>
    <th id="balance">Balance</th>
  </tr><tr>
    <td id="Q1">Quarter 1</td><td></td><td></td><td></td><td></td>
  </tr><tr>
    <th id="StoreAQ1">Store A</th>
    <td headers="Q1 receipts StoreAQ1">12,585</td>
    <td headers="Q1 salestax StoreAQ1">2,202</td>
    <td headers="Q1 costs StoreAQ1">4,155</td>
    <td headers="Q1 balance StoreAQ1">6,228</td>
  </tr><tr>
    <th id="StoreBQ1">Store B</th>
    <td headers="Q1 receipts StoreBQ1">15,221</td>
    <td headers="Q1 salestax StoreBQ1">2,663</td>
    <td headers="Q1 costs StoreBQ1">5,320</td>
    <td headers="Q1 balance StoreBQ1">7,238</td>
  </tr><tr>
    <th id="SubTotalQ1">Subtotal</th>
    <td headers="Q1 receipts SubTotalQ1">42,806</td>
    <td headers="Q1 salestax SubTotalQ1">4,865</td>
    <td headers="Q1 costs SubTotalQ1">9,475</td>
    <td headers="Q1 balance SubTotalQ1">13,466</td>
  </tr><tr>
    <td id="Q2">Quarter 2</td><td></td><td></td><td></td><td></td>
  </tr><tr>
    <th id="StoreAQ2">Store A</th>
    <td headers="Q2 receipts StoreAQ2">14,682</td>
    <td headers="Q2 salestax StoreAQ2">2,569</td>
    <td headers="Q2 costs StoreAQ2">4,650</td>
    <td headers="Q2 balance StoreAQ2">7,463</td>
  </tr><tr>
    <th id="StoreBQ2">Store B</th>
    <td headers="Q2 receipts StoreBQ2">21,166</td>
    <td headers="Q2 salestax StoreBQ2">6,704</td>
    <td headers="Q2 costs StoreBQ2">6,240</td>
    <td headers="Q2 balance StoreBQ2">11,222</td>
  </tr><tr>
    <th id="SubTotalQ2">Subtotal</th>
    <td headers="Q2 receipts SubTotalQ2">35,848</td>
    <td headers="Q2 salestax SubTotalQ2">6,273</td>
    <td headers="Q2 costs SubTotalQ2">10,890</td>
    <td headers="Q2 balance SubTotalQ2">18,685</td>
  </tr><tr>
    <td id="Q3">Quarter 3</td><td></td><td></td><td></td><td></td>
  </tr><tr>
```

```
    <th id="StoreAQ3">Store A</th>
    <td headers="Q3 receipts StoreAQ3">16,284</td>
    <td headers="Q3 salestax StoreAQ3">2,849</td>
    <td headers="Q3 costs StoreAQ3">4,840</td>
    <td headers="Q3 balance StoreAQ3">8,595</td>
  </tr><tr>
    <th id="StoreBQ3">Store B</th>
    <td headers="Q3 receipts StoreBQ3">24,374</td>
    <td headers="Q3 salestax StoreBQ3">4,265</td>
    <td headers="Q3 costs StoreBQ3">6,990</td>
    <td headers="Q3 balance StoreBQ3">13,199</td>
  </tr><tr>
    <th id="SubTotalQ3">Subtotal</th>
    <td headers="Q3 receipts SubTotalQ3">40,658</td>
    <td headers="Q3 salestax SubTotalQ3">7,114</td>
    <td headers="Q3 costs SubTotalQ3">11,830</td>
    <td headers="Q3 balance SubTotalQ3">21,794</td>
  </tr><tr>
    <td id="Q4">Quarter 4</td><td></td><td></td><td></td><td></td>
  </tr><tr>
    <th id="StoreAQ4">Store A</th>
    <td headers="Q4 receipts StoreAQ4">19,454</td>
    <td headers="Q4 salestax StoreAQ4">3,404</td>
    <td headers="Q4 costs StoreAQ4">5,520</td>
    <td headers="Q4 balance StoreAQ4">10,530</td>
  </tr><tr>
    <th id="StoreBQ4">Store B</th>
    <td headers="Q4 receipts StoreBQ4">27,366</td>
    <td headers="Q4 salestax StoreBQ4">4,789</td>
    <td headers="Q4 costs StoreBQ4">7,360</td>
    <td headers="Q4 balance StoreBQ4">15,217</td>
  </tr><tr>
    <th id="SubTotalQ4">Subtotal</th>
    <td headers="Q4 receipts SubTotalQ4">46,820</td>
    <td headers="Q4 salestax SubTotalQ4">8,193</td>
    <td headers="Q4 costs SubTotalQ4">12,880</td>
    <td headers="Q4 balance SubTotalQ4">25,747</td>
  </tr><tr>
    <th id="Totals">Totals</th>
    <td headers="Totals receipts">111,172</td>
    <td headers="Totals salestax">26,445</td>
    <td headers="Totals costs">45,075</td>
    <td headers="Totals balance">79,692</td>
  </tr>
</table>
```

This adds quite a lot of effort to the work of writing a table, but both the WCAG and Section 508 guidelines require that each cell should be associated with heading information, so you will have to use this attribute with any complex data tables you come across.

Guidelines for complex tables

For your complex tables to make any sense to those using assistive technologies, such as screen readers, you need to ensure that the markup indicates clearly which cells are header cells. The WCAG make this a priority 1 checkpoint:

> **WCAG 5.2 For data tables that have two or more logical levels of row or column headers, use markup to associate data cells and header cells. [Priority 1]**

The Section 508 guidelines are very similar:

> **Section 508 §1194.22(h) Markup shall be used to associate data cells and header cells for data tables that have two or more logical levels of row or column headers.**

Forms

Whenever you want to collect information from a visitor to your site, you have to use a *form*. Forms are used for all manner of purposes—from adding simple search boxes to complex registration and ordering forms.

Web users tend to find forms daunting at their best, and treat them with some trepidation, especially when they involve revealing personal information or paying for goods and services. Therefore, you can imagine that when a user cannot see the form, or has difficulty understanding it, their reservations are magnified.

Bearing in mind that online shopping facilities can be a real benefit to older Web users and those with disabilities, it should be a core aim of any online service to provide accessible forms that will attract these groups of users.

To create accessible forms, you will revisit a couple of the techniques that you met in the previous chapter:

❑   Using alt text on buttons that use images

❑   Ensuring that you do not rely on color alone to convey important information (such as which fields are required)

You will also have to address some new topics:

❑   How form elements gain focus (so that they can be interacted with)

❑   How to clearly label the purpose of each individual form control

❑   How to group sections of forms

Along the way, you will be introduced to some elements that are part of HTML and XHTML that you might not have encountered before. Indeed, few HTML authors have come across some of these because they are rarely used. However, adopting these elements can greatly increase the accessibility and usability of your form.

Labeling forms clearly

The first aim in making any form accessible is to ensure that the user can tell exactly what each form control is supposed to do, and what information they should be providing where. This means that each control must have a clear *label* or *prompt* that indicates to users what they should do.

One of the key aspects of adding a label or prompt to a form control is determining where it should be placed. Typically, prompts are placed in one of three places depending on the type of form control:

❏ To the left of text inputs and drop-down list (or select) boxes

❏ To the right of checkboxes and radio buttons

❏ On submit and image buttons

However, if you simply write prompts next to the form control, they do not tend to align well and therefore look a bit messy. Figure 7-6 shows a simple login form with two text inputs that do not align well.

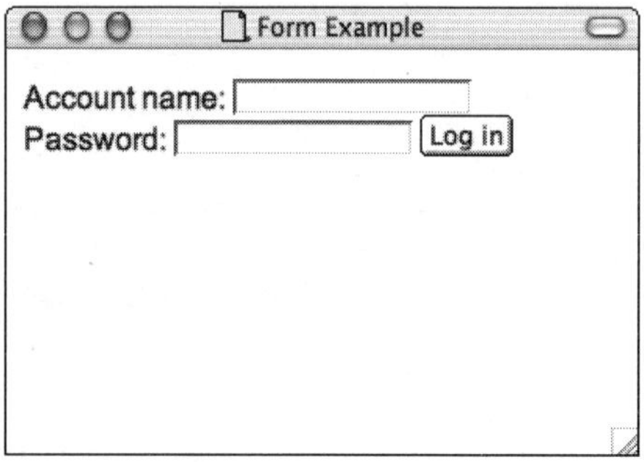

Figure 7-6

Following is the code for this example (ch07_eg07.html):

```
<form action="login.asp" method="post" name="frmLogin">
   Account name: <input type="text" name="txtLogin" size="20" /><br />
   Password: <input type="password" name="txtPwd" size="20" />
   <input type="submit" value="Log in" />
</form>
```

When text inputs do not align, they not only look messy but are harder to read or view on-screen. Although the form in Figure 7-6 is readable, it is only an example with two input fields. When you have several text input fields that are not aligned, it can be much more difficult to follow. As a result, designers often place forms in tables. Figure 7-7 shows this same login form placed inside a table.

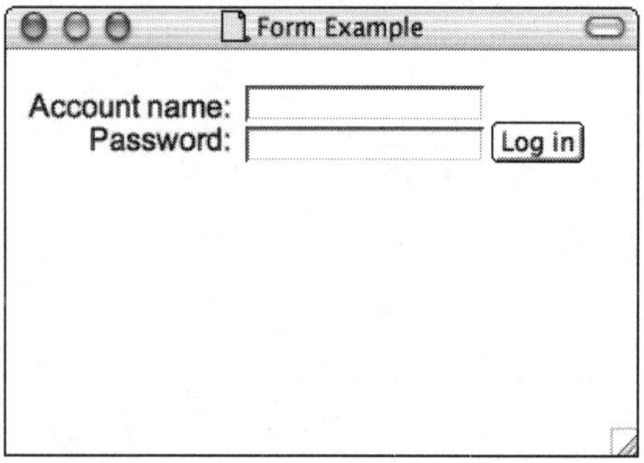

Figure 7-7

You can see the code for this example here (ch07_eg08.html):

```
<form action="login.asp" method="post" name="frmLogin">
  <table>
    <tr>
      <td align="right">
        Account name: <br />
        Password:
      </td>
      <td>
        <input type="text" name="txtLogin" size="20" /><br />
        <input type="password" name="txtPwd" size="20" />
        <input type="submit" value="Log in" />
      </td>
    </tr>
  </table>
</form>
```

This form does look a lot more attractive, but as you have already seen in this chapter, you need to make sure that your tables linearize correctly so that a screen reader can present them in a way that makes sense to users.

This example would cause problems for visitors relying upon a screen reader because both of the prompts are written in the first table cell, so both would be read out before the user gets to any of the form controls, which are in the second table cell.

If you are going to use tables to lay out your forms, the best way around this is to ensure that any prompts are on the same row as the form controls, and to use only one prompt and one form control per row. The following code demonstrates a far better way of ensuring that the parts of the form align correctly (ch07_eg09.html):

```
<form action="login.asp" method="post" name="frmLogin">
  <table>
    <tr>
      <td class="prompt">Account name: </td>
      <td><input type="text" name="txtLogin" size="20" /></td>
    </tr>
    <tr>
      <td class="prompt">Password </td>
      <td><input type="password" name="txtPwd" size="20" /></td>
    </tr>
    <tr>
      <td></td>
      <td><input type="submit" value="Log in" /></td>
    </tr>
  </table>
</form>
```

Note how both of the table cells that contain a prompt are given a class attribute whose value is prompt. This enables you to add a CSS rule in a style sheet to align the text of these cells to the right, which not only makes the form more attractive, but also more readable for sighted users. Here is the CSS rule for the prompts:

```
.prompt {text-align:right;}
```

At this point, it would be helpful to note some of the terminology used when it comes to labeling forms. The WCAG make a clear distinction between *implicitly* and *explicitly* labeled form controls.

❑ *Explicitly labeled* form controls use the <label> element, which was introduced in HTML 4, to indicate the label for an element (which you will meet in the next section).

❑ *Implicitly labeled* form controls simply place the text that describes the purpose of the form control next to the control (as we have been doing so far in this chapter).

Now that you have looked at examples of prompts for form controls that use implicit labels, you can turn your attention to creating explicit labels using the <label> element.

The <label> element

The <label> element enables you to specify a label that is associated with a particular form control. The <label> element carries an attribute called for, which is used to indicate the form control with which the label is associated. The value of the for attribute is the same as the value of the id attribute on the form control for which it is supposed to be the label.

In the following simple example, note how the first <label> element has a for attribute whose value is accountName. Meanwhile, the form control used to collect the account name has an id attribute whose value is also accountName (ch07_eg10.html):

```
<form action="login.asp" method="post" name="frmLogin">

  <label for="accountName">Account name:</a>
  <input type="text" name="txtLogin" size="20" id="accountName" /><br />

  <label for="password">Password:</label>
  <input type="password" name="txtPwd" size="20" id="password" />
  <input type="submit" value="Log in" />

</form>
```

Again, remember that the value of the id attribute has to be unique within the document; this ensures that each label can correspond with only one form control.

> *While the <label> attribute has been supported only since IE 4 and Netscape 6, older browsers will just ignore the opening <label> and closing </label> tags and display what is written between them, so you are free to use the <label> element in all of your pages.*

As you might imagine, on a complex form the addition of all of these <label> elements adds quite a lot of work. In addition, it is not really necessary on most forms where either the implicit label is right next to the form control or the table linearizes as you would expect it to. In such cases, where implicit labeling is sufficient, you do not need to use the <label> element. However, you will come across some more complex form layouts where it comes in very handy. In the example shown in Figure 7-8, the user is expected to indicate to what degree they agree with a comment — this kind of form layout is commonly used with surveys.

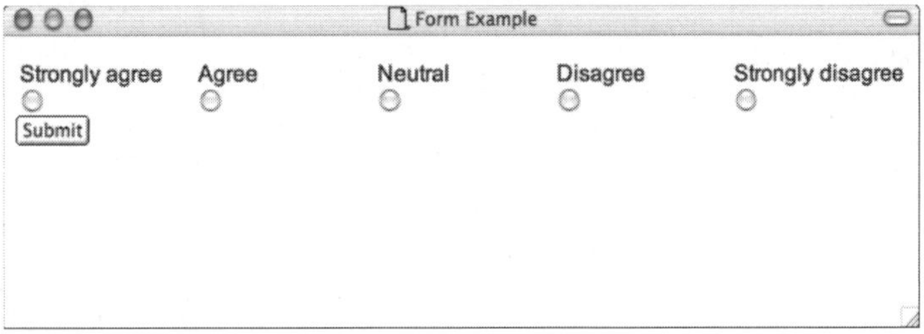

Figure 7-8

Now have a look at the code for this form, because to ensure that it aligns nicely, it has been placed inside a table (ch07_eg11.html):

```
<form action="surveyResults.asp" method="post" name="frmSurvey">
  <table>
    <tr>
      <td>Strongly agree</td>
      <td>Agree</td>
      <td>Neutral</td>
      <td>Disagree</td>
      <td>Strongly disagree</td>
    </tr>
    <tr>
      <td><input type="radio" name="radQ3" value="5" /></td>
      <td><input type="radio" name="radQ3" value="4" /></td>
      <td><input type="radio" name="radQ3" value="3" /></td>
      <td><input type="radio" name="radQ3" value="2" /></td>
      <td><input type="radio" name="radQ3" value="1" /></td>
    </tr>
  </table>
  <input type="submit" />
</form>
```

This form is a prime candidate for use of the <label> element because without it visitors using screen readers will hear all of the possible values in the top row, and then all of the radio buttons in the second row — without clearly knowing which radio button correlates with which opinion.

Ideally, the form should have been built as shown in this next listing (ch07_eg12.html):

```
<form action="surveyResults.asp" method="post" name="frmSurvey">
  <table>
    <tr>
      <td><label for="q35">Strongly agree</label></td>
      <td><label for="q34">Agree</label></td>
      <td><label for="q33">Neutral</label></td>
      <td><label for="q32">Disagree</label></td>
      <td><label for="q31">Strongly disagree</label></td>
    </tr>
    <tr>
      <td><input type="radio" name="radQ3" value="5" id="q35" /></td>
```

```
        <td><input type="radio" name="radQ3" value="4" id="q34" /></td>
        <td><input type="radio" name="radQ3" value="3" id="q33" /></td>
        <td><input type="radio" name="radQ3" value="2" id="q32" /></td>
        <td><input type="radio" name="radQ3" value="1" id="q31" /></td>
      </tr>
    </table>
    <input type="submit" />
  </form>
```

The explicit labels used on this form explicitly state which label is associated with which radio button.

This is an ideal time to point out the importance of all form controls having their own label. While this might sound obvious, you can find plenty of examples of voting forms (like the one you have just seen) where some form controls have not been given labels at all. This causes visitors that rely upon a screen reader a lot of difficulty, as shown in the example form in Figure 7-9:

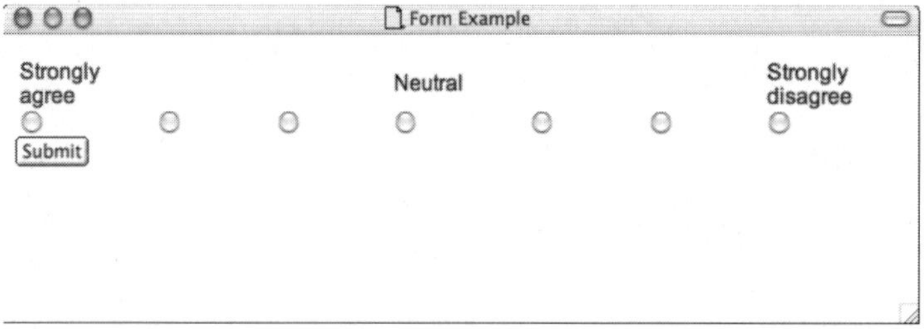

Figure 7-9

As you can see, this form contains seven options from which the user can select, but only three labels. Listening to a screen reader, a user would hear three options but be presented with seven form controls, which would be very confusing. You can see the code for this example here (ch07_eg13.html):

```
<form action="surveyResults.asp" method="post" name="frmSurvey">
  <table>
    <tr>
      <td>Strongly agree</td><td></td><td></td>
      <td>Neutral</td><td></td><td></td>
      <td>Strongly disagree</td>
    </tr>
    <tr>
      <td><input type="radio" name="radQ3" value="7" /></td>
      <td><input type="radio" name="radQ3" value="6" /></td>
      <td><input type="radio" name="radQ3" value="5" /></td>
      <td><input type="radio" name="radQ3" value="4" /></td>
      <td><input type="radio" name="radQ3" value="3" /></td>
      <td><input type="radio" name="radQ3" value="2" /></td>
      <td><input type="radio" name="radQ3" value="1" /></td>
    </tr>
  </table>
  <input type="submit" />
</form>
```

This form should also be using the `<label>` element to indicate which control the prompt applies to because all of the prompts are in the first row and will be read out before any of the form controls on a screen reader.

If you still choose not to show the labels for each of these radio buttons, one alternative way around the issue is to use a single-pixel trick again, like the one you saw with the skip navigation links in Chapter 6. This time, the single-pixel GIF becomes part of the label and has `alt` text indicating what value the radio button corresponds to. This example also uses the `<label>` element to indicate which image represents a label for which form control (ch07_eg14.html):

```
<form action="surveyResults.asp" method="post" name="frmSurvey">
  <table>
    <tr>
      <td><label for="q37">Strongly agree</label></td>
      <td><label for="q36"><img src="1px.gif" alt="agree" /></label></td>
      <td><label for="q35"><img src="1px.gif" alt="slightly agree" /></label></td>
      <td><label for="q34">Neutral</label></td>
      <td><label for="q33"><img src="1px.gif" alt="slightly disagree" />
          </label></td>
      <td><label for="q32"><img src="1px.gif" alt="disagree" /></label></td>
      <td><label for="q31">Strongly disagree</label></td>
    </tr>
    <tr>
      <td><input type="radio" name="radQ3" value="7" id="q35" /></td>
      <td><input type="radio" name="radQ3" value="6" id="q35" /></td>
      <td><input type="radio" name="radQ3" value="5" id="q35" /></td>
      <td><input type="radio" name="radQ3" value="4" id="q34" /></td>
      <td><input type="radio" name="radQ3" value="3" id="q33" /></td>
      <td><input type="radio" name="radQ3" value="2" id="q32" /></td>
      <td><input type="radio" name="radQ3" value="1" id="q31" /></td>
    </tr>
  </table>
  <input type="submit" />
</form>
```

If the majority of your visitors are using Netscape 6+ or IE 4+, a better option might be to set a CSS rule for those `<label>` elements you did not want to display and give the CSS `display` property a value of `none`.

It is also worth noting that you can use a `<label>` element to contain the form control, as shown in the following example (ch07_eg15.html). When the `<label>` element contains the form control it is labeling, there is no need to use the `for` attribute because it is automatically associated with the control it contains:

```
<form action="login.asp" method="post" name="frmLogin">

  <label>Account name: <input type="text" name="txtLogin" size="20" /></label>
  <br />

  <label>Password: <input type="password" name="txtPwd" size="20" /></label>
  <input type="submit" value="Log in" />

</form>
```

To a certain extent, however, this just adds work, as the label is probably clear in the first place because it is right next to the form control it labels.

Note that because HTML and XHTML require that any markup within a table nests correctly, you cannot have opening **<label>** *tags in one table cell and closing* **</label>** *tags in a separate cell. Any* **<label>** *element must be completely contained within that table cell.*

The title attribute on the <input> element

The <input> element can carry a special attribute that increases accessibility (and indeed the general usability of forms) called title. The value of the attribute can provide extra information to the user. Recent screen readers read the value of this attribute to users when present; and for sighted users, the value of this attribute is presented as a tooltip when the mouse hovers over the input.

This enables you to revise the code for the voting form in a different way than you have seen (ch07_eg16.html):

```
<form action="surveyResults.asp" method="post" name="frmSurvey">
  <table>
   <tr>
     <td><label for="q37">Strongly agree</label></td>
     <td></td>
     <td></td>
     <td><label for="q34">Neutral</label></td>
     <td></td>
     <td></td>
     <td><label for="q31">Strongly disagree</label></td>
   </tr>
   <tr>
    <td><input type="radio" name="radQ3" value="7" id="q35"
              title="strongly agree" /></td>
    <td><input type="radio" name="radQ3" value="6" id="q35"
              title="agree" /></td>
    <td><input type="radio" name="radQ3" value="5" id="q35"
              title="somewhat agree" /></td>
    <td><input type="radio" name="radQ3" value="4" id="q34"
              title="neutral" /></td>
    <td><input type="radio" name="radQ3" value="3" id="q33"
              title="somewhat disagree" /></td>
    <td><input type="radio" name="radQ3" value="2" id="q32"
              title="disagree" /></td>
    <td><input type="radio" name="radQ3" value="1" id="q31"
              title="strongly disagree" /></td>
   </tr>
  </table>
</form>
```

In my opinion, this solution is much better than using single-pixel tricks to add labels, as it is an attribute that is part of HTML 4 and XHTML. Ideally, you would combine this technique with providing a <label> for each form control and use CSS to hide the labels you do not want displayed.

The title attribute is also particularly useful to clarify exactly what information a user should enter into a text box, providing extra help to sighted users if they hover the mouse over the form control and to all users with screen readers. The following example shows a form that uses the `title` attribute to provide extra instructions (ch07_eg17.html):

```
<form action="surveyResults.asp " method="post" name="frmSurvey">
Product registration:
<table>
  <tr>
    <td>Enter the serial number for your software: </td>
    <td><input type="text" name="txt" size="20" title="Enter the serial number
        displayed in the About This Product option in the Help menu." /></td>
  </tr>
</table>
<input type="submit" />
</form>
```

Figure 7-10 shows you what this form looks like when a user hovers the mouse over the form control to get the extra information in the tooltip.

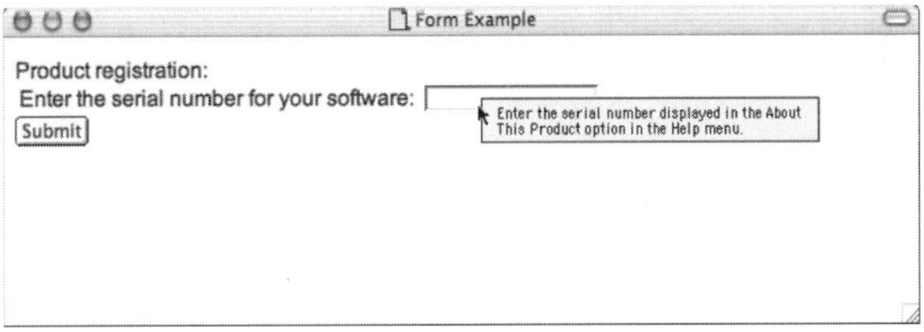

Figure 7-10

While use of the `title` attribute is not explicitly encouraged by the WCAG or Section 508 guidelines, it is likely to be included in the next version of the WCAG, and will therefore help "futureproof" your documents.

Grouping form controls using <fieldset> and <legend> elements

Because Web users often find forms daunting, anything you can do to help them use the forms on your site will help your site be more successful. For example, if you are running an e-commerce store but users find your registration forms too complex, you are unlikely to make any sales; people will never get far enough through the process to order goods.

By grouping related form controls you can help make a form less daunting for users. This not only helps those who rely on assistive technologies to access your site, it is a prime example of how learning about accessibility helps other visitors to your site (and in turn helps your business in general). In fact, in the case of the elements you are about to meet, they are of more use to those who can see your site because they create a visual grouping of elements (by default, drawing a line around the related elements), which helps users understand how the form is organized and why they are being asked for each set of information.

The form shown in Figure 7-11 contains two sets of information, and around the groups of form controls are thin lines (similar to those you might see in a Windows application). The first group contains the login details; these are kept together because they represent the user's online information. The second box contains user address information (this is for their home address).

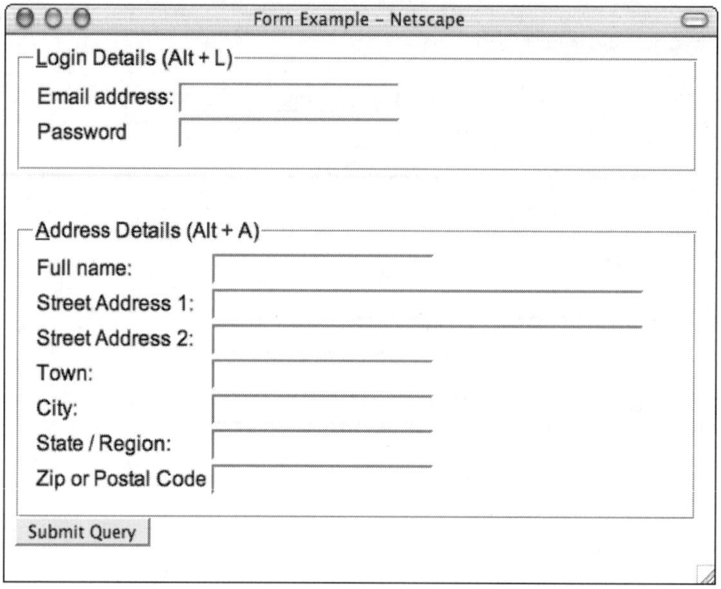

Figure 7-11

The element that creates these groups is called the `<fieldset>` element. Anything within the opening `<fieldset>` tag and the closing `</fieldset>` tag belongs to that group. You can also create a label for that group of form controls using the `<legend>` element, which should be the first element after the opening `<fieldset>` tag.

You can put markup other than just form controls inside the `<fieldset>` element, as you can see in the code for ch07_eg18.html that follows (which was used to create the page shown in Figure 7-11). The layout of the form elements is controlled using two tables, one inside each of the `<fieldset>` elements:

```
<form action="register.asp" method="post" name="frmRegister">
  <fieldset>
    <legend accesskey="l"><u>L</u>ogin Details (Alt + L)</legend>
    <table>
      <tr>
        <td class="caption">Email address:</td>
        <td><input type="text" name="txtEmail" size="20" /></td>
      </tr><tr>
        <td class="caption">Password</td>
        <td><input type="password" name="txtPwd" size="20" /></td>
      </tr>
    </table>
  </fieldset>

  <fieldset>
  <legend accesskey="a"><u>A</u>ddress Details (Alt + A)</legend>
    <table>
      <tr>
        <td class="caption">Full name: </td>
```

```
        <td><input type="text" name="txtName" size="20" /></td>
      </tr><tr>
        <td class="caption">Street Address 1: </td>
        <td><input type="text" name="txtStreet1" size="40" /></td>
      </tr><tr>
        <td class="caption">Street Address 2: </td>
        <td><input type="text" name="txtStreet2" size="40" /></td>
      </tr><tr>
        <td class="caption">Town: </td>
        <td><input type="text" name="txtTown" size="20" /></td>
      </tr><tr>
        <td class="caption">City: </td>
        <td><input type="text" name="txtCity" size="20" /></td>
      </tr><tr>
        <td class="caption">State / Region: </td>
        <td><input type="text" name="txtState" size="20" /></td>
      </tr><tr>
        <td class="caption">Zip or Postal Code</td>
        <td><input type="text" name="txtZip" size="20" /></td>
      </tr>
    </table>
  </fieldset>
  <br />
  <input type="submit" />
</form>
```

The `<legend>` element also enables you to create keyboard shortcuts to that `fieldset`. The keyboard shortcut is created using the `accesskey` attribute. When users hold down Alt on a PC or Ctrl on a Mac and press the key specified as a value of the `accesskey` attribute, they should be taken to that part of the form. As you can see from this code and Figure 7-11, to indicate the access key, it is common to underline that letter in the caption, like you would see in an application on a desktop computer. Access keys work well in IE 5+.

> Note that older browsers will ignore the **<fieldset>** and **<legend>** elements, simply reading whatever is within the **<legend>** element and not drawing the line around the edge of the **fieldset**. This means you are safe to add them to all of your designs without fear of breaking any pages.

You can also associate CSS rules with the `fieldset` to add further cues to the grouping of the elements, such as controlling the style of the border around the `fieldset` or the shading inside of it.

Grouping options in a select box with the <optgroup> element

Another element specifically designed to help group related items in forms is the `<optgroup>` element, which was designed to work on *select boxes* (also known as *drop-down list boxes*). The `<optgroup>` element is particularly helpful when you are creating select boxes with numerous option elements. For example, you might have a select box that contains U.S. states, Australian states/territories, and U.K. counties. This would create a very long select box, but you can make it easier to use by grouping the states into individual countries.

Figure 7-12 shows a slightly simpler select box that uses the `<optgroup>` element to group staff names in a select box according to the departments in which they work. It acts as a containing element for the `<option>` elements it is intended to group together. The `<optgroup>` element takes an attribute called `label` whose value is the label that should be used with the group of `<option>` elements it contains.

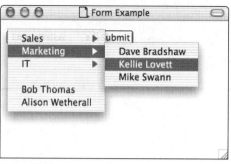

Figure 7-12

Here is the code for this example (ch07_eg19.html):

```
<select name="selStaff">
  <optgroup label="Sales">
    <option value="EmmaW">Emma Walker</option>
    <option value="SimonB">Simon Bolter</option>
    <option value="AndyP">Andy Pinnock</option>
    <option value="JayT">Jay Thomas</option>
    <option value="VernonM">Vernon Malhotra</option>
    <option value="SuzieF">Suzie Farnshaw</option>
  </optgroup>
  <optgroup label="Marketing">
    <option value="DaveB">Dave Bradshaw</option>
    <option value="KellyL">Kellie Lovett</option>
    <option value="MikeS">Mike Swann</option>
  </optgroup>
  <optgroup label="IT">
    <option value="AliceG">Alice Goodyear</option>
    <option value="ThomC">Thom Cooper</option>
  </optgroup>
  <option lable="Support">
    <option value="BobT">Bob Thomas</option>
    <option value="AlisonW">Alison Wetherall</option>
  </option>
</select>
```

Guidelines for forms

Section 508 assigns the Web page author the responsibility of making data input accessible:

> **Section 508 §1194.22(n) When electronic forms are designed to be completed online, the form shall allow people using assistive technology to access the information, field elements, and functionality required for completion and submission of the form, including all directions and cues.**

This guideline differs from many of the other points raised by Section 508 and WCAG in that Web page authors are to judge for themselves what makes the data input accessible (compared with other more precise explanations).

The WCAG have several checkpoints that specifically deal with how to make forms accessible. While they are only priority 2 checkpoints, you should consider them very important for users of screen readers. The first indicates that you should explicitly label form controls:

> **WCAG 12.4 Associate labels explicitly with their controls. [Priority 2]**

Another says you should ensure that your implicit labels make sense for those users with tools that do not associate labels with form controls:

> **WCAG 10.2 Until user agents support explicit associations between labels and form controls, for all form controls with implicitly associated labels, ensure that the label is properly positioned. [Priority 2]**

Still another checkpoint deals with empty text inputs; however, this point can reasonably be ignored because most modern screen readers can now handle empty text inputs:

> **WCAG 10.4 Until user agents handle empty controls correctly, include default, place-holding characters in edit boxes and text areas. [Priority 3]**

The preceding checkpoint addresses a problem that was common in older screen readers that used to literally read what they could see on the screen, but technology has advanced sufficiently that this is no longer an issue.

Finally, you come to a checkpoint that addresses the issue of grouping form controls:

> **WCAG 12.3 Divide large blocks of information into more manageable groups where natural and appropriate. [Priority 2]**

As you learned previously in this chapter, to specifically deal with this point you have two elements that help you group form controls: the `<fieldset>` and `<legend>` elements. You can even create shortcuts between different `fieldset` elements on a page. You can also use the `<optgroup>` element to group `<option>` elements.

PDF forms

It is possible to create forms that look the same as printed forms using the Adobe PDF (Portable Document Format) format. These forms are not based upon the main HTML form elements you are familiar with.

Originally, this format was designed to enable people to send documents that users could print themselves (so that the documents would look the same when printed no matter who prints them). Because this format was designed for print, it was not accessible. However, with Adobe Acrobat version 5, Adobe introduced the capability to create *tagged forms,* which enable a screen reader to indicate when it comes across a prompt.

Adding tags to a PDF document requires that the author manually add the tags. It is not part of the normal design process (usually, PDF documents are created from other programs such as Quark XPress or Adobe Photoshop). It therefore adds a whole new step to the construction of these forms.

In reality, PDF is still, the vast majority of the time, used to create forms that can be printed out, filled in, and then sent by mail. I have not come across a Web site that uses PDF forms, rather than HTML forms, on purpose.

Because Section 508 §1194.22(n) requires that forms be accessible, Adobe may have felt obliged to add the accessibility options to facilitate PDFs continued use on the Web:

> **Section 508 §1194.22(n) When electronic forms are used, the form shall allow people using assistive technology to access the information, field elements, and functionality required for completion and submission of the form, including all directions and cues.**

Because the Acrobat Reader plug-in is required in order to view a PDF document, any page that links to a PDF document should also include a link to an URL from which the plug-in can be downloaded.

> **Section 508 §1194.22(m) When a Web page requires that an applet, plug-in or other application be present on the client system to interpret page content, the page must provide a link to a plug-in or applet that complies with §1194.22(a) through (l).**

Timed responses

Sometimes you will need to require a user to fill in a form within a certain amount of time (for example, in a timed test when the form is automatically submitted after the allotted time is up, or when dealing with sensitive financial data and the connection is closed after a specified period of time). Section 508 has a specific point for such forms:

> **Section 508 §1194.22(p) When a timed response is required, the user shall be alerted and given sufficient time to indicate more time is required.**

The WCAG Version 1.0 does not include a checkpoint for timed responses, although the Working Draft of the second version did contain the following point:

> **WCAG 2 Working Draft Guideline 2.2 Allow users to control time limits on their reading or interaction unless specific real-time events or rules of competition make such control impossible. [Priority 1]**

If timing is critical to a task (for example, in a quiz where the time could be used to find an answer to a question), users should be informed beforehand that a timer will be running. This gives users the opportunity to not use the form.

The Section 508 point specifically relates to forms that will be cleared or sent automatically after the time is up; however, you should also consider the case of any page whose content changes after a specific time period. For example, some sites have a feature that automatically refreshes the content of a page or redirects the user to another page. In cases such as these, the user should be given the same options as with a timed response.

You should consider page refreshes and redirections in a similar light to that of timed responses.

On some sites (particularly news or sports sites whose content is updated regularly), automatic refreshes reload the page on a regular basis. This can be frustrating enough for sighted users, but users with a screen reader may never get to the end of reading a page if the refresh rate is too frequent (as it can take longer to go through a page with a screen reader). Therefore, you should provide an option to turn off automatic refreshing of a page. Alternatively, make just one section of the page — such as the latest news — refresh (rather than updating the whole page).

Accessibility issues for deaf people

You might assume that when creating Web pages you do not have to consider any issues for deaf visitors, because hearing impairments do not stop someone from seeing a page. Actually, you do need to address a couple of very important issues, including the following:

- ❑ Offer a transcription of any spoken words in audio or video footage
- ❑ Enable deaf users to indicate that their phone number calls a Telecommunication Device for the Deaf (TDD)

Offering transcriptions of audio/video footage

With increasing numbers of users having access to broadband, and with the rapid growth of multimedia features on the Web (using formats such as RealPlayer, Windows Media, MP3, QuickTime, and Flash), you have to ensure that visitors can access the information in these formats even if they cannot hear what the reader is saying.

Until the quality of video improves, users cannot be expected to lip-read from the images streamed on the Web, and with audio there is no option for lip-reading anyway. Therefore, it is important to offer users either captions for video or transcriptions of any audio or video that is spoken.

This should really come as no surprise, though, as this point reflects the guideline you were introduced to in Chapter 6 specifying that all content must be given a text equivalent.

Collecting phone numbers

You might require contact telephone numbers from your visitors for a number of reasons, from following up on sales leads to speaking to someone who has applied for a job. However, forms don't always offer an easy way for some people to let the caller know that they have problems using the phone — for example, if they are deaf or have suffered from a stroke and have speech difficulties.

Deaf telephone users often have a *TDD (Telecommunications Device for the Deaf)* telephone, but if the caller does not know how to use one when speaking with someone who is deaf, the caller might terminate the call. Therefore, you should try to provide a way for deaf users to indicate that they have a TTD, rather than a regular phone.

It is also good practice to offer users a choice of how they are contacted if they provide a number of contact forms — for example, street address, e-mail address, phone, fax, and mobile phone. This can also have advantages in other situations where a call might wake someone who works nights, wake a young baby, or be otherwise inappropriate (such as calling a work number regarding a new job interview).

Accessible frames

As a designer, you may sometimes need to use frames in the design of your site. However, this should be necessary only in situations such as the following:

❑ When you have a large amount of content in one frame, which you do not want to refresh. For example, with thumbnails in an image gallery, only the content in the other frame needs to change.

❑ To provide a table of contents or index in one frame that helps users to navigate a *very* large document in the other frame

For example, Figure 7-13 shows a site with two frames, or panes; the left contains several references to parts of the main document on the right-hand side main frame.

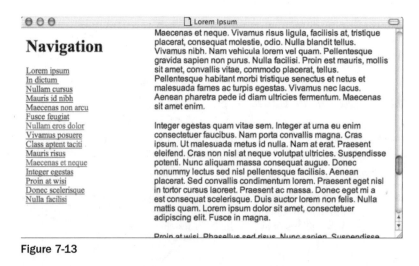

Figure 7-13

When users click on a link in the left-hand pane, they will see the appropriate section of the page in the right-hand frame, without needing to reload the annotations in the left-hand frame.

A *frameset page* is one that divides the screen into separate *frames*, or *panes*. These enable users to load one part of the page into the window without refreshing all of the other pages. This simple example in Figure 7-13 actually has three files:

- ❑ The frameset page that indicates how the screen should be divided into rows and columns (ch07_eg20.html)

- ❑ The index in the left-hand pane (ch07_eg20b.html)

- ❑ The main document in the right-hand pane (ch07_eg20c.html)

Here is the frameset page for this example:

```
<!DOCTYPE html
    PUBLIC "-//W3C//DTD XHTML 1.0 Frameset//EN"
    "http://www.w3.org/TR/xhtml1/DTD/xhtml1-frameset.dtd">
<html xmlns="http://www.w3.org/1999/xhtml">
  <head>
    <title>Lorem Ipsum</title>
    <meta http-equiv="Content-Type" content="text/html; charset=iso-8859-1">
  </head>

  <frameset cols="250,*" frameborder="NO" border="0" framespacing="0">
    <frame src="ch07_eg20b.html" name="NavigationFrame" scrolling="NO" noresize
        title="Frame containing the navigation shortcuts for the Lorem Ipsum text
        in the LoremIpsum frame" >
    <frame src="ch07_eg20c.html" name="LoremIpsum" title="Frame containing the
        Lorem Ipsum text">
  </frameset>
  <noframes>
    <body>
      This page requires a technology called frames. It appears that your browser
      does not support this technology. Please try again in a more recent browser
      (such as <a href="http://www.microsoft.com/ie/">Internet Explorer 6</a> or
      <a href="http://www.Netscape.com">Netscape 7</a>).
    </body>
  </noframes>
</html>
```

Unfortunately, frames can pose significant problems for those with vision impairments who cannot necessarily determine the relationship between frames (or indeed how many frames there are) in the same way that a sighted person can scan the whole page at once and see how the frames relate to each other. There are, however, methods you can use to help users understand the structure of the page and the relationships between the parts it contains.

You might have noticed in example ch07_20.html (which you just saw) how both the name and title attributes are used on each <frame> element, and how both are given values that describe the content of that frame.

❑ The name attribute is required so that the links in each document can load the content into the appropriate frames. For example, the links in the left-hand frame indicate that they should point to the appropriate part of the document in the right-hand frame.

❑ The value of the title attribute is what screen readers should use to tell users the purpose of the frame and the relationship between this frame and other frames in the frameset.

*Note that you cannot put a space in the value of the **name** attribute, although you can in the **title** attribute.*

In addition to using the title attribute on the <frame> element in frameset documents, it is also a good idea to give each individual document that represents a pane of the frameset a <title> element that describes the purpose of that frame.

If the title alone does not describe the purpose of the frames and how they relate to each other, you should then use the longdesc attribute or a description link to link to a resource where the relationship between the frames is explained in greater detail (you met both the longdesc attribute and description links in Chapter 6 when you looked at how to provide text equivalents for images).

Guidelines for accessible frames

The Section 508 guidelines have the following to say about frames:

> **Section 508 §1194.22(i) Frames shall be titled with text that facilitates frame identification and navigation.**

This means that not only should you title the individual frames; you should also explain the relationship between frames in a frameset. The WCAG checkpoint 12.1 is very similar:

> **WCAG 12.1 Title each frame to facilitate identification and navigation. [Priority 1]**

While neither of the guidelines indicates *how* the frames should be identified or titled, by using the title attribute and the <title> element, you will be satisfying these requirements, and hopefully "futureproofing" your documents.

However, if your methods of titling do not adequately describe the purpose of the frames and the relationships between them, you can provide a link to a fuller description using the longdesc attribute or a description link, as the WCAG state in their second point concerning frames:

> **WCAG 12.2 Describe the purpose of frames and how frames relate to each other if it is not obvious by frame titles alone. [Priority 2]**

Text only — the last resort

Some designers think that simply by offering a text-only version of their site they will be meeting accessibility requirements; however, this is quite a simplistic view of the situation. Although both the WCAG and Section 508 guidelines acknowledge that this is one possible way to increase the accessibility of your content, they both also indicate that you should use this option as a last resort and that you should attempt other means to create accessible pages first.

Both sets of guidelines highlight the fact that if you do create a text-only version of a site, you should ensure that it is updated as often as the main section of the site. They emphasize this because in the past, many sites offered text-only editions, but these sites were not kept as up to date as the main site, which is deemed unacceptable.

Here is what the WCAG have to say:

> **WCAG 11.4 If, after best efforts, you cannot create an accessible page, provide a link to an alternative page that uses W3C technologies, is accessible, has equivalent information (or functionality), and is updated as often as the inaccessible (original) page. [Priority 1]**

Here is what the Section 508 guidelines say:

> **Section 508 §1194.22(k) A text-only page, with equivalent information or functionality, shall be provided to make a web site comply with the provisions of this part, when compliance cannot be accomplished in any other way. The content of the text-only page shall be updated whenever the primary page changes.**

Even if you were to offer a simple text-only version of your site, it would be missing enhancements that you can make only if you really understand the recommendations. For example, without adding links that enable users to skip repetitive navigation, users would have to listen to the same set of links on every page. Similarly, without adding appropriate markup to data tables, their content may be very hard to follow.

As you can see, having learned about both the WCAG and Section 508 guidelines, you would be far better off designing accessible sites from scratch, rather than trying to maintain a text-only version of the site as well. If you are using XHTML and CSS, as you have learned to throughout this book (and you are using CSS, rather than tables, to control layout), you should not need a text-only version of the site.

Testing your site for accessibility

The ideal way to test your site for accessibility is to get users with disabilities who are used to working with assistive technologies to test your site on your behalf. Of course, this is not practical for every new site. Nor are developers likely to become familiar enough with assistive devices (and be objective enough) to determine whether the site is accessible. Therefore, when you have built your pages, you can use a number of tools to help ensure that you have met many of the requirements set out in the WCAG and

Section 508 guidelines. This section describes just a few of the most popular testing tools. In particular, you will meet the following:

❑ Bobby

❑ LIFT

❑ The W3C Accessibility checker

Note, however, that these tools will not perform a rigorous check, and there is no substitution for properly observing the guidelines. As you have seen throughout the last two chapters, several of the guidelines require a certain amount of human judgment—for example, whether or not `alt` text is meaningful or whether or not forms have been made accessible. Consider the following example of an image used as a link:

```
<img src="home.gif" alt="button" height="20" width="40'" />
```

This `alt` text, which merely states "button," does not indicate to users what the button is for.

Therefore, to test a site properly, you need to interact with the site in the ways in which it might be used, employing accessibility aids such as screen readers that read the content of the page to you. As mentioned in Chapter 6, some screen readers can take quite a while to learn (with their complex keyboard shortcuts). However, the IBM Home Page Reader is a lot easier than most for developers to learn. A free trial demo version can be downloaded from www.ibm.com/able/solution_offerings/hpr.html.

Finally, you should not just follow the minimum requirements of the guidelines set out in WCAG or Section 508; you should aim to meet as many of the guidelines (even priority 2 and 3 WCAG guidelines) as possible. In practice, there is no substitute for a designer who fully understands the guidelines and has experience with making different types of site accessible. Until then, however, several software tools can help you check your site. The following sections describe two such tools—Bobby and LIFT.

Bobby

Bobby is a piece of software developed by the Center for Applied Special Technology and is distributed by Watchfire. The Bobby home page is http://bobby.watchfire.com.

Bobby is available in two versions:

❑ A free online testing tool, which enables you to enter a URL for a page

❑ A standalone desktop program, which currently costs $299

Once your site has been tested by Bobby, you can display a Bobby Approved rating image on your site. The different icons represent the standard to which your site has been deemed compliant:

❑ A for priority 1 compliance

❑ AA for priority 1 and 2 compliance

❑ AAA for priority 1, 2 and 3, or 508 if using the Section 508 standard

You will see an example of Bobby in action in the "Solution" section of this chapter.

LIFT

Several different LIFT offerings are available from UsableNet at `www.usableNet.com`. They are divided into three categories:

Finding problems:

- ❑ **LIFT Machine** — A server-based application that checks Web sites for accessibility and usability solutions. It then generates reports to indicate how well the pages comply.

- ❑ **LIFT Online** — A hosted version of LIFT Machine

Fixing problems:

- ❑ **LIFT for Deamweaver** — This version enables you to select which guidelines should be checked against, evaluate a site upon these criteria, run a wizard to help you fix problems, monitor the site as you work, generate custom reports of compliance, and edit `alt` text, all within Dreamweaver.

- ❑ **LIFT for FrontPage** — Similar to LIFT for Dreamweaver but for FrontPage users

Delivering solutions:

- ❑ **LIFT Text Transcoder** — Used to automatically generate a text-only version of your site, thereby ensuring that any text-only content remains up to date

A free, basic accessibility test is also offered from `www.UsableNet.com`, which you will see in action in the "Solution" section.

Browser-based testing techniques

You can also use several techniques to test pages within your browser. These typically involve changing the settings or *preferences*. The main tests you can perform are described in the following sections.

Turning off images in your browser

By turning off images in the browser, you can see the alt text that you have provided for images. If the page does not make sense without the images displayed, you need to improve the quality of your alt text.

- ❑ In Internet Explorer, select Tools ➪ Internet Options, and select the Advanced tab. Check the option Always Expand ALT Text for Images.

- ❑ In Netscape, select Edit ➪ Preferences, and select the Advanced tab. Uncheck the option Automatically Load Images. (You might also need to clear the cache and restart the browser.)

Turning off CSS in your browser

By turning off CSS in your browser, you can confirm that both the presentation and the layout of the site are comprehendible to users without CSS support. If you are using CSS to control layout, this will also give you a better idea of the order in which information would be presented to those with visual impairments.

❑   In Netscape, select Edit ⇨ Preferences, and then select the Advanced tab. Uncheck the option Enable Style Sheets.

❑   In IE 6+, select Tools ⇨ Internet Options, and at the bottom of the General tab, click the Accessibility button. Then, under the heading Formatting, uncheck each option to ignore font styles and colors. (On the Mac, select Explorer ⇨ Preferences ⇨ Web Content and uncheck Show Style Sheets.)

Turning off JavaScript

As noted in Chapter 6, JavaScript should be used only to enhance the functionality of a site; users should not be required to view the site on a browser that supports JavaScript. By turning off JavaScript and ensuring that you can still achieve all of the tasks without JavaScript support, you will ensure that this requirement is met:

❑   In Netscape, select Edit ⇨ Preferences and then select the Advanced tab. Uncheck the option Enable JavaScript.

❑   In IE, select Tools ⇨ Internet Options and then select the Security tab. Select Custom Level of Security, and then select Disable under the Active Scripting option.

*You can find a lot of other sources of information related to accessibility on the W3C Web Accessibility Initiative pages at the W3C site (**www.w3.org/WAI/References**).*

Solution

Now that you have a good idea of how to solve many of the challenges you face when creating accessible sites that use tables, forms, or frames, you should take another look at the First Promotions site and ensure that it adheres to the guidelines you met in this chapter. In this section, you will also learn how to use the free versions of Bobby and LIFT to test the site.

The First Promotions site does not contain any forms or frames. However, tables are used on the pages that show individual products in detail. These tables show the prices for the product.

Product details pages

In the product details pages, you can see a data table that holds the price for different quantities and color combinations of a product. In the original designs for the site, this information was held in a table that contained all kinds of presentational markup, and which did not have clear headings for the column and row headings.

Here is an example of one of the original tables:

```
<table border="0" cellpadding="2" cellspacing="2">
  <tr>
    <td bgcolor="#D6D6D6"><font face="Arial, Helvetica, sans-serif" size="2">
      <b>Quantity</b></font></td>
    <td bgcolor="#D6D6D6"><font face="Arial, Helvetica, sans-serif" size="2">
      <b>150</b></font></td>
    <td bgcolor="#D6D6D6"><font face="Arial, Helvetica, sans-serif" size="2">
```

```
      <b>250</b></font></td>
    <td bgcolor="#D6D6D6"><font face="Arial, Helvetica, sans-serif" size="2">
      <b>500</b></font></td>
    <td bgcolor="#D6D6D6"><font face="Arial, Helvetica, sans-serif" size="2">
      <b>1000</b></font></td>
  </tr>
  <tr>
    <td bgcolor="#D6D6D6"><font face="Arial, Helvetica, sans-serif" size="2">
      <b>Unit price</b></font></td>
    <td><font face="Arial, Helvetica, sans-serif" size="2">$2.79</font></td>
    <td><font face="Arial, Helvetica, sans-serif" size="2">$2.69</font></td>
    <td><font face="Arial, Helvetica, sans-serif" size="2">$2.59</font></td>
    <td><font face="Arial, Helvetica, sans-serif" size="2">$2.49</font></td>
  </tr>
  <tr>
    <td bgcolor="#D6D6D6"><font face="Arial, Helvetica, sans-serif"
        size="2"><b>Additional colors (each)</b></font></td>
    <td><font face="Arial, Helvetica, sans-serif" size="2">$0.25</font></td>
    <td><font face="Arial, Helvetica, sans-serif" size="2">$0.20</font></td>
    <td><font face="Arial, Helvetica, sans-serif" size="2">$0.20</font></td>
    <td><font face="Arial, Helvetica, sans-serif" size="2">$0.20</font></td>
  </tr>
</table>
```

The following tasks need to be performed with a table like this (some of which would have been performed when you created the XHTML and CSS versions of the product details pages):

❑   All presentational markup needs to be removed.

❑   The <table> should be given an id attribute to clearly indicate that it is a price information table.

❑   CSS rules need to be added to control the table's appearance. These can use the value of the id attribute on the <table> element to identify just this table.

❑   The column and row headings should be placed inside <th> elements, rather than <td> elements, and different CSS rules should be written for these elements.

❑   The heading elements can have scope attributes added to clearly identify the scope of the header. Although the use of the <th> elements is enough to identify the headers, this will demonstrate their use again and make the identification of headings completely thorough.

Following these guidelines, here is what the table should now look like:

```
<table id="productPrices">
  <tr>
    <th scope="row">Quantity</th>
    <th scope="col">150</th>
    <th scope="col">250</th>
    <th scope="col">500</th>
    <th scope="col">1000</th>
  </tr>
  <tr>
    <th scope="row">Unit price</th>
    <td>$2.79</td>
```

```
      <td>$2.69</td>
      <td>$2.59</td>
      <td>$2.49</td>
   </tr>
   <tr>
      <th scope="row">Additional colors (each)</th>
      <td>$0.25</td>
      <td>$0.20</td>
      <td>$0.20</td>
      <td>$0.20</td>
   </tr>
</table>
```

Now take a quick look at the style sheet rules that apply to this table:

```
body {font-family:arial, verdana, sans-serif; }
th {
   font-weight:bold;
   background-color:#d6d6d6;
   font-size:small;}
td {
   margin:2px;
   font-size:small;}
```

The completed table, shown in Figure 7-14, should now look just like it did, but it is more accessible and uses CSS for presentation.

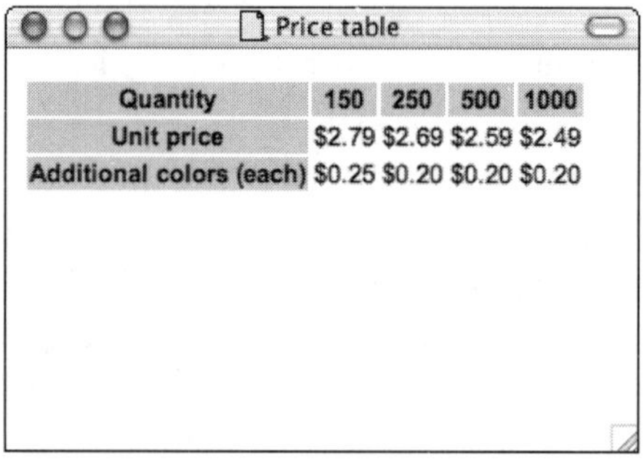

Figure 7-14

Testing with Bobby

Having made the tables accessible, you can now test your page using the free online version of Bobby, which is available at http://bobby.watchfire.com. On the home page of the site is a box in which you can enter the URL of the page you are testing (therefore, to try this out for yourself, you need to put the page on a Web server). You have to select either the WCAG or Section 508 guidelines (it tests only one set at a time).

If you try the version of the home page for the site shown in Appendix A (which contains the final version of the code for the First Promotions site), you should see that the page gets a AAA rating for the WCAG guidelines (the highest possible).

The page displaying the results also shows a version of the page without a style sheet attached (so it looks very different than you might expect). Beneath the rendering of the page is the Bobby report.

The Bobby report highlights a set of checkpoints that you need to manually check to ensure compliance with the regulations (with links to explanations of these checkpoints); these are checkpoints that the program is unable to check. Following are some examples of these checkpoints. Note how you are given line numbers (where appropriate) to indicate where the points are deemed relevant.

- ❑ If style sheets are ignored or unsupported, are pages still readable and usable?

- ❑ If this is a data table (not used for layout only), identify headers for the table rows and columns. (1 instance) Line 44

- ❑ If you use color to convey information, make sure the information is also represented another way. (8 instances) Lines 13, 24, 27, 29, 46, 47, 54, 55

- ❑ If an image conveys important information beyond what is in its alternative text, provide an extended description. (8 instances) Lines 13, 24, 27, 29, 46, 47, 54, 55

If your run the same page again, this time checking it against the Section 508 guidelines, you should find that it meets those, too.

You would need to repeat this process for every page of the site. If your site is based upon templates, it is a good idea to check with the first page before building all other pages that use the template so that you do not need to change each page individually.

Testing with LIFT

This section takes a look at testing the site using the free online LIFT tool available from www.UsableNet.com, which also enables you to enter a URL. For this tool, you have to enter an e-mail address, and a link to the report is e-mailed to you.

The LIFT test is not quite as easy to understand as the Bobby report, although it does address a number of usability issues as well as accessibility issues. Don't be alarmed if it indicates that you have a lot of errors to check. The First Promotions home page included a similar list of errors, most of which occur because LIFT is unable to check them itself. As with Bobby, you have to check these manually.

Summary

In this chapter, you have looked at accessibility issues regarding three main aspects of sites: tables, forms, and frames. You then learned how to test a site.

When you are dealing with tables, it is important to distinguish between layout tables and data tables, and to be aware that screen readers have different modes for dealing with the two types of table. When it comes to forms, the key issue is ensuring that users know what data they are supposed to enter into which form control. Forms are the principal way of getting data from visitors to your site, and if you are expecting them to fill one in, they must be confident that they are providing the correct information in the appropriate place.

Finally, when it comes to frames, you need to ensure that you have added a title for each frame that will describe its purpose, and use the title attribute on links to describe what is being linked to.

Having looked at these remaining issues to make Web pages accessible, you then looked at some of the tools that you can use to test whether your site meets the WCAG and Section 508 accessibility guidelines. While these tools are helpful, it is important to remember that they do not check for compliance with every guideline, and that these will still require human interpretation.

That brings us to the end of the chapters on accessibility. In the final chapter, you will learn about some of the technologies that are looming on the horizon for Web developers. This will help you "futureproof" your code and designs and help you stay abreast of skills you will need to keep current or acquire in the future.

8

Looking to the Future

In this final chapter, you will be looking at the future developments of XHTML and related Web technologies. So far, this book has brought you up to date with the skills of writing XHTML rather than HTML, styling and laying out pages using CSS rather than presentational markup, and creating Web sites that are accessible. Now that you are familiar with these aspects of designing an accessible site, it is time to look forward, so that you can anticipate and learn about the way in which your pages are likely to change.

If you are aware of likely changes; not only can you create Web sites with these possible changes in mind, you can also get an idea of the technologies you should be keeping an eye on. In particular, this chapter covers the following topics:

- ❑ XHTML 1.1 — Modularized XHTML
- ❑ Related languages — namely, SVG and MathML
- ❑ Mixing XML-based languages with XHTML
- ❑ Serving multiple devices

This last point, about serving multiple devices, refers to creating Web pages that will work on all kinds of devices, not just desktop computers. If you like to keep in touch with new technologies, you will no doubt have noticed increasing numbers of Web-enabled devices that complement PCs, including mobile phones, TV set top boxes, PDAs (personal digital assistants, such as Palm Pilots), and in-car entertainment and navigation systems; even kitchen appliances such as refrigerators and microwaves are getting in on the act. While some of these applications might sound a little bit far-fetched, as you will see, this future is a lot nearer than you might think.

By the end of this chapter, you will be prepared for several of the developments you are likely to see becoming popular in the next few years.

Problem

Because technologies move so fast, it can be very hard to hold down a full-time job *and* keep on top of new developments. Therefore, it helps to know what technologies are likely to be valued in the Web developer's toolkit, so that you can keep an eye on their progression and be aware of how they are likely to affect you.

Furthermore, because new devices are accessing the Web, you have two new major considerations:

❑ You have to develop sites that work with an increasing variety of browsers (not just IE and Netscape).

❑ Different devices have different capabilities, such as different screen sizes and different amounts of memory and power available to them.

These considerations mean that it is increasingly important that you write standards-based code that, as long as the browser has implemented the standards properly, will work on any platform.

This chapter will show you how emerging technologies are likely to affect the way in which you develop sites, and how XHTML makes it easier to develop sites for mobile devices.

Design

To make HTML relevant to the Web as it is today (and will be in the future), it was necessary for the language to evolve. You have seen the start of this evolution in XHTML 1.0; however, the next step of the process set out by the W3C was to create a modular version of XHTML, which you will be meeting in this chapter.

> *It is important to remember that part of the motivation for recreating HTML in XML was that it would make it easier to extend it in the future, either when people wanted to add new features to it or when new devices had to be supported.*

The situation today

In this book, you have been learning to write XHTML 1.0 documents. In particular, you have learned about the following three versions:

❑ **Strict XHTML 1.0**—which does not contain any of the presentational or stylistic markup that was present in HTML 4

❑ **Transitional XHTML 1.0**—which enables the use of the markup contained in HTML 4 but is no longer allowed in Strict XHTML 1.0

❑ **Frameset XHTML 1.0**—which is for use in creating frameset documents

You have also learned how to style these documents and control their layout using CSS, and how to make the pages accessible to visitors to your site who may suffer from disabilities and rely upon assistive technologies.

Having learned all of this, you might be a little alarmed when I tell you that a new version of XHTML, known as *Modularized XHTML* (or *XHTML 1.1*), has been released and is a W3C recommendation just like XHTML 1.0—but there is no cause for concern. You will learn everything you need to know about XHTML 1.1 in this one chapter. In fact, when designing pages for desktop PCs, the differences between XHTML 1.0 and 1.1 are mainly conceptual; only a couple of changes need to be made to the code. What sets Modularized XHTML apart from its predecessor is its ability to help you do the following:

❏   Create hybrid documents that contain markup from different languages

❏   Create new languages for different devices

Modularized XHTML, as the name suggests, involves splitting up the XHTML specification into separate modules — the idea being that languages for different devices would be able to use a selection of these modules that reflect their capabilities.

As you will see in this chapter, Modularized XHTML has already been put to practical use to create a version of XHTML specifically designed for use on mobile phones, and this language is already being used by market leaders such as Nokia.

The new devices

While the desktop PC is still the most popular way to access the Internet, many other devices on the market enable users to access the Web or e-mail. If you have the money (and the inclination), you can buy mobile phones, PDAs, TVs, digital book readers, and even refrigerators that are Web-enabled. However, each of these different devices has different capabilities:

❏   Some have monochrome displays; others are color.

❏   Sizes and shapes of screens vary between devices.

❏   Screen resolution varies among devices.

❏   Not all of the HTML 4 specification is relevant to all of these devices (for example, book readers do not need to know colors or sizes of fonts).

❏   Some devices require extra functions (beyond the capabilities of XHTML 1.0). For example, phones might need to respond to events such as the receipt of a call or SMS (Short Message Service) message.

❏   Portable devices tend to have less power available to them than those that run off mains.

❏   Some devices have less memory than others.

The differences in capabilities of devices mean that each device can have inherent limitations. For example, trying to fit the content of a large news site onto a phone screen is analogous to printing an entire page of a newspaper on a postage stamp. If the main news site controlled layout using tables (for example, 700 pixels wide) made up of two columns, then even if a mobile phone could display the layout table, the screen would be so small that the text would not be readable at such a small resolution. While you would not likely try to do this, if you were to try to fit the same amount of content on the screen of a mobile device, you would probably end up with very long pages that users would have to scroll a long way down through.

Furthermore, because mobile devices have limited power and memory, they cannot be expected to run browsers that require the same resources as IE 6 or Netscape 7 on desktop PCs (for example, Netscape 7.1 requires 52MB of hard drive space and 64MB of RAM).

Luckily, the W3C realized that not every device that can now access the Internet would be served using the one language — HTML — and that was one of the major motivations for creating XHTML, and XHTML 1.1.

Lessons from the mobile world

The capability of mobile phones to access the Internet first became a big feature in the market around 1999–2000. Mobiles were one of the first popular devices other than PCs that could access the Web, and the mobile phone manufacturers came up with several different specifications to enable their devices to display Web content. The specifications were designed with the limitations of the devices in mind (which had smaller screens, less memory, and required lower power consumption). These specifications included the following:

❑ **Wireless Markup Language (WML)**, which is commonly known as part of the Wireless Application Protocol (WAP) group of specifications.

❑ **Handheld Device Markup Language (HDML)**

❑ **Compact HTML (cHTML)**

If you take a close look at these competing specifications, each of which was created to support a different device, you will see that they share some common features. Each language enables users to mark up the following types of information:

❑ Basic text, including paragraphs and lists

❑ Hyperlinks and links to related documents

❑ Basic forms to capture data from users

❑ Basic tables to enable the presentation of data tables

❑ Images

❑ Metainformation (information *about* the Web page, rather than the content itself — such as the title of the page)

The fact that all of these separate specifications were created, all of which perform similar functions, teaches us a valuable lesson and highlights the reasons why XHTML was modularized: Rather than reinvent the wheel and have several competing languages for every new type of device, one key language (XHTML) is divided into modules that form the basis of the languages for new devices, enabling the following:

❑ The modules can act as building blocks for variations of XHTML designed for different devices (rather than having completely separate languages).

❑ If a new document type is created, it either supports a whole module or not at all, making it easier to develop for the device using the new specification.

In short, rather than create several different languages, each of which offers the same function (such as WML, cHTML, and HDML), XHTML enables you to build new languages for new devices from the same set of XHTML modules.

The abstract modules of XHTML

The first step in modularizing XHTML was to divide the markup from the XHTML 1.0 Strict recommendation into a set of *abstract modules* that could be used as the building blocks of future languages, each module containing related functionality. Any new languages based upon these modules would have to use a minimum set of *core modules*; and the new language would be referred to as belonging to the *XHTML family of languages*. In total, the W3C created 29 abstract modules for XHTML.

> *The W3C recommendation that covers the Modularization of XHTML can be seen at*
> **www.w3.org/TR/xhtml-modularization/**.

If you look at the XHTML 1.1 DTD (the Document Type Definition specifying the rules governing what markup can appear in a document and where each element or attribute can appear within a document), you will see that it contains 21 of the 29 abstract modules the W3C defined.

The following table shows the abstract modules, and demonstrates which module belongs to each of the following groups:

❑ **XHTML Core Modules**—The minimum list of modules that must be supported in order for a language to be part of the XHTML family

❑ **XHTML Basic**—A scaled-down version of XHTML designed as the basis of languages developed for use on small devices, which you will meet again later in the chapter

❑ **XHTML 1.1**—The modularized version of XHTML 1.0

Module Name	Core Modules	XHTML Basic	XHTML 1.1
Structure	Y	Y	Y
Text	Y	Y	Y
Hypertext	Y	Y	Y
List	Y	Y	Y
Applet			
Object		Y	Y
Presentation			Y
Edit			Y
Bidirectional text			Y
Frames			
IFrame			
Basic forms		Y	
Forms			Y
Basic tables		Y	

Table continued on following page

Module Name	Core Modules	XHTML Basic	XHTML 1.1
Tables			Y
Image		Y	Y
Client-side image map			Y
Server-side image map			Y
Intrinsic events			Y
Metainformation		Y	Y
Scripting			Y
Stylesheet			Y
Style attribute (deprecated)			Y
Link		Y	Y
Target			
Base		Y	Y
Ruby annotation			Y
Name identification			
Legacy			

XHTML 1.1 has similar functionality to Strict XHTML 1.0. However, the W3C recognized that some people would need to be able to support older devices and would require some of the features of HTML that had since been deprecated. This older markup has been added to a module called the Legacy module. Although this module is not part of XHTML 1.1, if you need to support these older devices, you can create a version of XHTML that includes this module, which would enable you to enjoy many of the benefits of XHTML, but also offer you the capability to support older devices.

XHTML 1.1

As shown in the preceding table, XHTML 1.1 supports 21 of the abstract XHTML modules, and the functionality of these modules offers something very similar to that offered by Strict XHTML 1.0. The importance of the fact that the language is made from modules will become apparent when you look at how to create new languages for use with different devices later in the chapter.

This section describes the following:

- ❑ The elements contained in each of the modules that make it into XHTML 1.1
- ❑ The differences between an XHTML 1.1 document and a Strict XHTML 1.0 document

While a couple of modules might initially seem like exceptions to you, upon further investigation, you'll find that they are not:

❏   The applet module is replaced with the functionality of the object module (and the `<object>` element should be used, rather than the `<applet>` element).

❏   The frame module is not included because frameset documents use their own separate DTD that supports the use of the `<frameset>` element as a child of the `<html>` element, rather than the `<body>` element, just as in XHTML 1.0.

XHTML 1.1 modules

This section describes each of the modules that make up XHTML 1.1; remember that each module contains a related set of functionality (and their names should be self-explanatory). By the end of this section, you will understand the purpose of the module, the elements that make up that module, and any notable attributes of the module.

Structure module

The structure module contains the elements that control the core structure (sometimes referred to as the skeleton) of an XHTML document:

```
<body> <head> <html> <title>
```

Text module

The text module contains elements that enable you to mark up text so that the markup describes the content and structure of the document. At the beginning of this module are the heading and paragraph elements:

```
<h1> <h2> <h3> <h4> <h5> <h6> <p>
```

These are followed by several other elements that should be used wherever appropriate:

```
<abbr> <acronym> <address> <blockquote> <br /> <cite> <code> <dfn> <em> <kbd> <pre>
<q> <samp> <strong> <var>
```

Interestingly, this module also contains the two grouping elements, although they can be used to group all kinds of markup — not just text:

```
<div> <span>
```

Hypertext module

The hypertext module contains only one element, which you will be very familiar with because it is used to create links:

```
<a>
```

List module

The list module enables you to create three types of list: ordered lists, unordered lists, and definition lists. The elements this module contains are as follows:

```
<ul> <ol> <li> <dl> <dt> <dd>
```

Object module

The object module is used to include all kinds of objects in a document, including Flash movies JavaApplets, and MP3s. This module contains two elements:

```
<object> <param>
```

Presentation module

The presentation module contains a set of elements that can be used to affect the presentation of text:

```
<b> <big> <hr /> <i> <small> <sub> <sup> <tt>
```

Note that you should really be using the `<em>` and `<strong>` elements for emphasis and strong emphasis, respectively, rather than the `<i>` and `<b>` elements; after all using the `<em>` and `<strong>` elements would enable a voice browser or screen reader to add the emphasis to the tone of voice using inflection.

Edit module

The edit module contains two elements that you can use to indicate which parts of a document have been deleted or inserted, so they can therefore be used to track the changes of a document:

```
<del> <ins>
```

These two elements are most likely to be used by authoring tools.

Bidirectional text module

The bidirectional text module contains just one element, which is used to handle pages that contain text from different languages that should be read in different directions (for example, Hebrew and French):

```
<bdo>
```

Forms module

The forms module contains the `<form>` element used to create the form:

```
<form>
```

This module also contains a set of elements that enable you to place form controls on a form:

```
<button> <input> <select> <optgroup> <option> <textarea>
```

Finally, it also has three elements to help divide and label the form:

```
<fieldset> <legend> <label>
```

Tables module

The elements in the table module are supposed to be used to display tabular data — not to lay out a page:

```
<table> <tr> <td> <th> <caption> <col> <colgroup> <thead> <tbody> <tfoot>
```

In XHTML 1.1 (as in Strict XHTML 1.0), you should use CSS to control the layout of documents — not tables — even though tables are still commonly used for layout.

Image module

The image module contains one element used to add images to a document:

```
<img />
```

In the future, the W3C is likely to encourage developers to start using the `<object>` element to insert images, rather than the `<img />` element.

Client-side image map module

The client-side image map module enables you to create client-side image maps. It contains two elements:

```
<area> <map>
```

Server-side image map module

The server-side image map module enables you to create server-side image maps and contains just one attribute, which should be used in conjunction with the `<img />` element:

```
ismap
```

However, as you saw in Chapter 6 when looking at accessibility issues, you should avoid using server-side image maps where possible; and where they are used, you should also provide redundant text links.

Intrinsic events module

Intrinsic events are attributes that can be used with elements that fire events when certain actions are performed by a user. When the intrinsic events module and the module that corresponds with each of these elements (shown in the right-hand column of the following table) are used, the following attributes can be carried on those elements:

Elements	Attributes	Corresponding Module
<a>	onblur onfocus	Hypertext (core module)
<area>	onblur onfocus	Client-side image map
<body>	onload onunload	Structure (core module)
<button>	onblur onfocus	Forms
<form>	onreset onsubmit	Basic forms or forms
<frameset>	onload onunload	Frames
<input>	onblur onchange onfocus onselect	Basic forms or forms

Table continued on following page

Elements	Attributes	Corresponding Module
<label>	onblur onfocus	Forms
<select>	onblur onchange onfocus	Basic forms or forms
<textarea>	onblur onchange onfocus onselect	Basic forms or forms

Metainformation module

The metainformation module contains one element, which enables you to add many different kinds of information about a document (such as title, description, and keywords):

```
<meta>
```

Scripting module

The scripting module contains two elements: one to contain a script and the other to indicate what should be presented if the browser does not support the scripting language:

```
<script> <noscript>
```

Stylesheet module

The stylesheet module contains one element that can be used to contain CSS rules within the <head> element of a document:

```
<style>
```

Style attribute module (deprecated module)

The style attribute enables you to specify inline CSS style rules on elements:

```
style
```

The use of this attribute (and therefore this module) is deprecated because it enables authors to mix stylistic markup (the CSS rules) with the structural markup in the document — and as you now know, one of the key aims of XHTML is to separate stylistic markup from presentational markup.

Link module

The link module contains one element whose purpose is to describe links between documents — for example, between a document and its style sheet, or between pages of a large document that has been divided into a set of smaller pages; in both cases, the file that is linked to is used with the file containing this element:

```
<link>
```

Base module

The base module enables you to specify a base URL for the page (so that all relative URLs in the page are appended to this base module):

```
<base>
```

Ruby annotation module

The ruby annotation module allows for small character annotations that are sometimes added to characters in ideographic scripts such as Japanese. The ruby are used to clarify the pronunciation (and/or meaning) of those characters. In vertical text, they are usually added in a very small font along the side of the ideogram, whereas in horizontal text they are used on the top:

```
<ruby> <rb> <rt> <rp> <rbc> <rtc>
```

Differences between XHTML 1.0 and XHTML 1.1

The functionality of the modules just described that makes up XHTML 1.1 is the same functionality as that found in Strict XHTML 1.0. Therefore, the only differences you need to observe when writing a document using XHTML 1.1, rather than Strict XHTML 1.0, are as follows:

❑ The DOCTYPE declaration *must* precede the root element; and if you use a public identifier, it should be represented as follows:

```
<!DOCTYPE html PUBLIC "-//W3C//DTD XHTML 1.1//EN"
        "http://www.w3.org/TR/xhtml11/DTD/xhtml11.dtd">
```

❑ The root <html> element should carry the xmlns attribute indicating the namespace for the document; that namespace is http://www.w3.org/1999/xhtml.

❑ The lang attribute on each element has been removed; instead, you should use the xml:lang attribute.

❑ The name attribute on the <a> and <map> elements has been removed; instead, you should use the id attribute.

❑ The ruby collection of elements has been added.

❑ The style attribute has been deprecated.

The following example is a very simple page that conforms to the rules of XHTML 1.1 (ch08_eg01.html):

```
<?xml version="1.0" encoding="UTF-8" ?>
<!DOCTYPE html PUBLIC "-//W3C//DTD XHTML 1.1//EN"
        "http://www.w3.org/TR/xhtml11/DTD/xhtml11.dtd">
<html xmlns="http://www.w3.org/1999/xhtml" xml:lang="en">
  <head>
    <title>My First XHTML 1.1 Document</title>
  </head>
  <body>
    <h1>My First XHTML 1.1 Document</h1>
    <p>This web page conforms to the rules of XHTML 1.1.</p>
    <p>You would not know that the specification was made up of different modules
       just by looking at (or writing) the code.
  </body>
</html>
```

You can see what this page looks like in Figure 8-1.

Figure 8-1

XHTML Basic

XHTML Basic was created as a *host language* for small devices — the idea being that, if you are going to create a new document type for a small device (such as a mobile phone or a PDA), rather than write the language from scratch, you should base it upon XHTML Basic.

The idea of building variations of a language upon this host language counters the problems met earlier in the chapter (recall how the mobile phone manufacturers created several competing specifications when they first tried to make the Web available on their mobile phones).

Any language that uses XHTML Basic as a host language has to support all of its features, which include the following modules and elements (for further description of the elements, see the preceding section). These basic modules can then be extended with other existing XHTML modules or new modules.

Module	Elements
Structure	`<body> <head> <html> <title>`
Text	`<h1> <h2> <h3> <h4> <h5> <h6> <p>` `<div> <span>` `<em> <strong>` `<abbr> <acronym> <address> <blockquote>   <cite> <code>` `<dfn> <kbd> <pre> <q> <samp> <var>`
Hypertext	`<a>`
List	`<ol> <ul> <li> <dl> <dt> <dd>`
Object	`<object> <param>`
Basic Forms	`<form> <input> <label> <select> <option> <textarea>`
Basic Tables	`<table> <tr> <td> <th> <caption>`

Module	Elements
Image	`<img>`
Link	`<link>`
Metainformation	`<meta>`
Base	`<base>`

Any new features that are required can be built upon these modules — for example, if you are working on a language for mobile phones, you might need event handlers that are triggered when a phone receives an SMS message or a call.

Using this modular approach offers many advantages, including the following:

❑ It is easier for document authors to create pages for multiple devices if they share common features, and the device either supports or does not support a set of the features.

❑ Because devices share the same language, more pages will work on different devices (without the pages having to be rewritten for each device); and more content will be available to all devices (because existing content that uses a subset of the same modules would automatically be available to the new device).

❑ It is easier to learn new languages for devices because the core set of modules remains the same.

> If you want to create a new language based upon an XHTML host language (such as XHTML Basic) and a feature you want is available in another module, you must always include the whole of the module that contains the feature you want, rather than recreate the feature or just include the one feature without the others.

I have already mentioned that it is not practical for small devices to support all of the features of HTML 4, so to understand a little more about XHTML Basic, take a closer look at what it leaves out:

❑ The `<style>` element was left out because you can use the `<link>` element to link to an external style sheet (therefore keeping the content separate from the rules that control presentation); and when you use external style sheets, you can specify different style sheets for different devices (because the style rules are not in the same document as the content).

❑ The `<script>` and `<noscript>` elements are not necessary because small devices might not have the resources (memory and power) required to execute scripts and programs. As you learned in Chapter 6, in order to be accessible, all pages should be able to run without scripts.

❑ Event handler attributes are not required because they are used to invoke scripts — and if scripts are not used, neither are event handlers. Furthermore, event handlers are the one aspect of a language that is most likely to be device-specific; for example, mobile units might have to deal with events such as SMS messages or phone calls, microwaves might have to deal with a timer, and car-navigation systems might have to deal with events triggered by GPS data.

❑   The more advanced features of forms are not applicable to all small devices because some of them will not have a local file system, and without a local file system they will not need to use file input types in forms. Furthermore, their screens might not support features such as `<fieldsets>`, encouraging the designer to create several smaller screens of related information instead.

❑   Advanced features of tables are not applicable to all small devices because their screens will not always be able to support features such as nested tables. In addition, tables should be used only for tabular data, not for layout purposes.

While XHTML Basic can be used as it is, as a *host language* it is intended to become the basis of other languages for small devices, and for additional features to be added to a particular implementation to support the requirements of the target device. Later in the chapter, you will see that this is exactly what has happened with a language called XHTML MP (XHTML Mobile Profile).

Hybrid documents

One of the powerful aspects of XHTML is that it can contain markup from more than one language. As you will see in this section, the ability to mix markup from different languages is something that increasing numbers of developers will be taking advantage of. However, to really understand this aspect of XHTML, it is important to understand XML namespaces.

Understanding XML namespaces

As you already know, XML is a language used to create other markup languages, and XHTML is just one example of a language written in XML. Different languages in XML look similar to a certain extent in that they all contain elements (whose names are surrounded by angled brackets), and these elements can carry attributes. What differs between languages is the names of these elements, the attributes they can carry, and where the elements are allowed to appear within the document (for example, in XHTML a `<li>` element can appear only inside an `<ol>` or `<ul>` element).

Every family of languages created in XML has its own namespace, and the namespace for XHTML is as follows:

```
http://www.w3.org/1999/xhtml
```

You have seen this namespace used on the root `<html>` element of many of the XHTML documents in this book. This namespace applies to all different versions of XHTML.

The namespace is used as a unique identifier for a family of documents; it does not actually specify a physical resource of a file. It is *not* the source of the DTD that contains the rules for this version of the language (that is specified in the `!DOCTYPE` declaration). You might find several versions of a language within the one namespace (each with separate DTDs).

One of the key points of languages created in XML is that they are supposed to be *self-describing*; the element and attribute names are supposed to describe the data that they contain. For example, the `<h1>` to `<h6>` elements indicate different levels of headings. Similarly, the `<table>` element contains tabular data. However, XML is not just used to create languages that present data to a user in a browser; it is commonly used to send data/messages between programs. Therefore, for example, there is nothing to stop a furniture manufacturer from creating a new XML language — to exchange data with suppliers — that also uses a `<table>` element, but their use of this element might be to represent a piece of furniture. Another language might be written to describe sports results, and that language might use a `<table>` element to indicate teams' positions within a league table.

Of course, if documents contained markup from only one language, and if programs were written to understand only one language, then this would not matter. However, not only is it possible for an XML document to contain more than one language, and for programs to work with many different languages, in many cases this is going to be a requirement.

XML namespaces solve the confusion that could arise if two languages use the same element names, by associating the markup with a URI that is a unique identifier for that language. Here is a simple XHTML example to illustrate how namespaces are used:

```
<?xml version="1.0" encoding="UTF-8" ?>
<!DOCTYPE html PUBLIC "-//W3C//DTD XHTML 1.1//EN"
          "http://www.w3.org/TR/xhtml11/DTD/xhtml11.dtd">
<html xmlns="http://www.w3.org/1999/xhtml" xml:lang="en">
  <head>
    <title>namespace example</title>
  </head>
  <body>
    <h1>Understanding Namespaces</h1>
    <p>Because the root element carries the xmlns attribute to identify the
        namespace, all child elements are expected to be from the same namespace
        unless otherwise stated.</p>
  </body>
</html>
```

If you go to `www.w3.org/1999/xhtml`, you will not see a set of rules for XHTML; this URI is just used to identify the XML namespace. When a namespace is declared upon the root element of the document, it indicates that this namespace is the default namespace for the document, and all child elements within the root element belong to the same namespace (unless otherwise stated).

The Web is actually a very good example of where you are likely to see increasing amounts of different XML vocabularies mixed into the same document; for example, not only do you have XHTML to mark up Web pages, you also have other XML-based languages intended for viewing in Web browsers that are gaining popularity, including the following:

❑ **Scalable Vector Graphics (SVG)** — A language for creating vector graphics on the Web. Vector graphics are similar to those created by programs such as Flash, Illustrator, and Freehand. One of the advantages of SVG is that graphics scale and can therefore be stretched or squashed to fit the device with which they are used. While SVG is likely to become widely used, more complex SVG code will probably be created by programs, rather than hand-coded.

❑ **MathML** — A language for marking up complex mathematical equations and formulae, which are not supported by normal character sets and layout methods and have therefore commonly been shown using images. This language has a powerful advantage over images because it is possible to programmatically analyze the content of the page — either for calculations or for searching.

The following example makes use of markup from two namespaces — XHTML with SVG (`ch08_eg2.html`):

```
<?xml version="1.0" encoding="iso-8859-1" ?>
<!DOCTYPE html PUBLIC "-//W3C//DTD XHTML 1.1//EN"
  "http://www.w3.org/TR/xhtml11/DTD/xhtml11.dtd">
<html xmlns="http://www.w3.org/1999/xhtml" xml:lang="en">
  <head>
    <title>XHTML and SVG</title>
  </head>
  <body>
    <h1>An XHTML Document Containing SVG Shapes</h1>
    <svg xmlns="http://www.w3.org/2000/svg" width="5cm" height="2.5cm">
    <rect width="150px" height="100px" rx="15" ry="15"
          style="fill:#ff0000; stroke:#000000" />
    <circle cx="35" cy="35" r="30" style="fill:#00ff00; stroke:#000000;" />
    </svg>
  </body>
</html>
```

The SVG markup is contained within the `<svg>` element, which carries another `xmlns` attribute. This indicates that the `<svg>` element and its child elements belong to the SVG namespace.

Unfortunately, the major browsers do not natively support SVG at the time of writing. They require the use of a third-party plug-in that requires an `<object>` element to load the plug-in. However, you can use a browser created by the W3C called Amaya to try out the example. You can see what this example looks like in Amaya in Figure 8-2.

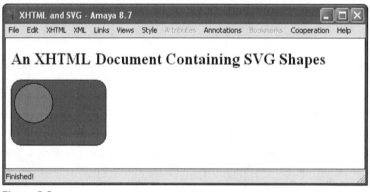

Figure 8-2

Amaya can be downloaded from `www.w3.org/amaya/`. Amaya is unlikely to ever get the mainstream support of other browsers, but it is a very powerful testing tool for developers.

Hybrid document types

It is not only documents that can contain markup from more than one language; entirely new document types (new languages) can be created using markup from different languages — these are known as *hybrid document types*.

Because XHTML was modularized, it is possible to create entirely new document types that mix parts of XHTML with other languages written in XML. For example, it would be possible to extend XHTML Basic with parts of SVG to create a language specially designed for financial reports, with text and basic tables of data in XHTML and graphs and charts in SVG.

Using the XML modularization framework, the W3C created a hybrid document type that incorporates XHTML 1.1, MathML 2.0, and SVG 1.1. The result is a language that can cope with the requirements of most documents: text, images, links, tables, and forms in XHTML; enhanced with graphics from SVG; and the capability to create complex equations using MathML. The home page for this language is `www.w3.org/tr/XHTMLplusMathMLplusSVG/` (it assumes you know each of the constituent languages, rather than explain each of them).

Here is an example of a document in this hybrid language (`ch08_eg03.html`):

```
<?xml version="1.0" encoding="UTF-8" ?>
<!DOCTYPE html PUBLIC "-//W3C//DTD XHTML 1.1 plus MathML 2.0 plus SVG 1.1 //EN"
          "http://www.w3.org/2002/04/xhtml-math-svg/xhtml-math-svg.dtd ">
<html xmlns="http://www.w3.org/1999/xhtml" xml:lang="en">
  <head>
    <title>XHTML plus MathML plus SVG</title>
  </head>
  <body>
    <h1>A Hybrid Document</h1>
    <p>This document contains markup from three separate namespaces that have been
       combined to create a hybrid document type. The host namespace is XHTML.</p>
    <p>MathML is used to add equations to the page.</p>
    <math xmlns="http://www.w3.org/1998/Math/MathML">
      <mroot>
        <mrow>
          <mi>x</mi>
          <mo>+</mo>
          <mn>1</mn>
        </mrow>
        <mn>3</mn>
      </mroot>
    </math>
    <p>SVG is used to add graphics to the page.</p>
    <svg xmlns="http://www.w3.org/2000/svg" width="5cm" height="2.5cm">
    <rect width="150px" height="100px" rx="15" ry="15"
          style="fill:#ff0000; stroke:#000000" />
    <circle cx="35" cy="35" r="30" style="fill:#00ff00; stroke:#000000;" />
    </svg>
    <p>You can look at the source of the page to see the markup from the three
       different namespaces.</p>
  </body>
</html>
```

While this example uses XHTML 1.1 as the host language and has been extended with MathML and SVG, it would be possible to use either MathML or SVG as the host language. For example, you might choose SVG as the host language if your documents were going to mainly consist of graphics and you just wanted to include a few modules from XHTML.

While this example uses XHTML 1.1 plus MathML 2.0 plus SVG 1.1 DOCTYPE declaration, you might have noticed that the root element still uses the XHTML namespace:

```
<!DOCTYPE html PUBLIC "-//W3C//DTD XHTML 1.1 plus MathML 2.0 plus SVG 1.1 //EN"
        "http://www.w3.org/2002/04/xhtml-math-svg/xhtml-math-svg.dtd ">
<html xmlns="http://www.w3.org/1999/xhtml" xml:lang="en">
```

It is not necessary to create a new namespace for the hybrid document type because the markup already belongs to three existing namespaces. By declaring the XHTML namespace on the root <html> element, it becomes the default namespace for the document. Then, when markup from the SVG or MathML namespaces is used, their namespaces are declared.

In the following example, the MathML markup lives inside a <math> element, which declares it is part of the MathML namespace (this is the code that inserts the equation into the example). This overrides the default namespace for the <math> element and anything inside it:

```
<math xmlns"http://www.w3.org/1998/Math/MathML">
    <mroot>
        <mrow>
            <mi>x</mi>
            <mo>+</mo>
            <mn>1</mn>
        </mrow>
        <mn>3</mn>
    </mroot>
</math>
```

Similarly, the <svg> element uses the SVG namespace (this draws the red rectangle on the page, which contains a green circle). The SVG namespace on the <svg> element again overrides the default XHTML namespace and indicates that the content of the <svg> element belongs to the SVG namespace:

```
<svg xmlns="http://www.w3.org/2000/svg" width="5cm" height="2.5cmv">
    <rect width="150px" height="100px" rx="15" ry="15"
        style="fill:#ff0000; stroke:#000000" />
    <circle cx="35" cy="35" r="30" style="fill:#00ff00; stroke:#000000;" />
</svg>
```

You can see what this page would look like in the Amaya browser in Figure 8-3.

This demonstrates that although new devices that can access the Web are being released with increasing frequency, by modularizing the languagesused to create Web pages, you can create hybrid document types that share common language constructs but can deal with the variety of devices that will be accessing the Internet. The permutations available should prevent the situation that occurred when several mobile phone manufacturers reinvented the wheel and created conflicting and competing specifications for similar devices.

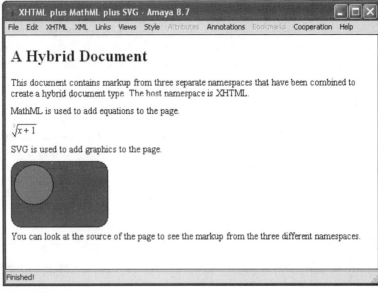

Figure 8-3

XHTML on different devices

As already mentioned several times in this chapter, developers no longer have to create sites solely for desktop PCs; there is now a demand for pages that will work on a range of new devices that can access the Internet — in particular, mobile phones and PDAs.

In this section, you will be looking at how Modularized XHTML makes it much easier to develop sites for different devices. In particular, this section covers the following:

❑ XHTML on mobile phones and the XHTML Mobile Profile specification

❑ Technologies used in creating sites for different devices, including database-driven sites, and how XSLT is used to transform pages from one version of XHTML to another (and indeed to other languages)

XHTML on mobile phones

Earlier in the chapter, you saw how mobile phone manufacturers created a competing set of specifications (such as WML, cHTML, and HDML) when the Internet was first becoming available to mobile devices.

In contrast to this practice of using separate languages, Modularized XHTML has offered the mobile industry a chance for unification (which would enable people to develop applications for more mobile users).

Many of the main players in the mobile industry — including NTT DoCoMo (the Japanese company who created the i-mode service that used cHTML) and the WAP Forum (a group of companies including

Nokia, Sony Ericsson, Microsoft, and Vodafone) — joined forces to form the Open Mobile Alliance and create standards that would be used across different phones. These included a new standard that combined the features of their previous offerings with the features of XHTML Basic. The new language was called *XHTML Mobile Profile (XHTML MP)*, which is based upon XHTML Basic and uses CSS to control rendering. Some of the features of XHTML that were not in XHTML Basic were added (such as `<acronym>`, `<address>`, `<br />`, `<big>`, `<small>`, `<hr />`, `<i>`, `<fieldset>`, and `<optgroup>`). Also added were some features from previous specifications that were not available in XHTML, such as different ways to control navigation, new events, and other features.

The XHTML Mobile Profile (XHTML MP) solution was ideal for the following reasons:

❏   The markup was very similar to (and shared common markup with) XHTML.

❏   It meets more requirements for usability (in particular, because it uses CSS to style the document).

❏   You can have several nonlink commands on a page.

Unfortunately, although they got very close to a unified solution, things didn't work out entirely as they should have, for the following reasons:

❏   Nokia decided to use XHTML MP without a namespace at all.

❏   The successors to the i-mode phone browsers used XHTML without the extended features of XHTML MP (which means usability suffers).

❏   Many others used the suggested namespace.

Therefore, there are still inconsistencies in implementations. However, these steps are a major improvement, and we can hope that there will be even more convergence in the future.

> In reality, at the time of writing, a lot of older phones still in circulation do not support XHTML MP (particularly older phones with monochrome displays). This, combined with the fact that many of the recent phones supported WAP for backward compatibility, means that a lot of the content is still made available using older technologies.

Creating sites for multiple platforms

As an increasing number of people use a variety of devices to access Web pages, you have an increased responsibility to serve pages to a variety of different devices. When you take a close look at the services offered to different devices, you can see that very few sites offer carbon copies of the same content for different sites; rather, they offer services that are tailored to the device (and how that device is used, and its physical limitations).

Part of the reason for this is because in different situations, you are likely to want very different information. For example, mobile phone users are far more likely to want movie showtimes on their mobile phones then biographies or photo galleries of their favorite stars. For other companies, there would be little purpose in providing information to mobile users (beyond perhaps their contact details and directions to find them); for example, a garden center would not need to show photos of all their plants/ seeds on a mobile phone.

The other part of the reason why services are tailored to devices is that different devices often have very different capabilities. Mobile phones and PDAs have much smaller screens than desktop PCs and cannot carry as much information on the screen at once; nor can they carry large, detailed images. Meanwhile,

TVs used with set top boxes often have lower resolution than computer screens. In fact, many of these new devices can behave so differently from desktop computers that it seems like they are completely different mediums. Therefore, physical limitations add to the reasons why users want different content from different devices.

Therefore, if you end up creating different versions of a site for different devices, you may well be wondering why this book began by saying that separating content from presentation was important if you need to enable the same content to be served to different types of new devices. A clear answer appears in the form of two key reasons that are apparent when you look at how the content is served to multiple devices:

❑ Different versions of the site are often created from the same content, which is actually stored within a database (rather than in XHTML documents on the server).

❑ It is possible to transform XHTML into XHTML MP (and other XML vocabularies) using a language called XSLT.

The following sections describe how content is served to multiple devices using these techniques.

Database-driven sites

When you start looking at larger sites in which content changes regularly — for example, news sites — you realize that coding every page by hand would involve a lot of work. Rather than hand-code these pages, the content tends to be put in a database, and then template pages are used to recover the appropriate information from the database and place it with the page that is sent back to the user.

Database-driven Web sites became very popular in the late 1990s with the advent of what are known as *server-side scripting languages,* such as ASP, PHP, and JSP.

The capability to store the content of the Web pages in a database and then access the information using scripting languages meant the following:

❑ It was far easier and quicker to create and maintain content for the Web. Previously, most sites would manually code an HTML page for each article. Therefore, the capability to simply add the relevant text into a form on the Web site, for this to be placed into the database, and then for template pages to show users the items in the database and format each article automatically saved a lot of work.

❑ Different people could add information to the database using the same forms, without all of them having to learn how to code the pages in the same way.

❑ It was possible to create pages that specifically answered users' queries, such as what time trains depart from London to Edinburgh on Sundays after noon. Users enter details of the information that they want to know, and this information is turned into something known as a *database query*. The database then retrieves information relevant to that query, which is formatted in a template page and returned to the user. After all, when you are creating a Web site to show a train timetable, you would not want to create a page for every possible journey from and to every stop on the line.

To get a better idea of how this works, imagine a site that contains regular new articles. The articles would be stored in a database table that might look something like the following table, with a unique ID for each article and fields for the title of the article, a summary, and the full text of the article (in practical applications you would likely have more fields for items such as images, author, and date created, but this will do for the purposes of this example).

articleID	Title	Summary	Article
25	Aliens Shopping at K-Mart	Multiple sightings of strange aircraft spotted in K-Mart car park	\<p\>On November 23, the Greatville police confirmed they had received...
26	Dog with Two Tails	A lucky canine in New Byron is wagging two tails	\<p\>Vets in New Byron were given a surprise when Lucky the dog came into their...

Rather than your having to create a separate page for each article, one page containing server-side script can collect the information for each article and display it within a template. You can also create a page that acts as a list of all the articles in the database, showing only the titles and summaries, which could retrieve the information from the database, rather than having to be manually updated.

Therefore, if a visitor requested the page www.example.org/news.asp, the news.asp page would do the following:

1. Select the articleID, title, and summary of the last 10 articles in the database.

2. Format the titles and summaries of the last ten articles in XHTML.

3. Create a link to a viewArticle.asp page for each article, appending the articleID to the *query string* on the URL, so the URL for article 25 might look like this: www.example.org/viewArticle.asp?articleID=25.

4. Send the XHTML back to the user who requested the page.

The resulting XHTML that contained the results might look like the following:

```
<table>
  <tr>
    <td><a href="viewArticle.asp?articleID=25">Aliens Shopping at KMart</a></td>
    <td> Multiple sightings of strange aircraft spotted in KMart car park.</td>
  </tr>
  <tr>
    <td><a href="viewArticle.asp?articleID=26">Dog with 2 Tails</a></td>
    <td>A lucky canine is in New Byron is wagging 2 tails.</td>
  </tr>
  <tr><!-- more article links here --></td>
</table>
```

When the user clicks on a link for the viewArticle.asp page, they would be asking the article template page to format the article for them using the following steps:

1. The article.asp page looks at the query string and determines which article the user wants.

2. It requests the title and article from the database.

3. The page then presents the title and article as XHTML using the template.

New articles could be added to the database using forms in the administration section of the site, and each new article would automatically be given a new articleID by the database.

While the `news.asp` page and the `viewArticle.asp` page might be used for the desktop PC version of the site, you might have other pages that could serve a subset of this information to smaller devices. For example, the titles and summaries of articles might be presented to mobile users from a different page that accessed the same database but presented the information using a different template. Using this technique, you need create only different templates for different devices, not an entirely new site with different versions of each article.

You can therefore see the importance of each field in the database containing XHTML markup for things such as paragraphs, emphasis, links, and subheadings. By ensuring that the database content is Strict XHTML, you ensure that the information in the database can be used with all kinds of clients.

Using XSLT to transform pages

Another way to create different versions of pages is to use a language called *XSLT*, which stands for *Extensible Stylesheet Language Transformation*. But XSLT style sheets are very different from CSS style sheets. XSLT style sheets are not used simply to control the presentation of pages; rather, they transform markup from one vocabulary (say, XHTML 1.0) to another vocabulary (such as XHTML MP), or indeed other formats, such as comma-delimited data.

This means that XSLT can be used to take a page written in XHTML 1.0 and create a version that uses the markup of XHTML MP, showing only the subset of information that you want to make available to users of mobile devices (because they have smaller screens).

You could even use XSLT to transform pages that are written in XHTML into versions of the page for older browsers that do not support, for example, CSS. For example, you could take the following element:

```
<span class="totalPrice">$22.50</span>
```

and transform it into something more like this for older browsers:

```
<font face="arial, verdana, sans-serif" size="2"><b>$22.50</b></font>
```

The one restriction is that the markup you are going to transform needs to be well formed; if you have missing closing tags and incorrectly nested elements, then XSLT might not be able to process the data.

XSLT is a huge topic in its own right and requires a book of its own to fully explain the language. However, to give you a sense of what it looks like, the rule that would transform the `<span>` element just shown into the older HTML might look something like the following:

```
<xsl:template match="span">
  <xsl:choose>
    <xsl:when test="@class = 'important'>
      <font face="arial, verdana, sans-serif" size="2"><b>
        <xsl:apply-templates select="." />
      </b></font>
    </xsl:when>
    <xsl:otherwise>
      <xsl:apply-templates select="." />
    </xsl:otherwise>
  </xsl:choose>
</xsl:template>
```

The `<xsl:template>` element is looking for elements whose name are span. When it finds them, it tests whether their class attribute has a value of important using the `<xsl:when>` element. If the class attribute does have a value of important, then the contents of this element are written between the `<font>` and `<b>` elements (as indicated with the `<xsl:apply-templates>`). If the `<span>` element does not have a class attribute whose value is important, then the `<span>` element and its content are written as they were.

In a full XSLT style sheet, you are likely to see many rules like this one, so a full XSLT style sheet can be quite complicated, as you can imagine.

> *If you want to learn more about XSLT, Beginning XSLT 2.0 by Jeni Tennison (Wrox Press, 2002) is an excellent starting point. The XSLT Programmer's Reference, 3rd Edition, by Michael Kay (Wrox Press, 2004) is another good resource.*

Switching CSS style sheets

Having seen how to offer different presentations of a page for different devices, you should also be aware that you can offer different presentations for the same device. This is possible because you can specify more than one CSS style sheet for the same XHTML page, and the browser will download all of them, enabling users to select their preference.

Although this technique is commonly used by people who want to offer different presentations, or *skins*, for their site, it can also be a very powerful tool either for visual effect or to make the page more accessible (by offering the page in different font sizes).

You have been writing a lot of style sheets in this book, but they have all been used with the page by default. However, the way in which you attach your style sheet can create different levels of precedence:

❑ A **persistent** style sheet is a style sheet that is always used by the browser; it has no title attribute, and the value of the type attribute is text/css:

```
<link href="persistent.css" rel="stylesheet" type="text/css" />
```

❑ A **preferred** style sheet is enabled by default, although users can switch it themselves. Preferred style sheets have a rel attribute with a value of stylesheet and a title attribute to distinguish between the style sheets the user can select:

```
<link href="preferred.css" rel="stylesheet" type="text/css" title="preferred" />
```

❑ **Alternate** style sheets can be selected by the visitor as an alternative to the preferred style sheet. An alternate relationship is specified by giving the rel attribute a value of alternate stylesheet and by providing a title attribute so that the user can select which style sheet to use:

```
<link href="alternate.css" rel="alternate stylesheet" type="text/css"
title="alternate" />
```

Some browsers, such as Netscape 6+, enable users to select which style sheet they want to use in the View menu, where a Page Style option should appear. Unfortunately, Internet Explorer does not.

However, you can enable users to switch between the preferred and the alternate style sheets using JavaScript. This is possible because in the DOM, the `<link>` element has a property called `disabled` that can be accessed by JavaScript. By default, alternate style sheets have this property set to `true`, and preferred ones have it set to `false`. Therefore, you can use JavaScript to loop through those with the `title` attribute (preferred and alternate) until the active one is found. Then you deactivate all others.

The following function is called `setActiveStyleSheet()` and was originally written by Peter-Paul Koch; it is used to switch between style sheets:

```
function setActiveStyleSheet(title) {
    var i, a, main;
    for(i=0; (a = document.getElementsByTagName("link")[i]); i++) {
      if(a.getAttribute("rel").indexOf("style") != -1
        && a.getAttribute("title")) {
        a.disabled = true;
        if(a.getAttribute("title") == title) a.disabled = false;
      }
    }
}
```

Here are the two style sheet links that are also in the `<head>` of the document (`ch08_eg04.html`):

```
<link href="preferred.css" rel="stylesheet" type="text/css" title="preferred" />
<link href="alternate.css" rel="alternate stylesheet" type="text/css"
    title="alternative" />
```

When the user clicks on the following links in the `<body>` of the XHTML page, it calls this function and switches the style sheet that is used:

```
<a href="#" onclick="setActiveStyleSheet('preferred'); return false;">
  default style sheet</a>
<a href="#" onclick="setActiveStyleSheet('alternative'); return false;">
  alternative style sheet</a>
```

In this very simple example, here is the preferred style sheet (`preferred.css`):

```
body {
    font-size:12px;
    font-family:arial, verdana, sans-serif;
    color:#000000;
    background-color:#ffffff;}
```

And here is the alternative style sheet (`alternate.css`), which has larger text and uses the opposite colors for the text and background:

```
body {
    font-size:28px;
    font-family:arial, verdana, sans-serif;
    color:#ffffff;
    background-color:#000000;}
```

This is quite a basic example, but it clearly demonstrates how you can offer alternative style sheets to users.

Several free articles on the Web extend the style sheet switching example by, for example, using cookies to store user preferences for page layout:

- ❑ www.alistapart.com/articles/alternate
- ❑ www.alistapart.com/articles/n4switch
- ❑ www.notestips.com/80256B3A007F2692/1/NAMO5GK2NM

You can also use server-side languages such as ASP, PHP, or JSP to switch style sheets, but JavaScript techniques enable pages to be restyled without requesting the page from the server again.

It is worth noting, however, that the browser does have to download all of the style sheets, which, if you had a lot of choices, could slow your pages down the first time the user views the page (although it should speed up after being downloaded once, because the style sheets are cached on the user's computer).

Looking to the future

The mobile phone is very different from the desktop PC in terms of capabilities, but that difference is just the beginning. You are likely to see many other kinds of devices that can access the Web. While a browser in a kitchen device such as a refrigerator or microwave, or a browser in a car, would not necessarily have the same restrictions related to screen size or power that mobiles have, it might need or want features used by mobile devices that are not available as standard on desktop PCs, such as the capability to read content to the user and respond to voice commands (for example, users in the kitchen might have food on their hands, and those in the car might be driving).

Visitors using browsers that read content, such as on a kitchen appliance or in a car, might not require visual formatting, but they could certainly benefit from aural properties that were introduced in CSS2, such as the ability to control the volume of voices or the position between stereo speakers (to the left or right).

In the future, users will not want all of the same features on all devices (how many people would want to watch a full-length movie on a microwave or a small mobile phone screen?). As a result, the best sites will tailor the content they offer to visitors according to the browser they are using *and* the situation in which their devices are usually used. For example, a news site might offer headlines to a mobile phone, with links to a synopsis of the story. The same site might offer full-length articles, along with background information to the story and related articles, to PC users. Similarly, a music site might offer songs and ringtones on mobile phones, and also offer forums, bios, and photo galleries on desktop versions.

Therefore, when you are thinking of developing for different devices, you need to bear in mind what your audience will be doing and what users will want to accomplish using each type of device. Different media and the aspects of various devices can complement each other. For example, you can see the value of databases to store content so that it can be repurposed, and why this content should be written in XHTML so that it will work with all devices.

Solution

What you have read about in this chapter already provides the solution to the problem of dealing with changing technologies. You have seen that the modularization of XHTML has created a framework that will take XHTML and related technologies such as CSS, SVG, and MathML into the future, with the framework being capable of dealing with browsers that have not even been created yet.

To see a real example of how pages are developed for different devices, however, you are going to develop a page for the First Promotions site using XHTML MP and test it on a mobile phone simulator.

The browser you are going to test this example on is the Nokia Mobile Browser (4.0), which can be downloaded from `http://forum.nokia.com/` (Nokia's developers Web site, for which registration is required). It is a piece of software that emulates the behaviour of a Nokia mobile phone browser.

*You can also download a handy authoring tool called the Nokia Mobile Internet Toolkit from the same site, which helps you create documents for mobile devices (it will create the basic skeleton of a document, including the XML Declaration, the **DOCTYPE** declaration, and minimal structure for a page).*

The page you are going to create is the page showing the list of available bags. You can see a screenshot of this page taken in the Nokia Mobile Browser 4.0 in Figure 8-4.

Figure 8-4

You begin with the familiar XML declaration, followed by the DOCTYPE declaration indicating that this document is written according to the rules of the XHTML Mobile Profile 1.0:

```
<?xml version="1.0" encoding="utf-8"?>
<!DOCTYPE html PUBLIC "-//WAPFORUM//DTD XHTML Mobile 1.0//EN"
        "http://www.wapforum.org/DTD/xhtml-mobile10.dtd" >
```

Next is the root `<html>` element, which carries the namespace declaration indicating that this document is part of the XHTML namespace (and therefore belongs to the XHTML family of documents):

```
<html xmlns="http://www.w3.org/1999/xhtml">
```

This is followed by the familiar `<head>` element with the required `<title>` element:

```
<head>
    <title>First Promotions :: Bags</title>
</head>
```

In the `<body>` of the document, you can see the `<h1>` element for the primary heading, just as you would on any standard XHTML page:

```
<body>
    <h1>Bags</h1>
```

Next up is the information for the first of the bags, which consists of an `<h2>` element for the name of each bag, followed by a `<p>` element containing the description, price, and a link to a photo of the bag:

```
<h2>City Conference</h2>
<p>Best selling low cost range of bags with detachable strap and
    interior pockets.<br />
    From $2.49 min qty 150<br />
    <a href="images/bags1_thumb.gif">View bag</a>
</p>
```

This same format is used for each of the bags:

```
<h2>Seattle Conference</h2>
<p>With rugged construction for added durability and zipped front
    pocket.<br />
    From $3.89 min qty 50<br />
    <a href="images/bags1_thumb.gif">View bag</a>
</p>
<h2>Cambridge Conference</h2>
<p>High quality bags in polyester with many pockets and features at a
    great price.<br />
    From $3.58 min qty 100<br />
    <a href="images/bags1_thumb.gif">View bag</a>
</p>
<h2>Jupiter Business</h2>
<p>Manufactured in 600D polyester in either blue or navy ideal for
    executives on the move.<br />
    From $2.99 min qty 100<br />
    <a href="images/bags1_thumb.gif">View bag</a>
</p>
```

After all of the bags, you have to close the document as usual:

```
    </body>
</html>
```

This kind of structure should be very familiar to you. It is just like any very basic XHTML document. Of course, if you were creating a more complicated page, you would have to ensure that all of the elements you wanted to use were available to you in the XHTML MP vocabulary, but all of these elements are part of the XHTML core modules required for every member of the XHTML family of documents.

The only part of the pages that are not part of the core set of modules are the images that are linked to that show each bag. Figure 8-5 shows you an example of one of the images of the bags.

Figure 8-5

In a real site, you would also require navigation for the site as a whole, and the images would be better served if they had their own pages with titles and links back to the main site, but the page suffices for the purpose of this example.

When you consider that some of the first mobile phones to access the Internet required that you programmed the pages using different languages, with different element names, and a far more restricted set of elements, you can understand how using XHTML makes things far easier. For example, a similar page created in WML (part of the WAP group of specifications) would look quite different; an example is shown next. WML did not contain heading elements. Pages were referred to as *cards,* and the title of the page was provided as an attribute on the <card> element. Furthermore, GIFs and JPEGs were not supported; instead, WBMPs were used. Here is what this page might have looked like:

```
<?xml version="1.0"?>
<!DOCTYPE wml PUBLIC "-//WAPFORUM//DTD WML 1.1//EN"
    "http://www.wapforum.org/DTD/wml_1.1.xml">

<wml>
  <card id="Bags" title="First Promotions :: Bags">
    <p>Bags</p>
      <p>City Conference<br />
            Best selling low cost range of bags with detachable strap and
            interior pockets.<br />
            From $2.49 min qty 150<br />
            <a href="bags1_thumb.wbmp">View bag</a>
      </p>
```

```
    <p>Seattle Conference<br />
        With rugged construction for added durability and zipped front
        pocket.<br />
        From $3.89 min qty 50<br />
        <a href="bags2_thumb.wbmp">View bag</a>
    </p>
    <p>Cambridge Conference<br />
        High quality bags in polyester with many pockets and features at a
        great price.<br />
        From $3.58 min qty 100<br />
        <a href="bags3_thumb.gif">View bag</a>
    </p>
    <p>Jupiter Business<br />
        Manufactured in 600D polyester in either blue or navy ideal for
        executives on the move.<br />
        From $2.99 min qty 100<br />
        <a href="bags4_thumb.gif">View bag</a>
    </p>
    </card>
</wml>
```

Beyond the differences apparent in the code, you must be aware of many other things when developing pages using WML: comments must appear between tags (not inside them), a WAP gateway (a special program sitting on a server) is required to serve WML pages, and it uses its own scripting language called WML script.

Therefore, when you compare learning a completely new vocabulary (such as WML) to using XHTML MP (based upon the familiar language of modularized XHTML), you can see how much simpler and clearer XHTML makes things, and how it makes it much easier to create and learn new vocabularies for new devices.

Summary

As you have seen in this chapter, in creating XHTML the W3C has devised a language that enables you to create more effective Web pages not only for today's needs, but also for devices that have not even been built yet, and whose capabilities are still unknown.

As you learned in the chapter, there is little difference between creating pages for a desktop PC using XHTML 1.0 and XHTML 1.1. You also learned how modularizing XHTML made it possible to create languages for new devices that are much easier to learn (such as XHTML MP for use on a mobile phone).

By using the same markup to deliver Web content to multiple devices, and using CSS to control its presentation, you find yourself in possession of a truly flexible content delivery format. In addition, those creating new devices have strong incentives to use this approach because it means more content is instantly available to new devices (as opposed to developers being required to create new content in a new language) and new devices are easier to program for, which will help those devices succeed.

Of course, this future where those creating new languages use the same basic modules of markup and extend it for their new devices relies on new developments following the W3C's approach. As you have seen, the mobile phone companies have had trouble doing this, but it is hoped that others will learn from their mistakes and see the difficulties created when people do not share a common vision.

Hopefully, the W3C's vision in creating a language that is capable of supporting a huge range of devices will be rewarded with its adoption, but only time will tell. In the meantime, at least you are armed with the best knowledge possible about how the Web is likely to develop, and if you read anything about languages based upon XHTML or the XHTML family of documents, you will know what it means and understand the architecture behind it.

That brings us to the end of this journey. By now, you have brought your skills up to date, and probably learned some new markup along the way. You will likely find you miss some of the old markup you are no longer supposed to be using, but if you stick to what you've learned in this book, you will create sites that will last a lot longer in the new Web world, sites ready for access from different devices, and sites that fulfill the accessibility requirements that the pages to be available to everyone. Having read this book and applied its principles, you should be well prepared for both current and future job requirements.

Final Example Code

This appendix contains the final code for the First Promotions project example that has been developed throughout the book. It incorporates many of the new techniques you have learned throughout the book. In particular, the code does all of the following:

❑   Uses strict XHTML

❑   Uses CSS to control layout of the page (not tables)

❑   Meets accessibility requirements (including the Bobby AAA rating)

❑   Has a more modern design than the original example

You will see three pages in this appendix:

❑   The home page

❑   A product details page

❑   A product list page

You will also see the full CSS style sheet. The style of these pages has been modernized, as promised at the beginning of the book.

The structure of the site is identical to the original version; only the content of the pages has changed.

You can download the entire code for this example, along with the code for the rest of the book, from the book's companion Web site, which can be found at www.wrox.com. Once you've extracted the download, you will find the code for the new site in a folder called new_site.

Home Page

The home page (and the other pages that are linked to from the top navigation and footer links) uses the following code (this is found in the new_site folder and is called index.html):

```
<?xml version="1.0" encoding="iso-8859-1"?>
<!DOCTYPE html PUBLIC "-//W3C//DTD XHTML 1.0 Strict//EN"
    "http://www.w3.org/TR/xhtml1/DTD/xhtml1-strict.dtd">
<html>

<head>
  <title>First Promotions :: Promotional corporate gifts (pens, notepads,
      mugs, and bags)</title>
  <link rel="stylesheet" href="interface.css" type="text/css" />
  <meta http-equiv="Content-Type" content="text/html; charset=iso-8859-1" />
</head>

<body>
  <p><a href="#content"><img src="images/interface/1px.gif"
      alt="Skip to main content" width="1" height="1" /></a></p>

<div id="page">
  <div id="byline">Promotional gifts, pens, note pads, bags, mugs, executive
      toys, corporate gifts, and lots more... </div>

  <div id="masthead"><img src="images/interface/logo.gif" alt="logo" width="364"
      height="77" />
    <a href="#endMainNav"><img src="images/interface/1px.gif" alt="Skip main
      navigation" width="1" height="1" /></a>
  </div>
  <div id="topNav">

  <div id="linkContainer">
    <a href="index.html" class="topNavLink">Home</a>
    <a href="howToOrder.html" class="topNavLink">How To Order</a>
    <a href="bestSellers.html" class="topNavLink">Best Sellers</a>
    <a href="customerGifts.html" class="topNavLink">Custom Gifts</a>
    <a href="contactUs.html" id="lastItem" class="topNavLink">Contact Us</a>
    <a id="endMainNav">
       <img src="images/interface/1px.gif" alt="" width="1" height="1" /></a>
    <a href="#endTopNav">
       <img src="images/interface/1px.gif" alt="Skip side navigation"
       width="1" height="1" /></a></div>
  </div>

  <div id="sideLeft">
    <a href="products/pens/index.html" class="pens">Pens</a>
    <img src="images/interface/nav_divider.gif" alt="" width="149" height="2" />
    <a href="products/pads/index.html" class="pads">Pads</a>
    <img src="images/interface/nav_divider.gif" alt="" width="149" height="2" />
    <a href="products/mugs/index.html" class="mugs">Mugs</a>
    <img src="images/interface/nav_divider.gif" alt="" width="149" height="2" />
    <a href="products/bags/index.html" class="bags">Bags</a>
    <img src="images/interface/nav_divider.gif" alt="" width="149" height="2" />
```

```
      <a href="products/keyrings/index.html" class="keyrings">Keyrings</a>
      <img src="images/interface/nav_divider.gif" alt="" width="149" height="2" />
      <a href="products/stressbusters/index.html" class="stessbusters">
        Stress busters</a>
      <img src="images/interface/nav_divider.gif" alt="" width="149" height="2" />
      <br /><br />

      <div class="leftPanel">
        <img src="images/interface/guarantee.gif" alt="our guarantee"
            width="124" height="22" /><div class="point">
            All orders will be delivered to your door within 14 days.</div>
        <a id="endSideNav">
          <img src="images/interface/1px.gif" alt="" width="1"
          height="1" /></a></div>
    </div>

    <div id="sideRight">
      <div class="rightPanel">
        <img src="images/interface/orderHotline.gif" width="138" height="28"
            alt="Order hotline 8 369 5972" />
        <div class="orderNumber">8 369 5972</div>
      </div>
      <div class="rightPanel">
        <img src="images/interface/howToOrder.gif" width="137" height="23"
            alt="How to order" />
        <div class="point">1 Select an item from our extensive catalog.</div>
        <div class="point">2 Send us the logo or text you want printed on the
            gifts.</div>
        <div class="point">3 We e-mail you an image of the item with your
            design.</div>
        <div class="point">4 Confirm the order, and we'll deliver the goods within 21
            days.</div>
      </div>
    </div>

    <div id="content"><br />
      <div class="item">
        <img src="images/interface/photo_pen.jpg" alt="Photograph of silver pen"
            width="75" height="75" id="homePenImage" />
        <p>Welcome to First Promotions, specialists in corporate gifts and
            promotional items. Our extensive range of promotional bags, mugs, pads
            and pens helps your customers remember your customers name.</p>
        <p>All of our promotional gifts can be personalized with your logo, name and
            Web address. First Promotions can even help with the design of your
            promotional gifts.</p>
      </div>

      <br/>

      <div class="featuredRow">
        <p id="left" class="mugs"><a href="#">
          <img src="products/mugs/images/mugs2_thumb.gif" alt="Marrow mug"
              width="88" height="80" /><br /><br />
          Marrow mugs from $1.25</a></p>
```

```
        <p id="right" class="pens"><a href="#">
            <img src="products/pens/images/pens2_thumb.gif" alt="Buggy Pen"
                width="150" height="75"  /><br /><br />
            Buggy ball pens from $0.25</a></p>
    </div>
    </div>

    <div id="footer">
      <a href="#">About Us</a> |
      <a href="#">Contact Us</a> |
      <a href="#">Terms and Conditions</a> | &copy; 2004 FirstPromotions.co.uk
    </div>

</div>
</body>
</html>
```

Product List Page

Each category of products has a page that lists all the items in that category. They follow the following
format (this page is called index.html and is in the new_site/products/bags folder):

```
<?xml version="1.0" encoding="iso-8859-1"?>
<!DOCTYPE html PUBLIC "-//W3C//DTD XHTML 1.0 Strict//EN"
    "http://www.w3.org/TR/xhtml1/DTD/xhtml1-strict.dtd">
<html>

<head>
  <title>First Promotions :: Promotional corporate gifts :: Bags</title>
  <link rel="stylesheet" href="../../interface.css" type="text/css" />
  <meta http-equiv="Content-Type" content="text/html; charset=iso-8859-1" />
</head>

<body>
  <p><a href="#content"><img src="../../images/interface/1px.gif" alt="Skip to main
      content" width="1" height="1" /></a></p>

<div id="page">

  <div id="byline"> Promotional gifts, pens, note pads, bags, mugs, executive toys,
      corporate gifts, and lots more...
  </div>

  <div id="masthead">
    <img src="../../images/interface/logo.gif" alt="logo" width="364"
        height="77" />
    <a href="#endMainNav"><img src="../../images/interface/1px.gif"
      alt="Skip main navigation" width="1" height="1" /></a>
  </div>

  <div id="topNav">

<div id="linkContainer"> <a href="../../index.html" class="topNavLink">Home</a>
```

```
<a href="../../howToOrder.html" class="topNavLink">How
To Order</a> <a href="../../bestSellers.html" class="topNavLink">Best
Sellers</a> <a href="../../customGifts.html" class="topNavLink">Custom
Gifts</a> <a href="../../contactUs.html" id="lastItem" class="topNavLink">Contact
Us</a> <a id="endMainNav"><img src="../../images/interface/1px.gif" alt=""
width="1" height="1" /></a><a href="#endTopNav"><img
src="../../images/interface/1px.gif" alt="Skip side navigation" width="1"
height="1" /></a></div>
  </div>

  <div id="sideLeft">
    <a href="../../products/pens/index.html" class="pens">Pens</a>
    <img src="../../images/interface/nav_divider.gif" alt="" width="149"
        height="2" />
    <a href="../../products/pads/index.html" class="pads">Pads</a>
    <img src="../../images/interface/nav_divider.gif" alt="" width="149"
        height="2" />
    <a href="../../products/mugs/index.html" class="mugs">Mugs</a>
    <img src="../../images/interface/nav_divider.gif" alt="" width="149"
        height="2" /><a href="../../products/bags/index.html"
        class="bags">Bags</a>
    <img src="../../images/interface/nav_divider.gif" alt="" width="149"
        height="2" />
    <a href="../../products/keyrings/index.html" class="keyrings">Key Rings</a>
    <img src="../../images/interface/nav_divider.gif" alt="" width="149"
        height="2" />
    <a href="../../products/stressbusters/index.html" class="stessbusters">
      Stress busters</a>
    <img src="../../images/interface/nav_divider.gif" alt="" width="149"
        height="2" />
    <br /><br />
    <div class="leftPanel"> <img src="../../images/interface/guarantee.gif"
        alt="our guarantee" width="124" height="22" />
      <div class="point">All orders will be delivered to your door within 14
          days.</div>
      <a id="endSideNav"><img src="../../images/interface/1px.gif" alt="" width="1"
          height="1" /></a>
    </div>
  </div>

  <div id="sideRight">
    <div class="rightPanel"> <img src="../../images/interface/orderHotline.gif"
        width="138" height="28" alt="Order hotline 0208 369 5972" />
      <div class="orderNumber">8 369 5972</div>
    </div>

    <div class="rightPanel"> <img src="../../images/interface/howToOrder.gif"
        width="137" height="23" alt="How to order" />
      <div class="point">1 Select an item from our extensive catalog.</div>
      <div class="point">2 Send us the logo or text you want printed on the
          gifts.</div>
      <div class="point">3 We e-mail you an image of the item with your
          design.</div>
      <div class="point">4 Confirm the order, and we'll deliver the goods within 21
          days.</div>
```

```
          </div>
        </div>

      <div id="content"><br />

        <div class="productListBox">
          <div class="productListImage">
            <img src="images/bags1_thumb.gif" alt="Photo of City Conference Bag"
                width="102" height="80" /></div>
          <a href="bag1.html">City Conference Bags</a> <br />Best-selling, low-priced
            bags with detachable straps and interior pockets.<br />
          <span class="price">From $2.49</span> min qty 150
        </div>

        <div class="productListBox">
          <div class="productListImage"><img src="images/bags2_thumb.gif"
              alt="Photo of Seattle Conference Bag" width="134" height="80" />
          </div>
          <a href="bag2.html">Seattle Conference Bags</a><br />
          With rugged construction for added durability and zipped front pocket<br />
          <span class="price">From $3.89</span> min qty 50
        </div>

        <div class="productListBox">
          <div class="productListImage">
            <img src="images/bags3_thumb.gif" alt="Photo of Cambridge Conference Bag"
                width="144" height="80" />
          </div>
          <a href="bag3.html">Cambridge Conference Bags</a><br />
          High-quality bags in polyester with many pockets and features at a great
          price<br />
          <span class="price">From $3.58</span> min qty 100
        </div>

        <div class="productListBox">
          <div class="productListImage">
            <img src="images/bags4_thumb.gif" alt="Photo of Jupiter Conference Bag"
                width="82" height="80" />
          </div>
          <a href="bag4.html">Jupiter Business Bags</a><br />
          Manufactured in 600D polyester in either royal blue or navy. Ideal for
          executives on the move<br />
          <span class="price">From $2.99</span> min qty 100
        </div>

      </div>

      <div id="footer">
        <a href="../../aboutUs.html">About Us</a> |
        <a href="../../contactUs.html">Contact Us</a> |
        <a href="../../terms.html">Terms and Conditions</a> |
        &copy; 2004 FirstPromotions.co.uk </div>
      </div>

  </body>
</html>
```

Product Details Page

Each product has a page that follows this format (this page is called `bags1.html` and is in the `new_site/products/bags` folder):

```
<?xml version="1.0" encoding="iso-8859-1"?>
<!DOCTYPE html PUBLIC "-//W3C//DTD XHTML 1.0 Strict//EN"
    "http://www.w3.org/TR/xhtml1/DTD/xhtml1-strict.dtd">
<html>

<head>
  <title>First Promotions :: Promotional corporate gifts :: bags</title>
  <link rel="stylesheet" href="../../interface.css" type="text/css" />
  <meta http-equiv="Content-Type" content="text/html; charset=iso-8859-1" />
</head>

<body>
  <p><a href="#productContent"><img src="../../images/interface/1px.gif"
      alt="Skip to main content" width="1" height="1" /></a></p>

<div id="page">

  <div id="byline"> Promotional gifts, pens, note pads, bags, mugs, executive toys,
      corporate gifts, and lots more... </div>
  <div id="masthead">
    <img src="../../images/interface/logo.gif" alt="logo" width="364"
      height="77" />
    <a href="#endMainNav"><img src="../../images/interface/1px.gif"
      alt="Skip main navigation" width="1" height="1" /></a>
  </div>

  <div id="topNav">

<div id="linkContainer"> <a href="../../index.html" class="topNavLink">Home</a>
<a href="../../howToOrder.html" class="topNavLink">How
To Order</a> <a href="../../bestSellers.html" class="topNavLink">Best
Sellers</a> <a href="../../customGifts.html" class="topNavLink">Custom
Gifts</a> <a href="../../contactUs.html" id="lastItem" class="topNavLink">Contact
Us</a> <a id="endMainNav"><img src="../../images/interface/1px.gif" alt=""
width="1" height="1" /></a><a href="#endSideNav"><img
src="../../images/interface/1px.gif" alt="Skip side navigation" width="1"
height="1" /></a>
</div>
  </div>

  <div id="sideLeft">
    <a href="../../products/pens/index.html" class="pens">Pens</a>
    <img src="../../images/interface/nav_divider.gif" alt="" width="149"
        height="2" />
    <a href="../../products/pads/index.html" class="pads">Pads</a>
    <img src="../../images/interface/nav_divider.gif" alt="" width="149"
        height="2" />
    <a href="../../products/mugs/index.html" class="mugs">Mugs</a>
    <img src="../../images/interface/nav_divider.gif" alt="" width="149"
        height="2" />
```

```html
      <a href="../../products/bags/index.html" class="bags">Bags</a>
      <img src="../../images/interface/nav_divider.gif" alt="" width="149"
          height="2" />
      <a href="../../products/keyrings/index.html" class="keyrings">Key Rings</a>
      <img src="../../images/interface/nav_divider.gif" alt="" width="149"
          height="2" />
      <a href="../../products/stressbusters/index.html" class="stessbusters">
        Stress busters</a>
      <img src="../../images/interface/nav_divider.gif" alt="" width="149"
          height="2" />
      <br /><br />

      <div class="leftPanel">
        <img src="../../images/interface/guarantee.gif" alt="our guarantee"
            width="124" height="22" />
        <div class="point">All orders will be delivered to your door within
            14 days.</div>
        <a id="endSideNav"><img src="../../images/interface/1px.gif" alt=""
            width="1" height="1" /></a>
      </div>
  </div>

  <div id="productContent">
    <div class="productDetail">
      <div class="productDetailLeft">
        <h1>City Conference Bag</h1>
        <img src="images/bags1.jpg" alt="Photo of City Conference Bag" width="300"
            height="236"  />
      </div>
      <div class="productDetailRight">
        <p>
          <b>DESCRIPTION</b><br />
          Excellent value for money, this conference bag has everything you could
          possibly want. Each bag is manufactured with a carrying handle,
          adjustable / removable shoulder strap and four internal pockets to
          hold all your documents and more! Ideal for exhibitions, sales
          conferences and product launches.
        </p>
        <p>
          <b>SPECIFICATIONS</b><br />
          <b>Size:</b> 390 x 290 x 58 mm<br />
          <b>Print area:</b> 200 x 150 mm<br />
          <b>Colors:</b> black, blue <br />
          <b>Lead time:</b> 2-3 weeks<br />
        </p>
        <p>
          <b>PRINT DETAILS</b><br />
          Price includes a single-color print in one position.<br /><br />
          Screens cost $35 per color, per position.
        </p>
      </div>
    </div>

    <table id="productPrices">
      <tr>
```

```
        <th scope="row">Quantity</th>
        <th scope="col">150</th>
        <th scope="col">250</th>
        <th scope="col">500</th>
        <th scope="col">1000</th>
      </tr>
      <tr>
        <th scope="row">Unit price</th>
        <td>$2.79</td>
        <td>$2.69</td>
        <td>$2.59</td>
        <td>$2.49</td>
      </tr>
      <tr>
        <th scope="row">Additional colors (each)</th>
        <td>$0.25</td>
        <td>$0.20</td>
        <td>$0.20</td>
        <td>$0.20</td>
      </tr>
    </table>

  </div>

  <div id="footer">
    <a href="../../aboutUs.html">About Us</a> |
    <a href="../../contactUs.html">Contact Us</a> |
    <a href="../../terms.html">Terms and Conditions</a> | &copy; 2004
        FirstPromotions.co.uk
  </div>
</div>

</body>
</html>
```

CSS Style Sheet

Here is the style sheet, which is commented so that you can see which rules apply to which parts of the page, and the parts of different pages (`interface.css`):

```
body{
  font-family: arial, verdana, sans-serif;
  color: #333333;
  margin: 0px;
  padding: 0px;
  background-color: #f1f1f1;}

img {border:none;}
a {text-decoration:none; color:#990000;}
#homePenImage {float:left;}

#page{
  position:absolute;
```

```
    padding:0px; margin:0px;
    top:10px;
    left:10px;
    width:800px;
    border: 1px solid #888888;
    background-color:#ffffff;}

#byline{
  color:#ffffff;
  background-color:#cbcbcb;
  font-size:xx-small;
  padding:5px;}

#masthead{
  border-bottom:1px solid #888888;
  padding:5px;}

#topNav {
  border-bottom:1px solid #888888;
  padding:5px;
  background-color:#999999;}

#sideLeft{
  float: left;
  width:150px;
  height:450px;
  border-right:1px solid #888888;
  background-color: #efefef;
  padding:10px 0px 10px 0px; }

#sideRight{
  float: right;
  width:165px;
  height:450px;
  border-left:1px solid #888888;
  background-color: #efefef;
  text-align:center;
  padding:10px 0px 10px 0px; }

#content{margin:0px 165px 0px 150px; }
#productContent{margin:0px 10px 0px 150px; }

#footer{
  clear: both;
  border-top: 1px solid #888888;
  padding:5px;
  font-size:x-small;
  text-align:center;}

/* CENTER CONTENT */

.item{
  margin:0px 35px 0px 35px;
  padding:10px;
  font-size:x-small;
```

```
    color:#888888;
    border-left:10px solid #990000;
    border-right:1px solid #888888;
    border-top:1px solid #888888;
    border-bottom:1px solid #888888;}

.item p:first-letter {font-size:large;}
.item img {margin-top:10px;}

/* NAVIGATION */
#topNav a:link, #topNav a:visited{
    padding:0px 5px 0px 5px;
    font-size:x-small;
    font-weight:bold;}

#topNav{
    width:100%;
    background-color:#888888;
    height:24px;
    padding:0px;
    margin:0px;}

#linkContainer{
    position:relative;
    top:4px;
    height:16px;
    padding:0px;
    margin:0px;
    z-index:1;}

a.topNavLink, a.topNavLink:visited{
    padding: 0px 5px 0px 5px;
    border-right: 1px solid #666666;
    color:#ffffff;
    font-size:small;}

a.topNavLink:hover{background-image:url("images/interface/topNavRollover.gif");
    color:#990000;}
a#lastItem {border-right:none;}


#sideLeft a:link, #sideLeft a:visited{
    display:block;
    color:#ffffff;
    font-size:x-small;
    font-weight:bold;
    padding:5px;
    background-color:#cbcbcb;}

/* The following rule prevents gaps appearing in between navigation items and
divider images Netscape and Firefox */
#sideLeft img {display:block;vertical-align:top;}

.pens {border-left:10px solid #003366;}
.pads {border-left:10px solid #990000;}
```

```
.mugs {border-left:10px solid #996699;}
.bags {border-left:10px solid #669900;}
.keyrings {border-left:10px solid #ffcc00;}
.stessbusters {border-left:10px solid #ff9900;}

#sideLeft a:hover {background-color:#999999;}


/* FEATURED ITEMS */

div.featuredRow {margin: 0px 35px 0px 35px;}

div.featuredRow p#left {float:left;}
div.featuredRow p#right {float:right;}

div.featuredRow p#left, div.featuredRow p#right {
  margin:0px;
  width:170px;
  height:120px;
  padding:10px;
  text-align:center;
  font-size:x-small;
  border-right: 1px solid #888888;
  border-top: 1px solid #888888;
  border-bottom: 1px solid #888888;}

/* hide from IE/Mac \*/
* html div.featuredRow p#left, * html div.featuredRow p#right {
  width:200px;}
/* end hiding */

/* SIDE PANEL BOXES */

.leftPanel {
  width:124px;
  margin:10px;
  border: 1px solid #888888;
  background-color:#ffffff;
  text-align:left;
  font-size:x-small;}

.rightPanel {
  width:137px;
  margin:15px;
  border: 1px solid #888888;
  background-color:#ffffff;
  text-align:left;
  font-size:x-small;}

.orderNumber {
  text-align:center;
  padding:5px;
  font-size:medium;
```

```
    font-weight:bold;
    color:#ff9900;}

 .point {
    padding:5px;
    color:#333333;
    margin:5px;}

.point:first-letter {
    color:#ff9900;
    font-size:medium;
    font-weight:bold;}

/* PRODUCTS LIST */

.productListBox {
    vertical-align:middle;
    width:400px;
    height:80px;
    margin:20px 30px 20px 30px;
    padding:5px;
    border:1px solid #888888;
    font-size:small;}

.productListImage {
    float:left;
    width:150px;}

span.price {font-weight:bold;}

/* PRODUCTS DETAIL */
h4 {margin-left:20px;}

.productDetail {
    border:1px solid #888888;
    margin:10px 15px 10px 10px;
    padding:0px;}

.productDetailLeft {
    float:left;
    width:310px;
    height:320px;
    text-align:center;}

.productDetailRight {
    margin-left:310px;
    height:320px;
    padding:10px 10px 10px 10px;
    color:#666666;
    background-color:#efefef;
```

```
    font-size:small;}

table#productPrices {margin:10px 10px 20px 10px;}

table#productPrices td, table#productPrices th {
  padding:2px;
  font-size:x-small;}

table#productPrices th {
  background-color:#d6d6d6;
  font-weight:bold;}

h1 {font-size:x-large;}
```

XHTML Element Reference

This appendix is a quick reference to the HTML and XHTML elements that are part of the W3Cs recommendations (browser-specific extensions are largely left out). The element names are listed in alphabetical order and the description of each element is followed by the attributes it may carry.

Elements that are marked as *deprecated* should be avoided, as they either have already been removed from Strict XHTML 1.0 or are going to be removed from future versions of XHTML. In particular, you should avoid using stylistic markup and aim to use CSS instead. The elements are still covered here, however, so that you have a more helpful reference.

Any attribute marked with an asterisk (*) is not part of the W3C HTML 4 or XHTML 1.0 recommendations (and therefore you cannot use it in any document you wish to validate against a W3C DTD), and those that are deprecated are indicated as such.

The first version of Internet Explorer (IE) and Netscape (N) that supported the element is shown next to its name, starting with IE 3 and N 3.

Finally, the word *all* indicates that an element is supported in all browsers from IE 3 and N 3 upward. Note, however, that not all of the attributes will work with the same versions of the browsers; some attributes were introduced in later versions.

Following are a few notes on syntax:

❑   All element names should be in lowercase.

❑   Any attribute listed without a value should have the name of the attribute repeated as its value in order to be XHTML-compliant; for example, the checked attribute on a checkbox would look like this:

```
checked = "checked"
```

❑   All attribute values should be inside double quotation marks.

Core Attributes

Unless otherwise stated, the core attributes can be used with all of the elements in this appendix.

class = *name*	Specifies a class for the element to associate it with rules in a style sheet
dir = ltr | rtl	Specifies the direction for rendering text (left to right or right to left)
id = *name*	Defines a unique identification value for that element within the document
lang = *language*	Specifies the (human) language for the content of the element
onclick = *script*	Specifies a script to be called when the user clicks the mouse over this element
ondblclick = *script*	Specifies a script to be called when the user double-clicks the mouse over this element
onkeydown = *script*	Specifies a script to be called when the user presses down on a key while this element has focus
onkeypress = *script*	Specifies a script to be called when the user presses and releases a key while this element has focus
onkeyup = *script*	Specifies a script to be called when the user releases a key while this element has focus
onmousedown = *script*	Specifies a script to be called when the user presses down on the mouse button while the cursor is over this element's content
onmousemove = *script*	Specifies a script to be called when the user moves the mouse cursor while over this element's content
onmouseout = *script*	Specifies a script to be called when the mouse is moved off this element's content
onmouseover = *script*	Specifies a script to be called when the mouse is moved over this element's content
onmouseup = *script*	Specifies a script to be called when the user releases a mouse button while the cursor is over this element's content
style = *style*	Specifies an inline CSS style rule for the element
title = *string*	Specifies a title for the element

<a> (all)

Defines a link. Either the `href` or `name` attribute must be specified.

accesskey = *key_character*	Defines a hotkey/keyboard shortcut for this anchor
charset = *encoding*	Specifies a character set used to encode the target document
coords = *x_y coordinates*	Specifies a list of coordinates (used for client-side image maps)
href = *url*	Specifies the URL of the hyperlink target
hreflang = *language_code*	Specifies the language encoding for the target of the link
rel = relationship (same | next | parent | previous | string)	Indicates the relationship of the document to the target document
rev = *relationship*	Indicates the reverse relationship of the target document to this one
shape = circ | circle | poly | polygon | rect | rectangle	Defines the shape of a region in a client-side image map
tabindex = *number*	Defines this element's position in the tabbing order
target = *<window_name>* | _parent | _blank | _top | _self	Defines the name of the frame or window that should load the linked document
type = *MIME_type*	Defines the MIME type of the target

<abbr> (IE 4+, N 6+)

Indicates that the content of the element is an abbreviation.

<acronym> (IE 4+ N 6+)

Indicates that the content of the element is an acronym.

<address> (all)

Indicates that the content of the element is an address.

<applet> Deprecated (all)

Used to place a Java applet or an executable code in the page. Takes only the following attributes:

align = top | middle | bottom | left | right | absmiddle | baseline | absbottom | texttop	Aligns the applet within the containing element
alt = *text*	Specifies alternative text to replace the <applet> for browsers that support the element but are unable to execute it
archive = *url*	Specifies a class archive that must be downloaded to the browser and searched for
class = *name*	Specifies a class for the element to associate it with rules in a style sheet
code = *classname*	Specifies the class name of the code (required)
codebase = *url*	Specifies a URL from which the code can be downloaded
height = *number*	Specifies the height of the <applet> (in pixels)
hspace = *number*	Specifies the width to allow to the left and right of the <applet> (in pixels)
id = *name*	Specifies a unique ID for the element
name = *name*	Specifies the name of this instance of the applet
object = *data*	Specifies the filename of the compiled code to run
vspace = *number*	Specifies the height to allow at the top and bottom of the <applet> (in pixels)
width = *number*	Specifies the width of the <applet> (in pixels)

<area> (all)

Used to specify coordinates for a clickable area or hotspot in a client-side image map.

accesskey = *key_character*	Defines a hotkey/keyboard shortcut for this area
alt = *text*	Specifies alternative text for the area if the image cannot be loaded
coords = *string*	Specifies a list of coordinates for the area
href = *url*	Specifies the URL of the hyperlink target
name = *string*	Specifies a name for the element that can be used to identify it
nohref	Specifies that no document is associated with the area

notab = notab *	Specifies that this element does not take part in the tabbing order for the document
shape = circ | circle | poly | polygon | rect | rectangle	Defines the shape of a region
tabindex = number	Defines this element's position in the tabbing order
target = *<window_name>* | _parent | _blank | _top | _self	Defines the name of the frame or window that should load the linked document

<b> (all)

Indicates that the content of the element should be displayed in a bold font. Where you are using the <b> element to add strong emphasis, you should use the <strong> element instead. If you are using it solely for visual formatting purposes, you should use CSS instead.

<base>

Specifies a base URL for the links in a document, enabling relative URLs to be resolved to the base URI. Supports only the following attributes:

href = *url*	Specifies the URL of the base for the links in this document
target = *<window_name>* | _parent | _blank | _top | _self	Defines the name of the frame or window that should load the linked document

<basefont> Deprecated (all)

Specifies a base font to be the default font when rendering a document. You should use CSS to control presentation of fonts instead of this element.

Supports the following attributes:

color = *color*	Specifies the color of text in this element
face = *font_family_name*	Specifies the font family in this element
size = *value*	Specifies the size of the font (required)

<bdo> (IE 5+, N 6+)

Turns off the bidirectional rendering algorithm for selected fragments of text.

class = *name*	Specifies a class for the element to associate it with rules in a style sheet
dir = ltr | rtl	Specifies the font family in this element
id = *id*	Specifies a unique identifier for the element
lang = *language* in HTML xml:lang = *language* in XHTML	Specifies the language of the element's content
style = *style*	Specifies inline CSS styles for the element
title = *string*	Specifies a title for this element

<bgsound> (IE only — IE 3+)

Specifies a background sound or audio file to be played when the page is loaded. Apart from being IE-specific, this element should be avoided because users should be allowed to control whether they hear a background sound (and should have the capability to stop it), and any audio content requires a text alternative.

balance = *number*	Specifies whether the sound comes out of a stereo pair of speakers equally (in which case it is given a value or 0) or whether it comes out of the left or right speaker more. Values range from -10,000 (indicating the sound should come out of only the left speaker) to +10,000 (indicating that the sound should come out of only the right speaker).
loop = *number*	Specifies the number of times the audio file should be played (can be an integer or the keyword "infinite")
src = *url*	Specifies the URL of the audio file to be played
volume = *number*	Specifies the volume at which the sound is played, from -10,000 to 0, with 0 being the full wave output volume

<big> (IE 4+, N 4+)

Renders text in a font size larger than its containing element. This should be avoided because it is a presentational element, so you should use CSS instead.

<blink> (Netscape only — N 3+)

This causes the content of the element to blink on and off (Netscape only). This element should be avoided because it is a Netscape-specific presentational element.

<blockquote> (all)

The content of the element is a quotation—usually used for a paragraph quote or longer (otherwise, use the <q> element for short quotations).

cite = *url*	Specifies a URL for the source of the quote

<body> (all)

Specifies the start and end of the body section of a page. Note that several of the attributes on the <body> element have been deprecated in favor of using CSS to control the presentation of the document.

alink = *color* (deprecated)	Specifies the color of active links
background = *url* (deprecated)	Specifies the URL for a background image to be used as wallpaper for the background of the whole document
bgcolor = *color* (deprecated)	Specifies a background color for the document
bgproperties = fixed *	Specifies that the image does not scroll with document content
leftmargin = *number* *	Specifies a margin, in pixels, for the left of the document
link = *color* (deprecated)	Specifies the color of unvisited links
onload = *script event handler*	Specifies a script to run when the page loads
onunload = *script event handler*	Specifies a script to run when the page is unloaded
text = *color* (deprecated)	Specifies a color for the text in the document
topmargin = *number* *	Specifies a margin, in pixels, for the top of the document
vlink = *color* (deprecated)	Specifies the color of visited links

 (all)

Inserts a line break. Supports only the following attributes:

class = *name*	Specifies a class for the element to associate it with rules in a style sheet
clear = left | right | none | all (deprecated)	Breaks the flow of the page and moves the break down until the specified margin is clear
id = *id*	Specifies a unique identifier for this element
style = *style*	Specifies inline CSS style rules for this element
title = *string*	Specifies a title for this element

<button> (IE 4+, N 3+)

Creates an HTML button. Any enclosed markup is used as the button's caption.

accesskey = *key_character*	Defines a hotkey/keyboard shortcut for this element
disabled = disabled	Disables the button—preventing user intervention
name = *name*	Specifies a name for the form control passed to the form's processing application as part of the name/value pair (required)
onblur = *script*	Specifies a script to run when the mouse moves off the button
onfocus = *script*	Specifies a script to run when the element gains focus
tabindex = number	Defines this element's position in the tabbing order
type = button | submit | reset	Specifies the type of button
value = *string*	Specifies the value of the parameter sent to the processing application as part of the name/value pair (required)

<caption> (all)

The content of this element specifies a caption to be placed next to a table. It should be the first child of a <table> element. While this element could carry the following special attributes, you should use CSS instead to control the positioning of the caption.

align = top | bottom | right | left (deprecated)	For IE, this specifies the horizontal alignment of the caption; in Netscape, it sets vertical position
valign = bottom | top *	Specifies the vertical position of the caption

<center> Deprecated (all)

The content of this element (and child elements) should be centered on the page.

<cite> (all)

The content of the element is a citation—and is typically rendered in italics.

<code> (all)

The content of the element is code and should be rendered in a fixed-width font.

<col> (IE 3+, N 6+)

Specifies default sets of attributes for cells within a column of a table.

align = center | left | right | justify | char (deprecated)	Specifies the alignment of the column
bgcolor = *color* (deprecated)	Specifies a background color for the column
char = *string*	Specifies the alignment character for text within the cells
charoff = *string*	Specifies the offset character to which the alignment character is set
span = *number*	The number of columns affected by the <col> tag
valign = bottom | top (deprecated)	Specifies the vertical alignment of content within the element
width = *number* (deprecated)	Specifies the width of the column (in pixels)

<colgroup> (IE 3+, N 6+)

Used to group together a set of columns within a table.

align = center | left | right | justify | char (deprecated)umn	Specifies the horizontal alignment of content within the column
bgcolor = *color* (deprecated)	Specifies the background color for the group of columns
char = *string*	Specifies the alignment character for text within the cells
charoff = *string*	Specifies the offset character to which the alignment character is set
span = *number*	Specifies a default for the number of columns in the group
valign = bottom | middle | top | baseline (deprecated)	Specifies the vertical alignment of content within the element
width = *number* (deprecated)	Specifies the width of the column group (in pixels)

<dd> (all)

The definition of an item in a definition list. This is usually indented from other text.

<del> (IE 4+, N 6+)

Indicates that the content of the element has been deleted from an earlier version of the document.

cite = *url*	Specifies a URL for justification of the deletion
datetime = *date*	Specifies the date and time of the deletion

<dfn> (all)

Defines an instance of a term.

<dir> Deprecated (all)

The content of the element is rendered in a directory-style file list.

<div> (all)

A containing element to hold other elements, defining a section of a page. This is a block-level container.

align = center | left | right (deprecated)	Specifies the alignment of text within the <div> element
nowrap = nowrap *	Prevents word wrapping within this <div> element

<dl> (all)

Denotes a definition list.

compact = compact (deprecated)	Makes the list more vertically compact

<dt> (all)

Denotes a definition term within a definition list.

<em> (all)

The element content is emphasized text and is usually rendered in an italic font.

<embed> (all) *

Embeds documents in a page that require another supporting application. This element is not part of the HTML or XHTML recommendations, and you should use the <object> element instead (although it is sometimes used for backward compatibility with older browsers and is often seen to include Flash movies).

align = absbottom | absmiddle | baseline | bottom | left | middle | right | texttop | top	Specifies the alignment within the containing element
border = *number*	Specifies the width of the border around the embedded object (in pixels)
height = *number*	Specifies the height of the embedded object (in pixels)
hidden = *hidden*	Specifies that the embedded object should be hidden
hspace = *number*	Specifies the amount of additional space to be added to the left and right of the embedded object
name = *name*	Specifies a name for the embedded object
palette = foreground | background	Sets foreground and background colors of the embedded object
pluginspage = *url*	Specifies the URL of the page where the plug-in associated with the object can be downloaded
src = *url*	Specifies the URL of the data to be used by the object
type = *MIME_type*	Specifies the MIME type of the data used by the object
units = en | ems | pixels	Sets units for height and width attributes
vpsace = *number*	Specifies the amount of additional space to be added above and below the embedded object
width = *number*	Specifies the width of the embedded object (in pixels)

<fieldset> (IE 4+, N 6+)

Creates a box used to group related items in a form.

align = center | left | right (deprecated)	Specifies the alignment of the group of elements
accesskey = *number*	Defines a hotkey/keyboard shortcut for this element

<font> Deprecated (all)

Specifies the typeface, size, and color of the font to be used for text within the element.

color = *color*	Specifies the color of text in this element
face = *font_family_list*	Specifies the family of font to be used for the text in this element
size = *value*	Specifies the size of the text used in this element

<form> (all)

Containing element for form controls and elements.

accept-charset = *list*	Specifies a list of accepted character sets the processing application can handle
action = *url*	Specifies the URL of the processing application that will handle the form
enctype = *encoding*	Specifies the encoding method for form values
method = get | post	Specifies how the data is sent from the browser to the processing application
onreset = *script*	Specifies a script that is run when the form values are reset
onsubmit = *script*	Specifies a script that is run before the form is submitted
target = <window_name> | _parent | _blank | _top | _self	Defines the name of the frame or window that should load the results of the form

<frame> (all)

Specifies a frame within a frameset. Supports only the following attributes:

[event_name] = *script*	The intrinsic events supported by most elements
bordercolor = *color* *	Specifies the color of the border of the frame
class = *name*	Specifies a class name to associate styles with the element
frameborder = 0 | 1	Specifies whether a frame border is present
id = *string*	Specifies a unique value for the element
lang = *language_type*	Specifies the language used for the content of the frame
longdesc = *url*	Specifies a URL for a description of the content of the frame

marginheight = *number*	Specifies the height of the margin for the frame (in pixels)
marginwidth = *number*	Specifies the width of the margin for the image (in pixels)
noresize = noresize	Specifies that the frame cannot be resized
scrolling = auto | yes | no	Specifies whether the frame can have scrollbars if the content does not fit in the space in the browser
style = *style*	Specifies inline CSS style rules
src = *url*	Specifies a URL for the location of the content for that frame
title = *title*	Specifies a title for the frame

\<frameset\> (all)

Specifies a frameset containing multiple frames (and possibly other nested framesets). This element replaces the \<body\> element in a document.

border = *number* *	Specifies the width of the borders for each frame in the frameset
bordercolor = *color* *	Specifies the color of the borders for frames in the frameset
cols = *list*	Specifies the number of columns in the frameset, enabling you to control the layout of the frameset
onblur = *script*	Specifies a script to run when the mouse moves off the frameset
onload = *script*	Specifies a script to run when the frameset loads
onunload = *script*	Specifies a script to run when the frameset is unloaded
rows = *number*	Specifies the number of rows in a frameset, enabling you to control the layout of the frameset

\<head\> (all)

Container element for heading information *about* the document; its content will not be displayed in the browser. Supports only the following attributes:

class = *classname*	Specifies a class to associate style rules with this element
dir = ltr | rtl	Specifies the direction of text within this element
id = *string*	Specifies a unique identifier for this element
lang = *language_type*	Specifies the language used in this element
profile = *url*	Specifies a URL for a profile of the document

<hn> (all)

Headings from <h1> (largest) through <h6> (smallest).

align = left	center	right *	Specifies the horizontal alignment of the header within its containing element

<hr /> (all)

Creates a horizontal rule across the page (or containing element). Supports only the following attributes:

align = center | left | right (deprecated)	Specifies the horizontal alignment of the rule
class = *classname*	Specifies a class for the element to associate it with rules in a style sheet
color = *color* (deprecated)	Specifies the color of the horizontal rule
id = *string*	Specifies a unique identifier for this element
lang = *language_type*	Specifies the language used in this element
noshade = noshade (deprecated)	Specifies that there should not be a 3D shading on the rule
size = *number* (deprecated)	Specifies the height of the horizontal rule (in pixels)
style = *string*	Specifies inline CSS style rules for the element
title = *string*	Specifies a title for the element
width = *number* (deprecated)	Specifies the width of the rule, in pixels or as a percentage of the containing element

<html> (all)

Containing element for an HTML or XHTML page.

class = *classname*	Specifies a class for the element to associate it with rules in a style sheet
dir = ltr | rtl	Specifies the direction of the text within the element
id = *string*	Specifies a unique identifier for this element
lang = *language_type* in HTML	Specifies the language used in this element
xml:lang = *language_type* in XHTML	

| version = *url* | Specifies the version of HTML used in the document — replaced by the !DOCTYPE declaration in XHTML |
| xmlns = *uri* | Specifies namespaces used in XHTML documents |

<i> (all)

The content of this element should be rendered in an italic font. If you are using italics to show the following, use as indicated:

❑ For **emphasis** — you should use the <em>

❑ For a **quote** — you should use <q> or <blockquote>

<iframe> (IE 3+, N 6+)

Creates an inline floating frame within a page.

align = absbottom | absmiddle | baseline | bottom | top | left | middle | right | texttop | top (deprecated)	Specifies the alignment of the frame in relation to surrounding content or margins
frameborder = 0 | 1	Specifies the presence of a border: 1 enables borders, 0 disables them
height = *number*	Specifies the height of the frame (in pixels)
longdesc = *url*	Specifies a URL for a description of the content of the frame
marginheight = *number*	Specifies the space above and below the frame and surrounding content (in pixels)
marginwidth = *number*	Specifies the space to the left and right of the frame and surrounding content (in pixels)
scrolling = auto | yes | no	Specifies whether scrollbars should be allowed to appear if the content is too large for the frame
src = *url*	Specifies the URL of the file to be displayed in the frame
width = *number*	Specifies the width of the frame (in pixels)

`<img>` (all)

Embeds an image within a document.

align = absbottom | absmiddle | baseline | bottom | top | left | middle | right | texttop | top (deprecated)	Specifies the alignment of the image in relation to the content that surrounds it
alt = *text*	Specifies alternative text if the application is unable to load the image (required); also used in accessibility devices
border = *number* *	Specifies the width of the border of the image (in pixels) — you must use this property if the image is a link to prevent borders from appearing
height = *number*	Specifies the height of the image (in pixels)
hspace = *number* *	Specifies the amount of additional space to be added to the left and right of the image
ismap = ismap	Specifies whether the image is a server-side image map
longdesc = *url*	Specifies a URL for a description of the content of the image
name = *name*	Specifies a name for the element
onabort = *script* *	Specifies a script to run if loading of the image is aborted
onerror = *script* *	Specifies a script to run if an error occurs while loading the image
onload = *script*	Specifies a script to run when the image has loaded
src = *url*	Specifies the URL of the image
usemap = *url*	Specifies the map containing coordinates and links that define the links for the image (server-side image map)
vspace = *number* *	Specifies the amount of additional space to be added above and below the image
width = *name*	Specifies the width of the image

`<input type="button">` (all)

Creates a form input control that is a button on which a user can click.

accesskey = *key_character*	Defines a hotkey/keyboard shortcut for this element
disabled = disabled	Disables the button — preventing user intervention
name = *name*	Specifies a name for the form control passed to the form's processing application as part of the name/value pair (required)

notab = notab *	Specifies that this element does not take part in the tabbing order for the document
tabindex = *number*	Specifies this element's position in the tabbing order
value = *string*	Specifies the value of the parameter sent to the processing application as part of the name/value pair

<input type="checkbox"> (all)

Creates a form input control that is a checkbox a user can check.

accesskey = *key_character*	Defines a hotkey/keyboard shortcut for this element
checked = checked	Specifies that the checkbox is checked (can be used to make the checkbox selected by default)
disabled = disabled	Disables the checkbox — preventing user intervention
name = *name*	Specifies a name for the form control passed to the form's processing application as part of the name/value pair (required)
notab = notab *	Specifies that this element does not take part in the tabbing order for the document
readonly = readonly	Prevents users from being able to modify content
tabindex = *number*	Specifies this element's position in the tabbing order
value = *string*	Specifies the value of the control sent to the processing application as part of the name/value pair

<input type="file"> (all)

Creates a form input control that enables a user to select a file.

accesskey = *key_character*	Defines a hotkey/keyboard shortcut for this element
disabled = disabled	Disables the file upload control — preventing user intervention
name = *name*	Specifies a name for the form control passed to the form's processing application as part of the name/value pair (required)
notab = notab *	Specifies that this element does not take part in the tabbing order for the document
onblur = *script*	Specifies a script to run when the mouse leaves the control
onchange = *script*	Specifies a script to run when the value of the element changes
onfocus = *script*	Specifies a script to run when the element gains focus

readonly = readonly	Prevents users from being able to modify content
size = *number*	Specifies the number of characters to display for the element
tabindex = *number*	Specifies this element's position in the tabbing order
value = *string*	Specifies the value of the control sent to the processing application as part of the name/value pair

<input type="hidden"> (all)

Creates a form input control, similar to a text input, but hidden from the user's view (although the value can still be seen if the user views the source for the page).

| name = *name* | Specifies a name for the form control passed to the form's processing application as part of the name/value pair (required) |
| value = *string* | Specifies the value of the control sent to the processing application as part of the name/value pair |

<input type="image"> (all)

Creates a form input control that is like a button or submit control but uses an image instead of a button.

accesskey = *key_character*	Defines a hotkey/keyboard shortcut for this element
align = center | left | right *	Specifies the alignment of the image
alt = *string*	Provides alternative text for the image
border = *number* *	Specifies the width of the border (in pixels)
disabled = disabled	Disables the image button — preventing user intervention
name = *name*	Specifies a name for the form control passed to the form's processing application as part of the name/value pair (required)
notab = notab *	Specifies that this element does not take part in the tabbing order for the document
src = *url*	Specifies the source of the image
readonly = readonly	Prevents users from being able to modify content
tabindex = *number*	Specifies this element's position in the tabbing order
value = *string*	Specifies the value of the control sent to the processing application as part of the name/value pair

`<input type="password">` (all)

Creates a form input control that is like a single-line text input control, but shows asterisks or bullet marks, rather than the actual characters, to prevent onlookers from seeing the values a user has entered. This should be used for sensitive information — although you should note that the values are passed to the servers as plain text (if you have sensitive information, you should still consider making submissions safe using a technique such as SSL).

accesskey = *key_character*	Defines a hotkey/keyboard shortcut for this element
disabled =disabled	Disables the text input — preventing user intervention
maxlength = *number*	Specifies the maximum number of characters the user can enter
name = *name*	Specifies a name for the form control passed to the form's processing application as part of the name/value pair (required)
notab = notab *	Specifies that this element does not take part in the tabbing order for the document
onblur = *script*	Specifies a script to run when the mouse moves off the element
onchange = *script*	Specifies a script to run when the value of the element changes
onfocus = *script*	Specifies a script to run when the element gains focus
onselect = *script*	Specifies a script to run when the user selects this element
readonly = readonly	Prevents users from being able to modify content
size = *number*	Specifies the width of the input, in numbers of characters
tabindex = number	Specifies this element's position in the tabbing order
value = *string*	Specifies the value of the control sent to the processing application as part of the name/value pair

`<input type="radio">` (all)

Creates a form input control that is a radio button. These appear in groups that share the same name attribute value and create mutually exclusive groups of values (only one of the radio buttons in the group can be selected).

accesskey = *key_character*	Defines a hotkey/keyboard shortcut for this element
checked = checked	Specifies that the default condition for this radio button is checked
disabled = disabled	Disables the radio button — preventing user intervention
name = *name*	Specifies a name for the form control passed to the form's processing application as part of the name/value pair (required)

notab = notab *	Specifies that this element does not take part in the tabbing order for the document
readonly = readonly	Prevents users from being able to modify content
tabindex = *number*	Specifies this element's position in the tabbing order
value = *string*	Specifies the value of the control sent to the processing application as part of the name/value pair

`<input type="reset">` (all)

Creates a form input control that is a button for resetting the values of the form to what they were when the page loaded.

accesskey = *key_character*	Defines a hotkey/keyboard shortcut for this element
disabled = disabled	Disables the button — preventing user intervention
notab = notab *	Specifies that this element does not take part in the tabbing order for the document
tabindex = *number*	Specifies this element's position in the tabbing order
value = *string*	Specifies the value of the control sent to the processing application as part of the name/value pair

`<input type="submit">` (all)

Creates a form input control that is a submit button for sending the form's values to the server.

accesskey = *key_character*	Defines a hotkey/keyboard shortcut for this element
disabled = disabled	Disables the button — preventing user intervention
name = *name*	Specifies a name for the form control passed to the form's processing application as part of the name/value pair
notab = notab *	Specifies that this element does not take part in the tabbing order for the document
tabindex = *number*	Specifies this element's position in the tabbing order
value = *string*	Specifies the value of the control sent to the processing application as part of the name/value pair

<input type="text"> (all)

Creates a form input control that is a single-line text input.

accesskey = *key_character*	Defines a hotkey/keyboard shortcut for this element
disabled = disabled	Disables the text input — preventing user intervention
maxlength = *number*	Specifies the maximum number of characters the user can enter
name = *name*	Specifies a name for the form control passed to the form's processing application as part of the name/value pair (required)
notab = notab *	Specifies that this element does not take part in the tabbing order for the document
onblur = *script*	Specifies a script to run when the mouse moves off the element
onchange = *script*	Specifies a script to run when the value of the element changes
onfocus = *script*	Specifies a script to run when the element gains focus
onselect = *script*	Specifies a script to run when the element is selected
readonly = readonly	Prevents users from being able to modify content
size = *number*	Specifies the width of the control, in characters
tabindex = *number*	Specifies this element's position in the tabbing order
value = *string*	Specifies the value of the control sent to the processing application as part of the name/value pair

<ins> (IE 4+, N 6+)

The content of the element has been added since an earlier version of the document.

cite = *url*	Specifies a URL indicating why the content was added
datetime = *date*	Specifies a date and time for the addition of content

<isindex> Deprecated (all)

Identifies a searchable index. Only the following attributes are supported:

accesskey = *key_character*	Defines a hotkey/keyboard shortcut for this element
action = *url*	IE only; specifies the URL of the search application
class = *classname*	Specifies a class for the element to associate it with rules in a style sheet

dir = ltr | rtl	Specifies the direction of the text within the element
id = *string*	Specifies a unique identifier for this element
lang = *language_type*	Specifies the language used in this element
prompt = *string*	Specifies an alternative prompt for the field input
style = *string*	Specifies inline CSS style rules for the element
tabindex = *number*	Defines this element's position in the tabbing order
title = *string*	Specifies a title for the element

<kbd> (all)

The content of the element is something that should be entered on a keyboard and is rendered in a fixed-width font.

<label> (IE 4+, N 6+)

The content of the element is used as a label for a form element.

accesskey = *key_character*	Defines a hotkey/keyboard shortcut for this element
for = *name*	Specifies the value of the id attribute for the element for which it is a label
onblur = *script*	Specifies a script to run when the mouse moves off the label
onfocus = *string*	Specifies a script to run when the label gains focus

<layer> (Netscape only, N 4+)

Defines an area of a page that can hold a different page (Netscape-specific). Not covered in this book.

above = *name*	Positions this layer above the named layer
background = *url*	Specifies the URL for a background image for the layer
below = *name*	Positions this layer below the named layer
bgcolor = *color*	Sets the background color for the layer
clip = *number [, number, number, number]*	Specifies the layer's clipping region
height = *number*	Specifies the height of the layer (in pixels)

left = *number*	Specifies the position of the layer's left edge from the containing document or layer
name = *name*	Specifies the name for the layer
overflow = none | clip	Specifies what should happen if the layer's content is larger than the specified box and clipping area. A value of `none` does not clip content, `clip` does.
pagex = *number*	Specifies the absolute horizontal (x) coordinate position of the left of the layer in relation to the browser window
pagey = *number*	Specifies the absolute vertical (y) coordinate position of the top of the layer in relation to the browser window
src = *url*	Specifies another document as the content of the layer
top = *number*	Specifies the position of the layer from the top of the containing document or layer
visibility = show | hide | inherit	Specifies whether the layer should be visible
width = *number*	Specifies the width of the layer (in pixels)
z-index = *number*	Specifies the stacking order of the layer

<legend> (IE 4+, N 6+)

The content of this element is the title text to place in a <fieldset>.

accesskey = *key_character*	Defines a hotkey/keyboard shortcut for this element
align = top | left | bottom | right (deprecated)	Specifies the position of the legend in relation to the fieldset

<li> (all)

The content of this element is an item in a list. The element is referred to as a *line item*. For appropriate attributes, see the parent element for that kind of list (<ul>, <ol>, <menu>).

compact = compact (deprecated)	Specifies that the vertical spacing of list items should be made more compact
type = *bullet_type* (deprecated)	Specifies the type of bullet used to display the list items
value = *number* (deprecated)	Specifies the number of the current list item in ordered lists

<link> (all)

Defines a link between the document and another resource. It is often used to include style sheets in documents. This element takes only the following attributes:

charset = *character_set*	Specifies a character set used to encode the linked file
href = *url*	Specifies the URL of the linked document
hreflang = *language_type*	Specifies the language encoding for the target of the link
media = *list*	Specifies the types of media for which the document is intended
rel = same | next | parent | previous | *string*	Indicates the relationship of the document to the target document
rev = *relation*	Indicates the reverse relationship of the target document to this one
type = *MIME-type*	MIME type of the resource being linked to

<map> (all)

Creates a client-side image map and specifies a collection of clickable areas or hotspots.

name = *string*	Name of the map (required)

<menu> Deprecated (all)

Renders the child elements as individual items. Replaced by lists (<ol> and <ul>). Deprecated in HTML 4.01.

type = *bullet_type*	Specifies the type of bullet used to display the list items

<meta> (all)

Allows for information about the document or instructions for the browser; these are not displayed to the user. It takes only the following attributes:

charset = *character_set*	Specifies a character set used to encode the document
content = *meta_content*	Specifies the value for the metainformation
dir = ltr | rtl	Specifies the direction of the text within the element

http-equiv = *string*	Specifies the HTTP equivalent name for the metainformation; causes the server to include the name and content in the HTTP header
lang = *language_type*	Specifies the language used in this element
name = *string*	Specifies the name of the metainformation
scheme = *scheme*	Specifies the profile scheme used to interpret the property

\<noembed> (N 2+)

The content of the element is displayed for browsers that do not support \<embed> elements or the required viewing application.

\<noframes> (all)

The content of the element is displayed for browsers that do not support frames.

\<nolayer> (N 4+ only)

The content of the element is displayed for browsers that do not support layers.

\<noscript> (all)

The content of the element is displayed for browsers that do not support the script. Most browsers will also display this content if scripting is disabled.

\<object> (IE 3+, N 6+)

Adds an object or non-HTML control to the page.

align = absbottom | absmiddle | baseline | bottom | left | middle | right | texttop | top *	Specifies the position of the object in relation to surrounding text
archive = *url*	Specifies a list of URLs for archives or resources used by the object
border = *number* *	Specifies the width of the border (in pixels)
classid = *url*	Specifies the URL of the object

codebase = *url*	Specifies the URL of the code required to run the object
codetype = *MIME-type*	Specifies the MIME type of the code base
data = *url*	Specifies the data for the object
declare	Declares an object without instantiating it
height = *number*	Specifies the height of the object (in pixels)
hspace = *number*	Specifies the amount of additional space to be added to the left and right of the embedded object
name = *name*	Specifies a name for the object
notab =notab *	Specifies that this element does not take part in the tabbing order for the document
standby = *string*	Defines a message to display while the object is loading
tabindex = *number*	Defines this element's position in the tabbing order
type = *MIME type*	Specifies the MIME type for the object's data
usemap = *url*	Defines an image map for use with the object
vspace = *number* *	Specifies the amount of additional space to be added above and below the embedded object
width = *number*	Specifies the object's width (in pixels)

<ol>

Creates an ordered list.

compact = compact (deprecated)	Attempts to make the list more compact vertically
start = *number* (deprecated)	Specifies the starting number of the first item in the list (if list type is a letter or other character, the corresponding number character will be used)
type = *bullet_type* (deprecated)	Specifies the type of bullet used to display the list items
value = *number* (deprecated)	Specifies the number of the current list item

<optgroup> (IE 6+, N 6+)

Used to group <option> elements in a select box.

disabled = disabled	Disables the group — preventing user intervention
label = *string*	Specifies a label for the option group

<option> (all)

Contains one choice in a drop-down list or select box.

disabled = disabled	Disables the option — preventing user intervention
label = *string*	Specifies a label for the option
selected = selected	Indicates that the option should be selected by default when the page loads
value = *string*	Specifies the value of this option in the form control sent to the processing application as part of the name/value pair

<p> (all)

The content of this element is a paragraph.

align = center | left | right *	Specifies the alignment of the text within the paragraph

<param> (IE 3+, N 6+)

Used to set a parameter on an `<applet>` or `<object>` element. You can have multiple `<param>` elements in any order, but they must appear directly after the opening tag.

id = *id*	Specifies a unique identifier for the element
name = *name*	Specifies the name of the parameter
type = *MIME_type*	Defines the MIME type of the parameter (only used when the `valuetype` attribute has a value of `ref`)
valuetype = data | ref | object	Specifies the type of the value attribute. `data` is the default value, meaning the value will be passed to the object as a string `ref` indicates that the value of the `value` attribute is a URI to a resource `object` indicates that the value of the `value` attribute is a reference to another object in the document
value = *string*	Defines the value of the parameter

`<pre>` (all)

The content of this element is rendered in a fixed-width type that retains the formatting (such as spaces and line breaks) in the code.

width = *number* (deprecated)	Specifies the width of the preformatted area (in pixels)

`<q>` (IE 4+, N 6+)

The content of the element is a short quotation.

cite = *url*	Specifies the URL for the content of the quote in question

`<s>` Deprecated (all)

The content of the element should be rendered with a strikethrough.

`<samp>` (all)

The content of the element is a sample code listing. Usually rendered in a smaller fixed-width font.

`<script>` (all)

The content of the element is a script code that the browser should execute.

charset = *encoding*	Specifies a character set used to encode the script
defer = defer	Indicates that the browser can defer execution of the script
event = *event name* (deprecated in HTML 4 dropped in XHTML 1)	Specifies the event for which the script is being written
for = *id* (deprecated in HTML 4 dropped in XHTML 1)	Specifies the value of the id attribute on the element to which the script is bound
language = *name*	Specifies the language used in this element
src = *url*	URL for the location of the script file
type = *encoding*	Specifies the MIME type of the script
xml:space = preserve (XHTML only)	Intrinsic XHTML attribute specifying that white space within the element should be preserved

`<select>` (all)

Creates a select or drop-down list box.

disabled = disabled	Disables the select box — preventing user intervention
multiple = multiple	Permits selection of multiple items from the list
name = *name*	Specifies a name for the form control passed to the form's processing application as part of the name/value pair (required)
onblur = *script*	Specifies a script to run when the mouse moves off the control
onchange = *script*	Specifies a script to run when the value of the element changes
onfocus = *script*	Specifies a script to run when the element gains focus
size = *number*	Specifies the number of items that may appear at once
tabindex = *number*	Defines this element's position in the tabbing order

`<small>` (all)

The content of this element should be displayed in a smaller font than its containing element. You should try to use CSS where appropriate instead.

`<span>` (all)

Used as a grouping element for inline elements (as opposed to block-level elements); also allows for the definition of nonstandard attributes for text on a page.

`<strike>` Deprecated (all)

The content of this element should be rendered in strikethrough text.

`<strong>` (all)

The content of this element has strong emphasis and should be rendered in a bold typeface.

<style> (IE 3+, N 4+)

Contains CSS style rules that apply to that page.

media = *media type*	Specifies the type of media/device for which the style sheet is written
title = *string*	An optional title for the style sheet
type = *text/css*	Indicates that the MIME type of the style sheet is CSS

<sub> (all)

The content of this element is displayed as subscript.

<sup> (all)

The content of this element is rendered as superscript.

<table> (all)

Creates a table.

align = center | left | right (deprecated)	Specifies the alignment of the table within its content
background = *url*	Specifies a URL for a background image
bgcolor = *color* (deprecated)	Specifies a background color for the table
border = *number*	Specifies the width of the border (in pixels)
bordercolor = *color* *	Specifies the color of the border
bordercolordark = *color* *	Specifies the darker border color
bordercolorlight = *color* *	Specifies the lighter border color
cellpadding = *number*	Specifies the distance between the border and its content (in pixels)
cellspacing = *number*	Specifies the distance between the cells (in pixels)
cols = *number*	Specifies the number of columns in the table
frame = above | below | border | box | hsides | lhs | rhs | void | vsides	Defines where the borders are displayed

height = *number* *	Specifies the height of the table (in pixels)
hspace = *number* *	Specifies the amount of additional space to be added to the left and right of the table
nowrap = nowrap *	Prevents the content of the table from wrapping
rules = all | cols | groups | none | rows	Specifies where the inner dividers are drawn
summary = *string*	Offers a summary description of the table
valign = bottom | top *	Specifies the alignment of content in the table
vspace = *number* *	Specifies the amount of additional space to be added above and below the table
width = *number*	Specifies the width of the table (in pixels)

\<tbody> (IE 3+, N 6+)

Denotes the body section of a table.

align = center | left | right (deprecated)	Specifies the alignment of the content of the body of the table
char = *string*	Specifies an offset character for alignment
charoff = *string*	Specifies the offset within the cells of the alignment position
valign = bottom | top	Specifies the vertical alignment of content in the body of the table
width = *number*	Specifies the width of the table body (in pixels)

\<td> (all)

Creates a cell of a table.

abbr = *string*	Specifies an abbreviation for the cell's content
align = center | left | right (deprecated)	Specifies the alignment of the content of the cell
axis = *string*	Specifies a name for a related group of cells
background = *url* (deprecated)	Specifies a URL for a background image for the cell
bgcolor = *color* (deprecated)	Specifies the background color of the cell
border = *number* (deprecated)	Specifies the border width of the cell (in pixels)

bordercolor = *color* *	Specifies the border color of the cell
bordercolordark = *color* *	Specifies the dark border color of the cell
bordercolorlight = *color* *	Specifies the light border color of the cell
char = *string*	Specifies the cell alignment character
charoff = *string*	Specifies the offset from the cell alignment character
colspan = *number*	Specifies the number of columns this cell spans
headers = *string*	Specifies the names of header cells associated with this cell
height = *number* (deprecated)	Specifies the height of the cell (in pixels)
nowrap = nowrap (deprecated)	Prevents the content of the cell from wrapping
rowspan = *number*	Specifies the number of rows the cell spans
scope = row | col | rowgroup | colgroup	Specifies the scope of a header cell
valign = bottom | top	Specifies vertical alignment of the content of the cell
width = *number*	Specifies the width of the cell (in pixels)

<textarea> (all)

Creates a multiple-line text input control in a form.

accesskey = *key_character*	Defines a hotkey/keyboard shortcut for this element
cols = *number*	Specifies the number of columns of characters the text area should be (the width in characters)
disabled = disabled	Disables the text area — preventing user intervention
name = *string*	Specifies a name for the form control passed to the form's processing application as part of the name/value pair (required)
onblur = *script*	Specifies a script to run when the mouse moves off the text area
onchange = *script*	Specifies a script to run when the value of the element changes
onfocus = *script*	Specifies a script to run when the element gains focus
onselect = *script*	Specifies a script to run when the text area is selected
readonly = readonly	Prevents users from being able to modify content
rows = *number*	Specifies the number of rows of text that should appear in the text area without the scrollbar appearing
tabindex = *number*	Defines this element's position in the tabbing order
wrap = physical | vertical | off *	Indicates how text should be wrapped if the text entered is wider than the number in the value for the `cols` attribute

<tfoot> (IE 3+, N 6+)

Denotes a row or rows of a table to be used as a footer for the table.

align = center | left | right	Specifies the alignment of the content of the footer of the table
char = *string*	Specifies an offset character for alignment
charoff = *string*	Specifies the offset within the cells of the alignment position
valign = bottom | baseline | middle | top	Specifies the vertical alignment of content in the foot of the table
width = *number*	Specifies the width of the table body (in pixels)

<th> (all)

Denotes a header cell of a table. By default, content is often shown in bold font.

abbr = *string*	Specifies an abbreviation for the cell's content
align = center | left | right (deprecated)	Specifies the alignment of the content of the cell
axis = *string*	Specifies a name for a related group of cells
background = *url* (deprecated)	Specifies a URL for a background image for the cell
bgcolor = *color* (deprecated)	Specifies the background color of the cell
border = *number* (deprecated)	Specifies the border width of the cell (in pixels)
bordercolor = *color* *	Specifies the border color of the cell
bordercolordark = *color* *	Specifies the dark border color of the cell
bordercolorlight = *color* *	Specifies the light border color of the cell
char = *string*	Specifies the cell alignment character
charoff = *string*	Specifies the offset from the cell alignment character
colspan = *number*	Specifies the number of columns this cell spans
headers = *string*	Specifies the names of header cells associated with this cell
height = *number* (deprecated)	Specifies the height of the cell (in pixels)
nowrap = nowrap *	Prevents the content of the cell from wrapping
rowspan = *number*	Specifies the number of rows the cell spans
scope = row | col | rowgroup | colgroup	Specifies the scope of a header cell
valign = bottom | top	Specifies vertical alignment of the content of the cell
width = *number*	Specifies the width of the cell (in pixels)

\<thead> (IE 3+, N 6+)

Denotes a row or rows of a table to be used as a header for the table.

align = center | left | right (deprecated)	Specifies the alignment of the content of the head of the table
char = *string*	Specifies an offset character for alignment
charoff = *string*	Specifies the offset within the cells of the alignment position
valign = bottom | top	Specifies the vertical alignment of content in the head of the table
width = *number*	Specifies the width of the table body (in pixels)

\<title> (all)

The content of this element is the title of the document and will usually be rendered in the top title bar of the browser. Supports only the following attributes:

dir = ltr | rtl	Specifies the direction of the text within the element
id = *string*	Specifies a unique identifier for this element
lang = *language_type*	Specifies the language used in this element

\<tr> (all)

Denotes a row of a table.

align = center | left | right (deprecated)	Specifies the alignment of the content of the row
background = *url* (deprecated)	Specifies a URL for a background image for the row
bgcolor = *color* (deprecated)	Specifies the background color of the row
border = *number* (deprecated)	Specifies the border width of the row (in pixels)
bordercolor = *color* *	Specifies the border color of the row
bordercolordark = *color* *	Specifies the dark border color of the row
bordercolorlight = *color* *	Specifies the light border color of the row
char = *string*	Specifies the row alignment character

charoff = *string*	Specifies the offset from the row alignment character
nowrap = nowrap *	Prevents the content of the cell from wrapping
valign = bottom | top	Specifies vertical alignment of the content of the cell

<tt> (all)

The content of this element is rendered in a fixed-width font, as if on a teletype device.

<u> (all)

The content of this element is rendered with underlined text (deprecated in HTML 4.01).

<ul> (all)

Creates an unordered list.

compact = compact (deprecated)	Attempts to make the list more compact vertically
type = *bullet_type* (deprecated)	Specifies the type of bullet used to display the list items

<var> (IE 3+, N 6+)

The content of this element is a programming variable and is usually rendered in a small fixed-width font.

C

CSS Properties

This appendix covers CSS properties that control the look of your documents. Each property has a brief description and an example of how it can be used. These are followed by two tables:

❏ The tables on the left show the possible values for each property and the first version of IE and Netscape to support them.

❏ The tables on the right indicate whether the property can be inherited, what its default value is, and the elements to which it applies.

This is not a complete reference to all CSS properties, but it does cover the properties you are likely to use most of the time and those covered in the CSS chapters of this book. At the end of the appendix, you can find the units of measurement for lengths that can be used in CSS.

Note that the tables indicating which browser version supports a value are based on browsers on the Windows platform. Internet Explorer 5 on a Mac has notably better support for many of the properties than its Windows counterparts.

*While Netscape supports the **inherit** value of many properties, if it is unable to set the property to some other value in the first place, it will have nothing to inherit.*

Font Properties

The font properties enable you to change the appearance of a typeface.

font

This is a shorthand property that enables you to set several font properties (covered in this section) at the same time by providing the appropriate values separated by space. You can specify the font-size, line-height, font-family, font-style, font-variant, and font-weight in this one property (all of these properties are covered in this section except `line-height`, which is covered in the section entitled "Dimensions" later in the chapter).

```
font {bold 12pt arial, verdana, sans-serif;}
```

Value	IE	Netscape
[font-family]	3	4
[font-size]	3	4
[font-style]	3	4
[font-variant]	4	6
[font-weight]	3	4
[line-height]	3	4
inherit	–	6

Inherited	Yes
Default	n/a
Applies to	All elements

font-family

This property enables you to specify the typefaces you want to use. It can take multiple values separated by commas, so if your first choice of font is not installed by the computer trying to view the page, it will try to use your second choice. You should end the list with a generic font-family (`serif`, `sans-serif`, `cursive`, `fantasy`, or `monospace`), which would be used if the computer cannot find the fonts you listed.

```
p {font-family:arial, verdana, sans-serif;}
```

Value	IE	Netscape
[generic family]	3	4
[specific family]	3	4
inherit	–	6

Inherited	Yes
Default	Set by browser
Applies to	All elements

font-size

This property enables you to specify a size of font. The `font-size` property can take four types of values (the absolute and relative values are specific to fonts):

❑ **Absolutes sizes** — `xx-small`, `x-small`, `small`, `medium`, `large`, `x-large`, `xx-large`

❑ **Relative sizes** — `larger`, `smaller`

❑ **Length** — A unit of measurement (as described at the end of this appendix)

❑ **Percentage** — Percentage of the parent font

Value	IE	Netscape
[absolute]	3	4
[relative size]	4	4
[percent]	3	4
[length]	3	4
inherit	–	6

Inherited	Yes
Default	medium
Applies to	All elements

font-size-adjust

This property enables you to adjust the aspect value of a font, the ratio between the height of a lowercase letter x in the font and the height of the font.

```
p {font-size-adjust:0.5;}
```

The less the difference between the height of an x and the font-height, the more legible the text should be when it is small.

Value	IE	Netscape
[number]	–	–
none	–	–
inherit	–	6

Inherited	Yes
Default	Specific to font
Applies to	All elements

font-stretch

This property enables you to specify the width of the letters in a font (note that this is the actual width of the characters; you can set the space between characters using the letter-spacing property).

❑ The **relative values** are as follows: normal, wider, narrower

❑ The **fixed values** are as follows: ultra-condensed, extra-condensed, condensed, semi-condensed, semi-expanded, expanded, extra-expanded, ultra-expanded.

```
p {font-family:courier; font-stretch:semi-condensed;}
```

Value	IE	Netscape
[absolute]	–	–
[relative]	–	–
inherit	–	6

Inherited	Yes
Default	Specific to font
Applies to	All elements

font-style

This property applies styling to a font. If the specified version of the font is available, it will be used; otherwise, the browser might attempt to render it using an algorithm.

```
p {font-style:italic;}
```

Value	IE	Netscape
normal	3	4
italic	3	4
oblique	4	6
inherit	–	6

Inherited	Yes
Default	normal
Applies to	All elements

font-variant

This property renders text using capital letters that are the same height as normal lowercase letters.

```
p {font-variant:small-caps;}
```

Value	IE	Netscape
normal	4	6
small-caps	4	6
inherit	–	6

Inherited	Yes
Default	normal
Applies to	All elements

font-weight

This property specifies the thickness of the text or its "boldness."

- ❑ **Absolute values**—normal, bold
- ❑ **Relative values**—bolder, lighter
- ❑ **Numeric value** between 100 and 900

```
p {font-weight:bold;}
```

Value	IE	Netscape
[absolute]	3	4
[relative]	4	6
[number 100–900]	4	6
inherit	–	6

Inherited	Yes
Default	normal
Applies to	All elements

Text Properties

Text properties change the appearance and layout of text in general (such as the spacing between characters as opposed to the font in which the characters are displayed).

letter-spacing

This property specifies the distance between letters as a unit of length.

```
p {letter-spacing:1em;}
```

Value	IE	Netscape
[length]	4	6
normal	4	6
inherit	–	6

Inherited	Yes
Default	normal
Applies to	All elements

text-align

This property specifies whether text is aligned left, right, center, or justified.

```
p {text-align:center}
```

Value	IE	Netscape
left	3	4
right	3	4
center	3	4
justify	4	4
inherit	–	6

Inherited	Yes
Default	Depends on the user agent and element (usually left except for <th> elements, which are center)
Applies to	All elements

text-decoration

This property specifies whether text should have an underline, overline, line-through, or blink appearance.

```
p {text-decoration:underline;}
```

Value	IE	Netscape
none	3	4
underling	3	4
overline	4	6
line-through	3	4
blink	–	4
inherit	–	6

Inherited	No
Default	none
Applies to	All elements

text-indent

This property specifies the indentation in length or as a percentage of the parent element's width.

```
p {text-indent:3em;}
```

Value	IE	Netscape
[length]	3	4
[percentage]	3	4
inherit	–	6

Inherited	Yes
Default	zero
Applies to	Block-level elements

text-shadow

This property creates a drop shadow for the text. It should take three lengths: the first two specify *x* and *y* coordinates for the offset of the drop shadow, while the third specifies a blur effect. This is then followed by a color, which can be a name or a hex value.

```
.dropShadow { text-shadow: 0.3em 0.3em 0.5em black}
```

Value	IE	Netscape
[shadow effects]	–	–
none	–	–
inherit	–	6

Inherited	No
Default	none
Applies to	All elements

text-transform

This property specifies capitalization of text in an element.

- ❑   none — Removes inherited settings
- ❑   uppercase — All characters are uppercase

❑ lowercase — All characters are lowercase

❑ capitalize — The first letter of each word is capitalized

```
p {text-transform:uppercase;}
```

Value	IE	Netscape
none	4	4
uppercase	4	4
lowercase	4	4
capitalize	4	4
inherit	–	6

Inherited	Yes
Default	none
Applies to	All elements

white-space

This property indicates how white space should be handled:

❑ normal — White space should be collapsed.

❑ pre — White space should be preserved.

❑ nowrap — Text should not be broken to a new line except with the <br /> element.

```
p {white-space:pre;}
```

Value	IE	Netscape
normal	5.5	4
pre	5.5	4
nowrap	5.5	6
inherit	–	6

Inherited	Yes
Default	normal
Applies to	Block-level elements

word-spacing

This property specifies the gap between words.

```
p {word-spacing:2em;}
```

Value	IE	Netscape
normal	6	6
[length]	6	6
inherit	–	6

Inherited	Yes
Default	normal
Applies to	All elements

Color and Background Properties

The following properties enable you to change the colors and background of both the page and any boxes.

background

This property is shorthand for specifying background properties for the `color`, `url`, `repeat`, `scroll`, and `position` properties (all covered in this section), with each value separated by a space. By default, the background is transparent.

```
body {background: #efefef url(images/background.gif) }
```

Value	IE	Netscape
[background-attachment]	4	6
[background-color]	3	4
[background-image]	3	4
[background-position]	4	6
[background-repeat]	3	4
inherit	–	6

Inherited	No
Default	Not defined (by default, the background is transparent)
Applies to	All elements

background-attachment

This property specifies whether a background image should be fixed in one position or scroll along the page.

```
body {background-attachment:fixed; background-image: url(images/background.gif);}
```

Value	IE	Netscape
fixed	4	6
scroll	4	6
inherit	–	6

Inherited	No
Default	scroll
Applies to	All elements

background-color

This property sets the color of the background. Colors can be specified as a color name, hex value, or RGB value. By default, the box will be transparent.

```
body {background-color:#efefef;}
```

Value	IE	Netscape
[color]	4	4
transparent	4	4
inherit	–	6

Inherited	No
Default	transparent
Applies to	All elements

background-image

This property specifies an image to be used as a background; the default is tiled. The value is a URL for the image specified using the following syntax, where the path to the image is given in parentheses following the keyword url.

```
body {background-image: url(images/background.gif);}
```

Value	IE	Netscape
[url]	4	4
none	4	4
inherit	–	6

Inherited	No
Default	none
Applies to	All elements

background-position

This property specifies where a background image should be placed in the page, from the top left-hand corner. Values can be an absolute distance, percentage, or one of the keywords. If only one value is given, it's taken to be horizontal. The following keywords are available: top, bottom, left, right, center.

```
body {background-position:center; background-image: url(images/background.gif);}
```

Value	IE	Netscape
[length – x y]	4	6
[percentage – x% y%]	4	6
top	4	6
left	4	6
bottom	4	6
right	4	6
center	4	6
inherit	–	6

Inherited	No
Default	top, left
Applies to	Block-level elements

background-positionX

This property specifies the position of a background image to run horizontally across the page. The values are the same as for `background-position` (the default is `top`).

background-positionY

This property specifies the position of a background image to run vertically down the page. The values are the same as for `background-position` (the default is `left`).

background-repeat

This property indicates whether a specified background image should be tiled, and if so, how it should be tiled (all over the page or just along the *x* or *y* axis).

```
body {background-repeat:no-repeat; background-image: url(images/background.gif);}
```

Value	IE	Netscape
repeat	4	6
repeat-x	4	6
repeat-y	4	6
no-repeat	4	6
inherit	–	6

Inherited	No
Default	repeat
Applies to	Block-level elements

Border Properties

The border properties enable you to control the appearance and size of a border around any box.

border (border-bottom, border-left, border-top, border-right)

This property is shorthand for specifying the `border-style`, `border-width`, and `border-color` properties (which are all covered in this section).

Value	IE	Netscape
<border-style>	4	6
<border-width>	4	6
<border-color>	4	6
inherit	–	6

Inherited	No
Default	none, medium, none
Applies to	All elements

border-style (border-bottom-style, border-left-style, border-top-style, border-right-style)

This property specifies the style of line that should surround a block box.

```
div.page {border-style:solid;}
```

Note that Netscape did not support properties for individual sides until version 6.

Value	IE	Netscape
none	4	4
dotted	5.5	6
dashed	5.5	6
solid	4	4
double	4	1
groove	4	4
ridge	4	4
inset	4	4
outset	4	4
hidden	–	–
inherit	–	6

Inherited	No
Default	none
Applies to	All elements

border-width (border-bottom-width, border-left-width, border-top-width, border-right-width)

This property specifies the width of a border line. It can be a width or one of the following keywords: thin, medium, or thick.

```
div.page {border-width:2px;}
```

Value	IE	Netscape
[length]	4	4
thin	4	4
medium	4	4
thick	4	4
inherit	–	6

Inherited	No
Default	medium
Applies to	All elements

border-color (border-bottom-color, border-left-color, border-top-color, border-right-color)

This property specifies the color of a border. The values can be a color name, hex code, or RGB value.

```
table {border-color:#000000;}
```

Value	IE	Netscape
[color value]	4	4
transparent	–	6
inherit	–	6

Inherited	No
Default	none
Applies to	All elements

Dimensions

The dimensions properties enable you to specify the size of a box.

height

This property specifies the vertical height of block-level elements.

```
table {height:400px;}
```

Value	IE	Netscape
auto	4	6
[length]	4	6
[percentage]	4	6
inherit	–	6

Inherited	No
Default	auto
Applies to	Block-level elements

width

This property specifies the horizontal width of a block-level element.

```
td {width:150px;}
```

Value	IE	Netscape
auto	4	4
[length]	4	4
[percentage]	4	4
inherit	–	6

Inherited	No
Default	auto
Applies to	Block-level elements

line-height

This property specifies the height of a line of text and, therefore, the leading (the space between multiple lines of text).

```
p {line-height:18px;}
```

Value	IE	Netscape
normal	3	4
[number]	4	4
[length]	3	4
[percentage]	3	4
inherit	–	6

Inherited	Yes
Default	Depends on the browser
Applies to	All elements

max-height

This property specifies the maximum height of a block-level element (the values are the same as for height).

```
td {max-height:200px;}
```

Value	IE	Netscape
auto	–	–
[length]	–	–
[percentage]	–	–
inherit	–	6

Inherited	No
Default	auto
Applies to	Block-level elements

max-width

This property specifies the maximum width of a block-level element (the values are the same as for width).

```
td {max-width:400px;}
```

Value	IE	Netscape
auto	–	–
[length]	–	–
[percentage]	–	–
inherit	–	6

Inherited	No
Default	auto
Applies to	Block-level elements

min-height

This property specifies the maximum height of a block-level element (the values are the same as for height).

```
td {min-height:100px;}
```

Value	IE	Netscape
auto	–	–
[length]	–	–
[percentage]	–	–
inherit	–	6

Inherited	No
Default	0
Applies to	Block-level elements

min-width

This property specifies the minimum width of a block-level element (the values are the same as for width).

```
td {min-width:200px;}
```

Value	IE	Netscape
auto	–	–
[length]	–	–
[percentage]	–	–
inherit	–	6

Inherited	No
Default	auto
Applies to	Block-level elements

Margin Properties

Margin properties enable you to specify a margin around a box and, therefore, create a gap between elements' borders.

margin (margin-bottom, margin-left, margin-top, margin-right)

This property specifies the width of a margin around a box.

```
p {margin:15px;}
```

Value	IE	Netscape
auto	3	4
[length]	3	4
[percentage; relative to the parent element]	3	4
inherit	–	6

Inherited	No
Default	0
Applies to	All elements

Padding Properties

Padding properties set the distance between the border of an element and its content. They are important for adding white space to documents (in particular, table cells).

padding (padding-bottom, padding-left, padding-right, padding-top)

This property specifies the distance between an element's border and its content.

```
td {padding:20px;}
```

Value	IE	Netscape
auto	4	4
[length]	4	4
[percentage; relative to the parent element]	4	4
inherit	–	6

Inherited	No
Default	0
Applies to	All elements

List Properties

List properties affect the presentation of bulleted, numbered, and definition lists.

list-style

This property is shorthand that enables you to specify `list-style-position` and `list-style-type` (both covered in this section).

```
ul {list-style: inside disc}
```

Value	IE	Netscape
<position>	4	6
<type>	4	4
<image>	4	6
inherit	–	6

Inherited	Yes
Default	Depends on the browser
Applies to	List elements

list-style-position

This property specifies whether the marker should be placed with each item of a list or offset to the left of the text.

```
ul {list-style-position:inside;}
```

Value	IE	Netscape
inside	4	6
outside	4	6
inherit	–	6

Inherited	Yes
Default	outside
Applies to	List elements

list-style-type

This property indicates the type of bullet or numbering that each list item should use.

```
ul {list-style-type:circle;}
```

The following table shows the list styles available in IE 6 or Netscape 7; the CSS2 recommendation also allows for the following types of bullet: hebrew, armenian, georgian, cjk-ideographic, hiragana, katakana, hiragana-iroha, and katakana-iroha.

Value	IE	Netscape
none	4	4
disc (default)	4	4
circle	4	4
square	4	4
decimal	4	4
decimal-leading-zero	–	–
lower-alpha	4	4
upper-alpha	4	4
lower-roman	4	4
upper-roman	4	4
inherit	–	6

Inherited	Yes
Default	disc
Applies to	List elements

marker-offset

This property specifies the space between a list item and its marker.

```
ol {marker-offset:2em;}
```

Value	IE	Netscape
[length]	–	–
auto	–	–
inherit	–	6

Inherited	No
Default	auto
Applies to	Marker elements

Positioning Properties

Positioning properties enable you to use CSS for positioning boxes on the page and are therefore very helpful in controlling the layout of a page.

position

This property specifies the positioning schema that should be used for an element. When an element is positioned, you also need to use the box-offset properties (top, left, bottom and right, which are covered next). Note that you should not use top and bottom or left and right together (if you do, top and left take priority).

❑ absolute can be fixed on the canvas in a specific position relative to its containing element (which is another absolutely positioned element); it will also move when the user scrolls the page.

❑ relative will be placed offset in relation to its normal position.

❑ static will fix it on the page in the same place and keep it there even when the user scrolls.

❑ fixed will fix it on the background of the page, where it will not move when the user scrolls.

```
p.article{position:absolute; top:10px; left:20px;
```

Value	IE	Netscape
absolute	4	4
relative	4	4
static	4	4
fixed	–	6
inherit	–	6

Inherited	No
Default	static
Applies to	All elements

top

This property sets the vertical position of an element from the top of the window or containing element.

Value	IE	Netscape
auto	4	6
[length]	4	4
[percentage; relative to the parent's height]	4	4
inherit	–	6

Inherited	No
Default	auto
Applies to	Positioned elements

left

This property sets the horizontal position of an element from the left of the window or containing element.

Value	IE	Netscape
auto	4	6
[length]	4	4
[percentage; relative to the parent's width]	4	4
inherit	–	6

Inherited	No
Default	auto
Applies to	Positioned elements

bottom

This property sets the vertical position of an element from the bottom of the window or containing element.

Value	IE	Netscape
auto	5	6
[length]	5	6
[percentage; relative to the parent's height]	5	6
inherit	–	6

Inherited	No
Default	auto
Applies to	Positioned elements

right

This property sets the horizontal position of an element from the right-hand edge of the window or containing element.

Value	IE	Netscape
auto	5	6
[length]	5	6
[percentage; relative to the parent's width]	5	6
inherit	–	6

Inherited	No
Default	auto
Applies to	Positioned elements

vertical-align

This property sets the vertical positioning of an inline element.

- ❑ baseline aligns the element with the base of the parent.
- ❑ middle aligns the midpoint of the element with half the height of the parent.
- ❑ sub makes the element subscript.
- ❑ super makes the element superscript.
- ❑ text-top aligns the element with the top of the parent element's font.
- ❑ text-bottom aligns the element with the bottom of the parent element's font.
- ❑ top aligns the top of the element with the top of the tallest element on the current line.
- ❑ bottom aligns the element with the bottom of the lowest element on the current line.

```
span.superscript {vertical-align:superscript;}
```

Value	IE	Netscape
baseline	4	4
middle	4	4
sub	4	6
super	4	6
text-top	4	4
text-bottom	4	4
top	4	4
bottom	4	4
[percentage; relative to line height]	6	6
[length]	6	6
inherit	–	6

Inherited	No
Default	baseline
Applies to	Inline elements

z-index

This property controls which overlapping element appears to be on top when boxes overlap; it works for absolutely positioned elements only. Positive and negative numbers are permitted.

```
p {position:absolute; top:10px; left:20px; z-index:3;}
```

Value	IE	Netscape
auto	4	4
[number]	4	4
inherit	–	6

Inherited	No
Default	Depends on the position of the element in the XHTML source document
Applies to	Positioned elements

clip

This property controls which part of an element is visible. Parts outside the clip are not visible. If the value is rect(), it takes the following form:

❑   rect([top] [right] [bottom] [left])

```
rect(25 100 100 25)
```

•

Value	IE	Netscape
auto	4	–
rect	4	6
inherit	–	6

Inherited	No
Default	auto
Applies to	Block-level elements

overflow

This property specifies how a container element will display content that is too large for its containing element.

```
p {width:200px; height:200px; overflow:scroll;}
```

Value	IE	Netscape
auto	4	–
hidden	4	–
visible	4	–
scroll	4	–
inherit	–	6

Inherited	No
Default	visible
Applies to	Block-level elements

overflow-x

This property is the same as overflow but only for the horizontal *x* axis. It was first supported in IE 5.

overflow-y

This property is the same as overflow but only for the vertical *y* axis. It was first supported in IE 5.

Outline Properties

Outlines look just like borders, but do not take any space up or add to the width of a box — it's as if they sit on top of the canvas. The outline-color, outline-style, and outline-width properties act just like the border-color, border-style, and border-width properties, and they can take the same values, so I will not repeat them here (plus, there is little support for them). The only other difference is that you cannot provide different values for the different sides of an outline (as you can with borders).

Outline (outline-color, outline-style, outline-width)

This property is shorthand for specifying the outline-color, outline-style, and outline-width properties:

427

```
outline {solid #ff0000 2px}
```

Note that `outline-color`, `outline-style`, and `outline-width` take the same values as `border-color`, `border-style`, and `border-width`. They are not covered individually, because they are not supported yet.

Value	IE	Netscape
<outline-color>	–	–
<outline-style>	–	–
<outline-width>	–	–

Inherited	No
Default	none
Applies to	All elements

Table Properties

Table properties enable you to affect the style of tables, rows, and cells.

border-collapse

This property specifies which border model the table should use (whether adjacent borders should be collapsed into one value or kept separate).

```
table {border-collapse:separate;}
```

Value	IE	Netscape
collapse	5	7
separate	5	7
inherit	–	6

Inherited	Yes
Default	collapse
Applies to	Table and inline elements

border-spacing

This property specifies the distance between adjacent cells' borders.

```
table {border-spacing:2px;}
```

Value	IE	Netscape
[length]	–	–
inherit	–	6

Inherited	Yes
Default	0
Applies to	Table and inline elements

caption-side

This property indicates the side of a table on which a caption should be placed.

```
caption {caption-side:bottom;}
```

Value	IE	Netscape
top	–	6
left	–	–
bottom	–	6
right	–	–
inherit	–	6

Inherited	Yes
Default	top
Applies to	`<caption>` elements in `<table>` elements

empty-cells

This property specifies whether borders should be displayed if a cell is empty.

```
td, th {empty-cells:hide;}
```

Value	IE	Netscape
show	5	6
hide	5	6
inherit	–	6

Inherited	Yes
Default	show
Applies to	Table cell elements

table-layout

This property specifies how the browser should calculate the layout of a table; it can affect the speed of rendering a large or graphics-intensive table.

Value	IE	Netscape
auto	5	–
fixed	5	–
inherit	–	6

Inherited	No
Default	auto
Applies to	Table and inline elements

Classification Properties

The following properties provide additional information about how boxes should be displayed.

clear

This property forces elements that would normally wrap around an aligned element to be displayed below it. The value indicates which side may not touch an aligned element.

```
p {clear:left;}
```

Value	IE	Netscape
none	4	4
both	4	4
left	4	4
right	4	4
inherit	–	6

Inherited	No
Default	none
Applies to	All elements

display

This property specifies whether and how an element is rendered, if at all. If set to none, the element is not rendered, and it does not take up any space. It can force an inline element to be displayed as a block or vice versa.

```
span.important {display:block;}
```

Value	IE	Netscape
none	4	4
inline	5	4
block	5	4
list-item	5	4
inherit	–	6

Inherited	Yes
Default	inline
Applies to	All elements

(Other properties are either not supported or not required for XHTML.)

float

This property specifies that subsequent elements should be wrapped to the left or right of the element, rather than below.

```
img.featuredeItem {float:left;}
```

Value	IE	Netscape
none	4	4
left	4	4
right	4	4
inherit	–	6

Inherited	No
Default	none
Applies to	All elements

visibility

This property specifies whether an element should be displayed or hidden. Even if hidden, elements take up space on the page but are transparent.

Value	IE	Netscape
visible	4	–
show	–	4
hidden	4	–
hide	–	4
collapse	–	–
inherit	4	4

Inherited	No
Default	inherit
Applies to	All elements

Internationalization Properties

The following properties deal with the direction in which text flows.

direction

This property specifies the direction of text from left-to-right or right-to-left. This should be used in association with the unicode-bidi property.

```
td.word{direction:rtl; unicode-bidi:bidi-override;}
```

Value	IE	Netscape
ltr	5	6
rtl	5	6
inherit	–	6

Inherited	Yes
Default	ltr
Applies to	All elements

unicode-bidi

The `unicode-bidi` property enables you to override Unicode's built-in directionality settings for languages.

```
td.word{unicode-bidi:bidi-override; direction:rtl; }
```

Value	IE	Netscape
normal	5	–
embed	5	–
bidi-override	5	–
inherit	–	6

Inherited	No
Default	normal
Applies to	All elements

Lengths

Following are the units of measurement for lengths that can be used in CSS.

Absolute Lengths

Unit	IE	Netscape
cm (centimeters)	3	4
in (inches)	3	4
mm (millimeters)	3	4
pc (picas)	3	4
pt (points)	3	4

Relative Lengths

Unit	IE	Netscape
em (height of the font)	4	4
ex (height of a letter x)	4	4
px (pixels)	3	4

Escape Characters

Escape characters enable you to include characters in your document that might:

- ❑ Not be part of the character encoding you are using (for example, US-ASCII does not include characters with accents such as a ç with a cedilla)

- ❑ Conflict with markup in the document you are writing (for example, the use of angled brackets inside elements)

Luckily, XML processors are required to support a language called *Unicode* that was designed to alleviate problems arising from different computers and programs supporting different character encodings (in particular, they are required to support UTF-8, which has been used in most browsers for several years). Unicode assigns a number to every character of every language, and as long as your computer can display that character set, you will be able to see the character intended for display (if not, your document will still contain the correct markup term).

In this appendix, you will meet things called *character entities* and *numerical character references:*

- ❑ **Character entities** use text to represent characters, and contain the reference between an ampersand and a semicolon — for example, &*xyz*;

- ❑ **Numerical character references** use numbers to represent the Unicode number for the character you want to represent, and contain the number between the ampersand followed by a hash, or pound, sign and a semicolon — for example, &#*123*;

Ideally, when writing a document, you should always try to use a character encoding that supports all of the characters you need, because escape characters can increase the size of your document. However, if the majority of your document is in ASCII text and contains only a few words with characters that are not supported, this is an ideal scenario for the use of escape characters.

Built-In XML Character Entities

XML has five built-in character entities that can be used in any XML document, and therefore can be used with XHTML too:

- ❑ < for the less than symbol <
- ❑ > for the greater than symbol >
- ❑ & for the ampersand &
- ❑ " for double quotes "
- ❑ ' for apostrophes '

You should generally use these entity references, rather than the symbols they represent, in markup to help prevent any processor from confusing these characters for part of the markup.

XHTML Character Entities

This section describes some other common character entities that you might find of use in your XHTML documents. You can find the full lists of character entities that are included in the XHTML recommendation at www.w3.org/TR/xhtml1/#h-A2.

Currency

Symbol	Character Entity	Numerical Entity	Description
¢	¢	¢	Cent sign
£	£	¤	Pound sign
¥	¥	¥	Yen sign/Yuan Sign
€	€	€	Euro sign

Trade Symbols

Symbol	Character Entity	Numerical Entity	Description
©	©	©	Copyright sign
			You can also use © to add a copyright symbol to an XML document.
™	™	™	Trademark sign (recent addition)
®	®	®	Registered trademark sign

Math and Measurement

Symbol	Character Entity	Numerical Entity	Description
−	&minus;	&#8722;	Minus sign
±	&plusmn;	&#177;	Plus-minus sign
÷	&divide;	&#247;	Division sign
°	&deg;	&#176;	Degree sign
¼	&frac14;	&#188;	Fraction one-quarter
½	&frac12;	&#189;	Fraction one-half
¾	&frac34;	&#190;	Fraction three-quarters
/	&frasl;	&#8260;	Fraction slash
√	&radic;	&#8730;	Square root
∝	&prop;	&#8733;	Proportional to
∞	&infin;	&#8734;	Infinity
∴	&there4;	&#8756;	Therefore
~	&sim;	&#8764;	Tilde operator
·	&sdot;	&#8901;	Dot operator
π	&Pi;	&#928;	Greek capital letter pi
′	&prime;	&#8242;	Prime = minutes = feet
″	&Prime;	&#8243;	Double prime = seconds = inches

Punctuation

Symbol	Character Entity	Numerical Entity	Description
–	&ndash;	&#8211;	En dash
—	&mdash;	&#8212;	Em dash
'	&lsquo;	&#8216;	Left single quotation mark
'	&rsquo;	&#8217;	Right single quotation mark
"	&ldquo;	&#8220;	Left double quotation mark
"	&rdquo;	&#8221;	Right double quotation mark
«	&laquo;	&#171;	Left-pointing double angle quotation mark (guillemet)

Table continued on following page

Symbol	Character Entity	Numerical Entity	Description
»	&raquo;	&#187;	Right-pointing double angle quotation mark (guillemet)
‹	&lsaquo;	&#8249;	Single left-pointing angle quotation mark
›	&rsaquo;	&#8250;	Single right-pointing angle quotation mark
			Nonbreaking space
§	&sect;	&#167;	Section sign
…	&hellip;	&#8230;	Horizontal ellipsis = three dot leader

Miscellaneous

Symbol	Character Entity	Numerical Entity	Description
•	&bull;	#8226;	Bullet (black small circle)
¹	&sup1;	&#185;	Superscript one
²	&sup2;	&#178;	Superscript two
³	&sup3;	&#179;	Superscript three
·	&middot;	&#183;	Middle dot
←	&larr;	&#8592;	Leftwards arrow
↑	&uarr;	&#8593;	Upwards arrow
→	&rarr;	&#8594;	Rightwards arrow
↓	&darr;	&#8595;	Downwards arrow

E

MIME Types

The value of the `type` attribute in XHTML is supposed to be a MIME type. MIME (Multipurpose Internet Mail Extensions) types were originally devised so that it would be possible to send e-mails that contained information other than just plaintext. MIME types were then adopted by Web servers as a way of telling Web browsers what type of material was being sent to them so that they could deal with the file appropriately, which is why they are used for values of the `type` attribute.

All MIME content types consist of two parts:

- ❑ A main type
- ❑ A subtype

The main type is separated from the subtype by a forward slash character — for example, `text/html` to indicate a text file written in HTML.

The MIME type conveys the following information:

- ❑ How the parts of a message, such as text and attachments, are combined into the message
- ❑ The way in which each part of the message is specified
- ❑ The way the items are encoded for transmission so that even software that was designed to work only with ASCII text can process the message

MIME types are officially supposed to be assigned and listed by the Internet Assigned Numbers Authority (IANA), although many of the most common MIME types, such as `audio/x-mp3`, are not assigned by the IANA and do not have official status despite their popularity in browsers and other applications.

- ❑ All MIME types that begin with x- are unofficial.
- ❑ All MIME types that begin with vnd are vendor-specific.

You can see the list of official MIME types at www.iana.org/assignments/media-types; however, some of the most popular ones are listed here.

text

Note that when specifying the MIME type of a content-type field (for example, in a <meta> element), you can also indicate the character set for the text being used, as shown in the following example:

```
content-type:text/plain; charset=iso-8859-1
```

If you do not specify a character set, the default is US-ASCII:

```
text/css
text/html
text/plain
text/richtext
text/rtf
text/xml
```

image

```
image/bmp
image/gif
image/jpeg
image/png
image/tiff
image/vnd.wap.wbmp
```

multipart

```
multipart/encrypted
multipart/form-data
```

audio

```
audio/MPA
audio/MP4A-LATM
audio/mpeg
audio/mpeg4-generic
audio/x-aiff
audio/x-midi
audio/x-mod
audio/x-mp3
audio/x-wav
```

video

```
video/DV
video/JPEG
video/mpeg
video/mpeg4-generic
video/quicktime
video/x-sgi-movie
video/x-msvideo (microsoft windows video *.avi)
```

application

```
application/pdf
application/postscript
application/x-java
application/x-javascript
application/x-gzip
application/x-msaccess
application/x-msexcel
application/vnd.ms-works
application/vnd.ms-wpl
application/x-zip
application/xhtml+xml
application/xml
application/xml-dtd
application/xml-external-parsed-entity
application/zip
```

Index

Symbols

& (ampersand), 53
/ (forward slash), 49
 # (hash sign), 92
" (quotation marks), 51

A

`<a>` ***tag***
  element references, 373
  `target` attribute, 60
`<abbr>` ***tag, 373***
abbreviations, content structure, 253, 255
absolute positioning, 207–210
absolute units of measurement, CSS, 97–98
`absolute` ***value,*** `position` ***property, 197***
abstract modules, XHTML, 329–330
accessibility
  assistive technology
    accessible sites, 10–11
    audio/video footage transcriptions, deafness, 313–314
    braille technologies, 96, 246
    discussed, 245–246
    HTML problems, 2
    screen readers, 10
    tables, 290–292
    TDD (Telecommunications Device for the Deaf), 314
    visual impairment technology, 10
  content structure, 253–256
  forms
    controls, grouping, 307–309
    drop-down list boxes, 309–310
    guidelines for, 310–311
    labeling, 299–302
    legends, 308
    PDF forms, 312
    select boxes, 309–310
    timed responses, 312–313
    titles, 306–307
  frames, 314–316
  functional limitations, 246
  Section 508 guidelines, 248–249
  situational difficulties, 246
  tables
    captions, 294
    complex, 295–299
    headings, 295
    layout guidelines, 289–290
    linearized, 287–289
    `scope` attribute, 293–294
  testing techniques, 317–320
  text-only site versions, 317
  WCAG (Web Content Accessibility Guidelines)
    abbreviations, 255
    acronyms, 255
    ASCII art, 262–263
    checkpoints, 247–248
    color and contrast, 268–270
    deprecated features, 250
    discussed, 243, 247
    document organization, 252
    document presentation control, 252
    dynamic content, 263–267
    frames, 315
    general layout information, 251
    guidelines, 247–248
    headings, correct use of, 254
    language clarity, 257–258
    lists, 255–256
    markup languages, 256–257
    metadata use, 251
    motion and flicker control, 267–268
    navigation, 270–274
    pop-up windows, 268
    quotations, 256
    relative unit use, 252
    scripts, 265
    structural elements, 256
    table headers, 292–293
    table layouts, 289–290
    tables, assistive technologies, 290–292
    text equivalents, 258–262
accessible sites, 10–11
`accesskey` ***attribute, 308***
acronyms
  `<acronym>` tag, 373
  content structure, 253, 255
`:active` ***pseudo-class, 163–164***